Vietnam Wives

Women and Children Surviving Life with Veterans Suffering Post Traumatic Stress Disorder

By Aphrodite Matsakis Ph.D.

Woodbine House

LIBRARY OF CONGRESS CATALOGUE CARD NUMBER: 87-51346

ISBN: 0-933149-22-0

    Library of Congress Cataloging-in-Publication Data
Matsakis, Aphrodite.
        Vietnam wives.
        Bibliography: p.
        Includes index.
        1. Military dependents—United States. 2. Veterans—United States—Family relation-
ships. 3. Post-traumatic stress disorder. 4. Vietnamese Conflict, 1961-1975—United States.
        I. Title.
UB403.M38   1988   355.1   87-51346
ISBN 0-933149-22-0

Cover Design: Carol Schwartz
Book Design and Typesetting: Wordscape, Inc., Washington, D.C.

Manufactured in The United States of America

1 2 3 4 5 6 7 8 9 10

From the beginning of time, men have fought each other and have suffered greatly as a result. Their women, children and other family members have also suffered. To the "forgotten warriors"—the wives, children and other family members of Vietnam veterans afflicted with Post-Traumatic Stress Disorder—this book is sincerely dedicated.

Goodbye: To My Vietnam Veteran Lover

I am powerless over you
Not all my love
Nor all my sweetness
Nor all my desire
To kiss your wounds
And give you
More and more
Of me
Can pierce your fears
Your basic mistrust
Of everyone
(Especially women)
I know
You've been hurt
But is that a reason to
Act like such a jerk?
I wait and I wait
But how long can I wait
Until you see
That mine is heart that's true
I wait and I wait
And while I wait
All I feel is blue
Missing you
Missing you
"Come in! I need you!" you sometimes say
But mainly
You wall me out
So you can go shout
About Nam
General P.
And your stinking job
You yell at me
Call it PTSD
And won't make love to me anymore

from "Goodbye: To My Viet Nam Veteran Lover,"
pp. 129-130, *Anti-War Poems Anthology*, Vol. II,

edited by Stephen Gill, Vesta Publications Limited,
P.O. Box 1641, Cornwall,
Ontario K6H 5V6, Canada, 1986

Table of Contents

Introduction xi

What It's Like to be a Vietnam Wife xvii

Chapter 1 What Post-Traumatic Stress Disorder (PTSD) Is . . 1

Chapter 2 Living with the Ice Man 27

Chapter 3 PTSD and Sex 49

Chapter 4 The Reality of Multiple Roles 83

Chapter 5 Alcohol And Drug Addiction 101

Chapter 6 Anger 121

Chapter 7 Battered Wives 135

Chapter 8 But Military Wives Never 147

Chapter 9 Wives of Black And Hispanic Vietnam Veterans . 163

Chapter 10 Children And PTSD 163

Chapter 11 Suicide and the Vietnam Veteran Family . . . 225

Chapter 12 I Believe In Love—The Hope of Therapy . . . 255

Chapter 13 Stay or Go 275

Epilogue 311

Coping Techniques for the Vietnam Wife 319

Summary of Vet Center Study Results 339
    Table 1–The Vet Center Survey 344
    Table 2–Common Problems of Vietnam Wives 345
    Table 3–PTSD and Marital, Sexual, and Emotional Intimacy 347
    Table 4–Reactions to Losses in the Family 348
    Table 5–The PTSD Afflicted Veteran's Relationship to His Children . 349
    Table 6–Psychological Problems Observed in Children of
      Vietnam Veterans with PTSD 351
    Table 7–Wife Abuse 352
    Table 8–Child Abuse 353
    Table 9–Obesity and the Vietnam Wife 354

Resource Guide 355

Veteran's Administration Medical Centers Nationwide . . . 363

Veteran's Centers Nationwide 375

Reading List 389

Endnotes 397

Index 417

Acknowledgements

Most of all I want to thank the Vietnam veterans and Vietnam wives who trusted me with their pain and who have often served as a personal source of inspiration.

This book was written with the support of the Veteran's Administration and I wish to extend my deep thanks for that support.

I also wish to thank Ms. Terry Rosenberg of Woodbine House for her interest in the plight of Vietnam wives and for her careful and creative editing of this book, as well as for her many excellent organizational suggestions. I also want to acknowledge Dr. Brenda Alpert Sigall of the University of Maryland, College Park, Maryland and of the Governor of Maryland's Task Force on Eating Disorders, for sharing so generously of her expertise in the areas of multiple roles, eating disorders, and the psychology of women.

I thank my parents, Dr. and Mrs. Nicholas Matsakis, not only for their moral support, but for teaching my brothers and myself the profound personal significance of historical events and the meaning of human tragedy. I especially want to acknowledge my mother, Theodora Matsakis, my grandmother, Sophia Matsakis, my great-aunt, Rego Makris and her daughters, Theodora Anagnos and Maria Caputo, for refusing to numb themselves, either emotionally or intellectually, to the Vietnam war as it was occurring, for weeping rather than eating during the dinner hour's televised bodycounts, for example. I also thank my brother Demetrios and his wife, Cindy, my brother Elias, and his wife, Joanne, and my friend Elias Vlanton and his wife, Jane, for their many insights into the political and emotional ramifications of war. I especially want to thank Cynthia Anderson Matsakis for sharing her writings and deep understanding of emotional numbing and sorrow in wives and girlfriends of Vietnam veterans. I must also thank my daughters, Theodora and Magdalena, for their extreme patience with me during the writing of this book.

I also want to thank Drs. Eric Gerdemen and Bennett Jennings of the Vietnam Veteran's Readjustment Counseling Program for sharing their experience and knowledge about PTSD and the readjustment process; Mr. William Washington, Team Leader at the Silver Spring, Maryland Vet Center, for giving me the opportunity to work with Vietnam veterans and their families and for his continuous support; as well as numerous other Vet Center counselors and colleagues who have shared so liberally of their expertise.

I want to acknowledge Dr. Carole Rayburn, Ms. Andrea Steinerman, and Ms. Ellen Salom for their contributions regarding family dynamics and the impact of PTSD on children and Dr. Bob Boyle for his perspectives on the recovery process. I also gratefully acknowledge Ms. Joyce Larson, Ms. Sheila Lane, Ms. Jane Conoly, as well as Mr. Irv Shapell, and Mr. Jim Peters of Woodbine House, for their support and encouragement during the writing of this book.

Introduction

To all of you Vietnam wives who think that your suffering is unique; I wish to reassure you. You are not alone. Your suffering is real. And there is help.

Over the past sixteen years, I have met with and counseled hundreds of Vietnam veterans and their wives. As a therapist both at one of the 172 Veteran's Administration Medical Centers and at one of the 189 Vietnam Veteran Outreach Centers in the United States, I have seen our knowledge of the effects of the Vietnam war grow and have come to realize how much we still have to learn. This book is my small contribution to helping you understand *why* your family is in such pain and to helping you see what you can do about it.

In 1972, when I started at the Washington, D.C. Veteran's Administration Medical Center, few knew what Post-Traumatic Stress Disorder (PTSD) was or how it could affect not only the veteran, but his family. One wife wrote:

> *Living with a veteran who suffers the effects of Post-Vietnam Stress is like running blindfolded with weights on. Nothing is easy; the smallest tasks become monumental. Nothing is reliable; the rules change the minute you understand them.*[1]

Approximately 58,000 American men died in Vietnam, but many more are dying emotional and spiritual deaths here at home. In many cases the troubled vet is being held together, emotionally or financially, by a woman—usually you, his wife. Until recently, the Vietnam veteran was shunned by society. Since he represented a painful episode in our history, he was often rejected. During the war he received bad press and after the war, he was victimized not only by a negative public attitude, but by job discrimination and fewer government benefits. Many mental health professionals, historians, and social commentators view what happened to the Vietnam veteran the first five years after the war as a "national tragedy."

In many ways, the Vietnam veteran has borne the burden of our national shame, guilt, and confusion regarding the Vietnam war. You, as his wife, however, have borne society's burden for him. More often than not, it is you and no one else who has nursed your husband through his flashbacks and nightmares, through his depressions and suicidal episodes, and through his mourning, as well as his rage reactions. Usually it is you and you alone who have maintained your husband's will to live and have served as a buffer between him and the world. At times, you have even served as the scapegoat for his anger: his anger toward himself, his anger toward the government, and his anger toward society.

As one wife states:

> Women did not go to Vietnam in great numbers, but great numbers have been scarred by the war. One by one, without the awareness of danger that strikes those who put on uniforms, we met and fell in love with men whose combat experience would change our lives....The men of our generation were called to Vietnam: some went off to war; some of them came home. We thanked God it was over. And wearing frilly nightgown smiles, we slept snuggled next to walking time bombs.[2]

Often the veteran repressed his anger and grief and experienced it as depression. In some cases, he tried to make it disappear by drowning it in alcohol, with drugs, or becoming a workaholic. In other instances, the vet vented his fury on you by inflicting you with either verbal or physical abuse or both. Yet even when abused by your husband, you often remained by his side, not only from fear, but from compassion, realizing that your husband's rejections of you or his explosions were not solely due to his individual temperament, but due to the frustrations and stigmas imposed upon him by others and by a variety of societal institutions. Intuitively you may have sensed that underneath your husband's abuse, lay enormous amounts of self-hate and confusion.

You have sacrificed much. Yet, despite your many sacrifices, you have been treated like a footnote. To date, outside of Vet Center women's support groups, you have received practically no acknowledgement of your pain, anger, or anguish. In many cases, you have been as misunderstood and unsupported by your family and community as your PTSD afflicted husband. To the extent that he has been perceived as "crazy," you have sometimes been perceived as "crazy" too—for staying with him, for loving him, and for helping him through his "PTSD attacks."

We don't know how many PTSD afflicted veterans there are still untreated, wandering in our society, haunted by a war that everyone wants to forget. We do know that since 1969 over 600,000 Vietnam veterans have sought government help for readjustment difficulties and that the number is steadily rising.[3] In 1987, there was an average of 7,300 new clients per month at our nation's Vet Centers.[4] While conservative estimates are that only 30%-35% of these new clients had PTSD[5] or significant elements of PTSD, according to Dr. Bennett Jennings, Clinical Coordinator at the Silver Spring, Md. Vet Center, "With Vietnam (psychological casualties) are increasing without war activities and it's still increasing. We still haven't seen the peak."[6] Since, by definition, PTSD is a delayed response to the war, many Vet Centers today are experiencing an increase, rather than a decrease, in their case load. With so many of today's books and films about the Vietnam war, with the return of Vietnamese-American children to this country, and with increased negotiations regarding American MIA's and POW's, more and more troubled vets are beginning to "come out of the closet" and admit to being psychologically scarred by their war experiences.

Experts disagree about exactly how prevalent PTSD is; however; several reputable authorities estimate that the number of vets eventually in need of psychiatric help may reach as many as 1.5 million.[7] Based on this figure, an estimated 900,000 Vietnam wives and partners and approximately 1,098,000 children may also be affected, not to mention the approximately 4.7 million members of the vet's extended family. Already school and emotional problems among children of PTSD afflicted Vietnam veterans are coming to the attention of school counselors and mental health professionals, suggesting that the negative psychological effects of the war extend not only to the veteran, but, in some instances, to his wife and children as well.

The numbers are staggering. It is my belief, one held by many of my fellow counselors, that society is partly responsible for your husband's suffering, and yours as well. The unwelcome and, in some cases, overtly hostile, homecoming given your husband and the subsequent discounting of his readjustment difficulties helped to create and solidify his PTSD. His problems, and yours, are compounded by the fact that we live in a culture with an inadequate understanding of human suffering. Our cultural ideal is often that of emotional coolness. In other societies, it is and has been, perfectly permissible for warriors to openly grieve about having been in a war. However, in our society, and in our military system especially, to be "emotional" is considered a sign of weakness or mental instability. If one is "too happy," "too sad," or "too angry," he may be judged by others, even by some mental health professionals, as being "neurotic" or "abnormal." Yet in other cultures, emotional intensity is the norm.

In such cultures there is no such thing as loving "too much," grieving "too long" or suffering "too deeply." Depth of emotion is not only expected but applauded. Individuals are allowed to suffer without being accused of "self-pity" or of "dwelling in the past." In the face of death or loss, they are permitted to rant and rave and wail loudly for as long as they need to. In contrast, in our society, the appropriate response to loss is often a form of stoicism. One is expected to "get over it" as soon as possible. "Don't cry, don't feel, don't suffer, or, if you do, don't show it," is the message. Yet what is disparagingly viewed as "falling apart," or "going crazy" may elsewhere be considered a "normal" emotional reaction.

As a result, your husband may have felt that he had to stifle his emotions. Similarly, you may have felt that you have had to keep your feelings to yourself lest you be judged as "weak" or "crazy." Yet your husband's responses to the trauma and horrors of war and your responses to your husband's PTSD are often entirely appropriate, even when judged by uninformed outsiders to be otherwise. In this sense, both of you can be seen as victims of our society's tendency to look down upon those who are in emotional pain.

Upon coming home from the war, your husband was probably faced with a society that did not want to hear about his pain, or his losses. He was blamed for his own plight. If only he was "stronger," he would not be having such readjustment difficulties. Similarly, you were often blamed for your own pain. The notion that both of you were "abnormal" undercut your self-esteem and probably strained your relationships with your extended family, your neighbors, and other natural support systems. Although you may not be as socially isolated as your husband, you too can suffer from profound feelings of loneliness and alienation.

In a few cases, veterans have expressed their anger and frustrations in dramatic hostage taking or other violent episodes widely publicized by the media. More typically, however, the vet with untreated PTSD internalizes his anger and frustrations and suffers alone. Or he may express his dissatisfactions in the context of his family. Yet when his wife seeks understanding and help from others, she, like her husband, often receives an unsympathetic response. Just as few want to listen to her husband, few want to listen to her. In many cases she is made to feel inadequate and like a failure as a woman because she cannot wave a magic wand and produce a home life as happy as that of Donna Reed or Ozzie and Harriet.

While this book describes some of the harmful effects of your husband's PTSD on you and your children, it is not intended to be yet another betrayal of the Vietnam veteran. Nor does it intend to support *any* of the many unfair negative stereotypes about Vietnam veterans or otherwise portray the vet in a negative fashion. Throughout the book, the vet's pain and social predicament are emphasized.

Society failed your husband in sending him to fight an unofficial and confusing war and then in denying him the psychological and economic support necessary for adequate readjustment. While today increased recognition and services are being given to him, in many cases, significant damage to his self-esteem, psychological health, and economic opportunities already exists. His PTSD may have already resulted in low self-esteem, anger, and other psychological problems in you and your children as well.

This statement does not mean that your PTSD afflicted husband wants you or your children to suffer because of his war experience, but rather that your family is an integrated, interdependent system. One part of your family cannot suffer without that suffering affecting the entire unit.

I have based this book on my clinical experience and research with Vietnam veterans and their wives or partners, who, like you, were looking for help, as well as on a nationwide survey of Vet Center counselors who work with individuals who are in sufficient emotional pain or who are having coping problems of such magnitude that they have needed to seek professional help. There is reason to believe that the majority of women seen at Vet Centers and Veteran's Administration Medical Centers are married or living with men who experience more severe symptoms of PTSD than the average Vietnam veteran. It is my belief that there are many thousands of Vietnam veterans and their wives who are suffering the way the ones referred to in this book have suffered.

While I believe that the numbers of untreated vets is in the many thousands, it is important to point out that numerous Vietnam veterans and their families have made adequate psychological adjustments following the war. This book is written for those whose suffering is not yet over and who wish to start the healing. *Vietnam Wives* was written with the support of the Veteran's Administration;

however, my opinions, observations, and suggestions are just that—mine. They do not necessarily reflect the opinions or policies of the Veteran's Administration Program or the Vietnam Veteran's Readjustment Counseling Program.

I have written primarily from the women's point of view. However, in many cases, I also heard the male partner's side of the story and incorporated that into the book. In cases of physical battering, however, I view the woman as the victim.

In writing this book, I reviewed the literature on PTSD and on the effects of PTSD on family life. In addition, I polled counselors at each of the 189 Vietnam Veteran Outreach Centers regarding the impact of the Vietnam experience on marital, emotional, and sexual intimacy, on the Vietnam wife's emotional and physical health, and on the veteran's relationship to his children. Only those problems and issues which apply to family members of Vietnam veterans nationwide are presented in this book. In general, the results from the 100 Vet Centers which responded confirm my clinical observations of the effect of PTSD on family life.

Since the Vet Center study is general and preliminary in nature, any conclusions must be considered tentative. In addition, there was greater response from some areas of the country than others. Clearly more research is needed to obtain more precise answers to the many questions surrounding how PTSD affects wives and children. Hopefully in the future other investigators with more refined research instruments will provide us with fuller information.

In this book I have attempted to describe the problems and issues facing you in a manner helpful to you. Just as your Vietnam vet husband may feel painfully "different" and apart from others because of his wartime experiences, you may feel different too. You may think you are the only woman in the world who is undergoing such struggles. Being in a Vet Center woman's group, where the effects of PTSD on marital intimacy and family life are discussed often helps dispel this burden of isolation. Hopefully, this book will serve the same purpose.

What It's Like To Be A Vietnam Wife

Laura's Story

I was eight months pregnant and sick with the flu when my husband shot the phones, barricaded the house, and threatened to kill the first person in uniform who tried to enter the door. When the postman ran screaming down the block about the "weirdo" acting up again, my eight-year-old hid under the bed crying. That "weirdo" was his Daddy, not his real father, but the only father he had ever known.

Meanwhile, my thirteen-year-old (also from my former marriage) started calling Dave a "baby-killer" and yelled at me for marrying a "crazy Vietnam veteran" and ruining the family. "Divorce him, divorce him," she shouted.

As the wife of a Vietnam combat vet, I have lived through many crises. My husband has suffered from the usual symptoms—the flashbacks, the nightmares, the emotional numbing, and the rage reactions. Every Fourth of July, Veteran's Day, or anniversary date of the death of certain buddies, I could expect smashed records, broken windows, or another hole in the wall. I could also expect that sooner or later, I would be up all night holding him. For Dave, as for a lot of Vietnam combat vets, anger and sorrow go hand in hand.

In the past fifteen years, Dave has held over twenty different jobs. If it weren't for my working, our family could not eat. In between his "Vietnam attacks" as I call them, however, he is a loving man. But he is scarred, emotionally and physically, and I blame the war for this and society for this also. If it weren't for me, he would have no one.

After 'Nam, he broke off most of his friendships and his family had no understanding of what he was going through. In fact, his father, a military man, only looked down on Dave for "falling apart" over a war that we "didn't win." My family rejected me too. They want to know why, after one bad marriage, I went and married a vet, a vet from "that war."

Over the years I've lost touch with my parents and brothers. I've also lost myself. I don't even know how I feel anymore. Maybe I'm depressed, maybe I'm not. All I know is that I must keep on functioning. My family depends on me. I'm constantly running, from one job to the next, one chore to the next. There's always some child who needs something and of course, I never know when Dave is going to act up again. I wish he would go get help, but he won't hear of it.

So I guess I'm Dave's therapist and most of my life is organized around arranging his life to be as comfortable and stress-free as possible. He simply can't handle pressures and if he goes "off," I'll have yet another problem. I am the buffer between him and the world, and at times, his only link to sanity.

I watch how I phrase my every sentence, for if I use even the wrong preposition, Dave might see this as insulting to him. I've also had to limit my friends and outside interests. Sometimes even the children have to take second place to his intense need for peace and quiet and for my attention—when he wants it, that is. At times, he walls me out entirely. We can coexist for days, barely talking, never touching.

In the early years, I did my best to pierce his wall and enter his world. But he wouldn't let me in—because I was a woman, because I hadn't been in 'Nam and therefore could not understand. Now, after ten years of marriage, I have given up. Now when Dave withdraws, as long as he withdraws quietly, I don't care. It's a relief. It gives me time to get other things done.

Don't ask me what it means to be a woman anymore. My life is too hard, and I'm too bitter, and too afraid of the anger and the pain inside me. I'm also afraid that someday my husband's depression will engulf him—that I will lose him entirely to that sad far-away look in his eyes, to that "other woman"—Vietnam.

Laura, wife of a Vietnam combat vet

Anna Marie's Story

*M*y husband was a P.O.W. During his nine months of captivity, he saw every horror imaginable and later inflicted those same horrors on as many V.C. as he could find. He has a special hatred for the South Vietnamese, whom he felt had abandoned him and allowed him to be captured.

When Bob came home with two b.k. (below knee) amputations, he proceeded to fry his brains with every kind of drug imaginable. For seven years, there wasn't a T.V. set in the family. He was so heavily into drugs, he'd steal from anyone, until, on the verge of insanity, he committed himself to a VA hospital. There he experienced a religious conversion and received the help which got him drug-free.

But some of the drugs he took had half lives. Even today, residues from these drugs trickle down from his brain into his system. At such times, he leaves home to avoid possibly hurting me or the kids. Sometimes he's gone for three or four days at a time. I never know where he is or when he's coming home. Frankly, after several years of this, I'm tired of making excuses for him and of shouldering the load alone. He needs to do something—take some responsibility for what goes on in our lives.

What Bob was like before 'Nam, I don't know. I met him afterward, while he was recuperating in an army hospital. He seemed kind and generous, and was making jokes about winning dance contests with his new prostheses. I felt sorry for him because he had lost his legs, but mainly because his family wasn't talking to him.

The whole family had marched against the war. Bob's father felt his son got what he deserved in 'Nam. In his view, God had punished Bob for killing people in Vietnam by taking away his legs. One of Bob's cousins had fled to Canada and another had been prepared to cut off either a hand or a foot to avoid the draft.

The only person who forgives Bob is his mother. Whenever I talk about leaving Bob, she begs me not to leave her crippled baby, the high school athlete who won every dance contest but who can dance no more.

My mother feels the same way: that I should stick it out because Bob is a good husband and a religious man who works hard for his family and is not cruel in any way. But they don't know the hell of living with a man who is half-dead and who has lost all passion.

Mainly, Bob just goes to work, comes home, watches T.V., then goes to sleep. There's no conversation other than about the house or the children. I can go anywhere I want, see my friends as often as I please, but Bob goes nowhere with me, or with the kids. He can't take crowds or noise. Sometimes he makes it to church, but that's it.

I almost enjoy it when Bob explodes. At least I know he's there. But his rage reactions are few.

A part of Bob is a stranger to us. His war medals sit in the middle of the living room and pictures of Vietnam decorate every wall. But neither I, nor my ten-year-old son and seven-year-old daughter, can mention the word "Vietnam." Newspapers, news magazines, and rice are forbidden, too, as are most feelings. Bob just can't take anger or tears. They give him headaches and make his legs hurt.

My son is learning to repress his emotions, too, just like his father. It's like pulling teeth to get him to talk about how he feels. For example, last night Bob was going up to his room to watch T.V. "Can I watch with you, Dad?" my son asked. Bob said no and walked up the stairs. For a brief moment, there were tears in my son's eyes, but he quickly pushed them back. Boys don't cry. That much his father had taught him.

When I tried to comfort my son, he shoved me away. He felt it was my fault Daddy was too tired to be with him. If I didn't nag Daddy so much, Daddy would be okay.

The worse part is that I have to be both father and mother to our son, who wants Dad, not Mom, to be at his games, take him places, and help him with his homework. He interprets his father's not wanting to do things with him as meaning that his father doesn't love him, which is not the case. However, as a result of my husband's distancing, I'm afraid my son is developing an inferiority complex. He's achieving below his potential at school and doesn't socialize much with other children. Most weekends he stays around the house, hoping his father will take him out, which hardly ever happens. I don't know whether to tell my son to give up hope or not.

Discussing these problems with Bob gets me nowhere. If I bring up a family problem, other than a mechanical one, Bob just listens and says nothing. The more I talk, the more he retreats into himself. "You handle it. I just can't take the pressure," he says.

No matter how much I do for the children, I can't be their father, too. I do everything I can for them, yet I always feel guilty for not doing enough. This guilt paralyzes me and prevents me from doing things for myself. I've repeatedly urged Bob to seek help, but he's afraid that going for help would open up feelings and memories that would destroy him.

I'm wondering if things are going to stay the way they are or whether Bob is going to crack up some day. Meanwhile, there are times I feel like a vegetable, emotionally numb, just like my husband. My sexual feelings have lessened also. I guess I just got tired of being the only person who could feel.

When I'm honest, I realize my life is being wasted. But I see no way out. Financially, I cannot afford to leave my husband, and emotionally, I don't have the strength to start all over again. Morally, I feel I must continue to plug it out one day at a time for the sake of my children. They love their Daddy and breaking up the family would devastate them. My leaving would also devastate Bob. After all he lost in Vietnam—his friends and his legs, too—I don't think he could handle yet another loss. The kids and I are his whole life.

Anna Marie, wife of a Vietnam
ex-P.O.W.

Elizabeth's Story

*A*ll *I want is even one day without the pain, without the hurt. Maybe I wasn't in the Army, but after being married to a Vietnam veteran for sixteen years, I have paid my price.*

I met my husband two years out of 'Nam. Basically, Big Al is a kind and giving person, but there's another side to him, the angry side. But I didn't see this side until after we were married. Big Al had lots of anger, which was directed at everything and everybody, including me. Just a few weeks after the honeymoon, he would go out and not come home, and he started drinking. He cared about me very deeply, yet he continually ran away from that caring.

I didn't understand what was going on—how he could switch from the good and kind Big Al to the angry one. When he put holes in the wall and had car accidents, I thought it was just the alcohol. But once when he ran into a pole, then went on to hit two or three more objects in the road, I realized that he had a death wish. Yet I never traced it to Vietnam because he never talked about it.

We had many problems: sexual problems, economic problems, depression, and loneliness. My husband was a loner. He tended to lose friends easily because he'd refuse to forgive. He withdrew from his parents and began to do poorly at work. At this point, I was starting to become depressed and withdrawn, too. I got sick with migraines and was angry a lot. Yet not being able to count on my husband for very much gave me a drive—a drive to succeed at work. Even though I started out a GS-5 secretary in the government without a college degree, I've worked myself up to a supervisory mid-level position and have enjoyed one professional success after another.

I had to succeed at work because I had to pay all the bills. My husband had trouble keeping jobs and there were always lawyer bills, fines, car wrecks, and other expenses. When Big Al would be out all night, I used to wonder if he was dead or in jail. I hate to admit it, but a part of me used to wish he was dead because we couldn't afford any more lawyer bills and court costs.

Even when he didn't come home at night, the next morning I'd go to work and function as if nothing had happened. I couldn't break, because if I did, where would I be? And what would happen to our three children?

I couldn't break, but I did internalize everything and began to withdraw even more. Besides, most of my friends couldn't cope with my problems. If I'd start talking about Big Al, they'd just tell me to leave him, not understanding that with three children, this is not easy. Also, I am a committed family woman. If Big Al had cancer, I wouldn't have left him. In my view, Big Al had a mental disease, not a physical one, and I was not going to abandon him.

Even when he would verbally abuse me, I knew a part of him didn't mean it—that it was somebody else being so nasty, not my Big Al. Besides, leaving Big Al would have felt like defeat and I was a fighter, just like he was. Deep inside, I knew Big Al was a good man and that the only reason he couldn't feel for me was because he couldn't feel for himself. Even when he'd get locked up in jail, he'd be as kind and good to me as could be.

All the while, neither of us suspected Vietnam. I was so naive to it, that eleven years into the marriage, I didn't even know he had been in the jungles. At that time, society didn't recognize, much less realize, what it was like to be a grunt in Vietnam. When we went to our family doctor and to two or three therapists for help, they listened, but they didn't know about PTSD either.

My children have not been deeply scarred by my husband's behavior because 99% of the time, he is a wonderful father. Also, I protected them from most of their father's depressions. Whenever Big Al would start lying around the house, smoking pot or drinking, I'd take the children out. I didn't want them to see their father unwashed and unshaven. I didn't know why he was acting like this and I'd just scream and yell. Now when I see my husband not taking care of himself, I know that he has reached the point of depression, and I beg him to go for help.

PTSD therapy has helped my husband a great deal, but we still have problems. I have problems too, mainly pent up anger from years of always having to be strong and responsible. I'm afraid that if someone would put their arms around me, I would start crying and never stop.

Elizabeth, wife of Big Al, a Vietnam
Army hero

Lorraine's Story

My husband slit his wrists in the shower, with one of the knives from Vietnam that he had sometimes used on me. I almost left him after he used me for target practice one night. But I blame Vietnam for this, not him.

Len had been a medic in Vietnam, where he was forced to choose who would live and who would die. He talked about Vietnam night and day, but not to me. He read every book on the subject, but I was not allowed to do the same. Not until the day of his funeral did I find out any details about what he had experienced or why he finally decided to end his life.

At the funeral, his war buddies told me that the week before, Len had made some mistakes on the job. They weren't life-and-death mistakes, but his errors in reading certain lab results had messed up some patient's treatment plan. Len was a dedicated lab technician. He simply could not handle the guilt, not on top of all the survivor guilt he felt about the guys he had had to let die in 'Nam. Len used to hear their voices in the night.

I also found out that Len had gone to great lengths to save a certain Vietnamese family. The family was massacred anyway. Len blamed himself.

Is that why he made my life miserable? When Len was angry, nothing was safe. Furniture flew, curtains were ripped, toys were smashed. The name calling was vicious and PTA meetings, visits to the grandparents, and all shopping trips for the children were cancelled. I could hardly ever take the kids to the movies and we never invited anyone over for dinner.

If I felt a beating coming on, I'd lock the children in their bedrooms, or, if there was time, drive them to my mother's. Eventually, however, Len would wear out and everything would be peaceful. Sincerely repentant, he would shower us with love and many gifts.

I'm sorry Len is dead, but a part of me feels released. I was tired of walking on eggshells and having one anxiety attack after another. My thinking had become distorted, too, as I was always trying to find answers to problems over which I had no control. I was always irritable and depressed and when he'd be gone for hours, wandering aimlessly in the streets, I didn't know who was closer to suicide, him or me.

Not knowing how I could change my life, I started taking Valium and then, alcohol. When I realized that my drinking was making me neglect my children, however, I went to AA and I have been a sober and good mother ever since. But Len remembered my drinking days and my mothering mistakes and sometimes used them as excuses to physically abuse me.

Vietnam was another excuse. Why I had to take the beating for something some lieutenant or Viet Cong did twenty years ago is a mystery to me. But when Len was banging my head against the toilet bowl or smashing my back against the refrigerator, the idea made perfect sense to him. Intellectually, I knew I was not to blame for the beatings, but emotionally I felt I deserved them. It didn't help that Len pointed out everything wrong with me all the time.

Usually around patriotic holidays, or even other holidays, like Labor Day, Len would get into one of his moods and not allow me to see or talk to anybody for two or three days. Sometimes he'd abuse me, but mainly he just wanted me around. He was paranoid about me leaving him. He was also afraid that if I went outside, somebody might hurt me. I'd get so lonely that sometimes I would call the operator just to hear a human voice.

Over time, I became increasingly passive and numb to my own emotions, as well as psychologically depleted from dealing with my husband's Dr. Jekyll/Mr. Hyde personality. He would be the brute one day and Mr. Wonderful the next, leaving me in a constant state of confusion about whether to stay with him or leave him.

Now that Len is gone, I miss him. I think he was basically a good man, but a misguided one. There were times he was so loving, so giving, so charming that he melted my heart. Yet I have trouble reconciling my affection for him with his abuse of me. I can't blame Vietnam for all his problems, but I am certain that if he hadn't been in that war, he would have been a different man.

I have never set foot in Vietnam. Yet I consider myself a veteran also. Most Vietnam vets only served for thirteen months. I lived, breathed, slept, and fought with that war for thirteen years.

Lorraine, formerly battered wife of a
Vietnam combat vet

One

What Post-Traumatic Stress Disorder (PTSD) Is

"I hate Vietnam!" Jessica sobbed. "Ed went over there a warm, outgoing person. He came back angry, withdrawn, taking out all his anger on me and the kids. Why he has to turn on us—the ones he loves the most—I just don't understand. The yelling, being called every name in the book; it hurts deep, very deep, even more than the physical abuse.

"He's angry at me, his own wife, almost all the time. It's like I'm another person to him, a stranger, not the wife who has stood by him for fifteen years."

Jessica is the petite, attractive wife of a Vietnam combat vet named Ed. Jessica met Ed just before he was sent overseas. They fell in love almost immediately and she has been his faithful partner ever since. For over two years now, Jessica has been attending a woman's group at a local Vet Center. All the women share Jessica's pain, fears, and profound loneliness. They are all wives of Vietnam vets.

Although still living with Ed, Jessica feels alone and abandoned. Her husband, it seems, is involved with another woman. The other wives have the same complaint: their husbands are involved with another woman, too—the *same* other woman.

Her name is Vietnam. She is ugly and battle scarred, but her power is great. Somehow this "other woman"—Vietnam—still controls the men who knew her.

Saigon fell years ago, but the Vietnam war still rages in the hearts and minds of many vets, robbing them of emotional closeness with the ones they love and preventing them from enjoying fulfilling lives. A significant number of Vietnam veterans suffer from Post-Traumatic

Stress Disorder, PTSD, the current psychiatric label given to a malady more commonly known as "shell shock," "combat fatigue" or "war neurosis."

> *Remembering is worse than being there.*[1]
>
> *I wish I didn't have PTSD, but I do. Even when I'm happy, I'm sad. 'Nam is like a permanent dent in my heart and mind. Tonight I was at a party with my wife. My favorite music was playing. I felt love for her and even for life itself. But this happiness only made me acutely aware of the pain of my past.*
>
> *As we did a fast dance, I found myself stomping the ground angrily, muttering, 'Damn you, bitch. Damn you, bitch. You caused my buddy's death.' When I started flashing, I knew it was time to leave. But, damn, where do I go to get away from my own head?*
>
> *I want to write, to heal myself, but depression has immobilized me. Can I even move this pen?*
>
> *This morning I could barely get out of bed. Would I ever get up? Would I ever want to.*
>
> *The world is cold and bleak. There's nothing to live for. I can't bear the deadness inside me anymore. All I feel is anger and pain about Vietnam. Yet I'm sick and tired of thinking about that place. Why can't I turn off the memories?*
>
> *I saw a pregnant woman crossing the street yesterday proudly caressing her belly. I hated her for being happy and wanted to rip her belly open, like I saw in 'Nam. Thank God, I never did anything like that, but I came close.*
>
> *I want to be normal, like everyone else, and enjoy the good things in life. I have a wonderful wife, who has stood by me though all my depressions and ex-plosions (not to mention my ten years of drinking) and a beautiful twelve-year-old daughter, too. But am I happy? Hardly ever.*
>
> *I'm constantly worried that my daughter is going to be raped or in a car accident. Whenever her school bus is late, even two minutes, I break out into cold sweats, hyperventilate, and want to call the rescue squad. I keep thinking that God is going to punish me soon for things*

*I did in 'Nam, or for things I was tempted to do by
taking away my child.*

*I can't forget. I can't drive in the rain or go to bar-
becues either. Hot, wet weather and burning meat
remind me of 'Nam. In my dreams, dismembered bodies,
and teeth without the gold fillings float in the air, I
make love to ugly Oriental prostitutes and then the dead
VC come back to life—angry at me.*

*I can't go home for Christmas, either. First there's
my father, the World War II hero who thinks we lost
the war because guys like me drank and drugged too
much. And then there's my cousin Ralph, Mr. Success.
'You could have gone to Canada, but, no, you had to
go prove something. So don't cry now.'*

*His old lady wears furs. Mine stands on her feet all
day for $4.54 an hour. My career was shot to hell by
'Nam, but I don't care. Deep down, I hate myself—hate
myself, hate myself, hate myself, for what I became in
'Nam, for things that weren't even my fault.*
                    Vietnam Vets

The Vietnam veteran with PTSD is a case of unwept tears, un-
suffered suffering, a numb heart full of pain, subject to unwanted
rage reactions which express not only a deep sense of betrayal and
alienation, but a profound sense of grief, helplessness, self-pity, and
self-hate as well.

One of my patients described his PTSD as an "inner agony that
has no name, yet has many faces." Some vets run from their PTSD
with drugs and alcohol. Others dry heave every morning, mistreat
their wives and children, and have difficulty keeping jobs. Some try
to escape by overcontrolling their wives and children or by overcontrolling themselves with impossible "to do" lists and other forms of
workaholism. Still other vets withdraw from society altogether and
live as virtual hermits in secluded parts of the country.[2]

The official definition of PTSD, adopted by psychiatrists and
psychologists, states that for a person to qualify as having the
syndrome, he (or she) must:
1. Have had a history of trauma;
2. Find themselves re-experiencing the trauma in the form of
   such things as dreams, flashbacks, and intrusive memories;

3. Experience a numbing of emotions and reduced interest in others and in activities in the world; and

4. Have at least two of the following symptoms (which did not exist prior to the trauma): difficulties with memory and concentration, sleep disturbances, hyperalertness (the startle response), or avoidance of people, places and activities which arouse memories of the traumatic event.[3]

In life, we all face crises, large and small, ranging from the loss of a wallet to the death of a loved one. Yet these events, while stressful, cannot be considered traumas. Traumas severe enough to cause PTSD are of such magnitude, horror, or duration that they overwhelm your emotional and physical coping mechanisms.

Basically, PTSD is a normal reaction to an abnormal amount of stress. Imagine being in a car accident, twenty times a month, for twelve months in a row. Imagine being raped, twice a week, for a solid year. How would you feel? Even if these terrible things were not happening to you directly, what if they were happening to persons all around you and you were powerless to stop it? What if you knew that at any moment, you might be the next victim?

That's what it was like in Vietnam, for all but a few. In a war where bar girls had hand grenades and even babies were booby trapped, almost anyone, man, woman, or child, could be a possible enemy. There were few, if any, "safe zones." Death was everywhere.

One reason for the delayed onset of PTSD in some veterans is that during the Vietnam war men were sent overseas for one year only. When they "broke down" or became dysfunctional during battle, they were not as readily removed from combat as during previous wars. They were usually treated for their symptoms, told to "hang on" just a little longer, until their DEROS (Date of Estimated Return from Overseas), and were "quickly reinstated in the unit."[4]

It is not only war veterans who can acquire PTSD. Anyone who has undergone a trauma outside the range of normal human stress can develop this disorder. The symptoms of PTSD have been noted in prisoners of war, survivors of the Nazi holocaust and the bombing of Hiroshima, as well as among severe burn and head injury patients. PTSD has also developed among victims of rape, incest, and other assaults; among survivors of natural catastrophes, such as earthquakes, fires, floods, hurricanes, and tornados; and among refuge children.[5,6] While PTSD is found among survivors of natural traumas or catastrophes, it is more prevalent, more long-term, and more intense among victims of manmade disasters.[7]

According to Sarah Haley, who has worked extensively with Vietnam vets, trauma consists of being made into an object.[8] Whether one's assaulter is a tornado, a rapist, or a Viet Cong, at the moment of attack, one does not feel like a human being with the right to safety, happiness, and health. At that moment, one almost becomes a thing, a vulnerable object subject to the will of a power or force greater than one's self. When the assailant is a natural force, such as an earthquake, the catastrophe can somehow be explained away as an "accident of fate." However, when the assailant is another person, the victim's trust in other human beings, and in society in general, can be severely shaken or shattered entirely.

PTSD symptoms are not signs of mental illness. The person who manifests PTSD symptoms is "responding to specific experiences" and "needs help in identifying and resolving the issues raised by these experiences."[9] Neither is PTSD a sign that an individual is psychologically "weak" or "disorganized," as shown by the fact that PTSD has been found to develop among a variety of survivors of natural catastrophes, many of whom had no previous significant psychological problems.[10]

Furthermore, PTSD can develop in persons who witness trauma on a daily basis or are subject to "persistent and unrelieved" stress as part of their job.[11] This statement holds true even for individuals who are carefully screened for mental health problems prior to admission to their field. For example, PTSD has been found among rescue workers, fire fighters, health care teams, and police officers.[12]

As human beings, we must all confront the fact of our mortality. We and our loved ones will die someday, no matter who we are or what we do. Usually this awareness comes to us and stays with us more powerfully in our middle or later years, when we see our parents and their friends dying, or when we ourselves acquire an illness. However, victims of catastrophes, individuals who work with life and death experiences on a daily basis, and combat soldiers confront the existential reality of death sooner than most. Like survivors of car accidents and assault, the Vietnam veteran touched his death in Vietnam. In addition, the seeming senselessness of the war compounded his or her reaction to the wounding and killing all around, resulting in a cynicism and sense of futility that, for some, can last for many years.[13]

In the face of trauma, such as combat, torture, or rape, a person usually shuts down emotionally. Feelings are not felt, but suppressed, so that the individual can survive the traumatic event. As a result of this suppression, however, a range of symptoms may develop. Among Vietnam veterans, the symptoms of PTSD include the following:

> Depression
> Anger
> Sleep disturbances
> Anxiety
> A tendency to react under stress with survival tactics
> Loss of interest in work or activities
> Suicidal feelings and thoughts
> Fantasies of retaliation
> Alienation
> Negative self-image
> Memory impairment
> Cynicism and distrust of government and authority figures
> Hypersensitivity to injustice
> Difficulty with authority figures
> Tendency to fits of rage
> Problems with intimate relations
> Emotional distance from others
> Survivor guilt
> Avoidance of activities that arouse memories of trauma in the war
> Fear of losing others and self-deceiving, and self-punishing patterns of behavior.[14]

PTSD, however, is more than a list of symptoms. The fundamental force underlying the symptoms of PTSD is the veteran's re-experiencing of the trauma followed by his attempts to bury memories of the trauma and the feelings associated with the trauma. He will repeat this sequence over and over. This cyclical recurrence is an essential characteristic of the syndrome.

As more than one Vietnam veteran wife has observed, her husband suddenly withdraws soon after openly sharing with her. "I was so excited when Tom finally talked to me about Vietnam," Joan told the women's group. "All these years, he hasn't said a word about it. Finally, maybe, I thought we could be close. He even told me he had more to tell me. But ever since he opened up last week, he's shut down more than ever. He won't even tell me what he wants for dinner and hasn't let me touch him for over a week.

"What did I do wrong? I didn't know exactly what to say when he told me about some of his firefights. I'm no psychologist, but I was sympathetic. Maybe I wasn't sympathetic enough. Did I turn him off somehow?"

Joan did not do "anything wrong." She didn't "turn off" Tom either. Tom turned himself off. Like many wives, Joan was shocked and dismayed at her husband's withdrawal and assumed that she was responsible. But her husband's withdrawal is not the result of her behavior: it is a predictable feature of the cyclical nature of PTSD.

Tom, like many vets with untreated PTSD, is in a state of emotional numbing. He has shoved many of his emotions, especially those surrounding Vietnam, out of his conscious awareness. But this does not mean that these feelings are not there, nor that they do not motivate him.

Feelings are real and powerful. Although we can't see or touch them, they can heavily influence our behavior, our thought life, and even our spiritual life. Like Tom, we can push down our feelings in an attempt to make them go away, pretend that they aren't there at all, or that they are relatively unimportant. But eventually the stifled emotions will surface and clamor for attention: "Here I am. Here I am. Deal with me. Deal with me."

In the case of the Vietnam veteran with PTSD, the emotions and the memories associated with them emerge in conscious or unconscious awareness over and over again in a variety of forms, ranging from intrusive thoughts and images to dissociative states. This process is called "re-experiencing the trauma."

It is as if the veteran keeps playing a video movie with a sad ending over and over again, hoping that perhaps this time the ending will be a happy one. Of course, his wish does not come true. But he keeps playing the movie time and time again, hoping against hope that with enough repetitions, the desired ending will come to pass. The veteran is so absorbed with the unresolved traumas of his past that he has less psychic energy and emotion to devote to his job, his friends and family, and most importantly, to himself, in the present.

"My husband can't be there for me when I'm sick," explained Joan. "He loves me and wants to give to me; he just doesn't have it to give. Because of his PTSD, his emotional resources are limited."

Because much of the PTSD afflicted Vietnam veteran's psychic energy is bound up with his war experiences, when there is a family crisis, it is not unusual for the veteran to shut down emotionally. According to the Vet Center survey, about 40% of the time, it is the Vietnam wife or some other family member, not the veteran himself, who takes charge and handles most of the practical and emotional matters involved.

The vet may avoid the crisis because he fears it will aggravate his memories and bring upon him the hell of re-experiencing the trauma. This re-experiencing the trauma may occur in the form of:

1. Intrusive thoughts and images of the Vietnam experience;
2. Dreams, nightmares, or night terrors; and
3. Flashbacks, both conscious and unconscious, sometimes called dissociative states.

During dreams or nightmares, the veteran may shake, shout, scream, and thrash about with considerable violence.[15] He may or may not remember the dream upon awakening. However, the feelings of terror and fear contained in the dream may persist for quite some time.

The insomnia which plagues some veterans can be seen as an attempt to avoid such dreams and nightmares. Some vets overindulge in alcohol or drugs before they sleep, in hopes that these substances will obliterate the dreams. Others can only sleep with weapons nearby or under their pillows.

Nightmares and dreams about Vietnam create a high level of anxiety for the veteran because he is forced to relive traumatic events. In addition, his daytime coping abilities—as well as those of his wife or partner—may be hurt because the dreams interfere with much-needed rest. Some families are awakened by the veteran's cries and screams. In other cases, men wake up their wives and children after nightmares, to make sure they are still alive, to ask them for reassurance, or for help in searching the home for Viet Cong. Another disturbing element about the nightmares is that they are unpredictable, making the veteran feel as if he is "out of control."[16]

The feeling of helplessness is found in most of these nightmares. For example, "being trapped in a foxhole with V.C. pulling at me and trying to drag me further down into the hole with them;" "V.C. sneaking up on me in my sleep and not being able to wake up in time;" "being wounded and put in a body bag and being carried to the cellar and I am screaming at people that I'm not dead, but they continue putting me there anyway;" "being chased by men with no faces through jungle and then I fall off a cliff," "malfunctioning weapon," and "four or five days per week I am being killed by a gun, knife, or an injection."[17]

Next to dreams, flashbacks of Vietnam veterans are perhaps the most publicized forms of re-experiencing the trauma. Basically, a flashback is a sudden, vivid recollection of the traumatic event accompanied by strong emotion. The veteran does not "black out" or lose consciousness but he does, temporarily, leave the present and find himself back in Vietnam. He may see the scenes of Vietnam, smell the smells and hear the sounds. He may or may not lose contact with present reality and he may or may not find himself acting as if he is back in Vietnam. During such flashbacks, he may easily confuse his wife and children for the "enemy." Wives report that sometimes their husbands alternate between recognizing them as their wives and seeing them as Viet Cong.

Veterans may be reluctant to acknowledge that they are "flashing" for fear of sounding "crazy." Yet their histories may reveal many instances of "'coming to' with a memory of having once again been engaged in a war experience, such as going out on patrol or driving on a road in the jungle....These episodes may last up to several hours and are not without risk. Serious injuries have occurred when veterans have prowled around backyards and alleys at night fully armed, re-experiencing a patrol in hostile territory."[18]

While a few dramatic cases involving flashbacks have been well publicized in the media, most Vietnam veterans who "flash" do so more quietly, in the privacy of their hearts and minds, without public commotion. While "extreme public episodes are rare," "flashing" is not.[19] Neither is "flashing" peculiar to Vietnam veterans. It has been observed in survivors of Nazi concentration camps and in World War II aviation personnel.[20,21,22] It tends to occur among persons who have had to endure situations where there was an "intense, chronic, or pervasive loss of security" and lack of safety.[23]

Flashbacks can be conscious or unconscious. In conscious flashbacks, the veteran experiences vivid images of war events and can later report what he has seen, even if he had temporary amnesia during or after the flashback.[24] During unconscious flashbacks, however, the veteran may find himself engaged in unusual behavior motivated by some memory of Vietnam, but he has no conscious awareness of any thoughts or emotions about Vietnam, either during the time of the flashback, or later. Upon examining the episodes in therapy, however, usually the episode will reveal itself to be a "repetition of some event(s) in the war."[25]

To the wives and children of Vietnam veterans, flashbacks are always frightening. When their loved one falls to the ground or commands them to "walk the point" with him, they fear not only for their own safety, but for his. His moves are unpredictable. He could easily hurt himself in so many ways. How can they protect him? How can they protect themselves? How long will it take until he "comes back" this time? What if he never "comes back" or kills himself to end his anguish?

Women in group have been held hostage anywhere from two hours to two days by men who have refused to let them out of their homes, or certain rooms, for fear that they would be killed by Viet Cong. Sometimes the home, or portions of the home, are barricaded with wire or rope. Phones are ripped off the walls, doors are chained shut, and, if the vet has weapons, knives, guns, and ammunition may be made ready for the first intruder.

In preparation, women keep extra supplies of groceries and medications on hand. If the flashback happens to occur while one of the children is out of the home, the woman must use utmost tenderness and cleverness to obtain her husband's permission to get the child or to allow a trusted friend to do so. If she must go herself, she worries about what will happen to her husband or other children while she is gone.

If she has other children, she may want to take them with her, but the vet might insist that the children stay with him "for protection." Or perhaps he may not believe that she will return. If he keeps the other children with him, then he knows she will come home again. Sometimes there are physical struggles over the children. Special problems arise when one of the children is ill and must be taken to a doctor while the husband is having an episode.

Women in these situations usually evidence extraordinary coping abilities. Many have managed to keep their husbands sane and alive, even while severely physically ill themselves or while caring for infants. Most of the women report little fear for themselves. "Mike would never hurt me or the kids," says Debbie. "Even when he confuses me with the enemy, I can bring him out of it by caressing his face and telling him, 'It's me, Debbie, your wife. You're home. You're safe. You're not in Vietnam. It's me, Debbie, your wife, I love you.'"

Debbie, like the other wives, usually dares not call the police. The mere presence of a uniformed person might drive their husbands "wild." Some husbands have threatened to kill any police that would come. If the veteran has had violent episodes since his return to the U.S., the wife has to take such a threat seriously. The women are also afraid to call the neighbors for help, for fear they too will be harmed. In some cases, the women are ashamed to tell the neighbors or do not feel the neighbors would be sympathetic. Furthermore, if the neighbors were told, they might become alarmed and ostracize the veteran and his family.

For the most part, women go along with whatever their husbands ask of them: whether it be hiding under the bed to avoid enemy attack, or building fires in the backyard. Children also become involved. While younger children might think it's great fun to tiptoe around the living room with Daddy at two in the morning with a flashlight, older children are saddened, concerned, angered, or confused by their father's behavior. Sometimes younger children imitate their fathers. They may hide under the bed whenever a helicopter flies by or refuse rice and other "gook food."

Older children may not imitate their father as readily, but they may not understand their father's problem either. They may be afraid to ask questions for fear of precipitating another flashback or family uproar. If the flashback has occurred in public, or in front of friends, the child might be embarrassed and ashamed of his father. If the flashbacks are numerous, the child may resent the interruptions. On a deeper level, however, the child feels helpless and at the same time takes on adult responsibilities. Many learn to assist their mother in "bringing Daddy home." They may wipe his brow and whisper words of love and reassurance just like Mommy. They may regularly help their mother remove objects from the room on which their father could hurt himself.

As Dr. Arthur Blank points out in *The Trauma of War: Stress and Recovery in Vietnam Veterans,* flashbacks have not received the scholarly attention of mental health professionals.[26] Sometimes, mental health professionals have misdiagnosed flashback behavior as "uncontrollable rage reactions" and oriented therapy toward helping the veteran with his "poor impulse control." Veterans with PTSD would be better served by an exploration of the history of their war experiences and the personal meaning of that history.[27]

Another form of re-experiencing the trauma, which may be related to unconscious flashbacks, consists of suddenly feeling certain painful or angry feelings which do not seem clearly related to any particular memory of Vietnam. For example, vets have reported rage reactions, panic attacks, or intense psychic pain without any conscious thought of the war.[28]

"I can understand when my husband sulks or explodes after hearing about some vet killing himself or about some buddy dying in a car accident. But many times he gets moody or angry for no reason at all," explained one wife. Yet what this wife, and her husband, may not fully appreciate is that often there is a reason for the emotional upset, even though that reason may not be obvious to either one of them. The reason may lie in the intensity of the vet's repressed emotions about Vietnam. The feelings may emerge even when they are not triggered by any specific reminder of the war or any particular war memory.

Since re-experiencing the trauma can be so painful and possibly dangerous, the PTSD afflicted veteran may find himself retreating, mentally, socially, and physically. For example, one vet stopped going to shopping malls after flashing and falling to the ground in the middle of a department store. As a result of his PTSD, the vet may also experience some memory loss or impairment or have trouble concentrating or remembering current information.

Wives report that their husbands "forget" not only therapy and doctor appointments, but also where they have put money or to pick up children from the babysitters. Perhaps the husbands are lying, but their forgetfulness may be the combined result of drinking or alcohol addiction and unacknowledged and untreated PTSD. As Dr. Arnold points out in *The Trauma of War: Stress and Recovery in Vietnam Veterans*, such mental difficulties are "clearly more" than boredom, laziness, or lack of intellectual ability. They can represent a form of escape, a "distressful impairment of the capacity to appreciate" the experience at hand.[29]

In sum, vets with PTSD alternate between re-experiencing the trauma and avoiding re-experiencing the trauma. Sometimes "triggers" in the environment can set off a memory. For example, the sound of popping popcorn or helicopters, the sight of plastic trash bags (reminiscent of body bags), or the advent of hot, humid weather can put a veteran psychologically back to the original event. Sometimes he may react with the exaggerated startle response so characteristic of Vietnam veterans. An airplane passes by overhead and suddenly he is out of bed, reaching for a weapon, waiting to shoot the Viet Cong. The only people to shoot at, however, may be his own family.

Also associated with PTSD but not essential to the diagnosis of the syndrome, is increased irritability, with little or no provocation, and impulsive behavior. In an attempt to escape their memories, some vets change from one job to the next, move from one part of the country to the next, with unusual frequency. These many moves are sometimes forms of running from the past or a desperate searching for a "geographical cure" for the hurting, confused self inside.

PTSD is, by definition, a delayed reaction to the war. Symptoms may emerge one, two, even twenty years later. Often stress in the present—economic difficulties, a death in the family, or the veteran's own midlife crisis—will bring out symptoms of PTSD which the veteran had previously been able to control. According to several Vet Center counselors, often it is a major loss in the family—the death of parent or child—which brings the veteran's PTSD to the surface and forces him to seek help.

Many women who have attended the Vet Center women's group report that their husbands were—or seemed—"normal" until the death of a sibling or parent. Tim, for example, had been working successfully as a dietician in a hospital for ten years following Vietnam. His wife had noticed no signs of PTSD in him, except a tendency toward withdrawal, which she attributed to his family background. Also, he would sometimes drink too much. "But what man doesn't?" she reasoned.

However, last year, Tim had to deal with multiple stresses: the death of two nieces, a major car accident, and an overload at work. These combined pressures brought to the surface memories of Vietnam which he had previously suppressed. His drinking increased, as did his absences from home. While he was able to function at work, he found himself increasingly irritated with some of his patients, especially when they were rude to him. One day, a patient was being particularly demanding and verbally abusive toward Tim. Unable to contain himself any longer, Tim threw the man out of the bed. What frightened Tim was not that he attacked this man, but that he wanted to kill him. Tim feels he would have killed the patient had nurses and the hospital police not stopped him. Fear of his own rage sent Tim to a local Vet Center for help.

The root of PTSD is a fear of loss—of personal annihilation, death, or dismemberment, or of losing others. Just as the concentration camp victims, rape victims, and prisoners of war are not "insane" for displaying the symptoms of PTSD, neither is the troubled Vietnam veteran.

War is seldom good for people. Even the ancient Greeks commented on the negative effects of war on man's psyche. So did Shakespeare and other writers. For decades, too, mental health professionals have noted the psychiatric effects of war and talked about "war neurosis."

Veterans of previous wars have suffered from PTSD, even though their distress was not labeled as such. Among American troops, PTSD-like symptoms caused the evacuation of some 10% of enlisted men during World War I and, at various points, of over 300% more, during World War II. The psychiatric casualty rate was high during World War II despite elaborate psychological screening procedures which supposedly "weeded out" "weak men" prone to mental collapse. After World War II, however, military experts concluded that the trauma of war was often enough to impair even the "strongest" and "toughest" of men.[30]

World War I and World War II veterans who suffered from PTSD often kept their problems to themselves—or drowned them in alcohol. If it is not "macho" for a man to admit that he has inner turmoil today, it was even less so in the past. The fact that numerous World War II and Korean war veterans are still suffering from nightmares and other symptoms of PTSD has recently been brought to the attention of the U.S. Congress as part of a movement to open Vietnam Veteran Outreach Centers to older veterans of previous wars who have never received help for their PTSD.[31]

During World War I the psychological stress of war was first recognized by mental health professionals. During the "Great War," the "idea developed that the high air pressure of the exploding shells caused actual physiological damage," which, in turn, lead to numerous psychological symptoms that were later named "shell shock."[32] By the end of the war, the malady that seemed to afflict so many survivors was called "war neurosis."[33]

During the Korean war, the military, now aware of "war neurosis," provided immediate, on-site help to afflicted servicemen. Such assistance reduced the percentage of evacuations for psychiatric reasons from 23% during World War II to 6% during the Korean conflict.[34] During the Vietnam war, in an attempt to further reduce the psychiatric casualty rate, the one year tour of duty was adopted. The military reasoned that if men were subject to combat for only a year, they would be less susceptible to psychological breakdown.

The symptoms of PTSD in Vietnam veterans are almost identical to those suffered by World War II and Korean war vets.[35,36] These symptoms have been found among Australian troops who served in Vietnam as well.[37] In fact, the psychiatric casualty rate among Australian Vietnam veterans is almost equivalent to that of American Vietnam veterans.[38]

It cannot be overemphasized that having PTSD does not mean that the veteran is "mentally ill" any more than the earthquake victim is "mentally ill" for exhibiting stress reactions due to his experiences. Two recent studies found that while many vets evidenced stress reactions to the war, they were, nevertheless, psychologically healthy.[39] This phenomenon—the co-existence of stress reactions with healthy adjustment—has been found to be characteristic of survivors of other catastrophes as well.

"Most of the vets I know," writes Harrington, a counselor of hundreds of Vietnam veterans and a Vietnam veteran himself, "are successful journalists, plumbers, lawyers, electricians and, yes, advertising executives. They are bound together by one tie: Vietnam. Some suffer in a dignified silence. Others just can't do that."[40]

Summary

PTSD is a normal reaction to an abnormal amount of stress. The symptoms of PTSD—which include depression, emotional numbing, and avoidance of people, places, and things which remind the individual of the original traumatic event—can be suffered by anyone who has experienced an event or series of events outside the usual range of human experience. The events must be life-threatening or of such magnitude of pain and horror that they would overwhelm almost anyone's natural coping mechanisms.

Women living with men who suffer from active cases of PTSD must cope not only with the normal stresses of marriage, but with the fact that their husbands suffer from emotional numbing as well as depression, low self-esteem, anger, survivor guilt, sleep disturbances, social withdrawal, and hypersensitivity to noise, rejection, and injustice. Some vets experience these symptoms regularly; others only during certain emotionally sensitive times such as the anniversary date of an important battle. "He loves me but he runs from that love all the time."

As a result of all these stresses, the women are under constant pressure and may suffer from severe emotional strain. They may become depressed, isolated, anxious, and angry. As their emotional resources become depleted, they begin operating on "remote control," and retreat from others. They may become emotionally numb just like their husbands.

Questions And Information On PTSD

How Many Veterans Really Are Suffering With PTSD?

Some 58,000 Americans died in Vietnam. Approximately 300,000 more were wounded, 150,000 requiring hospitalization. Another 75,000 were severely disabled. Over 5,000 lost limbs, with over 1,000 sustaining multiple amputations.[41] Staggering numbers, but the number of Americans losing their emotional and mental health to PTSD may be even larger.

Since 1969, over 600,000 Vietnam veterans have sought government help for readjustment difficulties. Nationwide, Vet Centers treat about 150,000 vets a year and an additional 28,000 are in treatment for PTSD in one of our nation's 172 Veteran's Administration Hospitals, thirteen of which have special PTSD units.

While experts disagree on the true extent of PTSD, most put the figure at from 500,000 to one million. Since PTSD is, by definition, a delayed response to the war, the number of vets eventually in need of psychiatric help may reach as many as 1.5 million or more.[42]

"With Vietnam (psychological casualties) are increasing without war activities and it's still increasing. We still haven't seen the peak," states Dr. Ben Jennings, clinical psychologist at the Silver Spring, Maryland Vet Center.[43] In response to the growing need, the Vietnam Veteran's Outreach Program was recently expanded to include 189 vet centers.

The truth is, however, that we do not actually know how many Vietnam veterans suffer from PTSD. It was not until 1980 that PTSD was officially recognized as a "mental illness" by the American Psychiatric Association. Before that time, vets with PTSD were sometimes given psychiatric diagnoses that either excluded or minimized the role of the war on their psychological well-being.[44] As more and more mental health professionals become familiar with the nature of PTSD, they will be better able to detect and treat the syndrome in their patients.

The diagnosis of PTSD, however, can be a very challenging task, for PTSD can coexist with a host of other psychological problems—depressive disorders, alcoholism, anxiety disorders, paranoia, and even schizophrenia. In addition, some of the characteristics of PTSD are remarkably similar to those of other mental illnesses.[45]

On the other hand, a veteran can have PTSD and have few, if any external symptoms of distress. It is perfectly possible for a vet to have PTSD and still function on the job and at home. In fact, one survey reports that about 80% of the Vietnam era vets have "adjusted well both during and following military service."[45] Notice, however that this 80% figure refers to Vietnam *era* vets (the 9 million who served in the U.S. military between 1964 and 1975), not to those 2.5 million who served specifically in Vietnam or to those who saw combat, the two groups which seem to be most affected by PTSD.

Another reason we do not know how many men suffer from PTSD is that some fail to seek help for fear of being labeled "weak" or "unmanly." Some vets, especially those with relatives who supposedly made it through previous wars without any problems, feel it is "shameful" to seek counseling. Embued with the masculine stereotype of the "real man" being one who is always strong and in control of his emotions, it is most difficult for some veterans to admit to themselves, much less to another human being, that they have any psychological problems.[47]

In addition, denial is a central feature of PTSD. Like alcoholism, drug addiction, and compulsive overeating, PTSD is a condition that tells its victims that they really don't have a problem. "That's what I told myself for years," explains one vet. "I thought if I ignored it, it would go away."

Some vets even pretend that the war "didn't really happen." This denial serves as a major defense against feeling the extremely uncomfortable feelings that often went along with the Vietnam experience: specifically, the fear, the guilt, the grief, and the rage, not to mention the moral confusion.

What Was So Special About The Vietnam War?

"What was so special about the Vietnam war?" I am often asked. "All wars are hell. World War II and Korean war vets had a hard time too, but you don't see them running around, exaggerating their problems to get sympathy and benefits from the government.

"PTSD is a bunch of baloney," the reasoning continues.

"Whatever problems those guys have now, they had before the war. Besides, the war was fought by rejects. That's why we lost."

Wrong. The men sent to Vietnam constituted the best educated army America has ever fielded. "Seventy-nine percent of the men who served in Vietnam had a high school education or better when they entered military service. In comparison, only 63% of Korean War vets and only 45% of World War II vets had completed high school upon separation from the military."[48]

Another unique feature of the Vietnam war was that it was American's first "teenage" war. The average age of the American soldier in World War II was twenty-six, but in Vietnam, it was nineteen. During late adolescence, the personality is not yet formed and the individual is more vulnerable to stress. According to many experts on PTSD, the age of the Vietnam veteran when he entered the service played a decisive role in the development of PTSD.[49] Dr. John Wilson explains: "...late adolescence (is) the time of life when people put their identities together, their occupation, their sex role, their commitments, the normal developmental process that leads to a human identity.

"So if you take a nineteen-year-old soldier and subject him to tremendous war stress for a year...you end up with people who in their own words say, 'I'm a different person,' 'I'm changed,' 'I don't fit in.' 'I'm twenty and feel like I came back fifty.' This diffusion of identity is a universal feeling among people suffering from PTSD."[50] Vietnam vets are sometimes called the "old young men" because they went to war at a significantly lower age than soldiers of previous wars, yet emerged "old men" with "aged hearts."[51]

For some of the teenage soldiers, it was not only their first exposure to death, but their first time away from home and their first time in another country. "I felt like I was back in the stone age," says one vet.

It is widely acknowledged, both by Vietnam veterans and the general public, that the combat performance of individual soldiers was not the sole or major factor accounting for the outcome of the war. Most combat vets strongly believe that we lost "because the nation's political leadership would not permit our troops to win a traditional military victory."[52] Even 75% of the general public "agrees that it was a failure of political will, not of arms," that was responsible for losing the war.[53]

Although the Vietnam war was not the first twentieth century American war in which guerrilla tactics were used, it was the first in which guerrilla warfare predominated. And the guerilla warfare was particularly savage. The prevalence of specialized, well-hidden booby traps, often aimed directly at castration or dismemberment, is a major reason why permanently disabling wounds were sustained at a "far greater rate in Vietnam" than in previous wars.[54] "The percentage of Vietnam veterans who suffer from amputation or crippling wounds to the lower extremities is 300% higher than in World War II and 70% higher than in Korea. Multiple amputations occurred at the rate of 18.4% compared to 5.7% in World War II."[55]

In contrast to previous wars, during the Vietnam war, the serviceman typically entered and exited alone. Each soldier had his own DEROS (Date of Expected Return from Overseas Service). Units were constantly in a state of flux, which "undermined unit integrity, cohesiveness, and emotional support." Furthermore, the "one year tour of duty led to the adoption of a 'survivor mentality' and a 'short timers syndrome' which often undercut the soldier's capacity to make a full commitment to the war effort."[56]

What Effect Did The Atmosphere At Home Have On The Vietnam Vet?

> *In the fall of 1968, as I stopped at a traffic light on my walk to class across the campus at the University of Denver, a man stepped up to me and said, 'Hi.'*
>
> *Without waiting for my reply to his greeting, he pointed to the hook sticking out of my left sleeve. 'Get that in Vietnam?'*
>
> *I said, 'Yeah, up near Tam Ky in I Corps.'*
>
> *'Serves you right.'*
>
> *As the man walked away, I stood rooted, too confused with hurt, shame, and anger to react.*
>
> A Vietnam Veteran[57]

It was not only the unique military and political features of the Vietnam war which contributed to the development of PTSD among its surviving warriors, but the disappointing homecoming. Instead of a hero's welcome, many vets describe being greeted with either apathy or hostility. For many, their "good warrior ethos" was destroyed not only by experiences overseas, but by the view of significant segments of the American public of the Vietnam veteran as a deranged, drug abusing "babykiller."

In previous wars, men may have felt guilt for killing, but their guilt was at least partially absolved because they were seen by friends, family, and society as "good warriors," that is, as "heroes" who were killing as part of their duty. In general, the Vietnam veteran did not have the advantage of this societal absolution. Hence, Vietnam vets can be seen as suffering from two traumas, first the trauma of war and secondly, the trauma of an unwelcome homecoming.[58] As research has shown, vets with PTSD are characterized by a "negative perception of their family's helpfulness in their return home."[59] In many instances the veteran received indirect or direct messages that he should not talk about the war or his feelings about the war.[60] Such sharing would simply create too much anxiety and discomfort in the family members. One veteran told how he had to go hide in a closet to cry because his open expressions of grief were not tolerated either by his parents or his wife.

What Effect Does Combat Experience Have On PTSD?

While it is not necessary to have been in combat to have PTSD, study after study reveals that the greater the exposure to combat, the greater the severity of the PTSD. PTSD has also been found to be prevalent among those who saw or participated in the abusive random violence that is part of any war.[61]

It is not clear whether there was more random violence in Vietnam than in previous wars. Some argue that Vietnam was not unique in its legacy of atrocities, only in the fact that the atrocities were more publicized than in previous wars. On the other hand, special factors did operate in Vietnam which, in some cases, induced "extra killings."

In "Some Remarks on Slaughter," Gault, a psychiatrist who served in Vietnam, describes six psychological, social, and mechanical factors which contributed to the slaughter of defenseless Vietnamese civilians:

1. "The universality of the enemy"—the fact that the enemy was everywhere;
2. The cartoonization and dehumanization of the enemy—Orientals were not perceived as human, but as strange childlike creatures—dinks—who did not value human life anyway;
3. "The dilution of responsibility"—the fact that entire squads simultaneously attacked villages or crowds;
4. "The pressure to act" to prove that one was masculine or to execute revenge;
5. "The natural dominance of the psychopath" in war situations; and
6. "The ready availability of firepower."[62]

Most of my patients are well aware that they are not the first soldiers in history to be unnecessarily cruel. Most will say they would not have done some of the things they did in Vietnam had they not been under so much stress and seen atrocities committed on their friends by the Viet Cong. Nevertheless, some vets feel that they, in Vietnam, were more "animalistic" and "brutal" than previous warriors. The resulting sense of shame and self-hate can be intense.

In some cases, however, the vet may be experiencing this shame and self-hate on an unconscious level. He may not even be able to articulate any such feelings. If asked if he has a self-image problem, he may say "no." After all, shame, self-hate, and a negative self-image are not signs of masculinity. Yet, if the veteran is not able to acknowledge his shame or self-hate, and deal with it in an open, constructive manner, he may act it out destructively. For example, he may project his own feelings onto his wife or children or some other family member. If, on some level, he sees himself as "incompetent," "evil," or "bad" he may find himself criticizing his wife or children for what he sees as *their* misbehavior.

Vets who believe that manliness means exerting power and control over others, may be especially prone to lashing out at their wives or children, mothers, or pets when they are feeling out of control of their own lives or out of control of their own emotions due to their PTSD.

"I am a murderer, I deserve to be punished," is implied in the veteran's low regard for himself.[63] Some vets may not wait for society or the God of their understanding to punish them. They punish themselves, with a relentless internal self-beating, often unconscious, often masked as boredom or depression. Or they abuse alcohol, food, or drugs; find themselves unwittingly making a series of "mistakes" on the job or at home; or find other ways of defeating themselves. Still others push away families and friends lest they inadvertently reveal their "secrets" to these significant others and thereby lose their love and respect.

The vet's basic fear is that if his wife or child knew the "truth" about him, they would reject him immediately. Perhaps he has heard stories about vets who shared war stories with their wives only to have the partner turn cold or begin divorce proceedings. However, if the vet retreats into his shell or verbally puts down his family, this can be a means of temporarily shoving them out of his life so that they will never guess that he has committed certain acts or experienced certain feelings which he has judged to be "immoral" or "cowardly."

For example, some vets are tormented by the fact that, after a certain amount of exposure to combat, or despite their moral scruples against killing, at times they actually enjoyed the fight and got "high" on blood. Other vets are troubled by the fact that in certain instances they were cowardly and that their cowardice may have caused the death or injury of some of their friends. Back home reflecting on his past, the vet may ask himself, "Was that really me? If it was, then what kind of person am I? How can I face myself, much less others? Would my wife continue to stay with me and my children continue to respect me if they found out what happened in Vietnam?"

Of the approximately 2.6 million troops actually stationed in Vietnam, only about one fifth served in the first echelon combat arms where the enemy was regularly pursued and engaged on the ground. However, given the guerilla nature of the war, actually 40% to 60% either fought in combat, provided close combat support or were at least fairly regularly exposed to enemy attacks.[64]

PTSD is not restricted to combat vets, but can be found among those who experienced near-death or life threatening situations or who were surrounded by death. Medics, nurses, doctors, therapists, as well as transporters, body bag counters, embalmers, administrative officers, and numerous civilians who served in Vietnam have also developed PTSD.

Similarly, during World War II, war neurosis was found not only among combatants where the "threat of annihilation and destruction...was very real and imminent," but also among soldiers in graves registration units, and in air corps emergency fire squad units.[65]

How Did The War Affect The Veteran
Spiritually And Morally?

"Even the best of men couldn't begin to realize what the war did to human beings. How it made good men bent and worse men blind."

An Army Medic in Vietnam[66]

PTSD is more than a psychological problem, it is also a spiritual and moral problem. War has always been a spiritual problem in that most religions teach "thou shalt not kill." Yet, throughout history, governments, and even certain religious groups, have made exceptions to this general rule for purposes of defending the nation or the faith itself. For example, killing is prohibited in the Muslim faith, but "Holy War" is permitted. Similarly, the Catholic church sanctioned the Crusades.

Under such conditions, where the warrior kills for a purpose which he understands and in which he believes and where the killing is confined to a clearly defined "enemy," a warrior can kill and still consider himself "good." In Vietnam, however, the enemy was not clearly defined; neither were the goals. Some who went to Vietnam believing in God came to question God's existence, or God's benevolence. How could God allow this war to happen? Those who went to war unsure about their religious beliefs often emerged even less sure. For atheists, the war just confirmed the fact that there was no God.

When they returned home, they rejected religion and made it difficult for their wives to continue normal churchgoing activities. Some wives withdrew from their religious communities under these circumstances. Others increased their spiritual activities because they found them a tremendous source of energy and strength.

For some veterans, the war intensified their faith with profound religious experiences on the battlefield. There are reports of being protected by guardian angels, feeling close to God, even "seeing the Lord." Some men who had near-death experiences report spiritual awakenings of great beauty.[67] If their wives are atheists or agnostics, however, the vet's spirituality or religious fervor may create yet another marital barrier.

The majority of vets with PTSD, however, left Vietnam spiritually empty and in moral pain. Their participation in the war conflicted greatly with the spiritual or religious values they had once held.[68]

The veteran may have additional problems if he happened to serve in a unit that developed a hedonistic pseudocommunity. In this pseudocommunity it was "okay" to abuse alcohol and drugs and be sexually free, as it was to freely kill. Moral restrictions were ignored because the soldiers were far from home and because of the threat of death. Yet many young soldiers often had conscious or unconscious ambivalence about these experiences.[69]

The veteran's unresolved conflicts about his participation in some of these hedonistic activities may contribute to his withdrawal from his wife and family and from the faith he once held. He may feel he is too much of a "sinner" to go back to his synagogue or church or to participate fully in family activities surrounding religious holidays. Baptisms and bar mitzvahs may be especially painful since they illustrate the contrast between how he was when he went through those ceremonies himself and what he has experienced since.

As a result, religious holidays, like patriotic ones, can be very difficult times for the Vietnam family. Even if the vet forces himself to participate, for the sake of the family, his wife and children know his heart isn't in it, which changes the entire tone and meaning of the event. Consequently, the religious event, which could have brought the family closer ends up driving the family further apart and creating more pain.

What Is The "Predisposition" Theory?

In its crudest form the predisposition theory states that Vietnam veterans who are "cracked," that is, have PTSD, were "cracked" before they ever set foot in Vietnam. The predisposition theory does not deny that war is traumatic. But it attributes the veteran's resulting psychological problems primarily to his "pretrauma personality characteristics," his "defects, flaws, and weaknesses," rather than the war experience.

Obviously, PTSD is only complicated by any previous problems or traumas. It is only reasonable to expect that men who had social or psychological problems prior to their tour of duty in Vietnam would be more adversely affected by the war than their better adjusted fellow soldiers. However, under the circumstances in Vietnam, even well-adjusted, well-educated men "cracked." In fact, given the circumstances of the Vietnam war, acquiring a combat-related disorder can be considered a more "'normal' response than repressing the war experience or coping with it in other ways."[70]

Two

Living With The Ice Man

He loves you, but he doesn't trust you and he wants to run away from you—that's the double message you get from someone with PTSD.

Looking back on the early years of my marriage, I don't know what was harder for me—Jim's anger or his depressions and his numbing. That numbing—it was, and is, one of the biggest problems we have. Sometimes I can't get through to him no matter what I do.

At first I tried to pierce his wall gently. No success. So then I tried rejection and anger. Maybe if I rebuffed and scorned him, he would come around. That worked-—sometimes. But if his wall was really up, I could throw a first-class temper tantrum and he'd just shrug his shoulders and walk out the door.

I soon discovered that pressuring Jim for a response, whether I used loving tactics or not, was self-defeating. Either way, I'd usually drive him further away from me.

But he would always come back. He loves me. I know he loves me. And he's a good man, an honest man, who is only hurting himself. But in hurting himself, he hurts all of us—me, and the kids.

'Why doesn't Daddy go with us to Aunt Vicky's or Grandma's or the mall?' the kids used to ask. Now they don't ask anymore. They just accept Jim the way he is. I'd like to tell them that because of Vietnam their father just can't take crowds and loud, noisy places and parties, but I just don't know how.

I came to group complaining about Jim's numbing, not realizing that, over the years, I had become numb myself. Just like Jim, I am afraid of the feelings inside me—the years of pent-up anger and hurt and my sense of loss about what I thought my marriage would be and what my marriage really is.

Sometimes I stay away from group because I don't want to face my feelings. When I face the truth about my life, it hurts so bad I pray for the numbing to come back.

Wife of a combat vet

Have you ever cut yourself and not felt the pain immediately? Have you ever been whiplashed in a car accident, but not felt the soreness or fatigue until several days later? The body often emits a natural anesthetic which permits us some time to take care of our wounds and to do whatever is necessary to protect ourselves from further injury. When the pain is overwhelming, we may even go into shock and lose consciousness entirely. Our bodies simply cannot tolerate the pain and nature, mercifully, spares us.

Just as, in self-protection, the body may temporarily anesthetize itself against physical pain, the psyche, in self-protection, can numb itself against onslaughts of unbearable emotional pain. During combat in Vietnam, the soldier had to turn off his emotions. Feelings had to be put aside because feeling them would have been not only personally disorganizing, but life-threatening. If the combat vet had connected with his grief during battle, he would have been less able to give and take directions or otherwise figure out what to do next in order to save himself and others.

This deadening, or shutting off, of emotions is called emotional or psychic numbing. It is a central feature of PTSD and has been found not only among combat vets, but also among survivors of other traumas—survivors of the bombing of Hiroshima and the Nazi holocaust; victims of earthquakes, floods, and fires; and victims of physical assaults such as rape, incest, child abuse, or muggings.

In the face of a traumatic event, emotional numbing is an entirely appropriate response, for it helps a person "to pass through a period of trauma or excessive stress" by dulling his or her "awareness of the death, the destruction, and the terror and the anguish about him (or her) and of his (or her) own helplessness in such a situation."[1]

Problems occur, however, when the individual remains in the state of numbing long after the original traumatic event. In these cases, the emotional numbing is carried over to other areas of life or to present day situations where there is no danger. Then it can severely-"interfere with human living," especially with personal relationships.[2]

Vets with unresolved PTSD are often "stuck" at the numbing stage. Until recently, the Vietnam veteran was aided in the numbing of his wartime experience by two factors outside of himself:

1. A military training which not only dehumanized the enemy, but which also "punished...(men) who experienced or expressed fear, sadness or grief or tenderness" by labeling them "faggot, sissy, or some other derogatory label;"[3] and
2. A society which for the most part did not want to hear about the veteran's wartime experiences.

Only in the past several years has our society begun to reflect on the Vietnam experience and appreciate its impact on the men who served. Before now, despite the well-publicized agony of the Vietnam war, much of the American public was in a state of "psychic numbing" about the war.

Some vets came home to supportive families and friends who were willing to listen, and not judge. However many found that their friends and family at home were not interested in their emotional experiences and traumas. The vet's soul searching questions, if he dared to ask them, were even less welcome.

One wife explains: "An unprecedented media blitz had made us all aware of the political morass, the atrocities, the ambiguities. We knew the veterans were not heroes even before they did, but we were not sure just what they were. And so we told them simply to get on with their lives (and ours); to bury whatever it was they had seen and felt, to become 'normal' again. We refused to allow them to defuse. We didn't know how to hear men cry; we were unable to find out how they had changed.

"We weren't being cruel. We just wanted to love them as they had been and still were in our fantasies. We hoped that we could make them smile. But...we were the first to see that the problems would not disappear in some washday miracle, would not respond to our nurturing."[4]

In addition, unlike previous wars where soldiers shared war stories with surviving members of their units during the long journey home, the typical Vietnam veteran returned home alone, with no opportunity to "decompress" or share experiences and feelings with his comrades. For the Vietnam veteran, there was no gradual comedown or psychological debriefing. Often he was in the jungle one day and back home the next.[5]

One vet explains: "I got out of Vietnam on the sixth of June, got home the eighth. All of a sudden I found myself at one in the morning standing outside Oakland Air Force Base in my dress greens. I was out of the Army. I wish I would have had a barracks to go to or to an EOD unit to settle down and relax and talk to people that could listen to me and understand—I wish it wouldn't have been so abrupt because it did fuck me up."[6]

Another vet killed a man an hour before he was put on a plane back home. Twenty-four hours later, in his mother's living room, he wanted to talk about it. "Oh forget it," his mother said. "Why do you want to upset everybody?"

Many vets complain that upon return home they were expected to recover from their war experiences quickly and to resume "life as usual" almost instantly. After Vietnam, however, life could no longer be "as usual," for them, or for their families.

Psychic numbing exists in different degrees, in different ways, in different vets at different times. There is no set pattern. However, the result is the same: a distressing inability on the part of the PTSD afflicted veteran to form a meaningful, sustained emotional connection with another human being.

The Effect Of Numbing On Relationships

The last time Lisa and Allen held hands was in 1973. Their last hug was four years ago. "And that's only because he forgot my birthday again and I reminded him," Lisa explains. "Allen was never that sentimental, but since 'Nam, he's done nothing about my birthdays or our anniversaries.

"If I didn't force Allen, he wouldn't show up at our son's birthday parties, either. Last time I had to beg Allen to come. He came, all right, but he left right after the candles were blown out.

"Jeff wondered what happened to Daddy. I told him his Daddy was sick. What else am I going to tell a five-year-old—that his dad has PTSD and can't relate to people?"

After several years of having their anniversary pass by unnoticed, Lisa finally insisted that Allen take her out to dinner. Allen agreed, provided that the restaurant not be an Oriental one. On the way to the restaurant, Allen kept reminding Lisa that birthdays, anniversaries, cards, and flowers no longer held any meaning for him. After the life and death situations he had encountered in Vietnam, most social formalities and "middle class sentimentalities" seemed trivial to him, if not outright "silly."

Allen's low tolerance for formal dinners was born in Vietnam where, on several occasions, he had been given contradictory orders and found himself in situations which baffled all human reason. He had also suffered immensely from the heat and a variety of jungle rashes and had seen children starving to death. At one point he had been near starvation himself.

Lisa was not heartless. However, she was tired of hearing about the war. "While we were waiting for the waiter, all I heard about was how in 'Nam, combat vets never ate in fancy restaurants, about how the restaurants were booby trapped, about how lucky I was to be a woman, not a man, and to have escaped Vietnam—the whole bit. I wanted to leave right then and there, but then I figured it was probably better that he talk about the war then go into numbing.

"Besides, if I had suggested leaving, Allen would have either blown up at me, punched a hole in the table, or tuned out entirely. Sometimes I don't know what's easier to take: the numbing or the anger.

"So I sat there pretending, wondering how I was going to get through three hours of this, when we ended up leaving early anyway because the waiter was Oriental.

"We went home, Allen went out drinking, and I went to bed alone. This is the thanks I get for fifteen years of being a loyal wife."

A majority of research studies support the existence of feelings of detachment and problematic interpersonal relationships among veterans with PTSD.[7] It must be remembered, however, that many of these studies are based primarily on veterans who seek help at Veteran's Administration Medical Centers or at Vet Centers, not on the Vietnam veteran population as a whole or on Vietnam veterans who seek help with private mental health professionals. Therefore, the results of the studies cannot be generalized to the entire Vietnam veteran population. However, in the Vet Center study, over 95% of the Vet Center counselors polled observed that coping with the veteran's emotional numbing—his tendency to "shut off" emotionally and to be reluctant or unable to share on a deep emotional level—was a common problem for wives of PTSD afflicted veterans. In addition, almost 90% of those polled reported that vets with PTSD have greater difficulty disclosing themselves and expressing themselves with their wives or girlfriends than non-PTSD afflicted veterans. It may well be that it is primarily women whose husbands suffer from numbing who seek help.

In some cases, the numbing of emotions is so severe that the veteran is rendered almost totally incapable of relating to others, especially women, on more than a superficial level. Some of these more alienated veterans are literally homeless street people, who wander from one part of the country to the other, unable to commit themselves not only to a family, but also to an institution or organization.[8] Some of these man have had such devastating experiences in Vietnam that they have been unable to reintegrate into the mainstream of society, much less establish a relationship with a woman.

Other vets work two jobs or 10-14 hour days, filling their lives with work, not people. Such a heavy work involvement may be an economic necessity. However, the wives of such vets point out that even during nonwork hours, when the vet could be with the family, he chooses solitary pursuits or "blanks out" in front of the television. Sometimes he does not even watch television with the family, but has his own set in another room.

Other men deliberately choose to work evening shifts, rather than day hours. They prefer to work alone and in relative quiet. By working nights, not only do they have fewer co-workers to deal with on the job, but when they return home, they can sleep rather than deal with their wife and children. The night job also functions to prevent the veteran from attending numerous social and family affairs.

A few of the women who have attended the Vet Center woman's group have even had husbands who worked in other states, cities, or counties, but who, nevertheless, wanted to remain married—even to have children. Yet the veteran may visit his wife only 10-12 times a year, sometimes less often. Usually it is the veteran who decides on the visits. He appears on his wife's doorstep when he wants to see her, not when she wants to see him.

Sometimes the visits are announced, sometimes not. "I can't go anywhere because he expects me to be home waiting for him all the time," explains one wife. "But sometimes he doesn't show up when he says he's going to. Then I get depressed. But I'm afraid that if I complain, he won't come see me at all."

The wife who tolerates this degree of distance in her marriage often is a woman of exceptionally low self-esteem. Typically, she has few career ambitions, no job motivation other than financial survival, and is a traditionalist in desiring to center her life around a man.

Her dreams of love and marriage, however, are shattered by the reality of a husband who is more like a part-time lover. Even when she is with her husband, she is often disappointed. He may be affectionate, but more often he is cool and distant, even though he may have traveled many miles to see her. His coolness may have been born from the sorrows and betrayals he experienced in Vietnam, or afterward. However, the sources of his behavior, however legitimate, do not make his behavior any easier for his wife to tolerate.

"Sometimes I wonder why he comes to see me," one wife states. "He doesn't want to talk that much and when we're in bed, he's like an ice man. He says he doesn't care whether we have sex or not, doesn't care whether we stay married or not. If I start crying, he'll tell me he loves me, but he just can't help it, he doesn't care about anything."

The couple does not always engage in sex during these visits. But if they do, the woman often feels as if she has been with a stranger rather than with a husband. However, she usually hesitates to bring up her complaints for fear of further alienating an already alienated man.

For most of the Vet Center women, however, their partners' psychic numbing and emotional distancing is not so extreme. While some of the men are described by their wives as being almost chronically numb, other husbands are described as fluctuating between being emotionally present and "walling" out their families with what one woman aptly calls an "invisible sheet of ice." The vet may have periods where he is a family man, followed by periods where he is almost always absent from family functions. Or if present, he may be emotionally unresponsive and detached. Furthermore, he may suddenly "freeze" at a family function, stare into space, or leave abruptly, especially if Vietnam is mentioned or if there is some trigger from the war—a passing airplane, a sudden noise. He might also distance himself by starting an argument, which gives him an excuse to leave the room.

Some men "freeze" during intercourse as well, perhaps because of an intrusive memory or because the emotional and physical closeness is intolerable. As the vet retreats into his shell, the woman may be left frantic, wondering what to do next and questioning her sexual desirability.

"I can tell the minute he walks through the door whether or not his 'wall' is going to be up for the night," says Lisa. "If it is, there's no chance of sex, or any kind of communication. Allen wants to be alone so much of the time, sometimes I wonder why he's married at all."

Typically, Allen wants two or three hours to himself after work before he can join the family. Sometimes his need for solitude conflicts with the children's schedules, so that he often misses spending time with them. When he is with his family, he seems disinterested or distant.

Lisa has read about PTSD and understands why Allen is silent and needs to absent himself. But, on some level, she still wonders if there is something she does or says that causes Allen's coldness. The children, however, have little comprehension of their father's problem. Like their mother, they have come to accept their father's numbing as "normal" also. A depressive blanket seems to cover the family and the major weight of the family's emotional life falls on Lisa.

"I don't even explain to the kids anymore why Daddy doesn't eat with us or isn't there to help them with their homework. If we plan to go on a picnic or game or even to my mother's for Christmas, and Allen, at the last minute, decides not to go, I've learned to go ahead without him.

"It's hard...but it's better than staying home with an angry vet—or with someone so numb sometimes that he's like a statue."

When Lisa first joined the woman's group, almost all of her complaints about Allen's numbing had to do with the effects on their children, not herself. "I don't care about me, only the kids," she would repeat. Eventually, however, Lisa was able to experience her own deep sense of rejection and hurt at Allen's walling her out.

"It's painful to love a man, who although he might love you, is incapable of showing it. And it's not the big rejections—the major blow ups, the horrible name calling, things like him not being there for Christmas—that do me under. It's the hundred little ways he ignores me every day. One hundred little rejections equal one big depression."

While the veteran in numbing may not intend to shut out his wife, she often experiences his numbness as a personal rejection. Even when she learns in group that her husband's iciness and need to be distant from her has more to do with his war experiences or his family background than her own physical, emotional, or sexual desirability as a woman, she may still feel rejected.

"Intellectually, I know it's the numbing, but emotionally, I need more from a marriage. Living with a Vietnam veteran is like being on a starvation diet," states one wife. Almost every wife counseled has complained of emotional neglect, or of not knowing whether she is "on" or "off."

The anxiety of not knowing whether she is going to be greeted with smiles, anger, or a blank look is especially prevalent among women who are adult children of alcoholics. For example, as a child, Lynn used to help calm her alcoholic father after his drinking binges and soothe her mother after her parents' frequent fights. Even before she reached puberty, both parents were turning to Lynn for "mothering" and comfort. The little girl in Lynn had a legitimate right to want to be taken care of, rather than thrust in the role of caretaker. However, Lynn repressed her natural child desires and received much praise from her parents and other relatives for her abilities to keep the family together and make her parents and her sisters "feel better."

Eventually she came to feel as if the continuation of the family depended on her. Whenever one of her parents was upset, she interpreted it as the result of something she had failed to do or had done wrong. She felt she needed to be perfect to keep the family from falling apart. As a child she had a persistent nightmare where her home was blown up because she failed to please one or the other of her parents.

Today, however, as the wife of a combat vet who suffers from intermittent numbing, Lynn is experiencing the same emotional instability in her home as she did when she was a child. Once again, she feels responsible for the continuation of the family. During her frequent anxiety attacks about whether or not her husband will be "pleased" with her, she hyperventilates, perspires, and burns much of her emotional energy. She worries about how her husband's emotional state is going to affect her children. She is often running in two directions, trying to cheer up her husband and smooth things out for her children as well. When home life isn't "happy" she fails to see her husband's role in the situation, but focuses on her own inadequacies and minor imperfections.

Because her present home situation is similar to her childhood situation, Lynn's anxiety attacks tend to be intense and, at times, frighten her immensely. Her conclusion, that she is "neurotic," creates even more self-doubts and anxiety for her.

Repressing Grief

Psychic numbing involves the repression of two powerful emotions: grief and anger. Grief repression has been cited many times as central to the vet's inability to emotionally connect with others.[9] The wall the vet builds around himself to keep others out, is essentially a reflection of the wall he's built around his own heart, to shield himself from his own pain and grief.

Some vets are afraid to grieve, for fear that once they start they might never stop. Having repressed their grief through numbing, they fear that once they begin to sorrow over one memory or incident, they will be flooded by other memories and drown in grief. So they fight their grief, trying to keep a tight lid on it, rather than experience the pain.

The depression which many vets experience is, in reality, repressed grief. It is often easier, or more comfortable, to be depressed than to actively hurt or suffer. Although depression is a way that grief can be expressed, it is not actually grieving. In order for healing to occur, the grief must be experienced in full, perhaps a little at a time and usually more than once, before the individual is able to let go of the loss and become more fully involved in the present.

Vets with PTSD often find themselves in the midst of deep depressions every year around the anniversary dates of the deaths of friends or certain other traumatic experiences. During such depressive episodes, the vet may continue to go to work. However, his working capacity is often impaired. At home, his involvement with the family often comes to a standstill.

Typically, wives severely curtail their outside activities and don't come to group during these periods. Even though their husbands may not be talking to them, they feel that their husbands need them around. At such times, the husbands may be unwilling to, or in the woman's view, incapable of, watching the children while she is gone. The men may also be unwilling, or unable, to perform other household duties, leaving more work for the woman. "How can I remind him to take out the trash when he's doing all he can to fight his depression and keep himself together enough to get to work the next day?" one wife asks.

While some of the wives are "understanding," others wonder if their husband's psychic numbing is an excuse to escape responsibilities. Even some male counselors at Vet Centers, most of whom are Vietnam veterans themselves, recognize that some vets use psychic numbing, as well as some of their other PTSD symptoms, as a way to get their wives to do more of the work, especially chores which they dislike or consider "women's work."

In some cases, it is relatively easy to determine whether the veteran is using PTSD as an excuse or not. But in others, the situation is complex. For example, Mike refuses to drive his daughter to cheerleader practice or to her basketball games. This angers his wife, who works full-time and must add another trip onto the end of her already long workday. "Why can't he do it?" she shouts in a marriage counseling session. "After all, he only works ten hours a week. I work forty. What is this? The middle ages when women did everything?"

But Mike insists that his sanity will snap if he sees one more basketball or pom pom girl.

When Mike's daughter first became a cheerleader for her junior high school's basketball team, Mike did all the chauffeuring. Yet he did not approve of his daughter's participation. Even though he had been a basketball champ in high school, he now viewed basketball and all competitive sports as microcosms of the military system. Furthermore, he thought that cheerleading was a sexist institution. Nevertheless, he could not fight his daughter's desire to join the cheerleading squad, nor his family's reaction to his objections.

It was not until the third or fourth basketball game, however, that Mike finally discovered yet a deeper source of his dislike of basketball. During this particular game, one of the players was knocked down. His knee cap was broken and his nose began to bleed profusely. As he was carried off the gym floor, he moaned loudly and left a trail of blood.

Mike's daughter began to weep, "Look at the blood! Look at the blood!"

As Mike looked, the heads of the basketball players seemed to pop off and, within seconds, their young bodies had become dismembered corpses strewn around the gym floor. Then, when his daughter leapt into the air yelling a cheer, Mike imagined her uniform full of blood stains and her legs bleeding with knife wounds. Howling in pain, she died in mid-air.

The sight of the blood and the young boy falling had brought to the surface a memory from Vietnam which Mike had almost totally repressed. It so happened that the number of combatants involved in this particular firefight, and their distribution and location on the battle ground, was remarkably similar to the number of boys involved in the basketball game, and their location on the gym floor. Futhermore, a member of Mike's basketball team, a friend whom Mike had encouraged to join the military, had died in that fight.

Mike had never dealt with his grief regarding that fight or his guilt regarding the death of his friend. Neither had he ever dealt with his horror at seeing the legs of a young Vietnamese girl hacked with knives. Soon afterward, he sought help at a local vet center.

One year later, however, he was not "over" Vietnam. His overworked wife, however, was waiting for the day when Mike would be able to relieve her of some of the chauffeuring. Furthermore, her son was going to join a little league next year. Then what "Vietnam problem" was going to prevent Mike from helping out with the driving? Would Mike at least allow his children to join a car pool? Up to this point, Mike did not trust his children with anyone but himself or his wife.

Mike's wife felt he was "paranoid" and "impossible." Mike, on the other hand, felt he was only being cautious. "No one outside the family can be trusted," he insisted. Besides, if anything happened to one of the children, he would kill the offender, and then himself.

"It's not the work I mind," Mike's wife explained. "It's Mike's attitude. Our daughter knows he doesn't like her being a cheerleader and she feels bad about it. She feels guilty about going against her father. In fact, she was ready to quit the team after Mike broke down during that game. But I made her stick with it.

"She deserves to have a normal life, so does our son, even if our family isn't normal because of Vietnam.

"Our kids need outside activities more than most kids because our home life is so depressing. Mike's depressed. I'm depressed. We're struggling to keep our marriage together and make ends meet. I don't know how we're going to end up, but I do want these children to have some good memories of their childhood."

As a compromise, Mike agreed to assume additional household chores and not make derogatory comments about sports. In addition, he felt he could tolerate picking up his daughter one day a week, provided he could wait in the parking lot and not have to observe any games. Furthermore, his daughter had to change from her cheerleader uniform into regular clothes. He did not ever want to see that uniform again.

Fear Of Loss

Often vets with psychic numbing can function quite well at work, where emotional awareness and responsiveness are not required. However, at home, where emotional exchange is essential, the vets may fail miserably. Their wall may not always be up but, some wives sense, it is always there.

Being with relative strangers on the job is usually much easier for the PTSD afflicted veteran than being close to those at home, where he might forsake his wartime vow "never to care about anyone."[10] "I swore I would never again let anyone matter to me, so I couldn't ever hurt that much again," states a veteran, remembering the combat death of his best friend.[11]

Fundamentally, vets are afraid of being close because they fear losing the ones they love now as they lost others during the war. When a family member is ill or injured, this fear is increased. According to the Vet Center study, in the face of a loss in the family—the illness, injury, or death of a wife, child, or other loved one—the vet with PTSD tends to shut down emotionally and experience an increase in his symptoms. Vet Center counselors report that in 40% of the cases, rather than rush in to help the hurting family member, the vet may build up his defenses and avoid the family. Despite his deep feelings for his wife, child, or partner, he may respond to their illness or injury by withdrawing. Even if the family is knowledgeable about PTSD and tries to understand, they may also feel angry at the vet for what they interpret as his emotional abandonment of them in time of need.

In the other cases, however, the vet does not react with withdrawal, but with a hyperstate where he cannot do enough. He may even become the "rock" on which the entire family leans. However, even when he is helpful and protective, unless he has been through PTSD therapy or otherwise learned to deal with loss, he will usually not be emotionally present. For example, while he can help make arrangements for a funeral, he may not be able to help others with their grieving, just as he himself may not be able to grieve at such times. At the same time, however, he may be wondering what is wrong with him that he does not feel sad or cry.

It is not clear why some vets respond to family crises by pitching in there and helping and why others respond by disappearing, both emotionally and physically. According to the Vet Center counselors, the vet's response to loss may depend not only on his upbringing but on the way in which he saw, smelled, and felt death in Vietnam: the sheer amount of death and destruction which he witnessed during his tour of duty. The way he reacted to loss in Vietnam can provide clues to his civilian response.

If, in Vietnam, he responded by going out and killing someone, he may have an angry outburst when there is a loss in his family. If he responded by numbing himself with alcohol, drugs, or emotional withdrawal, he may respond in the same way in the present. If he was in a unit that was mobile or under frequent fire, he may not have had the opportunity to mourn the death of his buddies and learned to numb himself emotionally.

Vets also respond differently to loss depending on whether or not they feel some sense of responsibility for the loss. If a vet's father dies of cancer, he may have no feeling of responsibility for his father's death. If, however, his child dies of cancer, he may feel that the death is his fault since he was exposed to Agent Orange. Similarly, if his wife or child is injured in a car accident, he may know he was not to blame. If his child is molested by a babysitter, he may berate himself for not being more selective in his choice of a sitter.

As more than one wife has affirmed, some vets stay emotionally distant from others because they are afraid that everything they touch will wither and die. On a subconscious level, the vet may blame himself for the family member's illness or injury, feeling that the "bad karma" or "death taint" which he acquired in Vietnam has followed him home. There may also be an element of guilt. Some vets feel that they are going to be punished for some of their thoughts and behaviors in Vietnam through the death or injury of one of their family members. Mike, for instance, was certain that God was going to punish him for not stopping the killing of an innocent child in Vietnam. Someday God would take away one of his own children.

Another example is Marie's husband, Dan. Shortly after Marie married Dan, her child by a former marriage contracted leukemia and died. From the time the child first became ill, until she died, some two years later, Dan refused to drive Marie to the hospital, talk to the doctors, or help in making any of the necessary decisions about the child's treatment.

When his stepdaughter would come home from the hospital for visits, either Dan would disappear or act as if she wasn't ill or in need of special attention. Sometimes Dan would even argue that the child's medications were not necessary because she was not "really sick."

At night, when Marie reached out to Dan for comfort, he would either get angry with her or lie next to her like a mummy, looking at her as if she was crazy. "You're overreacting," would be his only comment.

As the child's health deteriorated, Dan became colder and colder, absenting himself from the home even more. Sometimes he would promise to visit the child in the hospital or come to a doctor's conference, but he would never appear. "I just can't stand hospitals," he would say.

Since Dan had been close to her daughter, Marie knew that Dan's iciness was not due to his insensitivity, but due to his inability to feel his grief. One night, when Marie and Dan were informed that there was no longer any hope for the child, Dan began to mutilate himself with a razor blade and angrily shouted that he would kill the doctor if the child died. He also felt he had contaminated the child.

After that evening, however, Dan showed no further emotion, not even at the funeral. Despite all her understanding of PTSD, Marie was enraged. "He didn't help with any of the arrangements, hold my hand—nothing. I can forgive him his drinking, his other women—everything—but, at that moment, when I was burying my child and needing him the most, he wasn't there for me. I know my husband has PTSD, but this is carrying it too far!"

This same vet evidenced an almost identical reaction when his wife's grandmother died. Immediately after the phone call announcing the grandmother's death, the vet left the room. He ignored his wife all day, even though she was weeping. When dinner wasn't ready on time, he said, "Okay, I'll forgive you this time, but you should be over this thing by now."

Similarly, when a veteran's wife or partner becomes ill herself, the vet may be deeply concerned, but he may not show it. Often he may be reluctant to drive the woman to the hospital or the doctor's office and does not want to listen to her descriptions of her illness. He may even deny the existence of the illness to the extent that he blocks the woman's attempts for necessary medical treatment.

Some women have been forced to wait until their illnesses significantly progressed before they were allowed to seek medical attention. If they had sought a doctor without their husband's permission, their husbands would have been greatly offended. "He's so sensitive," the women often say. "If I go ahead and make a doctor's appointment without getting his okay, he'll interpret it as me being against him or not trusting his judgement. He's always putting me to the test, even when I'm sick."

In violent homes, the vet may even deny his wife the money necessary for medical care or punish her with a beating for seeking medical attention without his permission. Furthermore, as a form of economic battering, the vet may not give his partner the funds to visit a sick relative or to attend the funeral of a dead one. In such cases, his need to control the woman by economic means interacts with his wish to deny the existence of illness and death. It is highly probable that the vet suffers from personality problems in addition to his PTSD. In cases of extreme abuse, the vet's behavior more closely fits the patterns associated with abusive or character disordered personalities rather than the patterns associated with individuals who suffer primarily only from PTSD.

Another pattern which might develop is that when the wife becomes ill, the vet's symptoms increase. If the vet is emotionally or economically dependent on his partner, as she assumes a relatively helpless and dependent position, he may become frightened and regress emotionally. Hence, the wife must deal not only with her own medical problems, but with a husband who is becoming increasingly dysfunctional. He may become more helpless and dependent himself, or he may become more antagonistic to others in the home. He may increase his alcohol or drug intake, or even regress emotionally to the point of competing with any children for the wife's now limited attention.

He may even compete with his wife for attention. For example, if he is ill, he may feel that his illness is more severe than his wife's, even when this is not the case. His wife might have pneumonia but his cold is ten times worse.

Wives often ask if such behavior is a formal part of PTSD. Theoretically, it is not. While emotional withdrawal is an expected part of the illness, if the vet regresses severely or acts in an extremely childlike manner when there is illness in the family, his behavior may be more related to some other psychological problem which coexists with his PTSD.

It must be emphasized that, according to the Vet Center Study, less than half of the vets with PTSD tend to respond inappropriately to family illness or loss. Some of the wives report that their husbands are extremely attentive when they, or one of their children, are ill or when there is a death in the family. In fact, extreme protectiveness, almost to the point of overprotectiveness, is also characteristic of some Vietnam veteran homes. While at times wives and children experience the vet's protectiveness as love and caring, at other times, they feel stifled and restricted by his constant concern about their health and safety.

For some veterans, the pattern of withdrawal from the family during injury, death, or another crisis is cyclical. "There are months, or years, where he's right there for me during times of trouble. But then are other months, or years, where I can't rely on him at all for help," explains one wife. Other veterans are described as "trying" to be helpful, but ultimately abandoning the scene of the crisis—the hospital, the funeral parlor, or wherever—because they "could not tolerate the pain."

Furthermore, some of the very individuals described above demonstrated loving, caretaking behavior toward sick children and wives, after the wife, or a friend or counselor, pointed out to them what behavior was needed. In addition, it may well be that it is primarily women whose partners are unable, or unwilling, to be supportive during family crises who are seen at Vet Centers. Women whose husbands respond more appropriately may not need outside assistance.

Nevertheless, for the women who seek help at Vet Centers or Veteran's Administration Medical Centers, it is not unusual for their vet husband to withdraw in times of family trouble, even in instances where his wife or child has been physically assaulted. At such times, one might think that a Vietnam vet, with his warrior background, might want to take justice into his own hands and wreak vengeance on the assailant.

In some instances, this is definitely the case. For example, some of the husbands have physically attacked drivers who crashed into their wives' vehicles. Yet, in other instances, vets have responded to their wife being in a car accident, raped, or mugged, or their children being beaten at school as if "nothing" had happened.

Alice, for example, was raped and mugged in her office building one evening after work. When she phoned her husband, he sounded extremely concerned and sympathetic and said he would come get her immediately. Three hours later, he had not arrived. Alice took a cab home.

When she walked in the door, her husband stared at her bloodied, torn clothing blankly. "Did you remember to bring home the milk?" he asked.

"I could have killed him, but I was too exhausted," states Alice. When she asked him why he had failed to pick her up, he stated that he "forgot." Then he went to bed in a room other than their bedroom.

To this day, he still claims that the rape "never happened."

Similarly, when the family's dog died, Alice's husband seemed undisturbed. "It's just an animal," he muttered, even though the dog had been a family pet for ten years. After this dog died, however, no other pets were allowed in the home and the family was not permitted to even mention the name of the dead dog. Alice recognized that her husband suffered from severe war trauma, but she could not tolerate his degree of numbing. After five years of marriage, she filed for divorce. After losing his wife, Alice's husband entered treatment and eventually realized that his PTSD had made him self-defeating in many areas of life. Part of his self-destructiveness ruined his relationship with Alice. Due to Vietnam, and before entering treatment, he had not been able to envision himself as a success in any dimension of life, especially in a relationship with a woman.

This discussion of inappropriate responses to loss is not intended to slur the character of Vietnam veterans as a group, a group which has already been slurred and misunderstood enough. Rather, the purpose of the discussion is to point out the possible effects of the grief repression and psychic numbing acquired in Vietnam on the veteran's ability to cope with losses in the present. In some cases, especially in cases involving physical abuse or severe verbal abuse, the vet's response to loss may also be rooted in problems other than PTSD, as well as in a strong belief in male prerogative of a man's "right" to be cruel to his wife.

Social Isolation

"It doesn't take much to remind me of 'Nam," says Arnold, who has been in therapy for PTSD for over a year. "And when I remember, I don't feel like going out and pretending to be happy either. I used to pretend—to please my wife—but now I'm sick and tired of it."

His wife, Polly, however, is "sick and tired" of staying home. "We can't go to parties because Arnold can't stand small talk. We can't go to movies either, because sad ones make Arnold depressed. Comedies depress him too, because they remind him of his depression.

"Basically, Arnold isn't interested in people or fun anymore."

"I feel different from everyone else," Arnold explains. Arnold is also afraid of how he might react if someone mentions Vietnam, particularly if they make a derogatory comment about Vietnam veterans or a statement betraying gross ignorance about the war. Also, Arnold feels it is inconsiderate of him to impose his depression and cynicism on others. "Why should I ruin the party with my depression?" he asks. Like many depressed persons, he feels socially undesirable when he is "down" and only wants to be with others when he is "up," which, due to his mood swings, is often unpredictable.

Since Vietnam, Arnold has visited his father only twice. Arnold went to Vietnam very much a "hawk," preparing to make the military his life. He also wanted to make his father, a career officer, proud of him. Yet experiences in Vietnam made Arnold question certain procedures and personnel. Although Arnold still feels that the war was justified, he did not re-enlist and abandoned his plans for a career in the military.

He now distrusts most government institutions and prefers to avoid any contact with "the establishment," whether it be the Veteran's Administration, the Department of Labor, the IRS, or the local unemployment office. Despite his exceptionally high I.Q., Arnold has chosen to stack cans at a local grocery store rather than go on to college. He has also chosen to stack the cans at midnight, so as to keep his interactions with others to a minimum.

Arnold's father does not understand his son's survivor guilt and nightmares, nor his alienation from society. To him, Arnold is a "disgrace" to the family, not only because Arnold is not a better provider for his wife and son, but also because Arnold was not "tough enough" to endure the stresses of war.

Arnold's father lost a leg in World War II. While stationed in the Philippines, he saw "plenty of combat," as well as starving children shot to death for rummaging through garbage for food. "If I can get over that, why can't Arnold get over Vietnam?" he asks. "Besides, what's a mental problem compared to a wooden leg?"

As Arnold's case illustrates, social isolation and social alienation are frequent characteristics of the PTSD afflicted veteran. They not only reflect his depression, they perpetuate it. Deprived of human companionship, the vet can sink deeper and deeper into himself and into negative thinking. The vet's reduced interest and ability to relate to others, however, is not only detrimental to him, but to his wife and children.

In light of his experiences in Vietnam, social gatherings and other occasions often appear meaningless or superficial to him. He may, in some instances, belittle or trivialize his wife's desire to see friends or go out or request that she decline invitations and stay with him. In other cases, he urges her to go ahead without him. Yet often the woman stays home anyway, feeling morally obligated to be with her husband or protective of her children.

Almost universally, the women in group complain about their husband's isolative tendencies. But they also tend to accept his social isolation and their subsequent "hermitage" as a given. "Until he gets over his PTSD, I'm going to be a hermit too," states one wife.

Most of the women have "given up" trying to pressure their husbands into attending social functions or family gatherings. "It's too much pressure, not only on Arnold, but on me," says Polly. "If I insist that we go out with another couple or to my sister's, then I have to worry about whether or not Arnold's going to make a scene or feel so uncomfortable that he'll take it out on me later.

"Now I automatically say 'no' to every invitation. It got too embarrassing to be always cancelling out at the last minute and coming up with new excuses all the time.

"Even though Arnold has been in therapy for over a year, his emotions aren't stable yet. I never know what kind of mood he's going to be in before we go out. If something about Vietnam comes on the radio or one of his Vietnam buddies call, I can usually just forget our plans.

"Besides, we usually fight before we go out anyway.

"So now we don't make any plans. Nobody calls us anymore and we're stuck with each other."

Arnold has dropped most of his old friends from before the war, not an unusual pattern among vets with PTSD. While Polly has kept some of her friends, Arnold doesn't feel he has much in common with them and Polly usually sees them on her own, but she has limited time to do so. Most of Polly and Arnold's current friends are other Vietnam veterans.

"But they're mainly his friends, not mine," says Polly, "and when they talk about Vietnam, they expect me to leave the room. I guess they don't think a woman can take it.

"I used to leave meekly. But now I protest. After all, it's my living room they're sitting in—my food they're eating.

"After a while they forget I'm there and I fit right in. It's okay, I guess, but it would be nice to have conversations with people about something else besides Vietnam."

Despite Polly's wish for a broader scope of friends, she is grateful that Arnold at least socializes with other vets. Some vets do not even have this outlet. The husbands of many of the women who attend group are often virtual loners with few contacts outside their wives, and, perhaps, a few select friends.

Special problems can arise when the woman has children from a former marriage. In a few cases, vets have asked their wives to minimize their involvements with these children, and, in a few isolated cases, have even requested that the woman send the children back to their natural father or, if the children are over eighteen, that the children be made to leave home. While no woman has yet given in to such requests, the resulting tensions, not only between the couple, but between the children and the veteran, are obvious, in some cases leading to teenage children leaving home voluntarily, over the mother's protest. In other instances, Vietnam wives have had difficulty obtaining "permission" from their husbands to visit their children who are already living in another state with their natural father. In many of these cases, the veteran has been described as being extremely jealous of the wife's former spouse, more than her children.

When the Vietnam vet wife first comes to group, her initial feeling is often that of relief. At last, she doesn't have to "explain" her situation in great defensive detail and can communicate almost instantly with the other women without lengthy introductions. Also, she can share her conflicting feelings about her husband's social isolation and the social isolation which his problems impose upon her.

On the one hand, she may feel that her first obligation is to her husband. She respects his PTSD and wants to be supportive. On the other hand, she is lonely, feels cut off from family and friends, but is weary of figuring out new and better ways of preventing clashes between her husband and others.

"I agree that both Arnold's father and my mother are narrowminded about the war," says Polly, "but I still think that our son should know his grandparents."

After a lot of arguing, Arnold agreed that Polly's mother could visit. "But the minute my Mom walks in the front door, Arnold's already out the back.

"At first I was humiliated at Arnold not being there when my Mom came to visit. Now I don't care, for me, but I don't want my son to grow up in a home where Grandmother and Daddy can't even sit down and have a cup of coffee together."

In marriage counseling, Polly requested that Arnold be at least willing to greet her relatives and visit with them for a half hour before he made his exit. Arnold agreed, provided he did not have to interact with the relatives during the rest of their stay and that Polly ask them to refrain from saying anything about the war.

Obviously, long family affairs, such as Thanksgiving dinners, are "out" for Arnold and Polly. They are also problematic for other women, many of whom purposefully elect to spend holiday times alone with their children and husband—without their relatives—or with their families of origin—without their husbands.

Summary

Psychic or emotional numbing is a natural and normal human response to being relatively helpless in a situation of great danger. In order to cope with the crisis, the individual tends to shut down emotionally and focus all his attention on surviving. Problems arise when the emotional numbing lasts beyond that needed for survival or is extended to situations which are not life-threatening.

Numbing almost always causes havoc and misunderstandings in marriage and other relationships requiring the expression of deep feelings. The veteran's difficulties in feeling his feelings, his fear of loss, and his fear of emotional pain often prevent him from establishing an emotionally close relationship with his wife. In some cases, the vet's numbing alternates with periods of emotional openness. In other cases, he may shun emotional relationships with women entirely or be able to relate to his wife on only a very limited basis.

The veteran's wife may interpret her husband's coldness as a personal rejection. As a result, she may build her own defenses against the veteran, have low self-esteem, and become numb to her own emotions, just like her husband. The vet's wall is a formidable barrier to marital communication, leaving the wife feeling shut out and alone.

Three

PTSD and Sex

Come here, lie with me
And take away the pain
Then go away
I never want to see you again.

                                     Vietnam Veteran, August 1986

*B*ruce's body is covered with scars, but he is still a very sexy man. Even if he wasn't a Vietnam vet and endowed with all the aura (and the muscles) of a warrior, he would still be sexy to me. Quite frankly, one of the main reasons I married Bruce was because I was so sexually attracted to him.

Bruce is a terrific lover, but when I get into bed with him, I get into bed with Vietnam too—with the memories and the mood swings and with the times where it feels as if Bruce is just using me to forget. Other times, because of his depression caused by PTSD, he is almost totally uninterested in sex.

I can tell whenever Bruce doesn't want sex. Either he acts like I don't exist, or he starts a fight just to keep me away. I used to think there was something wrong with me because he didn't want me, until in couples therapy, he explained that sometimes he just can't handle his PTSD and his job, much less the emotional and sexual demands of a relationship. At such times he wants—and needs—to be alone, free from other people, to 'get himself together.'

But on any given day, he can't predict how long a period of 'cooling out' he may need. Sometimes all he needs is an hour or two. Sometimes the whole evening. Meanwhile I'm supposed to take care of the kids and *everything else and then be ready for that magic moment when he decides he wants me. And when he wants me, he wants me right then. No matter how tired I am from a rough day at work or from being home with sick kids, when he's ready, I'm supposed to turn into a heated sex kitten.*

Sometimes I give in to Bruce. Sometimes I don't. But if I give up other plans or push myself to have sex with him and then he all of a sudden stops right in the middle due to some Vietnam thing, I get mad. Maybe it's selfish of me, but I'm tired of having to be understanding all the time.

After ten years of marriage, I want something more out of sex than just sex. I want to feel cherished and loved, and emotionally close to my husband. For me, it's hard to keep up the passion when there's no communication.

But Bruce has periods where he can't communicate and if I insist on talking, he'll just withdraw even more. At such times, when he wants sex, I hate to turn him down, even if I'm angry with him, because his wanting sex is a sign that he's trying to get out of his depression and isolation. At least he's reaching for pleasure instead of pain. So I go to bed with him even when I don't feel like it, even when we haven't talked for days, or there's all this silent fighting going on. Sometimes I fake orgasm too, just to make him happy.

In this day of women's liberation, it's not easy to admit such things. It's even harder to admit that many times I go along with Bruce sexually because it's easier that way. Sex reduces his anger level and stops him from picking on me and the kids. Over the years, I've learned that if Bruce has his sex, for the next few days there's more peace at home for me and the kids.

Bruce's wife, Laura

Sex is important, not only as a physical means of releasing tension, but as a means of communicating affection and love. Sex is also a means of reducing individual loneliness. Through physical merger with another person, human beings seek not only physical thrills and the pleasure of sensual excitement, but also validation and appreciation of themselves as unique individuals.[1]

"The way we express ourselves sexually—our most intimate way of relating to another person—reflects how we value ourselves, how we value the other person, how that person values us. It reflects all the things that mean warmth, love, affection and security to us—and which we therefore seek and cherish."[2] This is especially true for women in their thirties and forties, most of whom have been taught to equate sex with love and with emotional, if not financial, security.[3] In contrast, some younger women, like many men, have been given cultural permission to enjoy their sexuality with a variety of partners. The majority of the Vietnam wives seen so far, however, hold relatively conservative sexual values. Due to their upbringing or their religious convictions, they tend to feel that their sexual expression should be reserved only for men with whom they have a strong emotional commitment.

Typically, the Vietnam wife's sexual values were ingrained in her prior to the sexual revolution. Hence, almost all the Vietnam wives seen so far have held traditional values regarding sex and love. While some Vietnam veterans returned home to find their wives or girlfriends sleeping with other men, these are not the women who usually come to Vet Centers for help. Rather, the Vietnam wife who seeks help is almost always one who remained sexually—and emotionally—faithful to her husband during his tour of duty and who continues to remain true despite her husband's PTSD. Even if her husband has had prolonged periods of sexual apathy, has insisted on sex regardless of her feelings, or has had sexual flings or otherwise manifested some form of obsession with sex, she has remained faithful, never seriously considering the possibility of an affair with another man.

In fact, when approached by other men, the typical Vietnam wife has felt guilt along with the exhilaration of being seen as sexually desirable by another man. A number of wives have even felt guilty about masturbating, even when self-gratification was made necessary by the veteran's physical absence from the home, his sexual disinterest, or his disregard of his wife's sexual needs.

Dora, for example, jokes about sleeping with the handsome young teller at her bank who propositions her almost every time she makes a deposit. "If my husband stays out all night again, I'm going to meet that teller for drinks," she often says. Once she even made a date with the teller, but, as expected, quickly broke it. Not only did guilt overpower her, but she was just too angry at her husband to consider having a relationship—even a primarily sexual relationship—with another man. Besides, her major desire was for love, not sex.

Most of the wives say that they value the comfort of being held and the pleasures of talking intimately with their husband in bed more than any purely physical gratification. Yet, as a result of the women's movement, often the women do expect sexual pleasure, if not orgasm, as part of their "due" in marriage. However, the wives of some troubled vets have been disappointed to find that not only their dreams of emotional intimacy, but their hopes for sexual gratification, have been shattered by the "other woman"—Vietnam. Not only has this "other woman" disturbed the veteran's emotional peace, but she has intruded even on his sexuality, robbing both him and his wife of one of the most important sources of human physical and emotional gratification: satisfying sex.

This chapter presents some of the ways in which PTSD has affected the sexuality of the afflicted Vietnam veteran and his wife. The ways in which PTSD affects the veteran's sexuality and his sexual relationships, however, have not been well-researched. To date, there have been only five studies of the effects of the Vietnam experience on the veteran's sexuality. In the first study, questions about sexual intimacy were mixed with questions about other forms of intimacy.[4] Therefore, no conclusions can be drawn specifically about the relationship of PTSD to male sexuality. In the next two studies, researchers found no evidence that combat was related to sexual problems.[5] In the fourth study, however, 90% of individuals with PTSD (including non-Vietnam veterans who suffered traumas) were reported as experiencing reduction of sexual capacity and interest. Extra-marital affairs were also noted.[6]

Similarly, the Vet Center study I completed, as well as clinical experience with Vietnam wives and veterans, has found that many veterans had sexual concerns or were reported by their wives or their counselors to have sexual difficulties.[7] Over 86% of the Vet Center counselors polled report that vets with PTSD often experience periods of sexual dysfunction. Yet counselors caution that such sexual problems do not characterize every vet and are not necessarily symptoms of PTSD. Rather, these sexual difficulties reflect the depression and anxiety suffered by vets in the readjustment process. In addition, approximately 67% of the counselors found that vets with PTSD often desire sex on demand.

These results must be interpreted with caution. The sample of Vietnam families on which the results are based may be biased in that it consisted of individuals and couples in sufficient emotional distress that they sought help. Since this is not a random sample, these individuals cannot be considered representative of the entire Vietnam veteran family population.

In general, it is difficult to draw any firm conclusions even from formal research. Studies of prisoners of war from previous wars have found that the prison camp experience often results in long-term sexual disinterest, impotency, and other sexual dysfunctions, especially if severe malnutrition and physical abuse were involved. However, some of the wives of Vietnam P.O.W.'s who have attended group report a totally different picture: not only are their husbands sexually interested and almost always sexually potent, but they insist on sex on a daily basis.

Once again, I want to stress that there is no "typical" Vietnam veteran or Vietnam veteran wife. In sexual matters especially, there is wide variability. However, even in my limited sample, certain patterns emerged. In general, Vietnam wives report four areas of sexual concern related to their husbands' PTSD: 1. his sexual disinterest or impotency; 2. his insistence on sex on demand; 3. the separation of affection and romance from sexual activity; and 4. his extra-marital affairs or other forms of obsession with sex.

These patterns are not necessarily constant over time for any given veteran. For example, some vets experience periods of sexual apathy or impotency when undergoing depressions due to PTSD. But when they find some relief from their PTSD, their sexual functioning returns to normal. Similarly, some vets desire great control over their marital sexual encounters. However, the wives of even the most controlling veterans describe their husbands as having periods where they can "let go" of directing every sexual move, or "be normal." According to the wives, the husband's need to be watchful during sex or to re-enact his role in combat in the bedroom seems to be related to some of the symptoms of PTSD—increased withdrawal and irritability or nightmares. Given such fluctuations in the veteran's sexual behavior, the Vietnam wife is often confused about what to expect sexually from her husband. If she is not assertive about her sexual needs and seeks instead to please her husband, she may not know whether to put on her flannel nightgown or her sheer negligee.

Sexual Impotence And Apathy

"Sex, what's that?" more than one wife has said, describing her husband's long-standing sexual apathy or sexual impotency.

Two of the possible major causes of impotency or lack of sexual interest or abilities in Vietnam veterans with PTSD are the depression and emotional numbing associated with PTSD. Depression and emotional numbing, especially when they involve anger turned inward or repressed grief, can lead to sexual disinterest, anorgasmia (lack of orgasm) or various other forms of sexual impotence even among persons who did not serve in Vietnam.[9] For example, Vietnam wives who say they are disinterested in sex often suffer from depression and emotional numbing as a result of having stifled their negative feelings toward their husbands, especially their anger at all the demands made upon them as a result of their husband's PTSD. Furthermore, they are often in a state of mourning about their own lives: about the years spent loving and caring for a man who does not, or cannot, return their love in kind. Under such emotional conditions, it is very hard for Vietnam wives to achieve high levels of sexual arousal on a consistent basis.

In the early years of her marriage when her husband sexually ignored her, Dora used to masturbate for relief. However, today she hardly ever does so. "I used to think I stopped because I was approaching 40, but that's supposed to be a woman's sexual peak. I guess it's my husband, not my age. Since I've numbed my anger at him, it's no wonder my sexual feelings have also gone dead. Funny, now that I think about it, the last time we had good sex was after a fight when we both told each other how much we hated each other. Maybe the sex was good because we finally let out our feelings."

As described in the previous chapter, psychic numbing occurs on three levels: the emotional, the mental, and the physical. Physically, the muscles constrict. According to Wilhelm Reich, in *The Function of the Orgasm: The Discovery of the Orgone,* this muscular constriction can result in genital disturbances.[10] Furthermore, "sexual energy can be bound by chronic muscle tensions."[11]

Some Vietnam wives experience little feeling, either on an emotional or sexual level, during sexual intercourse. True, they may have pleasurable sensations, even orgasm but they are distressed to find that they experience their sexuality in a detached and distant manner. "It's like my body doesn't belong to me," explains one wife, whose statement reflects a severe degree of psychic numbing. Similarly, her husband, like some of my other Vietnam veteran patients, while able to achieve erection and orgasm, describes his penis as "numb," and his orgasm as "dead." When physiological causes are ruled out, this muting of sexual feeling and pleasure can perhaps be related to the overall numbing of emotions in both the veteran and his wife.

Furthermore, sexual pleasure and potency can be inhibited, if not totally obliterated, in almost any man or woman, veteran or nonveteran, by the presence of anxious, painful, or other negative thoughts or memories.

Have you ever begun to worry about your bills or the health of one of your family members in the middle of making love? What was the effect on your sexual interest? If you were the victim of rape or some other form of sexual abuse, how easily could you blot out the memory of being violated? Wouldn't it take time to be able to respond sexually again, even when with someone you loved and trusted?

If the Vietnam wife has had painful sexual experiences, memories of her past may intrude on her present sexual experiences with her husband. Similarly, veterans who witnessed or participated in sexual acts in which there was also pain or violence may recall these events when they begin to become sexually excited. On the simplest, most innocent level, perhaps gunfire went off while the veteran was making love. Or perhaps the veteran witnessed or participated in rape. Or perhaps he or one of his comrades was attacked or "set up" by a Vietnamese prostitute or girlfriend. Such memories, even if they are not in the veteran's conscious awareness at the time he is initiating sexual contact, may function to decrease his level of sexual involvement. They may even result in an inability to achieve and maintain an erection. Unless the wife is aware of the many possible causes of erectile failure in men, especially in men with PTSD, she may interpret her husband's impotence as a sign of her lack of sexual attractiveness. This is especially the case if one sexual failure precipitates the vet's almost total sexual withdrawal.

For example, if the veteran experiences a sexual "failure" due to certain memories, he may be reluctant to initiate sex or respond to his partner's sexual overtures in the future for fear of "failing" again. After repeated sexual "failures," he may withdraw from sexual activity altogether. Consequently, neither the vet nor his wife receive the emotional and sexual stimulation conducive to full sexual expression. Once this vicious cycle is established, the wife may resign herself to a sexless marriage or feel like a sexual failure herself, just like her husband.

This has been the case with several vets I have counseled. Although they very much wanted to have sexual relations with women, they could not bear the embarrassment of repeated sexual failures. In general, their wives or girlfriends were described as being understanding and accepting of their impotence. Nevertheless, the men preferred to keep relationships at a nonsexual level.

Survivor guilt can also play a role in the veteran's sexual relations, with some vets reporting guilt feelings during the sex act. "Here I am, making love to my wife, when my buddy will never make love again. Just the thought of it kills my desire," explains one vet.

When the veteran is impotent or quickly loses his erection or interest in sex, his wife will usually have trouble reaching orgasm unless her husband uses manual or oral means of stimulation. Few of the wives, however, have proven assertive enough to ask their husbands to help them climax outside of intercourse.

> When my husband can't make it, that means his PTSD is bothering him and I know better than to press him for anything, much less sex. He pretends he's sleeping, but I know he's awake, thinking. The depression, or anger, just oozes out of him.
>
> If I ask him to touch me, I'm afraid he'll call me 'selfish.' Here he is suffering, and what am I thinking about? Myself. A few times I did ask him and he did what I wanted. But he did it mechanically, without love and no emotion whatsoever. It was no fun and made me feel like a whore.
>
> So I don't ask anymore, I just accept sexual frustration as part of living with a Vietnam vet. If our sex gets interrupted because he gets into a mood, I just roll over and pretend that I'm asleep. He's left me hanging sexually so many times, I've learned not to get too turned on when we start. Slowly but surely, my interest and enthusiasm for sex has diminished.

Wives and girlfriends of veterans who were sexually abused during the war are particularly sensitive to the fact that their veteran's memories may be exceptionally intrusive and troublesome. What they may not know, however, is that their veteran may withdraw sexually because he is plagued by sadistic thoughts. These sadistic thoughts may arise, in part, from an urge to retaliate against his abusers. For example, Fred was sexually abused by Viet Cong guards during his six months as a P.O.W. After he was released, he sought to kill his abusers, but they could not be found. He still harbors considerable rage toward them, however, which mere vocal ventilation does not begin to relieve.

Rationally, he knows his girlfriend is not "the enemy" and does not want to hurt her. But emotionally, he still finds himself making her the scapegoat for his unresolved anger toward his abusers. Although he has never been aggressive with his girlfriend, he is troubled by sadistic thoughts toward her. For example, during intercourse with her, he noticed that as his sexual excitement increased and his urge to penetrate her increased, he wanted to "pierce" her and "rip her open."[12]

These thoughts troubled him greatly, so greatly that he now shuns sexual activity not only with her, but with other women, in order to avoid the pain and shame of having such sadistic thoughts and to avoid the risk that he might "lose control" and actually act on his sadistic impulses.

If a veteran actually witnessed any mutilation of female breasts or genitalia or any intercourse with dead women, his sadistic fantasies may be particularly vivid and problematic for him. He may be especially repelled by sex if he has found some satisfaction or pleasure in the sadistic thoughts or, if in Vietnam, he found some satisfaction or pleasure in observing or participating in sexually sadistic acts.

A vet need not have been exposed to sexual abuse during the war in order to suffer the intrusion of wartime memories in his sex life. Such memories can be evoked by the mere sight of a naked body or any scars resulting from the war. Hence wives, especially those wives who have invested considerable time and energy in maintaining trim figures or other forms of attractiveness, are often disappointed and, in some cases, devastated, to find their men almost immune to their loveliness. They often fail to understand that every time the veteran takes his clothes off, or sees a woman disrobe, he may begin to automatically—and unwillingly—think of Vietnam. Jim explains: "Nudity was part of the death there. It was nothing to see naked bodies, wounded, dead, cut up or whatever." Before Vietnam,

Jim had associated nudity primarily with pleasure. But now it is paired in his mind with pain and violence.

Jim was not wounded in Vietnam, but for those vets who were and who still bear physical scars, disrobing and exposing their scars to themselves and their partner may serve as yet another reminder of the war. If, in addition, the veteran was wounded in or near the genital area or in or near sexually sensitive areas, his injuries or the mere sight of his scars may contribute to his sexual difficulties.

While some vets are proud of their scars and consider them signs of manhood, for others the scars engender pain and anger. Many of the vets I have counseled brush off their scars or injuries as "nothing," ever mindful of the fact that they managed to survive, while others died, or that they could have been injured more severely, as were others. "Sure there's a hole in my leg, but at least I have one," says Ron. "Some guys lost both or everything."

Where psychic numbing exists, there may also be a denial about the pain of having been injured or disfigured. A vet with a wooden arm insisted that the loss of the arm "didn't bother him at all." In fact, he felt superior to vets who were "cry babies" about their physical and emotional problems resulting from the war. He had never grieved his loss and instead comforted himself with feeling like a true patriot for having sacrificed for his country. Quite possibly his sense of superiority over other vets who openly complain about their injuries may stem, in part, from his suppression of his own sense of loss. He claims to be sexually virile, but he has been unable to sustain either of his two marriages, either sexually or emotionally.

While some wives say that their husbands complain about their injuries almost constantly, other wives report that the "no talk" rule applies to war injuries as well.

> Ron's body is covered with scars and punctured with gunshot wounds. Looking at his body objectively, it is ugly, horrible really. But I love him and don't mind caressing his ugly spots. I just close my eyes and kiss parts of him that would make most people shudder.
>
> I only wish he had told me about his body before we had sex the first time. I was shocked. But since he didn't say anything, I didn't either. Besides, I knew he was testing me. He kept staring at me to see how I would react.
>
> But his eyes had a faraway look, too and I could tell he wasn't really thinking about me, but about Vietnam.

> *We've been together five years. Our sex life was great in the beginning, but now it's almost dead. We never talk about his scars, or Vietnam. After the first couple of months together, he couldn't get an erection. I told him I didn't mind, that I just wanted to hold and love him anyway. But he'd push me away and sometimes wouldn't come to bed at all.*
>
> *I've caught him masturbating a few times, so I know he's not impotent. But he's definitely disinterested in me. I thought—hoped—his disinterest would be temporary, but now we're just like two friends living in the same house.*

Ron feels that Vietnam "ruined" his sex life. Yet even veterans who are not physically scarred sometimes say that Vietnam "ruined" sex for them, like it ruined other aspects of their lives. Several studies have found that battlefield trauma is related to "diminished interest in previously enjoyed activities."[13]

Some vets with PTSD have so much emotional pain to deal with and so much disillusionment about their country, the military, and, by extension, life itself, that sex seems unimportant, if not meaningless. "Nothing matters, not even sex."

For example, Harvey went to Vietnam an idealistic nineteen-year-old. His unit fried steaks and drank beer while watching whole villages and many Americans be blown to bits. Harvey became emotionally numb and his numbing was reinforced by his unit's jokes about the nearby slaughters.

Once Harvey and two friends were attacked by a group of Vietnamese women carrying razor blades. The women were aiming for a particular artery in the leg, which, if slashed, could make a person bleed to death. Rather than shoot the women, Harvey kicked them in the face, which made him wonder if he was a "good guy" or a "bad guy."

At the same time Harvey marvelled at the women's motivation. Didn't these women in ragged pajamas know he could have blown them away in a minute? Why were they willing to risk their lives just to kill a handful of American servicemen?

Harvey began to question the U.S. involvement in Vietnam. Am I on the wrong side? he dared to wonder. However, such questions severely conflicted with his dedication to the military and the patriotic fervor which had sent him to Vietnam in the first place. Since the conflict couldn't be resolved, Harvey entered a state of mental numbing which only compounded his emotional numbing, rendering him sexually disinterested, even in Vietnam.

After returning to the U.S., his sexual disinterest was aggravated by discovering that his wife had been unfaithful to him. He forgave her but she continued to betray him. After he divorced her, he had a short period of promiscuity followed by a long period of celibacy. Obviously Harvey's experience with the Vietnamese women, in addition to his experiences with his first wife, made him wary of being close to women.

In his present wife, Sue, Harvey feels he has finally found a loyal and loving partner. But Sue is allowed into Harvey's world and into his bed only a little at a time. Harvey wants Sue to want him sexually and to pursue him. Yet sometimes he feels threatened by the very sexual aggressiveness which he asks of her.

Sue is baffled. Does he want me or not? she wonders. She also wonders why she must pay the price for Harvey's past experiences with women. When Sue is physically ill or emotionally troubled, Harvey becomes highly anxious and then withdraws. At such times Sue wants moral support and physical affection, not a cold or empty bed.

There are many valid reasons for Harvey's behavior toward Sue, but Sue's emotional and sexual frustrations are equally real and painful. Already she is experiencing a lessening of sexual desire, as well as other signs of depression. Before she met Harvey, she liked to have sex almost every night. Now if they only make love once or twice a month, she says she "doesn't miss it." But in reality she does miss the soothing effects, not only of orgasm, but of the entire sexual embrace.

When either the vet or his wife is in denial about their pain, their psychic numbing may contribute to their sexual disinterest. But when either the vet, or his wife, is in therapy and their pain is beginning to surface, this can also result in a temporary disinterest in sex. When in pain, the vet may not want to be physically touched. In fact, his woman's touch utterly repels him. Some wives report that their husbands do not allow them to touch them for days.

When the Vietnam wife is in pain, she may feel like her husband: disinterested in sex, or in touching. However, she usually tries to explain to her veteran why she is not interested in physical intimacies. Sometimes she will even offer to be with him sexually despite her sexual disinterest. Yet, according to the wives, when the veteran is in a sexual "funk," rarely does he give his wife the courtesy of an explanation—unless, of course, the veteran has made so much progress in therapy that he is able to recognize, and acknowledge, his own emotional states. In addition, the wife's problem may be compounded by the fact that the veteran's sexual apathy toward her is often accompanied by an almost total emotional cutoff from her as well. Not only does he not make love to her, but he doesn't want to talk or communicate with her either.

Quite naturally, the wife who has not been informed about the nature—and power—of PTSD, can easily interpret her husband's withdrawal as a personal rejection or as a certain sign that she is not physically or emotionally appealing. As a result, she may suffer a mini-depression as a result of her husband's coldness. Or she may match her husband's withdrawal by withdrawing also. Or, out of a desire to reconnect with the man she loves, she may make a sexual advance, only to be rejected and further plummeted into depression and self-doubt.

Jim's wife, for example, felt lonely without emotional and sexual contact with her husband. When, after ten days, he had failed to even hug her, she woke Jim at 4 a.m. in hopes that he would make love to her. He was furious.

> *Damn her! That bitch! I told her not to wake me up in the middle of the night. She knows I have trouble sleeping. But a few weeks ago, it was I who woke her up at 4 a.m. and told her that was my best time for lovemaking. Maybe she thought she was doing what I wanted.*
>
> *I don't know and I don't care. I never thought I'd get so calloused that I wouldn't care how my wife felt. But right now all her desires to love and kiss me are just a pain to me. Outright nuisances! I wish she'd just go away.*
>
> *I've been thinking about 'Nam lately. The thoughts just interfere with everything. My depression takes over and I'm an utter flop in bed. My wife never minds when I can't perform. She always says she loves me just the way I am.*
>
> *Yet I can't stand to even talk to her and I despise her for loving me, maybe because I despise myself somehow. I turn my back on her too, because I don't want her to see my face. I want to hide what's going on inside of*

me—the fear, the anger, the hate. I want her to go away, but I also need her. Without her I have nobody.

After she woke me up, I had nightmares. I tried to turn them off. I could actually feel myself trying to manuever my eyelids so that the ugly drama would stop. But I couldn't stop the dream, the horror. At the end of the dream, I was so angry I wanted to kill somebody, something. The last thing on my mind was sex.

At the end of the dream, I was standing in the middle of a street, lost, confused, just like the first day I got back from 'Nam. I didn't know where anything was. Suddenly my wife appeared. She was there to help me, but I wanted her to go away because she couldn't possibly understand what I had been through.

In my mind, I began to tear her down, repeating to myself what was wrong with her. Yet I knew it was not her character defects that were making me mad.

I was mad because she was emotionally unscarred and I was mad that she, with all her love for me, couldn't take away the fear and anger in me, couldn't stop the panic.

I'm angry at her because she didn't have to go, because she didn't have to suffer, because her life has been so smooth in comparison. Sure, she's had her share of problems, but nothing like what I went through.

When I get like this, I feel crazy—here I am, pushing away one of the few people in the world who really cares about me.

Despite Jim's PTSD, he and his wife do have many tender moments. Nevertheless, too often in Jim's view, his Vietnam experience has impaired his ability to love. Furthermore, for him, as for other vets, Vietnam spelled the death of any belief in romantic love. Few of the vets I have seen still believe in romantic love and, among couples counseled, romanticism is almost nonexistent.

"Romantic love died in Vietnam, right next to my friends," explains Jim. "After you've seen enough death, injustice, and horror, you can't believe in love any more, at least not the mushy kind of love that's in the media and songs.

"For me now, romantic love is a joke. How can I think now that getting lost in someone's embrace is going to take away my pain?

When I hear love songs now, I get angry, then sad. I'm angry because I remember the times before 'Nam when I was young and innocent and half-believed those songs. But the stress over there and the stress back here since has rotted me out so much I'm no longer capable of feeling like that any more."

Another vet has similar feelings. "The most horrible feeling in the world to me, is not pain or anger, but not being able to love, to be in bed with someone who I think is almost everything I ever wanted in a woman and still have no feelings. The sensuality of touching her, even my orgasm, is dulled by the lack of feeling in my heart."

For most of the wives too, romantic love is now an adolescent fantasy. The harsh realities of having to work full time, of a husband with unpredictable mood swings, and of the intrusion of the war upon their lives, has nearly eradicated their romantic dreams. In fact, some of the wives consider themselves veterans also.

For example, even though Jim's wife has never seen Vietnam, she feels she has served "combat duty" just by being a Vietnam wife. Like her husband, she has lost much of her romantic feeling about her marriage. "I wish I could feel romantic toward Jim—he deserves it. But there's just too many holes in the wall, too many bills to pay, and too many hurt feelings on my part. I still love Jim, but it's sad, sad, sad, not to be able to love him like I used to."

Some vets are in touch with their sadness about their impaired capacity to experience romantic love. Others vets, however, are not. As a result, they may abruptly leave parties or gatherings where there is romantic music because, as they tell their wives, they "can't stand" the superficiality or "phoniness" of the other people. But what they also "can't stand" is their own anger and pain or the feeling of being "different" from everybody else.

Their wives can feel "different" too. Jim's wife explains: "At parties, I watch Jim like a hawk. The minute I see him getting too hot—or too cold—I know it's time to make some excuse and get him home. My friends wonder why I can't relax and make small talk at parties. But how can I? I'm always afraid that someone will say the wrong thing about 'Nam and make Jim go off or turn into a zombie."

Some veterans accept diminished sexual interest and activity as part of their PTSD. But others have attempted to fight it, using a variety of means to sexually stimulate themselves. Some have found that they can achieve erection or orgasm through the use of marijuana, cocaine, or other drugs. Without the drugs, they are impotent. Others have used pornographic videos or other pornographic materials. Still others insist that their wives adopt exotic positions or don erotic outfits. In instances where the vet has been habitually physically abusive to his wife, sometimes erection could only be achieved after the woman was physically assaulted or sexually humiliated, for example, after she was called derogatory sexual names, after her sex organs were abused or ridiculed, or after the veteran exposed her breasts or genitalia in public. Sexual abuse of Vietnam wives, however, is probably best explained by the veteran's psychological problems other than PTSD.

In my experience, men who have had to resort to such means to achieve sexual potency often, on some level, feel ashamed or inadequate because they cannot achieve erection and orgasm "naturally" as they put it. While abuse of the woman is obviously morally unacceptable, it can be argued that there is nothing inherently "wrong" with using sex videos or other visual means of stimulation. Yet the very men who use such means often feel it is "wrong" due to moral considerations or their view that their sexuality should not be dependent on external props. When the external props no longer work, they may panic and seek professional help. Or they may decide to become celibate.

After experiencing several sexual failures with his wife, one vet began to frequent topless bars in hopes of being aroused. For a while, his efforts proved successful. After viewing women at the bars, and sometimes sleeping with them, he was able to have successful intercourse with his wife. Eventually, however, his go-go dancers failed him. No matter how young or voluptuous they were, he couldn't "get it up." His subsequent desperate search for younger and more attractive go-go girls also failed. It was at this point that he began to acknowledge his depression, not only about Vietnam, but about certain life situations prior to his tour of duty.

The Vietnam wife who must tolerate her veteran's drug or alcohol addiction, his pornographic interests, or his other means of achieving sexual arousal often feels insulted and humiliated. Is she not enough? Why does he have to look elsewhere for sexual stimulation? Furthermore, she feels reduced to the status of a sexual plaything. When her veteran makes love to her, she frequently feels that the lovemaking is more an expression of his intense need to prove his masculinity to himself, rather than an expression of love.

If the Vietnam wife must also contend with her husband's extramarital affairs, she feels slapped in the face. Yet even if other women are not involved, the Vietnam wife whose husband suffers from sexual problems often feels not only sexually disappointed, but more importantly, emotionally abandoned. She has experienced a major loss: the loss of her hope for a mutually loving marital relationship. In marriage, she had hoped for a man's tenderness, adoration, and protection. But instead she found Vietnam—flashbacks and nightmares, emotional walls and emotional pain, power trips and insecurities, or a raw male sex drive, devoid of the usual preliminaries or of any romantic gestures. If the woman, like her husband, is incapable of grieving, depression will set in. Rather than recognize her loss, she may develop her own symptoms or find means of avoiding her husband sexually.

She may simply be cold toward him, always be tired or busy, or start arguments with him. Or she may gain weight; significant amounts of weight. While her weight gain may be seen as a way to "punish" her husband, in my view, it is primarily a means of expressing her sexual and romantic frustrations and disappointments or a means of punishing herself. She may be punishing herself because she feels like a failure as a woman due to her husband's lack of emotional and sexual responsiveness toward her.

Paranoia In The Bedroom

During the war, the veteran needed to be on constant alert. Combat readiness—if not overt paranoia—were qualities necessary for survival. Carol Vercozzi, in "The War That Refused To Die: Vietnam Again," explains:

"If the message of the military was black-and-white, the soldier's world was a hundred shades of green. Everything he had learned about order and logic and reason, even the things he had been taught about the war...fell apart in Vietnam. Nothing was real.... He stopped trying to apply reason, accepted that what you expected would not happen, that no one can be trusted, that everything outside yourself is subject to no rules you can ever uncover....Death was the new 'reality principle' and the paranoid combat-readiness state was the only hope of staying alive."[14]

In the bedroom, however, states of paranoid combat readiness are, to say the least, not conducive to satisfying sexual relations. Patterns vary from one couple to the next. Sometimes the vet's paranoia results in impotency: he becomes too frightened of the woman, or the sex act, to engage in sexual activity. In other instances, the vet's paranoia takes the form of not trusting that the woman "really loves him." He may require that the woman "prove" her love by engaging in longer or more frequent sexual activity than she desires or by trying certain sexual positions or practices which he, not she, desires.

If she is not cooperative, she is accused of being "unloving," "ungiving," a "cold fish" or "frigid." Some women have been taunted with pickles, squashes, or cucumbers when they have not desired intercourse. Some wives feel they must go along with their veteran's sexual desires or risk becoming the "enemy" in his mind and consequently, the possible target of his anger or other form of retaliation.

The vet's paranoia in the bedroom may not be constant. Some husbands act paranoid some days, but not others. Others undergo monthly or cyclical changes, alternating between periods of emotional stability and "normal" sexual relations and periods of severe mood swings and troubled sex.

The root of paranoia is fear—fear of being attacked or losing control. Certain aspects of the sexual relationship may serve to trigger such fears in the vet. Simply taking off his clothes or lying down may make him feel vulnerable and defenseless. He may also be threatened by shutting the bedroom door or by having the lights off. His wife, however, may want the bedroom door closed for privacy. Or she may want the lights dim or off for romantic or other reasons. Conflicts inevitably result.

More fundamentally, however, sex can be threatening to a vet, or to any man, because it requires "giving in" to a woman and surrendering to his sexual desire. While a man might very much desire sexual pleasure and release, he may fear the loss of control which such surrender implies. Or perhaps he views surrender as "feminine."[15] In a parallel manner, women who have difficulty achieving orgasm have often been described as unable to "surrender" to their partner or to their own sexual impulses. Just as women sometimes have trouble "letting go" sexually for fear that their partners will hurt them, men can have the same fears.

Staying In Control

"What if she bites me?" asks one vet, explaining his fears about oral sex. For him, letting go sexually is difficult because it increases not only his physical, but his emotional, vulnerability. For him, as for others, sex is the only time he feels emotionally close to his wife. Only during sex are his defenses down. While he describes the intimacy he experiences as sweet, he is also frightened by it. "I can't let her under my skin," he says, "so I limit the sex. I don't want to get hooked on anybody anymore. What if I lose her, like I lost others?"

For some vets, giving in to a woman's sexual requests, or even to their own desires for the woman feels like "giving in to the enemy." Yet the "ability to surrender" is a "prerequisite...for orgasm."[16] In some bedrooms, the woman actually becomes the "enemy." Perhaps she disappointed or "disobeyed" the veteran in some way, thereby "crossing the line" from friend to foe. The vet may view her as some-one to be conquered. Yet the very process of sexual conquest re-quires that the veteran let down his defenses and surrender to her.

For a few of my patients, such surrender has been impossible. As a result, they experience various degrees of impotence. Or they ar-range their sex lives so that they maintain almost total control over the sexual situation. For example, only the vet, not his wife or girlfriend, is allowed to initiate sex. Or he only will have intercourse facing the woman's back, never looking at her face.

Another way the vet can maintain control is to not permit the woman to stimulate him, orally or manually. He stimulates himself and uses the woman only for penetration. By stimulating himself, he not only protects himself from the possibility that the woman might hurt him, on purpose or by accident, but he can also monitor his own level of excitement and exert greater control over the timing and intensity of his orgasm.

If he does allow the woman to stimulate him, he may be very specific about how she is to do so. She may be allowed only to touch certain areas of his body and not others or to exert only certain amounts of pressure at various places. In one instance, a woman was instructed to caress only one particular segment of the rim of her husband's penis, no other part of his body, with only one of her fingers, not her entire hand. When she failed to follow directions, she was accused of not loving her husband and of trying to hurt him. Sex would be discontinued.

In still other cases, sex is divorced from affection at the veteran's request. This can be a way for the veteran to control the degree of closeness between himself and his partner. "If we have sex, we can't cuddle and talk. It's just sex, nothing else. But when he wants to be close and have us just hold each other, then the rule is that we can't have intercourse," explains one wife. "I guess my husband can handle only one form of contact at a time."

When the veteran rushes sex, when he wants to strictly control every sexual move, or in other ways enters into a paranoid or aggressive state in the bedroom, the Vietnam wife usually experiences minimal emotional satisfaction and minimal sexual arousal. Her attention is diverted from sexual pleasure to self-protection. Instead of concentrating on what she needs from her husband sexually or how to best arouse him, she's wondering what he's going to do next. Will there be violence or verbal abuse? Will he flashback? Where are the children? Where are those weapons from Vietnam? Will he pull them out to empower himself sexually, to protect himself, or just to reenact the past? If so, then what?

At the same time she is furiously processing the possibilities of what might happen and outlining what she may need to do to save herself, she is also trying to appease her husband sexually so as to minimize his agitation. Does he want her passionate? Does he want her quiet and receptive? Whatever he wants, she complies.

Under such conditions, sex becomes sexless, at least for the woman. Her sexual needs are often not considered, much less met. Insufficiently aroused and substantially diverted, both mentally and emotionally, from experiencing the sensuality of the moment, she may have difficulty enjoying sex as a sensual experience or achieving orgasm.

Yet, no woman thus far has seemed particularly concerned about not achieving orgasm. Those women who complain about the inadequacy of their sex life do not complain about not having a climax, but about not feeling loved or cherished. In fact, wives tend to be more concerned about their husbands not achieving orgasm than about their own lack of sexual fulfillment.

In three cases, the vet refused to have orgasm with his wife. He would initiate sex, get himself excited, then withdraw just prior to his orgasm and hers. While the reasons for this self-denial are not clear, two factors seem to be involved: a desire to punish the woman and orgasm anxiety.

All three vets frankly stated that they stopped intercourse just prior to their climaxing in order to "get back at" their wives. "I don't want her to have the satisfaction of knowing that she can make me come—that she has that much power over me," one vet stated.

Sex Now

While some wives complain of infrequent sex in their marriages, others moan that their husbands insist on sex a certain number of times a week (or day). For these men, sex is sometimes an imperative. When refused by their wives, they feel desperately unloved. There is an urgent quality to their desire which cannot be attributed solely to their need for sexual gratification. In the view of some wives, their men are not just seeking sexual release in the sex act, but security, self-esteem, a sense of superiority, or "victory" as well.

The vet's intense need for sex may not be a daily occurrence. While some wives describe their husbands as always, or almost always insisting on sex, others point out that their husbands seem to vacillate between being like "regular men," who are impatient, mildly aggressive, but also understanding, and being like "warriors" who demand gratification as their "due"—"or else."

On one level, this intense need for sex can be related to the veteran's loneliness. Socially isolated people are often lonely. Although they may desire to be separate, their isolation often results in their becoming "stroke deprived,"—they do not receive the smiles, the hugs, the compliments, or any of the visual, verbal, or physical recognitions (strokes), large or small, which naturally come about when with supportive others.

In this state of deprivation, the vet may turn to sex to meet his social and relationship needs. Sex becomes a substitute for in-depth emotional communication, or even for casual socialization. One vet called sex the "total stroke." For a long time, he believed that sex would satisfy all his hungers—his hunger for sex, as well as his hunger for human companionship and intimacy. Like many persons, he confused sex with love and with emotional closeness.

When sexual activity without communication left him unsatisfied, he increased his sexual activity. Even after more sex, however, he still felt restless and empty inside. Eventually he found that some communication with his sexual partner and more time spent socializing with others, not more "pure sex," helped satisfy him.

On another level, the vet's need for sex can be intense because, biologically, sexuality is the "antithesis of anxiety."[17] As has been repeatedly proven in studies of both men and women, anxiety interferes with sexual performance, especially with orgasm.[18] Conversely, it is difficult, if not impossible to be anxious while highly sexually aroused.

Hence, for some vets, sex is more than sex. It is a form of tranquillizer or sedative for their anxieties and other tensions. Not only does sex provide a sense of physical peace, but an emotional peace as well. "Sex takes away my anger," explains Tom. "After satisfying sex, for a few moments at least, all seems well, both within and without."

In this sense, sex can be used like a mood-altering drug. When the vet begins to feel pain, fear or confusion, he may feel overcome, not only by the specific emotions, but by the sheer fact of having such a powerful emotion. Not knowing what to do with his feelings, he may feel anxious and out of control. That his emotions are throwing him "off base" and won't go away "on command" also threaten his sense of masculinity.

He doesn't like the strength or power of his emotions. "Real men" are supposed to be in control of their emotions, not the other way around. It may be acceptable for women to let emotions dominate them, but former warriors cannot let emotion get the upper hand.

At this point, the vet needs a means of cooling his emotional waters, of feeling in control, of asserting his masculinity. Sex can obliterate, or at least temporarily mitigate, anxiety, emotional upset, and personal insecurities. Like alcohol and drugs, sex can be used as an escape, not only from emotional realities, but from other realities, such as children, bills, and other responsibilities.

In addition, sex helps affirm the vet's sense of manhood. Perhaps he feels emasculated in certain areas of his life, for example, on the job or because of a lack of a job. But when he is with a woman, he can, at last, "feel like a man." At least one person, his wife or girlfriend, is (literally) "under him."

Furthermore, for some vets, orgasm functions as a form of "shock treatment" for their depression. "If I don't have at least three orgasms a day, I get so blue I can't stand it. The minute I start feeling down, I reach for my wife. If she won't cooperate, I do something else," explains Peter. (He also needs to exercise daily in order to combat his depression.) When his wife refuses him sexually, it is not just sexual frustration which he suffers, but the full weight of some of his symptoms of PTSD.

The women, however, protest at being used as "human tranquilizers." "I'm tired of being his pill!" is the cry of the wives, who become especially resentful when their husbands' approaches follow days of being ignored or being taken for granted.

"Peter and I don't have a relationship, we have a *sexship*," says Jo. "I'm supposed to be there for him sexually, ready to jump in bed, whenever he needs me, no matter what else is going on. I could be upset, the kids could be crying, my mother could be on the way over—it doesn't matter. He wants it when he wants it, just like a baby.

"If I don't go along, he says he'll go find someone else. Sometimes once a day isn't enough. He wants sex two or three times a day. I just can't do it, so he goes out on me."

When sex is sometimes used as a means of dealing with emotions or life situations, as in the case of Peter, the need for sex may become progressive and all absorbing. One woman is not enough, so two are needed. Eventually two women are not enough, so three are needed. Or a different type of woman is sought.

Some vets become obsessed with sex, hoping that by having more (or different) types of women, they will find peace within. Their spare time may be spent in sex stores and watching sex videos. Or sex can become a major preoccupation in other ways, perhaps by counting the number and measuring the duration of various sexual activities. Sexual flings are not uncommon. More than one wife has had to put up with her husband's affairs. "It's not that Peter and I don't have sex," says Jo, "but it's never enough for him. So he has all these floozies. I think he's trying to recapture his youth or something."

Wives' Responses

In general, women have trouble being intimate with a man who is unhappy or angry, who is emotionally distant, or who is verbally or physically abusive. Some women, however, especially physically abused wives, cling to sex as a major means of keeping their marriage alive. While it is impossible to make global generalities about the sexual response of Vietnam wives to husbands with PTSD related sexual problems, several patterns do emerge.

1. **Denial of sexuality leading to sexual avoidance of the veteran.**

Some women respond to their husband's sexual dysfunctions, to his insistence on sex on demand, or to his obsession with sex, or his sexual flings by "turning off" their sexuality. They may go to bed with him, but, over the years, they may lose touch with their own sexual rhythms and desires. They may even deny that they have any sexual drive or desires at all. When they do engage in sex, it is usually in response to their husband's need, not their own. In this, the Vietnam wife is not different from many other married women, who learn to adapt their sexuality to their partners' timing and tastes.

The Vietnam wife, however, is under special pressures. She knows her husband is troubled and if sex is paramount to him, she may go along with his sexual desires to help promote his mental health and keep the peace at home. When she is aggressive in bed, her aggression may not be a reflection of her own sex drive, but a response to her veteran's request, if not insistence, that she be more active sexually. Hence sex becomes more like work than play.

In recent years, with the onset of the sexual revolution, sex has become an achievement situation for women, as well as for men. It is no longer enough for a woman to lie in bed passively. Now she may feel pressured to "perform" by having an orgasm or at least displaying heated passion. In addition, a new phenomenon has emerged—women insisting on their "right" to sexual fulfillment and demanding that men bring them to orgasm.[19]

However, Vietnam wives who make such demands on their husbands are, in my experience, relatively few in number. In most cases, the woman allows her sexuality to be monitored by her husband's desires. If he wants her to be sexually aggressive, she will be so, even to the point of pretending more passion than she is actually feeling. In a few instances, women have forced themselves to be sexually aggressive to please their veteran, only to have him eventually become angry, accuse the woman of trying to "emasculate" him, and insist that she allow him to take control.

Given such a double message, even sexually alive women could throw up their hands. "It isn't fun if you're always being judged," explains one wife. "Or if the rules keep changing," adds another. As a result the woman's sexual desires and most certainly her sexual spontaneity might become inhibited, leading, eventually, to the woman's avoidance of, if not outright hostility toward, marital sexual activity.

2. Decreased self-esteem.

When the Vietnam wife experiences love during sex only on occasion, she begins to feel like a whore even though she is making love with her own husband. She feels debased because she feels she is being used as a sex machine. Yet, she may engage in sex with her husband anyway, out of a sense of duty or because of her husband's insistence, or because he is, or seems, desperate. Or, she may pity her husband. "Sex is the only time he feels alive. How can I deny him?" I have heard over and over. Or she may fear that her veteran will become enraged or that he will "go crazy." He might regress further and further into his PTSD if she does not comply. Yet she often feels like a robot. "I don't know why I do it with him. I don't get anything out of it sexually or emotionally. He hardly touches me. We don't talk. What's the point?" asks Jean.

Jean has been in group for over a year. She is long past the point of blaming the poverty of her sexual relationship with her husband entirely on herself. Today, she clearly recognizes that her husband's PTSD and other psychological problems are contributing to the lack of love and good sex in their marriage. Yet even Jean, like most of the newcomers who come to group, on some level attributes her sexual and emotional difficulties primarily to herself, rather than to her husband's problems. "If only I was 'better,' then he would love me more," is Jean's underlying thought. More specifically, "If only I knew how to relate to him better," or "If only I was prettier," or "If only my breasts were fuller, or my thighs slimmer, or whatever, then he would respond to me."

Despite her awareness of her husband's PTSD, Jean's self-esteem suffers because, as a woman, she has been socialized to look to male approval and male responses as a measure of her self-worth. Even the women with significant career achievements and successes, and well-established identities outside their homes suffer from feelings of inferiority and inadequacy when their husbands avoid them sexually, or, when their sex life seems to lack love and tenderness. They often find it hard to love and esteem themselves or to validate themselves as women when the man they love either ignores them, treats them like a sex object, or fails to give them the love and affection they desire.

While many of the women might feel like failures as women on some level, they also realize that the lack of sexual gratification and emotional intimacy in their marriage is not all their fault. Most women are quick to point out that their husband's inability to be intimate and his fear of being close derive from several sources, including Vietnam. Despite their understanding of the sources of their husband's difficulties, most of the women nevertheless eventually voice resentments toward their husbands for failing to love them properly.

Anger, resentment, and feelings of betrayal usually exist in the women, right alongside their self-blame. Obviously, the woman's anger toward her husband, like her husband's anger toward her or toward his Vietnam experience, can mitigate, if not totally obliterate, her sexual response.

In cases where the veteran is sometimes loving and attentive during sex, but other times not, the Vietnam wife becomes not only depressed, but confused.

"Sex is great when Tyrone is his regular self. But when he's under pressure or something snaps him back into 'Nam, the regular Tyrone disappears and a warrior takes his place. He begins to heave and the blood in his veins visibly pulsates. Then I never know what to expect, in bed or anywhere else," says Beau.

Like other wives in group, Beau experiences many pleasurable times with her husband, who can be extremely tender and loving, as well as self-centered and cold. His "PTSD" moods, as she calls them, are unpredictable. At times they last for days, at times for months. In considering whether or not to stay married to Tyrone, she does not know on which Tyrone to base her decision: the "regular" Tyrone or the warrior one.

A few wives are so devastated by their husband's sexual rejection or iciness, they desperately pursue him sexually. If they can but engage him in sex, even purely carnal sex, then they feel loved and assured of their worth. So far, this pattern has evidenced itself only among some of the physically battered women who have attended group. As Walker, who has studied hundreds of battered women, points out, battered women typically use sex to create an illusion of love and as a means of establishing harmony in the home.[20] Yet the price they pay is loss of self-respect. Whenever a woman uses "sex in order to create love she may feel she is prostituting and degrading herself."[21]

Sexuality And Role Overload

Sexuality is more than any specific sex act or variety of sex acts. Sexuality encompasses all of a person's feelings about his or her physical self, as well as his or her general attitude toward life. A highly sexual person is usually a vibrant self-actualized person whose enthusiasm for sex is mirrored in his or her enthusiasm for other activities.

The sexual person enjoys and rejoices in his or her physical self, including, but not limited to, the aliveness that comes from sexual energy. Depressed persons are typically not sexual in this sense, even though they may reach for sex as a means of self-validation or become obsessed with sex as a means of avoiding other problems.

Fun sex, as opposed to "duty sex," requires an atmosphere of play and lightness, not the seriousness, strains, and sadness which often surrounds the Vietnam veteran with PTSD and his equally burdened wife. Sex is also robbed of its potential for maximum emotional and physical gratification when the couple is saddled with financial instability. The vet may be physically handicapped. Or his emotional problems resulting from the war or from job discrimination against vets may have reduced his career opportunities. There may be other "headaches" as well, such as conflicted relationships with the extended family, troubled children, and the normal emotional and physical fatigue of everyday life, all of which can lessen the quality and quantity of the couple's sex life.

In some couples, the sense of responsibility, as well as the actual responsibilities, are shared. Both the vet and his wife do about the same amount of work, and worrying. In other cases, however, one of the couple assumes psychological responsibility for the family's burdens to a greater extent than the other and actually does more than half of the work. Typically, this is the individual who suffers not only from physical, but also from mental, fatigue. This partner's life becomes organized around work and other responsibilities, not pleasures or emotional needs.

Sometimes it is the veteran who assumes the role of the "responsible one." He is the one who says "no" when his wife calls him to bed or asks for a night out because he's finishing up some work or worrying about the broken water heater or the unpaid car repair bills. Or perhaps he feels his free time is better spent helping one of the children. In light of the family's many problems, his wife's request seems irrelevant, if not outright "irresponsible" or "frivolous."

In my clinical experience, however, it is the Vietnam wife, rather than the veteran, who usually assumes the sense of responsibility for the family's emotional and financial well-being. Obviously there is a bias in this sample. Most likely it is primarily women who feel burdened by an enormous sense of responsibility for their families or who have relatively irresponsible partners who seek help.

As the family's official "worry wart," sex and other forms of playing are not high on her list of priorities. When her husband wants to go to a movie or "hang out" at a mall, she wants to finish the ironing and other chores and go to bed early because the next day she's working overtime to help pay some bills.

As the following chapter on multiple roles will explain in greater detail, role overload is a "given" in the lives of many Vietnam wives. Saddled with multiple responsibilities both outside the home, as well as in it, the Vietnam wife typically operates in her "responsible adult" mode, rather than in her "playful child" mode. It is as difficult for her, as for any other overcommitted person, male or female, to turn off the "responsible adult" mentality and become the "playful child" in bed, or elsewhere. Breaks or periods of relaxation or physical exercise are necessary in order to make the transition from responsible adult to playful child.

"Even when we're on vacation, there's no vacation from his PTSD," explains Jean, who feels her playful child died long ago. Her enthusiasm for sex, as well as for other forms of recreation, has also died a slow death in the traffic jams or got lost somewhere in the endless "to do" lists which accompany being a working wife and mother.

In addition, she has to work overtime in order to have the leave necessary to accompany her husband to his doctor's appointments. He refuses to go alone. Furthermore, Jean is afraid her husband will "go off" or even start fights if she is not along to smooth the path and calm him down should one of the medical staff be, or seem to be, insulting or incompetent.

> I've been on the go since 6 a.m. and what aggravates me more than anything is that after group I have to stop at the grocery store and pick up milk and cupcakes. The cupcakes are for my son's ball game tomorrow. The milk is for my other baby—my husband. He called me today in the middle of a staff meeting at work to remind me that we were out of milk.
>
> 'Why can't you go get the milk?' I wanted to scream. But I know better than to yell at a combat vet. In his view, I'm the woman, so I'm responsible for the home, the groceries, the laundry, our son—the works. Sure, my vet helps, but only when he feels like it.
>
> I can handle doing all the work, but what I can't handle is having to turn into a sex kitten every night. I hate those women on T.V. who can work all day and

purr all night. Some nights all I want to do is go to sleep. But all he wants to do is fool around. Sometimes he isn't even interested in sex, but he wants me to be there panting anyway. If I'm not in heat, he wonders if I have another man, or if I don't love him anymore, or if this group has turned me against him. I tell him repeatedly that I love him, that I enjoy sex with him, but sometimes I'm just too tired.

Well, he just can't understand that, nor can he understand the enormous emotional burden I feel for our son. My husband is a very good father, except when he's into his PTSD. Then he gets depressed or into one of his moods or can be gone for hours, if not days, at a time. Even if he's around, he just sits and doesn't talk to us. I can't count on him to take Pete to his ball games or be involved in any of Pete's school activities. Since I work, I can't be there all the time either. But I make all the arrangements for my son to get to his events and I try to spend a lot of time with him on weekends.

Of course all this arranging takes time and energy, which my husband thinks is done by a magic secretary. Then on weekends and my days off, he thinks that I should have hours and hours totally free to play around with him in bed. But, as a working woman, my days off are not days off. I have all these chores to do, as well as a need for time for myself. Instead, I feel pressured to turn into some kind of sex goddess, or at least be there, sexually. Sometimes sex feels like another job to me, rather than a pleasure. I'm ashamed to admit that there are times when I'm in bed with my husband that I'm planning my grocery list or thinking of all the phone calls I have to make after I get up.

Pretty sad, isn't it? I wish I could be more spontaneous and totally absorb myself in sex, like I used to, before our son was born and before PTSD came into the picture. Basically, I'm a very sexual woman and my husband is very good in bed—when he's not into his PTSD that is. But I'm just too wound up from all I've done during the day and from realizing all that I have to do

the next day to let myself go. I wish I could be more
playful, but I'm not.

It's frightening to realize how much a job, a home, a
child, and a Vietnam veteran can take out of a woman,
but reality is reality. We have to eat. He doesn't make
enough. So I have to work, which means that not only
my sexuality, but other things suffer.

While Jean resents her husband's expectation that she be sexual
and alluring after a hard day's work, she also berates herself for not
measuring up to his desires. Yet she, like so many other Vietnam
wives, fails to realize that her veteran's ability to relax, play, and have
the physical and psychic energy for sexual fun, is based on somebody else, specifically the wife, assuming the physical and emotional responsibility for much of the family's life. When the Vietnam wife
takes care of most of the bills, the housework, the children's emotional and physical needs, she is essentially giving her husband the
free time, and more importantly, the peace of mind, to pursue recreational activities and to achieve a mental and physical state which
permits sexual desires to surface.

Jean's husband can go out twice a week with his friends and attend therapy a third night, knowing that Jean is helping Johnny with
his homework and cleaning the house. Also, he can spend much of
his weekend with friends or engaged in sports, because, once again,
Jean is either managing the household or tending to Johnny. After
having enjoyed himself with his friends or with his sports, he's ready
to make love to Jean. But Jean's energies have been drained by having
fulfilled many family responsibilities, as well as by the lack of free
time in her life. While her husband has had the time to recharge his
"pleasure batteries," she has not.

Not only does Jean's husband spend more time relaxing and playing than Jean, but he has a different mind set about life. Due to his
PTSD and his sense of male prerogative, he is able to detach not
only from his own problems, but from the problems of the family.
For example, Jean reports that her husband can "simply forget" the
nights he keeps her up for hours talking about Vietnam or having
flashbacks. "The next night, he acts as if nothing happened," explains Jean. "He's ready to be Tarzan and I'm supposed to be Jane.
But I'm still tired from the night before and still in a state of confusion and upset over his emotional condition.

"Because he feels fine at the moment, he forgets about all the times he's in a rage or in turmoil. But I can't forget. Nor can I pretend that everything's all right. He thinks everything is all right as long as we are making love. It's like he's never heard me say that no matter how good he is in bed, if he doesn't deal with his PTSD—really deal with it—not play at dealing with it—and change some of his attitudes about women, then I might leave him."

When Jean's husband gets depressed, he takes leave from work, goes camping or fishing, or travels to see his war buddies. When Jean gets depressed, she goes to work, fixes Johnny's meals, and does the dishes anyway. Happy or sad, sick or well, Jean is working almost all the time. Most likely if she was relieved of some of her physical, and emotional responsibilities, her natural interest in sex, and other forms of fun, would come back.

Vietnam wives need not have jobs outside the home in order to suffer from mental and physical fatigue like Jean. The Vietnam wife who is home most of the day with small children may also find herself swamped with chores, as well as saddled with concern, if not agony, over her husband's mental health and the future of her marriage. In addition, she may suffer from the lack of stimulation, the loneliness, and the unfair lack of recognition and appreciation which often attend being a full-time homemaker in our society.

More than one full-time Vietnam wife and mother has sat in group weeping over the fact that her husband cannot comprehend how caring for a home and small children all day can be not only tiring, but frustrating, and certainly not conducive to being sexually alive at night. These wives feel they do not have the "excuse" of working outside the home in order to say "no" to sex or in order to explain their lack of sexual interest. Hence they sometimes feel under special pressure to be sexually enticing and available. Yet the very pressure from their husbands to be more sexual is a "turn off" and, combined with the many strains of being a full-time homemaker and mother, such pressure from her husband can produce a highly anxious, and therefore, sexually disinterested, woman.

Yet the Vietnam wife, despite her many emotional and physical responsibilities, is not inherently any less sexual than any other woman, as shown in the responses of Vietnam wives to a popular exercise used in group entitled "Your Free Self." After the Vietnam wife is thoroughly relaxed, she is asked to imagine her "free spirit"—what she would be like or what she would like to do if she were not feeling so responsible for her husband, the children, the laundry, work at the office, or if she were in a relatively problem-free marriage. To help her get in touch with her playful child, she is asked to remember any time in her past when she felt free of multiple demanding responsibilities. Under such circumstances, many Vietnam wives fantasize themselves as extremely creative and erotic.

Sexual Deprivation And Depression: A Vicious Cycle

While the Vietnam wife sometimes wishes she were more sexual in order to please her husband, she frequently forgets that often when she wants sex, her husband is simply not at home at night or is sexually disinterested or impotent due to depression or the prolonged effects of drug or alcohol abuse. She also forgets that if the two of them had greater communication and emotional intimacy, her sexual interest might soar. Yet the diminished frequency—and quality—of her sexual relationship with her husband only serves to lengthen the emotional distance between herself and her husband and to increase their communication problems.

In addition, the lack of sexual contact or meaningful sexual activity also perpetuates any existing depression in either the vet or his wife. While the vet and his wife may be depressed for different reasons, both suffer when their sexual relationship is suffering.

Since sexual activity and orgasm require energy, they are often seen as "draining." However, suppressing sexuality and fighting the need for sexual release also require energy. While a person may feel depleted immediately after intercourse, ultimately the sexual release functions to create more energy and an elevation in mood. When the Vietnam wife states that she is "too tired" for sex, part of her fatigue may stem from the very lack of sexual touch and fulfillment itself.

Summary

Sexuality is an issue in many homes, but especially in the homes of PTSD afflicted veterans. The veteran's sexual response may be diminished, or twisted, by the intrusion of wartime memories or survivor guilt into his intimate moments. Or the vet may fear the physical and emotional vulnerability inherent in disrobing and in the sexual act itself. If he is unable to maintain an erection, or otherwise enjoy his sexuality due to his PTSD, he may avoid sex altogether.

While some vets avoid sex, and others have only periods of sexual disinterest, in some instances vets are interested in sex almost all the time. An intense need for, and preoccupation with, sex may reflect the vet's need to combat his depression and anxiety and to forget not only Vietnam but his problems in the present. Sex may make him "feel good" if only briefly.

Meanwhile his wife may feel like a sex machine—a human tranquilizer—or a sexual reject. If her husband alternates his behavior, she may feel like both. Whether the veteran avoids sex or is obsessed with it, the Vietnam wife's self-esteem suffers if her needs to be cherished and loved, to be listened to and considered important by her husband are not met.

In homes where the Vietnam wife does the majority of the housework and childcare, sheer fatigue may deplete her sexual energies, especially if she is simultaneously working outside the home. And underneath the fatigue, which is real, lies anger. Even if she can't admit it, her sexual rejection or lack of response often betrays her anger at him—for failing her sexually, or for sexually using her. Primarily, though, she is angry at her husband for failing to meet her needs for intimacy and emotional bonding.

Some wives resign themselves to sexually unfulfilling marriages. They tend to find comfort in their children and their work, not other men. Some wives admit their bitterness, others bury their bitterness with denial or excess food. In many instances, the sexual happiness of the Vietnam veteran and his wife can be viewed as yet another casualty of the Vietnam war.

Four

The Reality of Multiple Roles

As the wife of a Vietnam combat vet with a flaming case of untreated PTSD, I have several full-time jobs. My full-time job at the office is just one of them. In fact, it is the easiest one of all.

First, and most important, I am a mother, and being the wife of a vet, this means that usually I function like a single parent. I don't know whether it's PTSD or male chauvinism or a combination of both, but the bottom line is that I am responsible for almost every detail of my children's lives—from their lunches to their health.

I am also responsible for most of the details of my husband's life—arranging his medical appointments, explaining and protecting him from his parents, my parents, the social workers, and the neighbors. I take care of all his paperwork too and since he's one of those vets who hates the IRS, I take care of all the family finances as well.

When my husband is in a good mood, he vacuums, does the dishes, and irons my blouses. But I never know how long his good moods are going to last and I can't count on anything getting done unless I do it myself. I hate to start a fight over something as trivial as an undone chore.

But all those undone chores pile up, and before I know it, I'm working all the time. Sometimes I get so tired I can't even fall asleep. But other times I purpose-

ly stay up until two or three in the morning just to have a little time to myself, and a little peace.

I wish I could socialize and do more for myself, but I don't have time. I have to think twice before I leave the kids alone with my husband. It's not that he's abusive to them, but since he won't go for help, I have to be around as much as possible in case he has a problem. If something happens to him while I'm out, the kids couldn't handle it without me. He wouldn't be able to handle it either.

I do everything for everybody else. I don't do anything for myself because that would be selfish. Yet when I do what everybody else expects me to do, no one ever says 'thanks.' Sometimes I feel so unappreciated that I want to run away from home.

> Melanie, mother of three and
> wife of a combat vet

Most of the Vietnam wives who have attended group work outside the home, some for personal fulfillment, but most out of economic necessity. In about one third of the cases, their husbands have been unemployed or only partially employed. In another third, the husbands, while employed full time, have expressed considerable job dissatisfaction to their wives. In the remaining third, the husbands have shown great pride and dedication to their vocations. However, among this third, in all but one instance, the veteran's employment record has been marred by one or more outbursts of temper or physical attacks on an employee or supervisor. Both the veteran and his wife usually trace the outburst to the husband's PTSD.

Many vets lost career opportunities due to the reduced educational and job training benefits available to Vietnam vets as compared to World War II veterans. The Vietnam vet also returned home to an economy suffering from inflation and unemployment and to employers who were hostile or ambivalent toward him due to his veteran status. Today, the old stereotype of the Vietnam veteran as a crazy angry baby-killer is slowly being replaced by the new stereotype of the Vietnam veteran as a "macho" or Rambo hero. However, even today, vets report that negative stereotypes about Vietnam veterans still exist. Furthermore, such negative stereotypes were certainly active some ten to fifteen years ago, when many vets were seeking employment. At that time, some vets purposefully did not mention their Vietnam service in job interviews or, if asked, denied it.

The vet's real or perceived need to hide his identity as a Vietnam veteran may have contributed to his job dissatisfaction and other job problems. Furthermore, the tendency of some veterans with PTSD to have interpersonal difficulties on the job and to mistrust authority figures has left them jobless, job hunting, or going from one job to the next.

The resulting instability deeply affects the wives who find themselves in financial limbo or in the process of constantly rearranging their work plans and schedules, the children's schedules, needed appointments, and any social plans to accommodate their husband's job changes, job hunting, or lack of employment. "I can't plan and there's no routine," states Dora. "If my husband gets a job, then maybe we can afford something we need or pay a certain bill. But I never know until the last minute. Then, once he gets a job, I never know how long he's going to keep it.

"Obviously we can't plan the chores or even our son's schedule. If my husband needs the car for a job interview, then our son can't get to his ball practice. No sense paying for the uniform if he isn't going to be able to participate.

"What we really need is a second car, but we can't afford one until George gets a job. But I'm not complaining.

"George's had six jobs since 'Nam, but some of his war buddies have had more than that. And at least my husband keeps trying to find work."

However, George is not motivated to work full time or to pursue an upwardly mobile career. Like some of his war buddies, he is "turned off" by middle-class values such as success and material gain. Problems arise, however, when the wife still desires a dream home with a two-car garage.

Another difficulty is that some vets are reluctant to accept or keep relatively menial or "unexciting" jobs after having held positions of considerable authority or more adventuresome positions during their tours of duty in Vietnam. "Do you know what it is to have to work 9 to 5 in an office and take orders from someone you don't respect after having been in command of millions of dollars worth of equipment in Vietnam?" asks a former officer. He resents having to write memos before he can do anything. In Vietnam, he had power of life and death over dozens of men and made his own decisions.

Regardless of the source of the veteran's employment difficulties, when he is unemployed or sporadically employed, his wife is not just a contributor to the family's income, but often the family's primary or sole source of funds. Hence all of the woman's issues and problems, whether with her veteran or within herself, exist in the context of a multiple role life style. The fact that she works both inside the home, as well as at an outside job, pervades every aspect of her life and emotional being. Yet it is a reality which she herself, as well as her partner, family and friends (and many therapists) overlook.

The strains of having primary responsibilities both inside and outside the home are obvious. Yet they are often overlooked because of media images of the working wife or mother as one who glides from one role to the next without anxiety, conflict, or effort, with her make-up intact and her figure perpetually slim. In addition, there is the cultural expectation that a woman should be able to "do it all," or at least "most of it," without complaining. "I don't know why we think that we have to do it all, but we do," the women in group often say.

In the past, women were strangled by the notion that women who worked outside the home were neurotic, unfeminine, or otherwise "abnormal."[1] But today women are strangled by society's denigration of traditional feminine roles. For many women, it is no longer "enough" to be a wife, mother, or homemaker.[2] In addition, economic changes during the past two decades have necessitated that many women work outside the home for sheer survival of the family or to improve the family's standard of living.[3]

Handling a full or part-time job in addition to home, means increased demands on time and energy, often resulting in overload and fatigue. With additional roles come additional commitments: more people to respond to, more appointments to keep, more deadlines to meet. In addition, the Vietnam wife must come to understand and grapple with any "office politics" as well as her interpersonal dynamics at home.

Essentially the Vietnam wife working outside the home faces the exhaustion of having at least two full-time jobs: one at home, one at work. In addition, she often has a third job: that of arranging all her roles. Since the cultural expectation is often that the woman's outside job is peripheral to her essential home roles, it is usually the woman who makes the arrangements necessary to execute all the various roles, for example, the phone calls regarding childcare and the transportation of children to and from school events. In most cases, the woman attempts to arrange that her working role does not interfere with her domestic role. However, the logistical difficulties involved, especially when children are young, can be enormous.

The Vietnam wife's burden is compounded by the fact that her sleep may be interrupted by her husband's nightmares or flashbacks, his anger or depression, or his unpredictable comings and goings from the home. Or she may have to spend the night in the car or at a friend's because she fears his anger. Furthermore, due to tensions in the home, the Vietnam wife often goes to work not only without sufficient physical rest, but without mental peace.

Since her husband's emotional capacities are impaired due to PTSD, she is often the emotional center of the home. Both her husband and her children may look to her for nurturing, guidance, and strength. Furthermore, she often assumes an active role in her husband's recovery by encouraging him to seek help, arranging his therapy appointments, helping him obtain his benefits, or whatever. If he cannot tolerate bureaucracies or waiting, then it will be she, not he, who calls the doctors and the hospitals, who contacts the Veteran's Benefits offices, who waits in line at the pharmacy, and does whatever else is necessary. If he must appear himself, usually she feels she must go with him, to keep him calm should he feel he is being treated unfairly or should he notice any incompetence or insensitivity on the part of the clerks or the medical staff. If he is hospitalized, there are frequent visits and, in some cases, participation in family therapy or conferences with doctors, all of which require, time, energy, and effort.

Her children might also have special needs. They may need to attend therapy or Al-A-Teen meetings. Children from violent homes often have learning problems which require tutoring or extra parental assistance. In most cases, it is the mother who helps her children with the homework, not the father. In addition, the Vietnam wife may be making special efforts to involve her children in outside recreational or social activities in order to offset the depressive mood in the home or compensate for their father's lack of involvement. In any of the above cases, the working woman's scheduling problems are even more complex.

At the same time, however, the Vietnam wife usually cannot afford the services that make being a working woman easier, like maid service or frequent restaurant dinners. If money is tight, she must also consider economic factors in executing her multiple roles. For example, she may need to shop at discount grocery and clothing stores, even though the stores are out of her way and the lines are long. She may also be unable to afford convenience foods, increasing her time in the kitchen.

Consequently, she feels pressured for time. Yet, she often feels she cannot complain about her time pressures to her partner because they seem "trivial" compared to his trials in Vietnam.

> If I mention to George that I feel pressured, he just laughs at me and says, 'You should have been in Vietnam. Then you would have seen real pressure. Why are you complaining about having to go to the grocery store again? At least you have one to go to, and a car to get there with. Why, when I was in the jungles...' and on and on.
>
> All I know is that my life is not my own. During the weekdays, my job consumes me. Then at night, I do everything and spend all my time getting me, and everybody else, ready for the next day. My weekends and holidays are not my own either. I clean, cook, take the kids shopping.
>
> Sure, I'm not surrounded by V.C., but my daily list of 'things to do' would blow away the minds of most men. All they have is one job—I have at least six: cook, laundress, chauffeur, cleaner, shopper, banker, not to mention my full-time job and being a mother.
>
> My husband laughs at my lists, but I couldn't survive without them. He doesn't understand that I'm working practically all the time. Neither do my kids.
>
> I don't know if they learned it from T.V. or what, but they complain when I'm five or ten minutes late to take them where they need to go, as if I'm late because I was taking a bubble bath or doing my nails.
>
> No. I'm usually late because I'm finishing up chores they said they would do, but didn't do. Yet I hate to nag the kids because they've got enough on them with their Dad in and out of the hospital with his PTSD.
>
> But I do blow up at them sometimes. Then I feel guilty because I really do want to be a patient mother and give them quality time. But how I can I be patient when I have so much to do?

Sex Role Stereotyping

Sex role stereotypes die hard. Often the woman faces the dual problems of a partner who is unwilling or unprepared to share domestic tasks and her own difficulty in giving up doing the traditional homemaking tasks which once defined her value to her family.

About one fourth of the women I have seen report that their husbands are "excellent" with the children, but not so excellent with domestic chores. The other three-fourths, however, report that while husbands help, they often feel and act martyred in doing so. Veterans who share domestic responsibilities often view themselves as "helping" or doing the woman a "favor" rather than "sharing" responsibilities. In general, they do not receive reinforcement for their work at home from friends, family, or community, except perhaps, for their involvement with their children.

If the vet has agreed to do something for the home or for the children, he may "forget" to keep his promise or decide to "do it later." The woman then has the dilemma of choosing to press her husband to keep his commitment and risk being called a "nag" or a "bitch," or suppress her resentment and do the work herself.

The Vietnam wife has special difficulties in getting her husband to complete his responsibilities at home, or to assume more of them. She is usually well-aware of her veteran's sensitivity to being "ordered around." On the other hand, she wants her vet to do much more. Yet she knows she might meet massive resistance if she makes her requests known. "He'll say he has too much pressure at work or from his PTSD to do anything more around the house," one wife reports. "He'll just get mad and walk out," says another. "If I push him too far, he might take it out on me and the kids later, or get into a funk and make me feel guilty," says yet another.

Often the woman is put in the impossible situation of having to choose between overextending herself or seeing one of her children's needs go unmet. For example, their child needs to be driven to music lessons or a sports event. The veteran has promised to take his child, but at the last minute, he says he cannot take the traffic.

He's had an exceptionally hard day. Somebody mentioned Vietnam and it set him back emotionally. It was enough for him to deal with his emotions and stay at work all day without him now having to go out again. He needs to be alone, to collect himself. What his wife is asking him to do seems minor compared to the pain, anger, or frustration he feels inside. Besides, taking kids places is "woman's work."

The wife might have had a hard day too. She is exhausted, but she cannot disappoint her child. Also, she may feel for her husband, have empathy for his pain, and not want to add to his burden. In addition, she may know that if her husband is in such a negative mood, even if she insists that he keep his commitment, she will most likely not get what she wants. Furthermore, there will also probably be a scene between them, which will only upset her child and other family members.

In order to spare the child, her husband, and herself the stress of yet another marital conflict, the woman usually ends up doing the driving. Furthermore, the child expects the mother to do the driving. After all, isn't this what mothers do, take care of children? Never mind that the mother has worked all day. She is expected to be a source of boundless energy at night and "compensate" for the fact that she works all day by doing whatever she can for her children at night.

In addition, in some homes, one or more of the children is sensitive to the fact that their father has been "put down" as a Vietnam veteran or has problems due to the war. Hence they may greatly resent their mother "putting down" their father, even if the mother's complaint is legitimate. If their father has war injuries or is handicapped due to the war, the child's resentment at the mother for asking the father for more help may be even greater.

"When George and I fight, it's torture for our son. If he's supposed to go to a party, and George and I argue over who is going to take him, our fight ruins his fun. By the time we decide who's going to take him, he's decided not to go. He knows that his father has back problems from the war and doesn't like to drive. On the other hand, I work longer hours than my husband, so I feel he should help out more at home," says Janet.

"But it doesn't matter who's right or wrong. When George and I fight, our son gets hurt and doesn't want to go anywhere.

"Bad enough my husband is a recluse and is trying to turn me into one. But I don't want our son to be a hermit. So, I do all the driving."

In some Vietnam vet homes, there is a complete or almost complete role reversal. The vet is on permanent disability due to war injuries or unemployed or only partially employed for other reasons. He becomes a househusband and the woman works full time. In some instances, the role reversal works smoothly. "It took a lot of training, but I finally got my husband to have dinner ready on time and to do the dishes afterward without me having to tell him ten times," says one wife.

"At first he used to call me at work to ask me about every little thing. But after I told him that if he could handle the Viet Cong, he could certainly figure out the vacuum cleaner and the mop, his phone calls stopped."

But not all wives are this fortunate. Most find that their husbands do not househusband automatically; they need to be reminded to complete certain chores. Sometimes the woman tires of doing all this reminding and begins assuming some of the domestic chores herself. In some cases, one chore at a time, the woman eventually reassumes many of her previous domestic responsibilities.

Furthermore, when the househusband vet becomes depressed due to PTSD, he cannot be relied upon to keep his commitments. If there are no children in the home, the woman can let go of certain nonessential household chores until her husband regains his strength. But if there are children, much of the work cannot be left undone. The woman has no choice but to do it herself.

For example, Kate, who worked full time, and her husband, Ron, who worked ten hours a week, established an elaborate division of labor chart. Ron's heart wasn't in it, yet he realized that the old days when men could read the newspaper while their wives cooked dinner and cleaned the house, were over. Kate, who managed an office by day, wanted to rest after work—"not too much—just a little bit." After hammering away at Ron for years about the unfairness of it all, Ron reluctantly agreed to carry his own weight and stop assuming that his wife was a superwoman who could do it all well and without any feeling of resentment.

The first week Ron attempted to do his chores. But he wasn't used to doing three things at once like his wife. Furthermore, when he got tired or bored, he wanted to quit, even if he hadn't completed everything on his list. After all, he reasoned, he had stressed himself enough in Vietnam. He was home now, not in the military. Breaks and slight infractions of the "rules" were permitted here. Beside, folding the laundry was really not a life-and-death issue compared to loading machine guns with ammunition.

For two consecutive days when Kate came home from work, she found half of Ron's chores undone. The first day she found Ron taking a nap. She was angry about the chores but she was also glad to see that Ron was able to get some rest. He suffered from insomnia and nightmares and Kate worried about him. The next day, however, the chores weren't done and Ron wasn't sleeping. He was out with his friends. Once again, Kate was resentful over the chores but a part of her was glad. In fact, she was delighted that her husband was finally socializing, rather than isolating himself, which had been his pattern. On the other hand, she was determined not to do his work for him.

The next day she picked the children's clothes for school out of the laundry but left her clothes, and the filled dishwasher untouched. That night she quietly confronted Ron and he promised to do better next time.

Two days later the laundry was still unfolded and the dishwasher was still full. At this point Kate was tempted to do Ron's chores for him. It seemed easier than nagging him or having him say that she was making "a big deal about nothing." In fact, Kate calculated that just in terms of time, it would probably take her longer to nag Ron into doing the work than to simply do it herself. But she left the chores undone, set the table with paper plates, and wore a dirty blouse to work.

She planned to confront her husband once more, but he was so angry that particular evening that she felt it best to drop the subject until a better time. A few days later she considered approaching him but he was so distant and depressed that she once again decided to wait. In the meantime she quietly unloaded the dishwasher and did Ron's laundry chores.

For the next few days, she waited for Ron to be in a good mood and for the right time to talk to him about the chores. The right time never came. Meanwhile, the household's needs continued and the children needed clean clothes. When Kate did speak with Ron he seemed so aggravated or distant that she quickly dropped the subject. Even though Kate was angry and resentful about the situation, within weeks she had reassumed responsibility not only for the laundry and the dishwasher, but for several of the other chores which had been Ron's tasks.

In many cases, it is not only her husband's resistance to helping with the domestic work which burdens the multiple role Vietnam wife, but her own difficulties in giving up traditional homemaking activities. In assuming responsibilities outside the home, the woman experiences the loss of a clearly defined, socially approved feminine identity.[4] When she finds that she no longer has time to make cakes for the church bake sale or to be a room mother for her children's school, she may be criticized by others. If she tells her husband she cannot attend yet another Vietnam conference with him or take in a homeless vet, he may criticize her, too. But more importantly, the woman may criticize herself and feel pain at not being able to be the type of mother, wife, or family member she could have been were she not employed outside the home.

"It hurt not to be there when my baby took his first step and to have to have a babysitter tell me about it," explains one wife. This same wife feels deep guilt that she cannot do more for her invalid father. "I'd like to visit him more, prepare his favorite dishes, but I can't, because I work." She would also like to attend more Vietnam veteran parades and other such events with her husband, but she's simply too exhausted and overextended as it is.

For the multiple role woman, the security of the old home roles is gone. In the world of work, she must face new situations, take risks, and be evaluated on the basis of her skills, not her personality, or her recipes. If she is in a low-paying or dead-end job, or if she is experiencing some form of sexism at work, she may begin to serious-ly question the "glamour" of being a working woman.

The woman's self-doubts about her working role are only increased when she encounters a loss of approval from others. While social mores have changed and working women and mothers are much more acceptable today than they were ten or twenty years ago, it is not unusual for some of a woman's relatives to question the woman's departure from domesticity.[5] If the woman must work for economic reasons, she may be "excused." But to the extent to which she works for her own enhancement of skills, for stimulation, or for pleasure, she may be "suspect."

"After Dan got out of treatment for PTSD and was able to work again, my family expected me to quit my job," explains Marie. "When I tried to tell them that I'd go crazy home all day with four children, they told me they thought I was crazy. Didn't I have enough to deal with, what with Dan still quite not his old self and the problems with the children?

"If I told them that I liked to work, they wouldn't understand. For me, working, even if it's at a job I hate, is easier than being home all day, dealing with all the tensions and problems there. Actually, working is a vacation in comparison.

"My husband understands why I like to work, but my parents and in-laws have combined forces and convinced our kids that I should stay home and be 'more of a mother' to them. Now what do I do?"

The social system may not support the woman either.[6] Despite some improvements in recent years, the woman may still have difficulty finding adequate child care, part-time work or flexible work schedules. In some instances the veteran proves to be a thoroughly reliable babysitter. But when he is not available, due to his work schedule, or is untrustworthy, the woman may have "great practical, even sometimes insurmountable obstacles" in arranging her roles. At the same time, her colleagues and superiors may question her investment in her work, given that she is simultaneously committed to a family.[7]

Many Vietnam wives are already socially isolated because of the veteran's tendency to isolate himself or his jealousy of the woman's involvements with other persons except himself. This pre-existing social isolation is compounded by the isolation which stems from the demands of working and the pressing needs of the family. Typically, the working Vietnam wife does not have time for recreational, social, religious, or community activities. At work she may not "fit in" with younger, single workers. In her neighborhood or in certain social groups, she does not "fit in" with full-time homemakers "whose interests, responsibilities and schedules are different from hers." [8]

All persons, both men and women, have multiple roles. Men function as workers, fathers, sons, citizens, and in other capacities. Even traditional women have numerous roles such as sexual partner, companion, family social secretary, house manager, housekeeper, cook, laundress, interior decorator, caretaker of older relatives, and hostess.

Invariably, there are conflicts between the roles. Any person, male or female, who manages numerous responsibilities must often juggle competitive demands and, eventually, compromise. For the multiple role Vietnam wife, as for all working women, conflicts between home roles and job or career goals are inevitable. Of particular importance, however, is how the conflicts are reacted to.

In the case of the stay-at-home woman, her various roles are not viewed as mutually exclusive. While the stay-at-home mother must often choose between taking care of her children and taking care of her home, all her roles are service or family oriented and therefore considered appropriate for women. In the case of the working wife or mother, however, career goals and job obligations are viewed as being competitive with or noncomplimentary to her home roles.[9]

In contrast, for a man to be simultaneously a father, husband, and worker is usually considered "normal" and appropriate. In reality, many men experience considerable conflict and difficulty in integrating their career and home lives. However, unlike the multiple role woman, they do not also struggle with the societal attitude that their roles are mutually exclusive. Neither do men struggle with the peculiar tug-of-war between roles which working wives and mothers experience due to the low status ascribed to women's home roles.

In this day and age, very few women feel that they must strictly adhere to the traditionally feminine role which restricts her to home and family-oriented activities and which dictates that she be passive, dependent, and always emotional in relation to the world. Like their brothers, girls from middle class homes are encouraged to achieve. At the same time, however, they are also instructed to be attractive, emotionally responsive, and appropriately "feminine." Many girls are also told that any academic or professional successes they might have are secondary to finding a husband and having a family.

For many of the women who have attended group, it has been a monumental achievement to recognize that they have desires and ambitions outside of the family and to decide to take steps toward achieving those ambitions, even if those steps required that they be out of the home an extra evening or morning a week. Some of the women decided to take courses which would promote their careers. They had been putting off doing so until their husband recovered from PTSD or until such time as their course work would not inconvenience their families. However, after waiting several years and growing increasingly impatient, some of the women decided to go ahead and at least take one small step toward pursing their career objectives.

One wife explains: "My 'real job,' for which I'm not paid, is at home. But I am paid and receive more recognition and respect for my other 'real job' at the office. When I wanted to take a cooking course, nobody in the family objected. But when I wanted to learn computer programming to advance my career, you should have seen the fireworks.

"My mother-in-law refused to babysit for the kids, saying 'Isn't it enough you work all day? Now you have to go out at night, too? Who's going to mother those kids and take care of that husband of yours? Put your career off for later.' But when I took the cooking course, she thought it was 'great.'

"I'm surprised that her guilt trip sunk in, that it's still hard for me to do things for me, just for me. I was brought up to think I belonged to the family, but I thought I had outgrown that. I guess I haven't.

"But I'm going to go ahead and take the course anyway, guilt and all. If I have to go to school guilty, well, I'll just go there guilty, because if I put it off any longer, I might never get to it."

Responses To The Multiple Role Dilemma

One common response to the problem of competing demands is the attempt to be "superwoman." Because the new values for women have not eliminated the old values, but have been merely superimposed upon them, many women expect themselves to fulfill traditional roles while working outside the home to the same extent as if they did not have job responsibilities.

Another not uncommon response to the multiple role dilemma is overeating. According to the Vet Center survey, approximately 20% of the wives seen were not just chubby or slightly overweight, but obese. Although definitions of obesity vary, in general obesity is defined as excess weight which is life threatening. If a woman is more than 40% over her ideal weight, she is considered severely overweight or obese.

In some instances the Vietnam wife's extra pounds have already created health problems for her. But even if the woman's health is not yet impaired, psychologically the excess pounds usually decrease her self-esteem and her sense of control over her life.

For almost all the obese Vietnam wives seen so far, overeating has been a coping mechanism, not only since their marriages, but since early childhood or adolescence. They turned to food for comfort or as a means of alleviating stress. Now married to Vietnam veterans who usually have not completed the healing process, they are beset not only with the stresses of the multiple role dilemma, but also with the stresses of problem-filled marriages. They turn to food once more.

Hardworking Vietnam wives who have little time, or energy, for pleasurable activities and whose sex lives may be either sporadic or unfulfilling may be easily tempted to turn to food for gratification. However, this does not mean that the veteran is responsible for his wife's difficulty with food.

Just as the alcoholic or drug-addicted veteran is responsible for what he does to his body, so is the wife responsible for what she puts in her mouth. Food is a fast fix. It is also an easy fix. Since women tend to do the shopping, cooking, and feeding of the family, food is readily available. Hundreds, if not thousands, of calories can be consumed in the grocery aisles or during food preparation. Furthermore, unlike drugs or alcohol, food is legal but it can serve the same purpose.

Food can sedate the emotions and anesthetize the woman to pain, anger, and hurt. Food can also be used to quell inner turmoil or as a way of dealing with—or not dealing with—relationship difficulties and external stress. The physical act of eating is not only pleasurable, but tension-reducing.

Dora, for example, is overwhelmed with demands, both inside and outside her home. Her sex life with her husband is troubled, as is her entire marriage. In the midst of feeling overwhelmed by responsibilities and wondering what the outcome of her marriage will be, she turns to food to give her "a lift," to make her feel better, and to give her the energy she needs to execute her multiple roles.

But she doesn't really need the calories to complete her work. Furthermore, any good feelings she might get from the satisfaction of having eaten something delicious are temporary when her scale, her clothes, and her husband remind her that she is "fat."

Yet Dora can't stop eating. For her food is a way out. Like many Vietnam wives, Dora feels that her whole life is being "gobbled up" by the needs of her PTSD afflicted husband, her children, and her full-time job. In response, she gobbles up whatever she can find.

When she gets home from work, she simultaneously juggles making dinner, helping her son with his homework, and worrying about her husband. What psychological state will he be in when he gets home? Will he get home at all tonight? She has situations at work that she needs to figure out. She is also exhausted. But she can't just finish the dinner dishes and go to bed. She has to pay the bills her husband "forgot" about and do the laundry he promised to do.

Dora is tired of worrying about her husband, of constantly placating him, of doing his work for him, and tired of all the fighting. When her son asks her to take him to the crafts store to buy clay for a school project, she wants to scream. Instead she gulps down the leftovers from his lunchbox and finishes off the ice cream. Then she has to go to the grocery store to buy more ice cream so her husband doesn't find out that she binged and yell at her again.

Under the intense pressure of so many obligations and feeling unsupported by her husband, Dora often gives up. "I might as well eat, what else is there for me?" she sometimes asks, not realizing that what she really needs is more rest, more love, and more time for herself. Like many Vietnam wives, Dora wants desperately to exert more control over her life but doesn't know how to do so. Feeling powerless, she turns to binging, but that only makes her feel less powerless and gives her less, not more physical and emotional energy with which to cope with her multiple roles.

Helping The Multiple Role Woman

In group, when women discuss their multiple roles, the purpose of the group discussion is not to help the women become more efficient in doing it all. Rather, group discussion is focused on how the multiple role woman can learn to appreciate herself more for what she does do. She is also encouraged to examine how she might structure her life so that all her various roles are expressions of her individuality rather than her conformity to some sex-role stereotype of the ideal woman. Specifically, Vietnam wives who work outside the home usually need help in:

1. Understanding that family problems are due not to personal inadequacy but to characteristics inherent in her multiple role situation.
2. Accepting conflict as inevitable.
3. Making choices: examining early teachings about the female sex role.
4. Acknowledging personal strengths and assets.
5. Learning self-nurturing.
6. Exploring alternative ways of fulfilling roles.
7. Expanding career horizons.

Most of the Vietnam wives I have counseled have high expectations of themselves. They want to be thorough and excellent workers, as well as loyal, sensitive, and giving wives and mothers. When problems arise, the Vietnam wife tends to define the problem as her inability to manage or cope. Given a life style that includes the schedules and tasks involved with work, school, childrearing, marriage, and homemaking, as well as the intense emotional needs and unpredictable behavior of a veteran who is suffering from a stress disorder, occasional interruptions in the routine and unfulfilled expectations are inevitable. The woman needs to be reminded that these occurrences are natural, not signs of her personal failure.

In fact, the woman may need to be *continually* reminded that conflict is inevitable and that conflict or other problems in the family are not the result of her personal inadequacies. She also usually needs help to appreciate the complexity of her life style and the weight of the multiple burdens she is carrying. Part of her burden stems from the traditional assumption that it is the responsibility of the woman to take care of everyone's needs. Not only does the woman tend to believe this, but her husband and children do also. Therefore, it is often difficult for the woman to ask her husband, or her children, for help.

At the same time, the woman may fear being successful in her career or work roles. Often she anticipates that her achievement will threaten her husband, who is perhaps struggling emotionally and financially, or that she will be ostracized as a "woman's libber" either by him, his family, or even her own friends and relatives.[10]

Summary

All working women who are also wives or mothers struggle with the burden and the conflicts inherent in having two major commitments—one to their families and another to their jobs. In addition, women are usually also assigned the job of arranging all their roles so that they do not conflict with one another and so that they can meet the needs of the entire family.

Unfortunately, in many families when the woman assumed a working role outside the home, there were few subtractions made from her home roles. This is especially the case in Vietnam homes where the veteran holds traditional values about the woman's role and is reluctant to participate in childcare and housework. Consequently, even the most hardworking and efficient Vietnam wife will inevitably have times when she is overwhelmed by the demands on her time and energy. Beneath the surface, she will also be angry and resentful of all that is expected of her in her multiple roles.

The Vietnam wife's multiple role dilemmas are similar to those experienced by other working women. However, the Vietnam woman's burden is increased significantly by her husband's PTSD and any resulting employment or emotional dysfunctions. Often the Vietnam wife carries with her to work the mental agony of worrying about her husband's psychological condition and possible self-destructive behavior. At the same time she must be careful to be productive at work and in no way endanger her job since her income may be essential for the family's survival.

In addition, because of her husband's PTSD, she often assumes major multiple caretaking functions with respect to her vet. She may arrange his appointments and serve as a buffer between him and the world. If he is unable or unwilling to perform as a parent then she also shoulders the massive responsibilities of being both mother and father to their children. She also has the responsibility for "explaining" their father's actions and illness to the children.

Self-care, fun, and pleasurable activities fall by the wayside as the Vietnam wife goes endlessly from one chore to the next; from one crisis to the next. When she becomes tired and depressed, she wonders what's wrong with her. Like many multiple role women, the Vietnam wife tends to interpret the conflicts and stresses in her life as reflecting some personal deficiency on her part. In truth, however, many of her problems are inherent to the multiple role life style, not the result of some personality problem on her part.

Five

Alcohol and Drug Addiction

*I feel very confused. I'm just beginning to under-
stand PTSD and why my husband acts like he does.
To see a good person run himself and me into the
ground is heartbreaking.*

I don't understand the drinking, how can anybody
drink so much? I don't understand the lying, can't he
ever tell the truth?

Even though he's the man, I'm in charge of all the
money and bills. He's an alcoholic and a drug addict
and he cajoles and threatens me—does anything he can
to get money out of me, whether the bills are paid or
not. When I won't give in, I'm accused of not caring
about him. Then Vietnam is thrown in my face, as if
that excuses all behavior.

Alcohol and drugs have caused him to steal my checks,
forge my name, and pawn my possessions, never telling
me, letting me be sued, and put in financial binds. He's
supposed to pick the girls up from the babysitter's, but
I can never count on him. Many times he's left them
there because he was off on some drug deal or he passed
out at a bar. Also, because of his PTSD, his mind strays
a lot.

I don't know what the kids think about all this. Maybe
they're too young to understand. But already they sense
that I'm nervous a lot and they seem to resent my preoccupation with their father. 'I wish you wouldn't be so
busy worrying about Daddy and spend more time with
me,' my five-year-old told me yesterday.

I've tried to talk to my husband, but have had no success.

If I try to discuss my feelings or respond with something he doesn't want to hear, then I am hit to make me shut up. I worry about my daughters, because they see and hear all this. I'm scared for myself too, afraid that he'll pull me down with him.

Terrie

Living with PTSD while juggling multiple roles is stressful enough, but when the Vietnam wife must also contend with her husband's alcohol or drug addiction, her daily life stresses are multiplied in manifold ways. Financially, emotionally, socially, and sexually her life becomes more complex and more unrewarding. Depending on the degree of her husband's addiction, she must assume a great degree of responsibility for her family's finances and the welfare of their children. When, and if, her husband begins to use essential family funds, to write false checks, or to sell family belongings in order to support his addiction, the woman may have to take drastic measures in order to assure the survival of the family.

Women become enraged when they find their credit cards abused by their husbands or when they find their grandmother's T.V. set at the local pawnshop. But they become especially enraged when their husbands embarrass or neglect the children due to drunken behavior (or drug abuse) or when they drink or engage in drug transactions in front of them. Some Vietnam wives assume the role of protecting the children from finding out about their father's addiction or otherwise protecting the veteran's image as the "good father" or "war hero." Or, if the women are honest about the veteran's problem, they must deal with their children's denial, hostility, grief, or other reaction to this information.

If children are not carefully educated about alcoholism or drug addiction, they may be angry at their mothers for implying that their father is a "wino," "drunk," "pothead," or "junkie." The children's self-esteem will suffer as they begin to perceive their family as being "different" both because of PTSD and the addiction. If the children go into denial, they may feel the alcoholism or drug addiction is a figment of their mother's imagination or they may blame her for it. For example, the mother may explain that father is not present because he is out drinking, only to have one of her children insist that father is not drinking but working overtime. Another child might mutter angrily, "If you'd be nicer to Daddy, he'd be home now."

In situations where the Vietnam wife denigrates her husband for his addiction, the children may resent her for talking against their father. Even if they agree with her about the inappropriateness of the father's behavior, they may have mixed loyalties and not like hearing negative facts about their father. Like most children, they might prefer to idealize their father and see him as "good" and "strong" or as a war hero. In addition, they may blame their mother for not being able to stop their father's drinking.

Approximately half of the women who have attended the Vet Center women's group have had alcoholic or drug addicted husbands. However this figure of 50% cannot be considered at all representative of the Vietnam veteran population as a whole. In fact, considerable controversy exists regarding whether or not Vietnam veterans have higher rates of alcohol and drug addiction than other veterans or than their nonveteran peers. Some researchers contend that Vietnam veterans, especially combat vets or vets with PTSD, have higher rates of addiction than other groups. Other researchers, however, emphatically state that drug addiction and alcohol abuse among Vietnam veterans is part of a worldwide problem of substance abuse and that service in Vietnam has not been established as a predictor of any form of substance abuse.

A search of the existing studies on alcohol and drug abuse among Vietnam veterans revealed an important distinction between alcohol and drug abuse. While it was found that drugs were widely used in Vietnam, it was not found that this drug use persisted upon return to the U.S.[1] In general, research has shown that "Vietnam veterans dependent on narcotics generally had high rates of recovery soon after returning to the U.S."[2] For example, the peak use of heroin occurred in Vietnam in the early 1970s when a high quality, relatively inexpensive form of heroin became readily available. During these years, there was also an international epidemic of heroin use and great concern that the Vietnam veterans would bring their heroin and other form of drug abuse back home with them.[3]

This fear, however, did not materialize. One researcher found that less than 10% of Vietnam veterans who used narcotics in Vietnam were using narcotics one year after discharge.[4] Some studies have found that the rate of recovery from drug abuse among Vietnam veterans is substantially higher than the rate of recovery among other addicted groups.[5]

Much of the confusion in these and other studies of drug abuse among Vietnam veterans stems from the fact that some are based on Vietnam *era* vets—*all* vets who served during the years of the war whether or not they actually served in Vietnam—whereas others are based only on veterans who served in Vietnam itself. Also, definitions of drug abuse vary from one study to the next.

This confusion spills over into the research on alcoholism among Vietnam veterans, with researchers varying not only in their definition of "Vietnam veteran" but in their definition of alcohol addiction or alcohol problems and in the types of statistical methods used. Not everybody who drinks is or becomes an alcoholic. Similarly, not everybody who uses drugs is or becomes physically addicted to them. Yet such distinctions are not made in some studies or are made differently from one study to the next.

Some researchers insist that there are no significant differences in alcohol abuse between Vietnam veterans and other groups. More frequently, however, researchers have found that war veterans, especially those who saw heavy combat, have a higher level of alcohol consumption, binge drinking, and alcohol related problems than comparable groups of other veterans and nonveterans.[6]

Regardless of what research studies show about the rate of alcohol and drug addiction among Vietnam veterans, it is the experience of many therapists who work with Vietnam veterans that PTSD and alcohol or drug addiction frequently go hand in hand. Some vets turn to alcohol or drugs in order to numb their emotions.[7] "He can't sleep, so he drinks (or smokes a joint)," more than one wife has stated. In a few isolated instances, husbands were *not* addicted prior to Vietnam *nor* during their Vietnam tour of duty. Upon return to the U.S., however, they turned to alcohol or drugs as an attempt to medicate themselves and suppress the symptoms of PTSD. More often, however, the use of drugs and alcohol was either learned, or reinforced, in Vietnam where both alcohol and drugs were readily available.[8]

By now, it is well known that alcohol, marijuana, opioids and other drugs were widely used in Vietnam for entertainment, anxiety relief, or as a means of coping with the boredom, or the terror.[9] What is less known, however, is that Vietnam is the first war in which tranquillizing drugs and the phenothiazines were dispensed on the combat front.[10] One vet claims that it was his commanding officer who introduced him to, and forced him to take, certain drugs. "The sarge pulled me in his office my first week there and said that if I didn't take these drugs, he'd blow my brains out. I had never taken any drugs and didn't plan to—ever—even though almost everyone around me seemed high.

'Look,' the sarge said, 'Do as I say.'

"He waited there until I had swallowed the pills. At first I thought he was picking on me because I was a country boy from Boise, Idaho, but now I see that he was trying to save my life. If the others had found out I wasn't on drugs, they might have thought I was a spy. I might have gotten fragged or something.

"Turns out, I needed those little pills to do what I had to do and stay sane. After a while, those little pills made even the blood seem pretty."

Perhaps this was an isolated instance. Perhaps not. Such instances are not frequently reported in the literature. In most cases American servicemen obtained drugs from the Vietnamese, not their commanding officers.[11] The military did, however, dispense certain mood and consciousness altering drugs to help control some of the medical symptoms which interfered with combat performance. For example, "antinauseants and potent antipsychotic agents like procholoperazine (Compazine R) and chlorpromazine (Thorazine R)" were "commonly used for symptom control in combat troops with diarrhea and nausea."[12] These drugs did have a psychological effect—mainly that of impairing the veteran's "capacity to integrate emotional experiences" regarding the war.[13]

Another factor contributing to the use of drugs or alcohol during the war was that the option of obtaining a psychiatric discharge was not as available to soldiers in Vietnam as to those in previous wars. The thrust of military psychiatry and psychology during the Vietnam war was to encourage soldiers to "hang on" until their one year DEROS.[14] Hence for the soldier experiencing psychological difficulties during the war, yet obstructed from obtaining a psychiatric discharge, drugs and alcohol might have been a means of escape or coping.

Servicemen on drugs or alcohol who were disruptive were often given administrative discharges with the diagnosis of character disordered personality, rather than PTSD.[15] The authorities often failed to distinguish true character disordered individuals from those who were using drugs and alcohol as a means of coping with acute combat reaction. Hence many men were not only not treated for their PTSD, but were also saddled with a diagnosis of "character disordered personality," a diagnosis which carries with it an extremely negative connotation. It is the view of many clinicians (myself included) that combat is not a prerequisite for PTSD. For example, American civilians who worked in Vietnam developed PTSD. Furthermore, while substance abuse may have many origins in a particular individual, one of the functions of substance abuse for some vets is self-medication for the symptoms of PTSD.[16] Some of my patients used alcohol and drugs prior to Vietnam, but increased their usage overseas. Upon return to the U.S., their alcohol or drug usage diminished but remained at a somewhat higher level than prior to the war. While alcohol or drugs were a part of their life style prior to the war (for various reasons), now another reason was added to the list: suppression of wartime memories and some of the symptoms of PTSD.

Alcohol helps the veteran to sleep, reduces his anxiety levels, and helps "ease muscle tensions and sometimes depression, irritability, and agitation." If the vet or his wife feel that using drugs or alcohol is "legitimate" because these substances help lessen the nightmares, the insomnia, or other symptoms of PTSD, then their denial of the dangerous effects of the veteran's addiction, on everybody, may be reinforced. The vet will have yet another justification for abusing himself and his wife; yet another excuse for accepting unacceptable behavior.

"I never know what I'm dealing with," states Rhoda, wife of an alcoholic veteran, "Don, his PTSD, or his booze." Rhoda has educated herself about alcoholism, knows that it is a disease and that she is "supposed" to distinguish the disease from the person. "But when Don is drinking, he becomes the disease and it's very hard to deal with."

As the wife of an alcoholic Vietnam veteran, Rhoda must contend not only with her husband's flashbacks, extreme irritability, and hatred of rice, slanty eyes, and anything Oriental, but with his weekend drinking binges and his unavailability as a companion and lover to her and as a father to their children. "Don loves his kids," Rhoda is always quick to say, "But he has no idea what they're thinking about, or what they're doing in school. He's never abused any of us, ever, but he's usually off to himself or out drinking."

Rhoda is lucky. Her husband is only in the early stages of the disease of alcoholism. He is still able to function on the job and does not suffer from memory lapses or blackouts or any of the diseases which attend the later stages of alcoholism.

Although Don and Rhoda's sexual relationship is sporadic and their emotional communication is limited, Rhoda can still count on Don to go to work and not drink in front of the children. But that's all.

She pays all the bills, assumes almost total responsibility for the children, and never knows when, and if, her husband will be joining her for dinner, for the children's school play, or for their anniversary. So far, she hasn't found any bottles hidden throughout the house. "But it's coming," she predicts.

She knows the disease of alcoholism well. Her father was an alcoholic, as was her grandfather, and she saw them both progress through the various stages of alcoholism to early deaths. Rhoda is well aware of the latest view of alcoholism as primarily a physical disease, rather than a psychological one but this understanding does not ease her loneliness or her fears about the future.

Rhoda first began to suspect that Don was an alcoholic when he would go shopping and forget to buy the food, but always bring home the liquor. Furthermore, when he would come home from work, he would head straight for the liquor cabinet. He didn't always take a drink at that time, but he needed to be sure that the liquor cabinet was full. Whenever it wasn't, he would become extremely anxious and even get up in the middle of the night to go search for an all-night liquor store. "He wouldn't always drink what he would buy," explains Rhoda, "But if the liquor wasn't there, he'd be a nervous wreck."

Rhoda also observed that liquor was always first on his shopping list and that he spent a lot of time in liquor stores just cruising down the aisles examining the various bottles.

At this point Rhoda's husband was still in the first stages of alcoholism. If she had not had such a discerning eye, his drinking patterns may not have appeared different from the drinking patterns of others. During this first stage, the alcoholic is able to consume increasing amounts of alcohol without any significant impairment to his abilities. In fact, during the first stage, his functioning may even be improved by drinking.

During the middle stage, the alcoholic begins to experience some of the effects of the physical damage caused to his body by his drinking. He also begins to experience a loss of control over his drinking, an intense craving for alcohol, as well as important personality and emotional changes—nightmares, depression, insomnia, sweating, memory impairment, and tension. When Rhoda's husband reached this stage, she observed major mood swings in her husband and found that his sexual performance suffered, or became dependent on having consumed a certain "right" amount of alcohol. During this second stage of alcoholism, alcohol, the poison, now becomes the medicine as the alcoholic comes to need more and more alcohol to counteract symptoms of withdrawal.

The third stage of alcoholism is characterized by extreme physical and mental deterioration and the need to drink almost constantly to combat withdrawal symptoms, which by now have progressed to include paranoia, convulsions, hallucinations, shaking, delirium, mental confusion, an inability to walk, and poor motor coordination.[17]

Like alcoholism, drug addition is also progressive. Although the particular symptoms and stages of drug addiction are specific to each drug, as with alcoholism, drug addiction often involves physical problems. In addition, there are numerous interpersonal problems caused by excess moodiness, jealousy, irritability, suspiciousness and fearfulness (sometimes bordering on paranoia) and, in some cases, violence.

The symptoms of drug abuse and drug withdrawal are many and vary from one drug to the next. Some of the common withdrawal symptoms include panic, confusion, irritability and restlessness, dilated pupils, nausea and vomiting, abdominal cramps and diarrhea.[18]

The symptoms of drug abuse and withdrawal depend not only on the drug used, but on the amount and quality of the drug and its reaction with the individual's unique body chemistry, his environment, and with any other drugs or alcohol he has taken. Often a wife can detect if her husband is on drugs if he becomes unable to keep appointments or other commitments or if he leaves his job for unexplained absences (especially on Mondays and Fridays or the day after pay day) or short bursts of energy followed by extremely low periods of productivity.

A wife can also suspect drug addiction if her husband spends an unusual amount of time in the bathroom or in other locked rooms, gives up old friends to take up with other drug-addicted persons, or becomes unable to keep a job or stay in school. Furthermore, she should not be surprised if her personal belongings are taken from her and sold or if her accounts and other assets are depleted by her husband's increasing need to support his addiction.[19]

Betty's husband used to squander her salary on drugs until she deposited her check in an account with just her name on it. Even then, he would present himself at the bank as Betty's husband and try to make withdrawals. Unsuspecting tellers complied with his wishes until Betty strictly instructed them not to allow him to make any withdrawals or to cash any of her checks, since at times he would forge her name on them. Afterward, her husband started taking her credit cards, charging items, then returning them to pay for drugs. Eventually Betty had to cancel her credit cards. Other wives have had to keep their credit cards, their bank books and other financial papers and assets under lock and key for protection against desperate husbands.

It is not unusual for a woman, even for a woman who is relatively well informed about alcohol or drug addiction, to initially be in a state of denial about her husband's illness. It is only human to want to avoid painful realities and observing a loved one suffer from a life-threatening, financially and emotionally disruptive problem hurts. True, the woman may be angry at her husband for being an alcoholic or a drug addict, but beyond her anger, is her pain.

Even if she does not assume a shred of responsibility for her husband's alcohol or drug addiction, if she loves or cares for him, just seeing him suffer causes her to suffer also. Even if she no longer loves him, but instead feels a loyalty to him as the father of her children or as the man to whom she has given many years of her life, she will also feel pain at observing him progressively deteriorate. Later on, her pain may well be mixed with anger, disgust, or even hatred toward her husband for the ways in which his illness has destroyed part of her life and the negative impact of his illness on the mental, and sometimes physical, health of her children.

While a part of the woman's initial denial may stem from her reluctance to feel pain, part of her denial may also be rooted in shame and guilt at being married to an alcoholic or a drug addict. She may not want to acknowledge her fears about the possible disastrous consequences of her husband's addiction, not only to him, but to herself and their children as well. Rather than face reality, she pretends she didn't find the needles in the bathroom or the half empty liquor bottles in the hall closet. She may pretend to her husband that she doesn't know. More importantly, however, she pretends to herself, to spare herself the anguish of having to face the responsibility and difficulty of making certain changes in her life or decisions about the family's future due to her husband's illness.

If she is the adult child of an alcoholic, she may be reluctant to "face the nightmare" once more. Wilma, for example, hoped that if she pretended her husband didn't have a drinking problem it would just go away. Similarly, as a child, she wished that her father was not a "drunk" and believed that if only she wished hard enough her father would be "normal" like the fathers of her friends.

Wilma had spent much of her childhood and adolescence crushed between two warring parents, an angry discontented alcoholic father and an equally angry discontented mother. When her father would come home at 3 a.m., drunk, demanding a meal he would never eat, Wilma's mother at first would comply. But eventually she would tell her husband to cook his own damn dinner and berate him for ruining the family with his drunkenness. At this point, Wilma would be awakened by the shouting matches, then asked to cook for her father, or to sweep up the broken glass from the liquor bottles which her mother had furiously smashed in protest to the father's drinking.

Even though Wilma sympathized with her mother's plight, Wilma also loved her father and resented her mother for "nagging" him and not supporting him. To Wilma, her father was her "hero," in spite of his disease. When, at the age of thirteen, her father, a prominent physician, abandoned the family, Wilma blamed her mother, but she also blamed herself. If only she were a "better" or "more lovable" daughter, her father would have never left home.

After Wilma's father left, her mother went to work full time during the day and collapsed into depression during the evenings, leaving Wilma to mother the two younger children. But Wilma had always "mothered" her sisters, for as her father's alcoholism had progressed, her mother had become increasing preoccupied with him and his drinking (as well as her own distress) and left much of the housework and child care up to Wilma.

Now Wilma was finding herself "mothering" her husband. Women who are adult children of alcoholics or who are married to physically handicapped veterans or to veterans with severe bodily injuries are especially prone to assume a maternal or caretaker role toward their husbands, especially if the vet feels he has not been adequately compensated by the government. Wilma met Todd when he first returned from Vietnam. Laden with medals, handsome and smart, Todd seemed like a "hero" to her. Her teenage years had been so unhappy and lonely that when Todd proposed to her, she said "yes" almost without thinking. By marrying Todd she hoped to get away from her depressed mother and end her unconscious search for her missing father. Like many returning vets, Todd initially idealized his wife and for a brief while, Wilma and Todd had an idyllic relationship.

When Wilma married Todd, he was only in the first stages of alcoholism and his illness was not apparent. She first began to suspect that Todd was alcoholic when he would come home late because he had stopped off at a local bar or when he seemed to prefer to go drinking with his war buddies rather than stay home with her. But she so desperately wanted her present life to be better than her past life that she could not believe her new "hero" was an alcoholic, too. When her husband reached the middle stage of alcoholism and the signs of his illness became unmistakable, Wilma could no longer deny reality. Todd was drinking at five in the morning and there were cash register receipts for large amounts of liquor in the trash, as well as evidence of affairs with other women.

Wilma began to make excuses for Todd: he drank because his compensation check was late, because a war buddy had threatened suicide, or because someone had taken him to see a movie like *Deerhunter*, *Platoon*, or *The Hanoi Hilton*. Furthermore, Wilma began to berate herself. She felt Todd's drinking was her fault, just as a child she had felt responsible for her father's drinking. Although the women in the Vet Center group challenged her on this, Wilma's sense of inferiority and responsibility persisted.

After Wilma shed her denial, her next posture toward her husband was that of "enabler." Not realizing that her husband had a problem which she could not "fix," she attempted to try to "help" him by hiding liquor, by being as pleasant and loving as possible, and by protecting him from all reminders of his war experiences and the consequences of his drinking. For example, she made excuses for him to his relatives, his employer, and even to their own children. When he would become intoxicated and unable to drive, she would pick him up from any place in the city, any time of the day or night. When he blamed her for his drinking, she didn't talk back. Instead she hid anger and hurt and became more determined to "help" him.

Wilma did not want to be a "nag" like her mother and lose her husband, like she lost her father. As the adult child of an alcoholic, Wilma had a well-developed tolerance for alcoholic behavior and family chaos. But when her husband impulsively gave away a huge sum of money to some less fortunate Vietnam veterans at a drinking party leaving no money for the family's bills, Wilma felt she had to confront her husband about his alcoholism, and she did so, many times. But she would quickly back off when he'd flare up at her. Even though he had never physically hurt her, she knew he had smuggled an M-16 home with him from Vietnam. While she feared the weapon, what she feared most was being abandoned. As an adult child of an alcoholic, her abandonment fear was profound.

Like many of the wives of alcoholic or drug addicted veterans, who do not value their own happiness, fulfillment, and peace of mind as much as they do that of their husbands and children, Wilma was shaken out of the stages of denial and enabling into the stage of active coping not so much by her own suffering, but by that of her husband and children. When her husband, under the influence, fell down some steps and nearly cracked his skull and when, on several occasions, he failed to feed the baby her dinner or strap her seat belt in the car properly, Wilma knew she could no longer be passive or limit her action to words.

In other cases, women have been forced to confront their husband's alcoholism (and their own enabling) due to his car accidents, job losses, or his arrest on drug charges. Or their children began to evidence unmistakable signs of low self-esteem and self-blame or to be ashamed to bring friends home for fear Daddy will be drinking, drunk, or high.

Unpaid bills, emptied wallets, and missing nest eggs also jar the woman out of her wishful thinking that the problem will magically disappear. More than one woman has walked into the Vet Center group shocked at the latest debt her husband's addiction has incurred for her, debts ranging up to $96,000.00. While financial hardships tend to be greater for the wives of drug addicted veterans than for the wives of alcoholic veterans, both groups of women suffer not only from the high costs of liquor and, especially drugs, but from the spending sprees and poor financial judgement and planning which often characterize the addictive personality. In some cases, women have had to shoulder the expenses of their husband's gifts to mistresses.

Such circumstances have forced women with little previous experience or training in financial matters to become virtual financial experts and to take complete control of the family's assets. The veteran, however, often will protest this affront to his masculinity. But faced with her children's deprivation, the wife has often had no choice but to "be hard." She puts her husband on a strict budget, puts as many of the family's assets as possible in her name only, and makes almost all major financial decisions on her own. When she is impeded in taking financial control of the household by her husband's threats of violence, she may have to resort to stealing from her husband in order to meet household bills and pay for food.

Cleo, a Vietnam wife jailed for theft, tells how her circumstances led her from an unhappy home to an unhappy marriage, and ultimately to prison.

My father abandoned our family when I was five years old. My Mom had to work two jobs to keep bread on the table. She was grouchy and angry when she came home from work and didn't have much time for any of us. I can understand now why she was so irritable, but I didn't understand it then.

I had a lot of anger in me, but I was never an aggressive kid in school. In fact, I did pretty well considering that my older sister usually forgot to fix me breakfast. I was shy and never part of the gang. My shrink says that by the time I was in the fifth grade, I had an inferiority complex and that's why, in my teen years, I was easy prey for manipulative men.

Most of my boyfriends and my first husband used me. I think Johnny was the first man who really loved me. He bought me gifts and understood what I had gone through in life because he had been through a lot in 'Nam too. The only problem was that Johnny had gotten hooked on drugs over there. But at least he wasn't violent, like the other drug addicts I knew. Also, he had a good job, even though he was getting high a lot.

When I met Johnny, I had two children by my former husband. He had deserted me just like my father had left my mother. I found myself in my mother's position, working all the time and hating it. At times I would get so tired of carting the kids from one babysitter's to the next that I could scream. I was also tired of the loneliness and the constant worry about trying to pay my bills.

So when Johnny proposed, promising that he would help support me and the kids so I would only have to work a part-time job, I said 'yes' immediately. At last I would have some time to be home with my children, like a 'regular' Mommy.

The first few months everything was fine, except that Johnny kept quitting one job after another. He always found a new one, but he would never stay long enough to establish health benefits. Because I had quit my full-time job, we didn't have my health insurance either, which meant we had to pay our doctor bills out of our pockets.

Our finances were manageable, even with Johnny's drug bills, until my son developed a serious medical problem that ate up most of our savings. At the same time, Johnny seemed to be spending more and more time and money on drugs. I resented it, but whenever I'd mention the cost of his drug habit, he'd remind me about my son's doctor bills. He also threatened to leave me if I couldn't accept him the way he was. After all, he had accepted me the way I was, with all my hang-ups and problems.

Johnny was the only person I had in the world. Also, I couldn't afford to leave him. My children and I needed his income, even if he did squander too much on drugs. As he needed more and more drugs, our money got lower and lower and he started stealing. Then he asked me to steal too.

I had a government job then. The first time Johnny mentioned that I should help myself to the money lying around the office, I was shocked. But he assured me that the government had plenty of money and that as a lower income private citizen, the government was always ripping me off anyway. Furthermore, the government had certainly cheated him, as a Vietnam veteran, out of his well-deserved benefits. Stealing from the government, he argued, was an act of justice.

I knew these were rationalizations, but I went along anyway. I was afraid of losing Johnny if I didn't help him get his fix. The first time I stole, I burned with shame. But afterward, it became easier and easier, almost a game, until the day I got caught and landed in jail. The worst part is that now my kids have a convict for a mother.

Like Cleo, some of the incarcerated wives and girlfriends of Vietnam veterans (seen at a local correctional facility, not at the Vet Center) were imprisoned for shoplifting or other forms of stealing in order to support not *their* drug habit, but their husband's. They often came from economically and emotionally deprived backgrounds. At least one-fourth of these women had been physically or sexually abused as children. They often stated that they "stole for love." Usually their husbands were drug addicted prior to Vietnam, but increased their drug usage during and after the war. While the imprisoned women often stated that they stole in order to keep their men "happy" and attached to them, some stole to protect themselves from physical assault. Drugs, they claimed, helped sedate their husbands' tempers and reduced the number of nightmares and flashbacks, resulting in fewer instances of wife beating.

Cleo's husband was not violent, but Viola's husband was. He terrorized both her and the neighborhood. She was glad to steal to buy drugs that would cool his heat and purchase her safety. While Viola was serving time for shoplifting, her husband was shot to death by another drug addict.

The Vietnam wife with an alcoholic or drug addicted husband needs first to educate herself about alcoholism or drug addiction. Suggested books are included in the Reading List. In addition, attendance at Al-Anon (for wives of alcoholics), at ADCIO (Al-Anon Adult Children of Alcoholics) or at Nar-A-Anon (for family members of drug addicts) could also help.

Secondly, she needs to emotionally detach from her husband's addiction as much as possible. Whether it takes one Al-Anon or Nar-A-Non meeting or a hundred, the woman needs to realize that she is powerless over her husband's illness. Confronting him, placating him, covering up for him, verbally attacking or otherwise punishing him will not work. Just as she needs to "let go" of a sense of responsibility for her husband's addiction, she also needs to stop trying to "fix" her husband. The only way she can truly help him is to encourage him to seek treatment.

Thirdly, she needs to examine her role as an enabler of her husband's addiction. Without blaming herself for her husband's habit, or even for inadvertently supporting it by trying to be a "good wife" or "family peacemaker," she needs to become aware of all the specific ways, both large and small, in which she protects her husband from the consequences of his behavior.

Next, she needs to assure her physical safety, and that of her children, as well as the financial survival of the family. While she cannot control her husband's spending or other alcoholic or drug-influenced behavior, she can take charge of as many assets as possible, realistically assess her financial situation, and make a budget.

Some women hesitate to take such actions because they were raised to believe that finances are the man's responsibility and that they are not competent at making financial decisions. Even if a woman is unfamiliar with money matters, however, she can seek information and advice. Furthermore, if she is not a substance abuser and she has her family's best interest in mind, she is more likely to make sound economic choices than her husband who has not only PTSD, but an addictive illness as well. While the wife may fear taking the risks inherent in making financial decisions for the family, she needs to consider the fact that if she abdicates control of the family's finances to a man whose thinking abilities are impaired and whose judgement abilities are clouded by substance abuse, she is allowing her entire family to sink into a form of economic suicide. Some women do not feel it is "feminine" to take economic control over the family. But poverty and economic hardship are not "feminine" either.

Finally, the woman needs to examine her personal life and decide what behavior she will accept from her husband and what behavior she will not. She can make such decisions without necessarily divorcing or formally separating from her husband. One wife had put off going to college until her husband recovered from a leg injury received during the war. Although he was left crippled, he was able to continue to drive his cab. She had thought his drinking would stop once his leg operations were completed, but she was mistaken. While she did not like his drinking, she decided to remain married to him. However, she would not remain in the house with him when he was intoxicated and potentially violent. Without criticizing him for drinking, she would simply go stay with friends. She always had a suitcase packed and extra money saved for gas or for a hotel, should friends not be available.

At one point, however, her husband invited two of his homeless war buddies to come stay with them. One alcoholic was "bad enough," but three, she just "couldn't handle." They expected her to cook and clean for them and verbally abused and roughhoused her when she refused to do so. After five years in Al-Anon, she understood that their rude, aggressive behavior was a function of their alcoholism, but she also understood that she could not change them.

In group, she overcame her feelings of selfishness and guilt and decided that in order to assure her safety and to give herself the peace of mind and quiet necessary to finish her college degree, she would not leave her husband permanently. However until such time as the war buddies moved out or became sober and her husband sought help, she would live with a friend. After two years, her husband tired of his war buddies and joined A.A. The couple is now reunited, but the veteran understands that the minute he resumes drinking, his wife will move out. Furthermore, while she is willing to compromise and negotiate with him, she will no longer let his illness arrest her own emotional and professional development.

Not only does the Vietnam wife need to examine her own personal life carefully to see how her husband's drinking has affected her life goals, she also needs to take a close look at how her husband's alcoholism may be affecting her children. In most cases she will need to confront the painful reality that her husband's alcoholism has, or will, affect her children. Even children as young as one or two have been found to respond negatively to an alcoholic father. If the vet has forgotten to feed the child or otherwise mishandled it due to his drinking, the child may cry upon seeing its father.

Alcoholism is aptly called a family disease because the drinking affects everyone, not just the problem drinker. First, over time, the whole family becomes isolated, not only from the community at large, but also from relatives, neighbors, and friends who must not know about the father's drinking or his PTSD. The child may even be asked not to invite friends home. Or, when the child becomes older, he may hesitate to have friends over lest his father be drinking. If the father also suffers from a severe and untreated case of PTSD, the child may also fear finding his father in the midst of a flashback or in some manner acting as if he were in Vietnam. Since both alcohol and PTSD can cause emotional regressions and flashbacks, when the two are combined, some vets exhibit very unusual behavior. A child may fear finding his father both drinking and crawling around the house as if he were in the jungle.

The children may feel responsible for their father's drinking. Young children may feel the father is drinking because they made too much noise or didn't behave "well." Older children blame their marks in school or their undone chores. As the Vet Center and other studies have shown, some PTSD afflicted veterans are intolerant of children's noises and games and tend to be critical of their children when the children do not obey the "rules" of the house.[20] In some cases, the vet has imposed a military-like regime upon the household and severely scolds the children when they fail to "measure up" or "obey orders." If the father is drinking at the time of the scolding, or afterward, the children can easily conclude that his drinking is the result of their failure to obey his instructions.

While children from PTSD afflicted alcoholic homes tend to blame themselves for their father's drinking and other signs of distress, they may also learn to hide their feelings and their needs. Because their father is so preoccupied with his drinking and his PTSD, and because their mother is so preoccupied with their father, the children are often left to take care of themselves.

Not only is mother often too busy, but often she is angry, crying, anxious, or withdrawn as well. Children can be as concerned, and as angry, at their nonalcoholic mother as at their alcoholic father. In light of her emotionality and fatigue, they may become frightened and insecure. If mother "falls apart" like father, who will take care of them?

Children of alcoholics are often characterized as having a profound fear of abandonment. They are afraid that if they do not help mother, or father, there will be no one left to provide for them. As a result, even at a young age, many of these children learn to hide their needs and to help take care of one or both of their parents instead.

All children do not react in the same way. However, almost all children in alcohol and PTSD afflicted homes are exposed to inconsistencies and many family crises as well as to a considerable amount of anger and bitterness on the part of both parents. Not uncommonly, one or more of the children may adopt almost a parental role and try to help either the father or the mother. Since the mother is often trying to be nurse, doctor, and counselor to her husband as well as mother, homemaker, and wage earner, there are many times she simply cannot meet all the responsibilities thrust upon her. In such cases, it is not unusual for a child even as young as eight or nine to assume major household responsibilities—cooking, cleaning, babysitting, or even balancing the checkbook.

For example, Judy, who is in the eighth grade, is the eldest of three children. She doesn't play sports after school. She doesn't hang out with her girlfriends. She doesn't participate in any extracurricular activities. She comes straight home to help her mother. She looks for her father's hidden bottles, helps prepare dinner, keeps track of the household expenses, does the cleaning, and spends the weekends taking care of her younger brother and sister. When asked to go to slumber parties or other social events, she usually refuses so that she can stay home with her mother. What if her father stays out all night and leaves her mother alone? Acutely aware of her mother's loneliness, Judy tries to be her mother's friend as well as her helper.

Judy also declines invitations because she feels she cannot count on her parents to drive her. There is only one car and if her father is drunk and needs to be picked up, her mother may not be available for transportation. Once Judy was left stranded at a party because her father was in a car accident. Another time, Judy's father just forgot. Yet another time, it was Judy's mother, who in her role overload, forgot.

Judy has suppressed her anger and is a "model child." Her brother, on the other hand, displays some of his aggressive feelings. When playing with other children, he needs to be "right" and to "win" or else he stomps off making threats. Since he idealizes his father, whenever he hears his mother talking about his father's PTSD or alcoholism, he overturns trash cans or tears up some of his sister's papers. He also suffers from insomnia and will watch hour after hour of war videos in order to get to sleep. His favorite videos are those with ample amounts of blood and slaughter.

This child's preoccupation with power and violence is, in part, natural for his age and for our culture. However his interest in death and killing also stems from knowledge of his father's war experiences. In this, he is like a minority of children of Vietnam veterans found in the Vet Center study who display an inordinate interest in power and death. In addition, his persistent need to watch such videos serves a psychological need related to his living in an alcoholic and PTSD afflicted home. Specifically, the aggression and violence acted out in these videos can be seen as giving vicarious expression to the hostility and confusion which the child harbors within.

Summary

Alcohol and drugs became a way of life in Vietnam, as many servicemen used these substances in order to cope with the horrors and absurdities of war. After returning to the U.S., some servicemen quit their alcohol/drug use but others had become physically addicted and continued to abuse these substances. Still others continued to or began to use alcohol/drugs in order to suppress their emerging symptoms of PTSD.

When the Vietnam wife confronts her husband's alcohol or drug habit, she often does not know if she is dealing with a true alcoholic or drug addict or with an individual who is self-medicating for his

PTSD. In some cases, this self-medication evolves into an addiction, or at least into a life fraught with emotional and financial insecurity.

When there is heavy drug/alcohol usage in the home, the Vietnam wife can expect even less emotional and financial support from her husband than if he suffered only from PTSD. Furthermore, her husband's addiction, in combination with his PTSD, will detract from his ability to parent his children and can create an even wider range of emotional problems for the children with which she will have to cope, if not now, then in the future.

While not all children react in the same way, feelings of shame, guilt, and low self-esteem are prevalent in the homes blighted by addiction and PTSD. In addition, the children sometimes have ambivalent feelings toward both parents. The Vietnam wife may find her children blaming her not only for the father's war-related problems, but for his alcohol or drug problems as well. Or she may find herself trying desperately to create some semblance of a home life.

Furthermore, as her husband's drinking/drug addiction progresses, she may find herself and her children increasingly alienated from family members and friends, from the community, and even from their own emotions.

Six

Anger

*I*n the early days, before Joel started PTSD therapy, there was a lot of verbal abuse. But by and large, Joel's anger at the time was not really focused on me. Although rationally I recognized that he was a loose cannon ball ready to be fired, emotionally I pretty much blocked out the reality of his anger. That's not a healthy way to deal with things, but most likely he and I would not be together if I hadn't.

Nowadays, it's the eggshells under the feet, constant tension, a constant testing of the atmosphere to decipher Joel's mood, whether it be angry or depressed, that keeps the whole family wound up most of the time. Also, Joel is starting to blame me for more and more of his dissatisfactions. If a line is too long or one of the kids cries too loud, that's my fault. If his mother forgets to call or calls too much, that's my fault too.

Now that Joel is aware of his PTSD, he wants to run away even more. But he has no place to go, and that's my fault, too.

At my very first counseling session, the therapist suggested that I was a very angry woman. The idea was totally unacceptable to me. To me, anger was ugly and to be an angry woman, well, that was almost the same as being a "bad" one. "Good" women, I had been taught, forgave quickly and did not harbor resentments. They were also experts at turning lemons into lemonade and at keeping their mouths shut when their husbands were upset.

Because my husband had seen so much death in Vietnam and was still pulling shrapnel out of his skin, I didn't feel entitled to be angry. My problems seemed *petty compared to his. I was also afraid that if I aired my grievances with him, his entire storehouse of anger from Vietnam would land on me or the children. Many times it has been in my best interest and in the best interests of my children to follow my grandmother's advice and keep my mouth shut.*

Andrea

Many of the women in group readily cry and easily admit to feeling helpless and depressed, but rarely express any anger. Anger is a major problem for them, as it is for their partners. Despite popular psychology books which often suggest "let your anger out," old religious and societal sanctions against expressing anger still exist, especially for women.

Perhaps today's young women are being taught differently, but most of the women who have attended group were raised to believe that anger is not "feminine." Rebecca, for example, was taught that anger was a "sin" and that God would strike her dead if she ever sassed her parents or expressed anger toward them or any other authority figure.

While Rebecca now laughs at this old-fashioned thinking, emotionally she is still bound by it. So are many of the other women. They fear that if they express their anger, especially toward their partners, they will be struck dead by a thunderbolt. In most cases, the thunderbolt the women fear the most is not a physical attack, but an emotional one. As with many women of their generation, their self-esteem is closely intertwined with their partner's view of them.

In addition, many of the women were raised to assume the traditionally female role of family peacemaker. They fear that expressing anger will cost them what they have been taught to value most: family peace and harmony. Some Vietnam wives also teach their children, "Don't get angry in front of Daddy and upset him." Such a message either perpetuates the denial of the powerful emotion of anger from one generation to the next or else forces the child to find another outlet for his or her anger.

When anger cannot be freely or safely expressed at home, some children act out their frustrations in school. Counselors who have worked with children of Vietnam veterans with PTSD report that school is the arena where children are most likely to vent the anger they cannot reveal at home. The anger is usually expressed in terms of minor acts of disobedience toward the teachers or minor infractions of school rules.

Most of the women *are* angry. Some are in touch with their anger, others are not. Most have ambivalent feelings about their anger. On the one hand, they feel their anger is a legitimate response to being mistreated, unloved, and overburdened; on the other hand, since their partners suffered through various hardships in Vietnam, they "should" be more "understanding" and "patient."

Most of the women hide their anger from their partners. Some fear being hit. Others do not want to in any way interfere with their partner's therapy and recovery from PTSD. Still others keep quiet because their partners have talked about suicide, a real possibility for some Vietnam veterans. Although the Veteran's Administration calls it a "trash statistic," research completed in California alleges that as many vets (some 58,000) have died by their own hand as were killed in Vietnam.[1] Equally distressing are the high number of deaths and injuries due to single car collisions and other "accidents" among Vietnam veterans, which could have been suicidal in nature.

Most of the women would readily describe their partners as "angry." Some even call their men "human volcanos," ready to erupt at any moment. Indeed, the Vietnam veteran with unresolved or untreated PTSD is often a very angry man.[2]

In Vietnam, when friends were killed or atrocities witnessed, there was no time for the normal grieving process. Grief, like many other emotions, was suppressed. Both during the war and afterward, drugs or alcohol often were used as a way to avoid feeling grief, fear, homesickness, and many other feelings which the war created.

Anger, however, was one of the few emotions the soldier felt free to express in Vietnam and it was often the expression for a wide range of feelings. He could easily deal with anger or any other emotion by going "off" in the next firefight or engaging in some form of brutality, often without any official reprimand. "Kill or be killed" was the rule of the day. To assure survival, usually there was no time for moral considerations, or even much thought. "If it moved, we shot it," explains one vet.

Given the guerrilla nature of the war, responding with violence became almost automatic. Some vets describe being "shocked" at how "easy" and "pleasant" it became to kill. "There was a terrific release, a power rush," explains one veteran. "For a while, I thought I became addicted to killing."

This quick action response, however, while appropriate to the combat situation in Vietnam, was no longer useful (or condoned) upon return to the U.S. Vets had to quickly unlearn the violent tendencies which had been expected of them and served them so well during the war.

Yet, after the glow of coming home alive had passed, many veterans found themselves angrier than ever. First, at having been asked to fight in an unofficial war where political considerations often undercut military objectives and second, at the U.S. public in general and at those in their immediate families whom they felt failed to acknowledge, much less appreciate, their sacrifices in Vietnam.

Some vets also brought home with them unresolved anger toward certain individuals in the war whose ignorance, avarice, or selfish career interests caused the possibly preventable deaths or injuries of buddies and others. Some of this anger was acted out during the war, with its well-known incidents of "fraggings" of officers.

On a deeper level, some vets came home angry at themselves for surviving when others didn't, for acts of cowardice as well as any senseless killings or even for killing in the line of duty. "In my nightmares I see a V.C. I killed. As he dies, his face turns into my face. Now I realize that whenever I killed, I killed a part of myself," says one vet. Not uncommonly, vets in therapy report that while they may have felt little remorse about killing while in Vietnam, they now feel as if they lost "parts of their soul."

Nancy's husband, Bob, for example, was ordered to send three men into a dangerous area. He suspected this would result in their deaths, but he "had" to obey orders. In another instance, Bob was asked to repair some machinery under heavy enemy fire. His attempts to work efficiently were impeded by the moans of the wounded and the increasing numbers of dead around him. Furthermore, the tools he was given for the repair work were not appropriate for the task. Many died as a result of what Bob calls his "incompetence."

Upon return to the states, Bob never discussed these or any other incidents. Instead, he drank to drown his anger at himself, at the officer who had ordered him to send three men on a suicide mission, and at the person responsible for giving him the wrong tools. He quit jobs because he could not tolerate "stupid" orders and wanted to attack superiors who pointed out any of his mistakes. Bob also tended to suffer from rage reactions whenever he had to repair something in his home.

"After 'Nam, Bob could barely deal with his own feelings, much less mine," says Nancy. "So I learned to be quiet.

"If Bob was mad about anything, from the long line at the supermarket to something his mother said, he'd blame me for it. Even if I was trying to help him, he'd jump all over me. I've found that if something isn't my fault, I just leave the situation alone.

"Like last night, he was trying to fix our refrigerator. I could have done a better job of it, but didn't dare say so. Even when he started cussing and asking me for help, I stayed away. I knew if I went over there, even just to help, I'd end up getting yelled at or hit.

"The last time he fixed the refrigerator, he threw the tools all around, smashed some plates, and put a hole in the wall. Now there's another hole right next to it.

"At least I wasn't in the kitchen when it happened. Last time he said that it was my fault he put a hole in the wall.

"I don't care what women's liberation says. I'm staying quiet."

Nancy had suffered five years of intermittent physical abuse before she threatened to leave Bob. But the "mental abuse was much worse." Bob has stopped the physical abuse, but Nancy, like many of the women, still "walks on eggs."

"It helps when I don't call him names back or make nasty remarks about Vietnam veterans," Nancy admits. "Therapy helps too. At least now he sometimes warns me, 'Get out of the way, Nancy, I'm having a PTSD attack.'

"Or sometimes he'll chew me out and apologize later, saying he was really mad about something about Vietnam, not about me. He's never had this awareness before. Before, anytime he had a feeling, any kind of feeling about anything, it would come out as anger— toward me, the T.V., the cat, anything, but usually me.

"Now that I understand PTSD I don't take Bob's explosions so personally any more. But still, it isn't easy, and I'm still wondering when he's going to fix that hole in the wall."

While the Vietnam veterans with PTSD are subject to angry outbursts, the major problem presented by help-seeking vets is more often fear of becoming violent, rather than actually being violent. Sarah Haley, who has worked with many dozens of Vietnam veterans, describes the veteran as caught in the grip of a "paralyzing passivity" born of fear of losing control and hurting others.[3] Having learned what he could do in terms of killing and maiming others in Vietnam, the veteran often strives to suppress his anger for fear of hurting family members.

This "impacted anger," however, is a powder keg, which, on occasion, is ignited and can explode. Unfortunately, sometimes the targets for the anger are the very persons the veteran loves most—his wife or their children. Sometimes the anger emerges dramatically. Stereos are smashed, pets are hurt, and women are slammed against walls or hurled through glass doors. But more often the anger emerges less violently, in the form of small cutting remarks or verbal outbursts over relatively trivial matters. These minor outbursts, however, can do as much to erode a relationship as a major physical assault.

For example, normally Rebecca's husband does not pick on her for not keeping accurate financial records, for not having been a virgin when they married, or for yelling at the children. However, if he is angry about some other matter, especially a matter having to do with Vietnam, he will freely vent such complaints. Intuitively sensing that her husband's anger runs deeper than the issues he is talking about, Rebecca does not fight back. What she would like to say, but doesn't is: "After all the women you had in Vietnam, you're complaining about me not being a virgin at the altar? And how dare you criticize my bookkeeping and my parenting when you do precious little of either? If you'd help me a little, I wouldn't be making so many mistakes with the checkbook or need to yell at the kids so much."

Rebecca's husband also tends to criticize their children for not doing better at school. Yet he fails to reinforce his children for the efforts they do make, just as he often fails to acknowledge all that Rebecca does on behalf of the family. When children receive primarily negative reinforcement and very little positive reinforcement from a parent, their motivation to please that parent tends to decrease, not increase. This may only intensify the parent's criticalness and establishes a cycle of mutual anger and hurt.

The child feels that if his father really loved him, he wouldn't be so judgmental. On the other hand, the father may feel that if the child really loved him, he would try harder at school. Without the feeling that his father believes in him, the child may lose confidence in himself or lose the motivation to discipline himself in order to achieve in school. As the child's grades worsen, the father's critical remarks increase, until either a confrontation or a stalemate occurs.

Stalemates often occur in Vietnam homes where the vet is overly critical because, over time, both the Vietnam wife and her children learn to "tune out" the vet. If the Vietnam wife, or her children, sense that they are being used as scapegoats, they will then have a good reason to ignore the vet or discount his comments. In addition, they will also have double anger: one anger stemming from the specific critical remarks and the second anger from being used as an inappropriate target for the vet's anger about his own issues.

Upon first coming to a Vet Center for help, however, many wives and children suffer from low self-esteem and guilt because they have taken their vet's destructive comments or actions to heart. They have yet to realize that often they are not the fundamental cause of his angry comments or behavior. As the result of counseling, some wives learn to tell if their husband is truly angry at them or if he is merely venting his fury about some other issue; using his wife as a whipping girl.

Often, however, the situation is mixed. The vet is aggravated about something his wife did, but the intensity of his anger is related to an unresolved Vietnam or pre-Vietnam issue, not to his wife's action. Similarly, as the result of therapy, sometimes children as young as twelve or thirteen have been able to discern whether their fathers are "really" angry at them or whether they are "really" mad about something else, like Vietnam, or a flat tire, or a demanding boss. They may also come to recognize when their mother is scapegoating them too—when she is truly angry with them, or is, in reality, angry at their father, but merely taking it out on them because they are smaller, and safer.

Once a Vietnam wife or child comes to realize that she is being used as a scapegoat, she may not only become relatively immunized to the veteran's comments, but may lose some respect for the vet and disregard his wishes or directives. Even if the wife, or child, fails to recognize when the vet's anger does not belong to her, but believes instead that she deserves the vet's anger, she may also block out his rage or treat him like a crazy man. She may need to ignore the vet or set up some other protective barrier between herself and the vet if his angry or critical remarks are too painful or overpowering to be absorbed on a frequent basis.

However, if the vet's family denigrates him, either verbally or inside their own minds, and communicates this disrespect or disregard to the veteran, he may become furious. Even if the wife and child are not outwardly disrespectful, but merely, in self-protection or, as a form of retaliation, ignore him, he may also become furious. At this point, he may either withdraw, or he may escalate his verbal criticisms in order to obtain his wife's or child's attention and regain a sense of power and control. In some cases, he may even feel he needs to resort to violence in order to be heard or command respect. After each explosion, the veteran typically redoubles his efforts to suppress his anger, which, in turns, leads to a further build-up of impacted anger. Unless the real cause of the anger is dealt with directly, the possibility of another "explosion" in the future is imminent.

Like the men, the women have their war stories too. Their chief complaint is that their husbands often use them as scapegoats for the problems having to do with Vietnam or with life in general.

"I don't know why the traffic jams are all my fault, too," says Rebecca. "But if we get stuck in one, Eric starts yelling at me and I get scared. Last time he put a hole in the windshield. Another time he nearly pulled out the steering wheel."

To avoid such angry outbursts, the vet might withdraw. As explained in the introductory section on PTSD, certain events or conditions, like national holidays, humid weather, barbecues, or Oriental restaurants, may bring forth conscious or unconscious flashbacks to Vietnam experiences. During these times especially, but also at other times, the veteran, fearing loss of control, medicates himself with drugs or alcohol, sinks into a deep depression, or leaves home.

Time after time, women have reported that suddenly their men leave the room, go hide in the basement, or walk out of the house. Sometimes they are gone for many hours, if not days or weeks. Some men go visit other Vietnam veterans, often traveling to other cities to do so, or go to the Vietnam Memorial in Washington, D.C. Others simply go out to drink or to find drugs.

"Is this a marriage?" asks Rebecca. "When Eric goes off with his war friends, what am I supposed to do? And what am I supposed to tell our son? A lie—that Daddy's working overtime, or the truth—that Daddy's down at the Vietnam Memorial smoking pot?"

Left alone, the women feel unloved and abandoned. They also resent having to shoulder all the responsibilities for the household, as well as for any children. Not only must they answer their children's questions and help them with their emotional reactions to their father's absence, but they must also explain to relatives and friends why they are alone and why they do not know where their husband is or when he will return. In those instances where a woman's parents, relatives, or associates look down on her for having married a "crazy" Vietnam veteran, the woman's embarrassment, confusion, and anger toward her partner is doubled.

In one case, a husband left for four months; in another, nine months. The wives report that afterward their husbands came home "as if nothing had happened," offering no explanation about where they had been. So far, three women have been abandoned entirely. In two instances, the men clearly stated that they were leaving because they were afraid of hurting their wives. These men were not habitual wife abusers. They had lost control on only one or two occasions, but they did not want to lose control again. According to the wives, these men, now in other cities, work long hours, have practically no friends, and do not socialize with other women.

Most of the women entered their marriage or relationship with the expectation that they would be "taken care of" by their partner, to some degree, both financially and emotionally. Some had never envisioned themselves as having to work outside the home, much less as having to be the "strong one." Yet, most of the women who have attended group are not only the emotional, but the financial, mainstays of the family, holding down at least two jobs—one at home, one at work.

Anita holds down two jobs while also caring for two school-age children. Her husband, Paul, has been unemployed ever since Vietnam and has been in and out of treatment for his PTSD for several years. Sometimes he is so depressed he can do little around the house. His major contribution to the family has been his disability check, which depresses him further.

In deference to Paul's ego, Anita keeps her complaints to herself and shares them only with the group. Like the majority of the women in the group, Anita feels deep loyalty to her husband and is very sensitive to the fact that he endured a great deal in Vietnam.

"Paul lost his hearing in one ear and has permanent back injuries. Half his unit was wiped out too. After all he went through, maybe I have no right to moan. But it's been thirteen years of me being supermom. I'm worn out and I keep wondering when is he going to get over this thing?

"I try to be patient, but when I come home and the dishes aren't even done, I blow up. Then he says I'm aggravating his PTSD."

Most of the men are described as being willing to help with only a minimal amount of household work or childcare. Some men leave all the chores to their wives. In general, the men seem somewhat more interested in childcare than in housecleaning.

Perhaps the women would be less resentful if their contributions to the family were acknowledged and appreciated. But most of the women report working long hours with minimal reinforcement or positive regard from their spouse or lover. "I know it's the numbing that makes him unable to show affection and I know that he's too depressed himself to even ask me 'how was your day?' when I walk in the door. But it still hurts," says Anita.

While most of the women are angry, they fail to acknowledge their anger because, on some level, they blame themselves for their partner's distress. According to the Vet Center survey, approximately 84% of Vet Center counselors polled indicated that the Vietnam wives they have seen suffer from self-blame for the veteran's depressions, his rage reactions, or his wide fluctuations in mood. Often Vietnam wives have mistakenly interpreted their veteran's emotional or sexual withdrawals as signs of some inadequacies in themselves as women. When their veteran doesn't talk, they wonder what they did to "turn him off;" when he explodes, what they might have done to "set him off."

In group, the women learn about Vietnam and PTSD. It comes as a surprise, and a relief, for them to hear that they are not responsible for the symptoms of their partner's stress disorder. The Al-Anon slogan, "C-C-C"—you didn't Cause it, you can't Control it, you can't Cure it—is emphasized.

Yet it takes months for the majority of the women to absorb this message. Most of the women, now in their early or late thirties, entered marriage with a 1950s mentality, believing that if only they were "giving" enough, then their husbands would be happy and all would be well. Many have tried to be the "perfect" wife and have expended a great deal of psychic energy trying to make their husbands "feel better." Some have even become frantic in their attempts to "fix" their partner.

Yet, they learned that their love was not enough—that while they were wanted, they were also not wanted; that while they were needed, sometimes desperately so, they were also functionally useless in the face of symptoms of PTSD. Yet if they expressed their feelings, especially anger, only more anger or rejection was sent their way.

Their men, struggling with PTSD, simply could not tolerate the emotional overload. Women who complained were frequently called "selfish" or "ungiving" or reminded that they could not possibly understand the horrors and deprivations endured in Vietnam. In some cases, the woman received the same guilt-evoking message from the veteran's family and friends: she should put her own feelings and needs aside until the veteran "got himself together." She should especially keep her anger to herself, since the veteran was already "upset enough as it is."

Some relatives and friends even overlooked the physical battering of the wife. Pat, for example, was physically abused all during her seven year marriage to Joe. She also supported him financially and was his only friend. She came to group severely depressed because the last beating had resulted in a miscarriage. She was also in danger of losing her job because of missing so many days from work due to her injuries.

With the group's support, Pat rallied the courage to ask Joe to stop the abuse. When Joe refused, Pat moved out, making her return conditional on his seeking help. Joe promptly moved in with his mother, who immediately called Pat and begged her to return to Joe, who was "falling apart" because he missed her so. The mother added that if only Pat were a "better wife" (and lost 20 pounds too) Joe would be able to get over Vietnam and not be abusive.

It must be emphasized that the abusive men referred to above were not in treatment for their PTSD and had refused all help, not only for PTSD, but for their alcohol and drug addictions as well. It is highly probably that these particular combat vets were suffering from other difficulties in addition to PTSD.

One of my major therapeutic goals has been to help the women get in touch with their anger and learn how to deal with it in a constructive, rather than destructive, manner. While it has never been my intention to encourage women to blast their partners with anger or produce further alienation in sometimes already well-alienated couples, mental health requires that women recognize, and take control of, the powerful energy contained in their anger. In some cases, the woman's marriage has been saved as a result of having her acknowledge her resentments and share them with her partner. Otherwise, she may have simply left.

Many of the women suffer from impacted anger just like their partners. If a woman has repressed her anger over time regarding a series of incidents, then each new conflict with her partner brings to the surface not only the anger appropriate to that particular incident, but all the built-up angers from the past. Like her veteran, the woman becomes afraid of erupting and tries to keep her anger to herself. She may hesitate to speak up even about minor incidents, for fear of "thunderbolting" her husband with all her past angers or with threats of leaving. Rather than risk his retaliation or her shame at such an unfeminine display, many of the women have done their best to hold in their anger.

Whereas the veteran may turn to alcohol or drugs to sedate his feelings, his woman partner may use a more socially accepted drug: food. As stated previously, approximately 20% of women seen at the Vet Centers polled were significantly overweight. Some were even double their ideal weight. It is possible that these women literally swallowed their anger as well as other feelings. For example, when Sybil overeats, she is literally stuffing down her anger with food. On her way home from work, she often stops to buy one of her favorite binge foods. "It's the only way I can cope with walking through the door and having him ignore me or blow up at me," she explains. When her husband ridicules her body, Sybil usually vows to go on a diet. But the minute her husband walks out the door, she's in front of the refrigerator stuffing down her hurt, and her rage, with food.

In fact, whenever her husband denigrates her about anything, Sybil ends up eating, if not immediately after the incident, then a few days later. Sybil is one of those Vietnam wives who "learned to be quiet." In addition, her self-esteem is so low that she doesn't feel entitled to be angry. "Fat slobs like me don't have rights," she once said. "I should be grateful he's still married to me." Whenever her husband disappoints her or cheats on her, she has difficulty expressing her anger toward him directly. Instead, she eats. "Each of his blondes has cost me thirty pounds," she sighs.

Sybil dares not admit it to herself (much less to her husband), but she harbors tremendous rage toward him. For example, Sybil claims to have forgiven her husband for his extramarital affairs. But her forgiveness, although sincere, is superficial, for she has never experienced the full depth of her fury.

"I've forgiven him," she tells the group, candy bar in hand. "After all, boys will be boys and this boy had to make up for the time he lost in Vietnam."

"Would you be saying that if you were thin?" asks a group member.

Sybil throws the candy bar across the room. "Hell, no! If I were thin, I'd kill him."

Like Sybil, other Vietnam wives have engaged in "revenge eating" in response to their husbands' extramarital affairs. On the surface it may appear that the woman is trying to punish her husband for his infidelity by gaining weight. Yet on a deeper level, the eating is a form of self-abuse. Upon introspection, many of the women blame themselves, not their husbands, for the affair. They think that if only they were sexier, more loving, more intelligent, more "something," the affair would not have occurred in the first place. By overeating, the women are consciously or unconsciously punishing themselves for their perceived inadequacies as women by destroying not only their bodies, but their self-respect and self-esteem.

Summary

According to the Vet Center survey, coping with the veteran's verbal abuse and his outbursts of anger is a major problem for the wives and girlfriends of PTSD afflicted veterans. The Vietnam wife often fails to understand that her husband's verbal tirades and his angry outbursts may reflect his unresolved angers regarding his Vietnam experience, rather than the appropriateness or inappropriateness of some action or inaction on her part. Similarly, children who are overcriticized by their father often cannot discern that the intensity and frequency of their father's stinging remarks stem primarily from his own problems, not their failings as children.

While the Vietnam vet is often portrayed as a violent individual, this image is false. In reality, the vet who suffers primarily from PTSD more accurately suffers from impacted, or suppressed anger, and consequently, from depression, which is often anger turned inward. When the vet is no longer able to keep a lid on his anger, however, rage reactions do occur. Yet, unless the veteran suffers from problems in addition to his PTSD, his rage reactions may be intermittent and followed by remorse and even greater efforts to suppress his anger.

Whether the vet is overly critical, explodes, or withdraws, his wife and children are often angered by his behavior. However, they often do not feel free to express their anger at the vet directly because they fear that the storehouse of anger he harbors inside may be unleashed upon them. Anger is also a "no-no" for Vietnam wives and children because of sanctions against women expressing anger toward men and against children expressing anger toward their parents.

Nevertheless, the wives and children may be angry. Yet their anger toward the vet, like the vet's anger toward certain aspects of his Vietnam experience, goes underground, where it only tends to grow, rather than disappear. Like their husbands, some Vietnam wives harbor years of resentment and, because they have no outlet for their anger, suffer from problems such as depression, medical problems, and, in some cases, obesity. Some children also have been treated for depression, stemming primarily from having internalized their anger toward their father, their mother, and the entire family situation.

Seven

Battered Wives

I met Bill right after the war. He seemed kind and compassionate and was extremely charming. My parents and friends, however, protested my seeing him. They felt he had a "dark side." But I thought they were just prejudiced against Vietnam veterans.

Not until six months after the wedding did I find out they were right. Bill really did have a dark side. The abuse began slowly and insidiously. I didn't count his slapping me and sitting on top of me as abuse. Even when he threw things at me or locked me up in rooms, I didn't consider myself battered.

Me, an educated woman with a master's degree, battered? My shrink had to be out of her mind. When she first used the word "battered," I was not even fully aware of what she was talking about. Sure, Bill and I had our difficulties. But didn't every married couple? He wasn't that bad, was he? If Bill was angry, it was my fault, or Vietnam's fault, I supposed. All I had to do to make things better was to keep improving myself and help Bill readjust to civilian life.

I first realized I was an abused woman last Veteran's Day, when Bill pushed me out of the car into the rain. It was midnight and he had taken my house keys, my credit cards, and my pay check. At that moment, I realized that I spent my entire life avoiding his anger and arranging people, places, and things so as not to 'set him off.'

I had lost my identity in constantly placating him and I was sacrificing the emotional and physical health of my children just for the sake of a wedding ring. I couldn't even make a doctor's appointment for the children without obtaining his 'permission' first, even though I earned most of the money in the family.

Up until this point, I had lived in denial, just like he did. Together we minimized my physical injuries and my mental sufferings and blamed everything on Vietnam. I firmly believe that Vietnam did play a role. Bill was a trained killer who had somehow not gotten the fight out of him. The military had flown him straight from the jungle back to his home town, with no time to unwind. He had also been asked to kill innocent civilians. Having learned violence as a problem-solving technique in Vietnam, he felt free to use it in our marriage. His war experience had also taught him that it was okay to push around women.

I left Bill several times, but he would always hunt me down. Once he kidnapped me and the kids from a friend's home. After the jungles of Vietnam, breaking into my friend's house was peanuts to him. He was skilled at scaling walls and other such tactics.

After each episode of violence, however, he was the most loving and wonderful husband and father imaginable. The children would scold me for having wanted to leave him. Since Daddy was being so 'nice' now, they felt I should forgive him as I did them whenever they misbehaved.

My children were still in grade school then. They knew nothing about what went on behind closed doors or about all the sacrifices I had made to keep the peace at home.

I finally left Bill. But while I was married and trying to tell people about my marriage, they usually turned around and told me I was as 'sick' as Bill was. Even my therapist thought I was crazy. Very few people, it seems, understand the powerful forces that keep a woman trapped in an abusive situation. They also fail to understand how the Vietnam war could ruin a man. Sure, Bill had problems before the war, but I am certain that my life with Bill would have been altogether different if he had never gone to Vietnam and did not have PTSD. There was a lot of good in Bill, despite his abusiveness.

> Tessa, wife of a Special
> Services officer

All Vietnam veterans are not wife abusers. Yet domestic violence is a problem in some Vietnam veteran homes, as it is in society at large. While definitions vary, most researchers agree that a battered woman is one who has received at least two or three deliberate and severe physical assaults. The physical abuse can include a wide variety of bodily assaults—slapping, hitting, punching with fists, attacks with broken glass or weapons, burning, biting, pushing, slamming against walls, and shoving down steps.[1,2]

Battering is not inherent to PTSD. It is not a symptom of the disorder. Yet some vets do batter and, for some, the battering is PTSD related.

If the vet adheres to the traditional male sex role stereotype, which dictates that "real men" should appear unemotional, always strong, and never confused, he might panic when his feelings about Vietnam rise to the surface. Feeling out of control and emasculated (by his own emotions, which, except for his anger, he may view as "feminine"), he may attempt to regain a sense of control and affirm his manhood by battering. Battering also helps release the mounting adrenaline caused by his pent-up emotions and inner turmoil.

The vet may also try to feel "strong" and "manly" by attempting to control his wife or girlfriend by other means, such as by making excessive demands on her, by restricting her financially, or by isolating her from others. However, if she resists his attempts to control her, or otherwise frustrates him, he may resort to violence in order to assume a position of dominance.

Vietnam veterans who batter are similar to other wife abusers in that they may batter out of a need to control and feel masculine and because they have few other means of expressing their needs and frustrations. However, physically abusive Vietnam veterans differ from other batterers in that their military training and experience not only gave them permission, but, in some cases, greatly encouraged them to give in to, rather than to restrain, their violent impulses. In addition, most vets received intensive training in a variety of fighting techniques. In some cases, wife abuse is the direct result of the vet's confusing his wife with the Viet Cong in the midst of a flashback or seeing her as "the enemy" in the midst of a paranoid state.

However, more usually it is the vet's economic or emotional dependency on his wife or his need for her to provide him with physical or psychological comfort which precipitates battering in the home.

In my experience, violence in the home seems to erupt when the wife does not meet the veteran's expectation that she can make life smooth for him, when he feels threatened by her need for intimacy, or when he somehow feels emasculated by her strengths. While these dynamics also exist in nonveteran homes, in my experience they are especially prevalent in homes where the vet is still struggling with untreated PTSD, suffers from extreme emotional numbing and feelings of powerlessness, and, in addition, has not yet adjusted to recent changes in the woman's role.

While the vet was fighting in the jungles, the woman's liberation movement was beginning to make concrete progress in emancipating women from their traditional roles. Upon return from Vietnam, the veteran may have (understandably) focussed on his own readjustment process, rather than on social changes. To the extent that PTSD hinders personality development and keeps the veteran focussed on Vietnam, rather than present realities, the veteran may still be holding on to what are now severely challenged, if not totally outmoded, notions of the woman's role. When his wife's behavior or attitude contradicts his beliefs about how a woman "should" be or act, he may batter in an attempt to reinstate the traditional sex roles with which he is more comfortable and which assign him a position of dominance.

PTSD related wife abuse, as opposed to other forms of wife abuse, is usually sporadic and lessens when the vet learns to identify and express his leftover anger and grief from Vietnam constructively and when he learns to root his sense of mastery, competency, and achievement in developing his skills and talents rather than in dominating a woman. He also must learn to accept his own emotions and see them as part of the human condition, rather than as signs of "feminine weakness."

Renewed pride in himself, as a Vietnam vet and as a competent person, usually reduces his need to batter in order to feel powerful, important, or masculine. Stopping battering, however, is usually more difficult for the veteran from a violent home: one who saw his mother being beaten and who, perhaps, was beaten also. Socialized to see violence as "normal," it may be harder for him to unlearn violence as a coping mechanism, especially if he still harbors unresolved painful and angry feelings regarding the abuse he saw or endured as a child.

Furthermore, if his mother spent most of her time avoiding beatings, or recovering from them, the vet may have suffered from inadequate physical and emotional nurturing as a child. In his wife, he may hope to find the mother he never had. When his wife fails to meet his needs, he may become quickly furious.

In my experience, the most severe and long-term cases of wife abuse existed in homes where the vet came from a violent family. Wife abuse is also especially prevalent in homes where the veteran is alcohol or drug addicted, where he suffers from a neurological disorder, or where he is character disordered or overtly paranoid. In all these instances, where PTSD interacts with another condition, it is difficult to determine which is primary: the PTSD or the other condition. However, the result is the same—a physically abused and deeply emotionally scarred Vietnam wife.

While psychological humiliation and degradation almost always accompany the physical abuse, the threat of violence must exist in a relationship if it is to be considered a battering one. The woman must know that her partner is capable of directing severe blows at her and perhaps, ultimately, of killing her.[3,4,5,6,7]

Yet, it is not necessary for a woman to be continually beaten in order to feel terrorized or humiliated into a submissive posture. One or two beatings or threats of violence, accompanied by infrequent inflicting of physical pain or actual torture, are sufficient to establish a pattern of male domination by force.[8] One wife, for example, was beaten twice soon after her husband's return from Vietnam. For fifteen years since, she has kept quiet, hiding her innermost needs and feelings from her husband for fear of being hit. A few months ago, she summoned the courage to assert herself and ask some questions about a touchy issue. As expected, she was assaulted. She lives in fear. These infrequent assaults are enough to "keep her in her place."

Current estimates are that one third of all married couples engage in spousal assault. The number of women being beaten by their husbands is close to 1.8 million per year.[9] However, many researchers, as well as official military and other government documents, note that wife abuse, like child abuse, tends to be underreported.[10,11]

More than one million abused women seek medical attention for injuries caused by battering each year.[12] Some studies show that at least 20% of the visits to emergency rooms by women are the result of wife abuse.[13] Four women a day in this country die as the result of domestic violence. In fact, wife abuse causes more injury to women than auto accidents, rapes, or muggings.[14]

Men from all social groups batter—rich men, poor men, white men, black men, professors, and even clergymen.[15] To date, we do not know whether Vietnam veterans batter their wives more or less than any other group of men. Candice Williams of the Disabled American Veteran Vietnam Veteran's Outreach Program in Denver, Colorado reports wife abuse in approximately one half of couples seen.[16] Rick Ritter at the Fort Wayne, Indiana Vet Center reports that about one-third of veterans seeking help there admit to striking their partners.[17] According to the counselors polled in the Vet Center study, approximately one-fourth of wives seen at their Vet Centers report not just mental, but physical abuse.[18]

Many more women have been hit at least once. However, only about one-fourth fit into the battered woman category where the husband exercises a financial and emotional, as well as physical, stranglehold over the woman. In these cases, women are not just hit on occasion, but thrown down stairs, slammed against (and through) walls, cut with knives, and locked in rooms without food or heat for hours. Some wives have been seriously sexually abused by their husbands, forced into obscene situations, or punched in the stomach, even when pregnant, causing some miscarriages.

I have also treated Vietnam veterans' wives and girlfriends who are incarcerated at a local correctional facility for a variety of crimes ranging from theft and drug dealing to attempted murder and murder. One of the women, Peggy, is serving time for killing her veteran husband, a man who, during his numerous flashbacks, would brutally assault her and their seven-year-old son.

"He thought we were V.C.," she explained. This man never sought help. Years after the war, he would simulate Vietnam by building fires in their backyard and sleeping outside. Whenever airplanes flew overhead in hot and humid weather, Peggy would anticipate a beating. In self-protection, she would hide at the homes of relatives and friends. But her husband would seek her out, drag her home, barricade her inside, and terrorize her, sometimes for days on end.

Peggy was afraid to call the police. Her husband had threatened to kill any police who came and then, kill her. She had good reason to believe him, for he had souvenir guns from Vietnam and had been in a Special Forces Division where he had killed many persons. Furthermore, he had often stated that even if the police shot him dead or imprisoned him, he would not care. Life was meaningless to him.

Peggy felt trapped. The only way she saw out of her marriage was murder. "But I'm still not free of him," she would often say. "In my dreams, I see him running around in our backyard, acting like he was in the jungles, then coming at me. If I didn't kill him, he would have probably killed himself someday."

Another imprisoned wife, whose husband also failed to recognize his PTSD, reported that her husband beat her during nightmares about Vietnam and, on one occasion, tried to cut her ear off with an opened lid from a can of baby formula.

"I'm not a Viet Cong! I'm not a Viet Cong!" she screamed and hit him on the head with a broomstick until he "came back to the U.S.A."

While these examples may seem extreme, they are real, and while the figure of one-fourth may seem high, actually, it is not strikingly different from the figure given for the rate of wife abuse in our society as a whole—a figure which ranges from 15%-50% according to the studies cited above.

It cannot be overemphasized that the one-fourth percentage is based on estimates from only half of the existing Vet Centers, as well as on an extremely limited sample: help-seeking veterans, not on the Vietnam population as a whole. The percentages from these highly specialized samples cannot be generalized.

In addition, there is evidence that with the increased public recognition given to Vietnam veterans in recent years, the incidence of domestic violence has decreased. "In the last few years, there has been a reduction in the external causes of anger by the dedication of 'The Wall,' by the willingness of television to discuss Vietnam, by therapy and rap groups conducted by Vet Centers, and by society's more accepting attitude toward Vietnam veterans," explains Mark Kaufki, Vet Center Team Leader, Wilmington, Delaware.[19]

"'The Wall' is a real focus for grieving," he continues. "It's as if society says it is okay to grieve. Veterans can do that now. Grieving can dissipate a lot of internal pressure," pressure which perhaps was relieved in the past through woman battering.[20] On the other hand, abused women and battering couples are less likely than others to seek help and, despite recent public awareness, may not report the abuse. Therefore, the true extent of wife abuse among Vietnam veterans is undetermined.

While wife abuse is not limited to any particular population of men, it has been found to be more prevalent among families experiencing financial pressures, frequent moves, and isolation from peer groups and family support systems—characteristics of some Vietnam veteran families.[21] A related problem is that in some homes, the vet is economically or emotionally dependent on his wife. He may sense his dependency and resent it. It insults his masculinity and sense of control. As a result, he may batter to maintain superiority.

Veterans, like other men, grew up in a society where the marriage license was sometimes perceived as a "hitting license." Furthermore, some veterans had extensive military training and wartime experiences which emphasized the value of power and violence and quick-action responses.[22] As one veteran stated, "I was just a mealymouthed clerk until the military turned me into a trained killer. Is it any wonder I beat my wife?"

"The military portion of our society, which is a microcosm of the larger society, contributes to the learning of violence and specifically to the battering of women and children," explains Rick Ritter, a former Vietnam veteran who now specializes in helping vets who batter.[23]

"Basic training encourages woman hating (as does the whole military experience)," Ritter continues. "Each man strives to outdo the next, i.e., to 'top him.' Inevitably, someone has to be on the bottom. Somebody has to be the scapegoat, the enemy (when all else fails women are always available for that role in the mind of the military.)"[24]

"Most men in basic training are teenagers—the time when their concept of womanhood is crystallized," writes Shepard Bliss in "The Military, Masculinity and the Men's Movement." "Many men have their first experiences with sexual intercourse while in the military, not the best context for what can be such a loving act, but can also become an instrument of control, power and domination.

"Speaking about Vietnam, a soldier explains...'You either had to be satisfied with masturbation or find someone to rape.'"[25]

According to Savina, who writes extensively on battered women, "During the Vietnam war, as in all wars, women were raped, mutilated, and tortured. Rape was often a method of interrogation, even though it was less than 10% effective. Assault on Vietnamese women was also sometimes a way for American soldiers to vent their frustrations regarding the war or to retaliate against the Vietnamese for the deaths of buddies or military defeats."[26] "After a hard day at the battle it was okay to go into town and brutalize a woman. If (we) had already won the land then it was okay to defile the defeated foe's woman as a conqueror," writes one veteran.[27]

"Certainly not all Vietnam veterans raped or otherwise victimized women. But some did, and those who did not actually participate in such crimes witnessed them or at least heard about them. Undoubtedly such experiences serve to lower inhibitions against expressing violence against one's wife or girlfriend in the U.S."[28]

One psychological factor leading to wife abuse among Vietnam veterans can be the unresolved grief and rage which underlie the symptoms of PTSD.[29] For some men, it is easier to lash out at a wife or girlfriend than to deal with the seemingly insurmountable amounts of pain and anger within. Some of their pain and anger may be leftover from Vietnam, but some of it stems from their frustration and disappointment with the present, as in the case of David.

"Why do I hit her when she's all I got?" asked David.

"Why do you think?" I asked.

"Because she's there, the safest available target."

"Who do you really want to hit?"

"The V.C., my C.O., my boss, myself."

David entered therapy in an extreme state of psychic numbing. As his emotions began to surface, he began to panic. The feelings seemed to overwhelm him at times. He felt "out of control," almost powerless, over his inner life.

Most people do not like to feel powerless over anything. For men, especially, it isn't "masculine." They may batter as a defense against such feelings.

David, for example, frequently felt powerless in Vietnam. Once he was ordered to shoot into a deserted hut. David objected, but his C.O. insisted. As it turned out, inside the hut were two abandoned toddlers.

"I swear, I didn't know there were two kids in there, I swear," David bawled in one session. "And I could have killed my C.O." But, David didn't kill his C.O. He didn't even say anything to the C.O. about the killing. Soon afterward, however, as a means of atonement, David began to visit a nearby village and brought small presents for the children. Five weeks later, the V.C. blew up the village. All the children were killed. "After that, I gave up," says David. "I didn't care about nothin' except getting home alive."

Upon his return to the states, however, David's wife did not want to hear about Vietnam. He could not find a job he liked. He felt cheated by the government over his benefits. Once again, he felt powerless. Once again, he decided "not to care."

He claims to have put Vietnam out of his mind until ten years later, when his wife, at thirty-nine, unexpectedly became pregnant. He was also in the midst of a midlife crisis. Only then did he begin to attack his wife immediately after she came home from work, threatening to throw her down the stairs or puncture her ovaries if she ever became pregnant again. Or, fearing his anger, he'd withdraw from her altogether and spend his nights in a park or go to the mountains for days. If she would not consent to an abortion, he planned to leave her. On the other hand, he felt that abortion was a form of murder. Seeing no solution to the problem, he became angrier and angrier at his wife, who he felt had tricked him into impregnating her. His wife, however, claims that the pregnancy was a total surprise.

As David's case illustrates, unresolved PTSD can play a key role in wife abuse, with a greater frequency and severity of wife beating occurring among couples where the veteran has yet to deal with his grief and rage. A significant event can sometimes precipitate an episode of wife abuse.

For example, incidents seem to occur when there is a death in the family or when one of the children is seriously injured. The veteran, in a state of psychic numbing, may show no apparent emotion about the event. However, when the wife begins to grieve or openly react, the veteran may batter her as an attempt to cope with the pain which her emotional response brings to his awareness.

In one instance, a vet's sister-in-law died in childbirth. The veteran showed no emotion until his wife picked up the phone to make plane reservations to attend the funeral. Screaming that there was no need for airline reservations because his sister wasn't "really" dead, the vet pulled the phone out of the wall and punched his wife in the stomach and face.

In another instance, a child received second degree oil burns in a kitchen accident. The vet refused to accompany his wife to the hospital. In his view, the child was not injured. Even when the child returned home in bandages, the vet was emotionless and said nothing. The next day the wife began to cry as she changed the dressings on the child's wounds. The vet accused her of "overreacting" and choked the cat. When the wife intervened, the vet choked her.

Beatings also may occur on patriotic holidays or when a veteran encounters frustrations with bureaucracies—like delays in obtaining benefits and waiting in long lines—even though the wife may be the veteran's right-hand partner in the process of obtaining his rights. Mary Elizabeth, for example, was constantly contacting veteran's benefits offices for her husband, Walter, who became "irrational" or "overly depressed" when he had to deal with government officials. Since Vietnam, Walter had been unable to work and she also was the sole support of the family. Yet Walter abused her, especially on patriotic holidays.

One holiday she phoned in the middle of the night. Walter had tied her to the bedpost for two days. He had not only assaulted her, but also used one of his knives from Vietnam to scrape designs on her stomach. When he left to buy some beer, he came back with a dozen live crabs also. He put Mary Elizabeth in the bathtub with the crabs and tried to recreate water tortures he had seen overseas. When a neighbor unexpectedly came to the door, Mary Elizabeth somehow managed to slip away and lock herself in her bedroom. She now wanted to kill herself.

My suggestion that her desire to commit suicide might reflect her suppressed anger toward Walter was not well received. Mary Elizabeth insisted that she "understood" why Walter was violent and listed all the traumas he had experienced in Vietnam which, in her mind, "excused" his behavior.

Similarly, Amy, who arrived at her first group meeting with a black eye and two missing teeth, felt that the military was responsible for her husband's outbursts. He had been wounded in Vietnam and did not receive proper medical care. Whenever he was in pain, he would prevent her from leaving the home and, sometimes, batter her.

While not all wives are so "understanding," many blame anything but their husbands for his behavior. Such thinking, however, is a form of denial which only serves to help the woman "forgive" and resigns her to a life of violence.

Other wives report that husbands hit them and then ask for forgiveness because, after all, it was just their PTSD acting up. There is, however, no excuse for a beating, not even PTSD.

Summary

While some vets recoil from all forms of violence after their firsthand experiences with blood and death in Vietnam, others find themselves "on guard" and "ready to attack" even at home. According to the Vet Center study, some 25% of Vietnam wives complain of physical abuse. This rate, however, is based on a limited sample and is not significantly different from rates of wife abuse found among other groups in our society.

In homes of Vietnam veterans, wife abuse tends to occur during certain flashbacks to Vietnam, in times of family loss or injury, or when the vet is feeling powerless over some aspect of his life, for example, his financial or employment situation, his personal relationships, or even his own emotions. Through battering he hopes to recapture a sense of control and to affirm his strength and masculinity. If the vet became anesthetized to violence in Vietnam, he may trivialize his wife's injuries, and thereby support her denial that she isn't hurt "that bad."

Battered Vietnam wives, like their husbands, sometimes blame Vietnam for the violence at home, not realizing that such violence cannot be entirely attributed to the veteran's PTSD. In fact, in cases of extreme or persistent wife abuse, usually the veteran suffers from problems in addition to PTSD.

Like other abused women, battered Vietnam wives often fail to realize the extent to which they are being abused until they are severely injured, or until one of their children develops a problem.

Even if children do not become directly involved in the violence, they will suffer psychological scars from living in a home where they see their mother being abused. Since domestic violence tends to escalate over time, eventually the children will discover the parental "secret" and imitate the parental patterns of victim or aggressor. Like children from alcoholic homes, children from violent homes tend to feel responsible for the family turbulence and, in some cases, suffer from long-term guilt complexes over what they did or didn't do to cause the assaults or to prevent them from occurring.

Eight

"But Military Wives Never"

I was born in a military family and, as a child, was proud of it. I thought it made me special. When my father served in World War II, my mother received a tremendous amount of support from the other military wives and members of the military community. I didn't like the frequent moves, but the warm reception we received at each new base almost made up for the home and friends we had left behind.

I was proud to be a military wife too, until my husband came back from Vietnam and both he and I were shunned, not cheered like my parents had been. In many ways, large and small, I found myself hiding the fact of my husband's tour of duty from the others on the base. Although Alex had served honorably, he was seen as being part of the war which had brought disgrace to the military and which had made the military a four-letter word to some people.

Popular military woman's magazines, and other military wife publications wanted no stories about Vietnam wives and there were no special clubs where we who had sent our men to the jungles could share our struggles and concerns. If we had trouble coping, well, that was our fault. After all, as military wives, we were supposed to be strong, keep a stiff upper lip, and stand by our man 100%, no matter how he might be destroying our peace of mind, as well as his own.

Given this atmosphere, I found dozens of clever ways of disguising the fact that my husband had served in

'Nam and invented yet another ingenious list of excuses for not attending certain military functions. Of course, nonattendance at social and other functions was a definite 'no-no' for a military wife, but there were times I was needed at home. If my husband was severely depressed or being self-destructive, I had to be there to help keep him, and our children, together.

At the time I had nowhere to turn. Ten or fifteen years ago, understanding of PTSD was just developing in our society. In the military particularly, PTSD was largely unheard of, or seen as an excuse for cowardice or as some kind of moral or masculine failure. Even today, among certain groups, the active duty Vietnam vet afflicted with PTSD is looked down on.

I left my husband three years ago, divorcing not only him but the entire military, the only life I had ever known. Of course I was accused—by his parents and mine—not only of breaking up the family, but of ruining my husband's military career and my children's financial security. I was also disgracing his particular unit which boasted few divorces. Yet I could no longer live a lie.

My military benefits are gone and I live close to poverty with several children to support. The most painful part of the divorce, however, was giving up access to my husband, surrendering my desire to save Alex from his depression, drinking, and his bouts of combat memories. And he was getting worse. My most vivid memory of him is seeing him lying on the couch, disheveled and bloated from beer, bags under his eyes from the nightmares, saying he didn't have a problem. The only problem was me. If I would only leave him, he would be fine.

I pleaded with him to get help, threatening to divorce him if he didn't. But he simply couldn't share his psychological problems with anyone in the military. It would have felt like a complete emasculation to him, a total antithesis of the 'macho' hero he was expected to be. Furthermore, since there is little confidentiality of records in the military, he feared that his attempts to seek help would have become a matter of record and

*possibly held against him for the rest of his military
career.*

*I often wonder how Alex is today. Rumor has it that
he is deteriorating rapidly. But because he is a lifer and
holds a high position, special exceptions are being made
for him. He is also the object of much sympathy because he was 'deserted' by his 'irresponsible' wife. My
years of loyal wifely service and personal martyrdom for
the sake of the family count for nothing.*

The ex-wife of a
high-ranking officer

Military wives have often been strangled by what the "good military
wife" should do. For example, when Evelyn, a formerly battered
military wife, sought help from her husband's commanding officer
and the army chaplain, she was advised to stop wallowing in self-
pity, "toughen up," and support her fighting man. Soon he would
be going to Vietnam. She might lose him. No sense filing charges
or making a fuss now. Besides, if she exposed her husband's wife
(and child) abuse, it would hurt his career. What if he was demoted
from officer to grunt status and had to fight in the front lines? If
he died in 'Nam, it would be all her fault.

Brought up in a military home, Evelyn was indoctrinated into the
"shoulds" of being a "good military wife" at a relatively young age.
She was also brought up in a religious household, which emphasized
the virtues of female submission, self-sacrifice, and the sanctity of
the family. These "shoulds" were reinforced by her military neighbors and those in her husband's chain of command. As a result, she
found it impossible to leave her husband until several years after his
return from Vietnam, when his physical abuse endangered the life
of their youngest son.

Like Evelyn, the military wife is under a special set of pressures
related to the military community. The demands that community
makes on her are numerous and difficult to follow even without a
husband suffering from PTSD. If the husband is afflicted with PTSD,
her life becomes almost unmanageable.

Military wives have listed the following demands as those must
difficult for them to accept when trying to cope with PTSD as well.

1. Always put her husband's career above her personal needs and
   the needs of the family;

2. Be willing to tolerate frequent moves and separations from her husband without undue complaint;

3. Be prepared to bear and raise her children alone;

4. Assume complete responsibility for the children, the home, the car, and finances during her husband's absences, but then allow him to feel he is the head of the household when he returns;

5. Be willing to give up anniversaries and birthdays and accept that the military comes first and she, second;

6. Attend all parties and mixers and always act in a way which promotes her husband's career;

7. Conform to group expectations and especially any expectations or orders from the "higher-ups;"

8. Always be compassionate, understanding, and obedient and plan special homecomings for her husband;

9. Keep her home spotless even if she works full time and doesn't have help;

10. At all times, keep up the pretense of having a home life;

11. Never, ever, under any circumstances, expose her husband's weaknesses, defects of character; and

12. In general, be willing to accept a subordinate wife role because not to do so would endanger her husband's status and potential for promotion.

One wife wrote, "I'm a perfect military wife. I've already moved 35 times in my life and taken full responsibility for all the moves and the children. I accept not being allowed to pursue my own career and having to be a yo-yo of dependence and independence—being super-strong while my husband's away and acting helpless when he's back. But I cannot accept alcohol coming first, the Marines second, and me last. What should I do?"

This wife, like other military wives, was particularly bitter about the excessive use of alcohol which she felt was encouraged by the military. "The military made an alcoholic out of my husband." She was also bitter about having to downplay her husband's involvement in Vietnam. Yet she, like others, felt there were many positive aspects to being a military wife, specifically, the feeling of belonging and security. "It was fun, like being in a big family. Even in the best of families there were secrets. Mine just happened to be that my husband was a Vietnam vet. Sure I couldn't talk about Vietnam the way I wanted and sure, there were cliques but I felt like part of the group. Money was tight too, but we knew the military would meet most of our basic needs."

Some of the wives enjoyed the travel and the semi-mandatory socializing and did not mind being constantly uprooted. But they also spoke of loneliness and the loss of their personal identity. "It's hard to make friends, because you and everyone else is always moving," explains Evelyn. "Plus, when your husband is gone and you have to handle everything, you get too busy to socialize, even though there's a lot of pressure on you to do so.

"But the hardest part is not being treated like an individual. You are not yourself, but someone's wife. Your husband's rank determines your life. It's like you don't exist." Evelyn found that almost everything she did, from cashing checks to buying cleanser at the commissary, was dependent on her husband's status.

Even military wives who are wage-earning members of the military in their own right are often rendered economically dependent on their husbands by the structure of the military. In addition, military values usually place the husband's career ahead of the wife's.

Evelyn's face is lined. Although only thirty-nine, she looks much older. Before Vietnam, her career officer husband physically abused her only on Saturday nights. In fact, during the early years of their marriage, there was no abuse. But soon after their first child was born, the beatings began. Evelyn has openly shared her story in the group several times. Like the traumatized vet with PTSD, she keeps telling and retelling the sad story of her own Vietnam, hoping that perhaps if she tells it often enough, the pain will go away. Yet, like a "good military wife," she has never cried.

"I didn't know what to do when Hank started crunching my skull and punching my stomach with his fists," she explains. "I'm not a fighter and I was raised in a family where there were certain things you just didn't talk about. I didn't know you could talk to people about family problems."

The walls of their apartment on base were paper thin. Certainly the neighbors heard the beatings, but everyone, Evelyn included, joined in the conspiracy of silence which shrouded wife abuse until public exposure of the problem in recent years.

All four of Evelyn's children were born while Hank was away at training or overseas. She managed everything during his absences, but had to do a complete turnabout when he returned home. She didn't like having to do whatever he wanted, but she felt she had no choice. Her husband was "aggressive" and "possessive" and always "picking fights." He was six foot six inches tall, she, five foot two. He weighed 270 pounds; she, 104. Also, he was a trained killer.

At times Evelyn had fleeting thoughts of leaving him. "But I had four kids and no place to go. As a military dependent, I would have been destitute without him."

Once she sought help from a military counselor, who, she claims, "sloughed over" her problem, did not believe her, and advised her to stay married. "If it's that bad now, how can it get worse?" he pointed out.

But it did get worse. After Vietnam, her husband insisted that she have another child and name it after one of his dead war buddies. When Evelyn wanted to go to college instead, her husband held a knife to her throat and raped her repeatedly until she conceived. "Nobody had ever heard of marital rape then," Evelyn remembers. "Besides, he said that since I was his wife he had a right to rape me."

When she miscarried, Hank "punished" her by cutting her thirty times on the face, neck, and arms with a broken bottle. Evelyn told the military hospital personnel that she had fallen through the glass shower door. They acted as if they believed her, even though on that particular base all shower doors were plastic, not glass.

After Vietnam, her husband was tortured by nightmares and self-hate and abused not only Evelyn, but mutilated himself as well. "In 'Nam they put a rifle in his hands and told him to 'go to it.' He killed—tortured—innocent men, women, and children or maimed them for life. The minute he walked off the plane from 'Nam, I knew he had changed, that he had all that on his conscience. I begged him to go see a psychiatrist or a priest, but he wouldn't hear of it.

"After 'Nam he started going into the bathroom and trying to scald himself or drown himself in the tub. I'd stop him. Other times he'd cut his arms and legs with razor blades, not enough to kill himself, but enough to get blood everywhere. He also plucked out most of his eyelashes, threw knives at pictures of himself, and went around saying he should be tortured to death.

"Once he gave me a gun and begged me to kill him. I didn't pull the trigger, of course, but he held my hand so tight I was afraid the gun would go off anyway.

"I felt so sorry for him then. I knew the way he was wasn't all his fault. After 'Nam, he'd isolate for days too, drinking and holding me hostage. Because he was an officer, when he'd call in sick, they believed him. They didn't know he was sitting on me in the living room for hours and not letting me go to the bathroom or take care of the kids.

"My three older children knew to go to a neighbor's house whenever he was into one of his moods. But my three-year-old was still around, in his room playing mostly. But every now and then he would come out and ask what we were doing on the floor. 'Daddy and Mommy are arm wrestling,' I'd say.

"There were other bizarre things too, like his insisting we make love with the lights on and the doors open, even when the kids were around, or opening the windows when it was below zero and making me freeze with him—or else."

Evelyn tried to talk to Hank's parents, but they were military and didn't want to face the fact that their son had PTSD and an alcohol problem. Evelyn approached her husband's commanding officer, asking him to urge her husband to seek help. But the commanding officer said that since her husband was an officer, he could not become involved and that if Evelyn continued to expose her husband's many problems, she would severely damage his military career.

For two years after her husband returned from Vietnam, Evelyn describes him as "unbalanced." There were two sides to her husband, the bad and the good. He could be so very loving and kind to her and the children, but then, turn around and choke her, or their youngest son, for wetting the bed, or any other reason that came up. This child also had a learning disability which the father could not tolerate, or accept. When the child abuse became severe and Hank continued to refuse help, Evelyn finally packed her bags and left.

Evelyn was one of the few members of the Vet Center women's group who was already separated upon coming to group. She came to group seeking greater understanding of PTSD and hoping to find ways of helping her husband, even though she was planning to divorce him. She was also seeking help for herself as she was coming out of her own numbing.

The extent of wife abuse in the military is unknown. Certain factors, common in the military, however, seem to affect the frequency and severity of abuse. Sociologist Murray Strauss, found wife abuse to be more prevalent among families with 2 to 5 children and among families experiencing financial stress, frequent moves or separations, and isolation from peer and family support systems.[1]

According to a recent Army Family Advocacy Progress report, the majority of both military battered wives (some 65%) and military who batter (some 70%) are between 21-30 years old.[2] Furthermore, high school graduates are more likely to be spouse abusers than men with either more or less education.[3] With over half of all servicemen having a high school education and military training emphasizing the use of violence, the military wife is at a high risk for battering.

Yet official military statistics indicate a very low rate of spouse abuse (.6 per 1000 per year) and do not differentiate between families of Vietnam veterans and other military families. The rate is higher for overseas families (5%), probably due to the stresses associated with overseas postings.[4] Most experts, however, both within and outside the military, feel that these statistics grossly underestimate the extent of the problem.[5]

According to an Army Family Advocacy report, "The relationship between official reports and the actual incidence of spousal maltreatment is unknown."[6] As Dr. Beryce MacLennan of the Government Accounting Office points out, one of the major problems in estimating the extent of family violence in the military is the fact that although each branch of the military and the Department of Defense have a reporting system, the systems are inconsistent. Furthermore, "families, service providers and military personnel may be reluctant to identify or report domestic violence."[7]

If the civilian wife is reluctant to report abuse, due to shame, guilt, or fear of retaliation, how much more so the military battered wife? So often she desperately fears that reporting the abuse will jeopardize not only her husband's career, but her own financial security as a military dependent as well.

To avoid such consequences, many battered military wives do not seek help or turn to civilian resources instead. These civilian service centers, however, are under no obligation to report to the military and rarely do so.[8]

In perhaps the most exhaustive study of wife abuse in the Armed Forces completed to date, researchers West, Turner, and Dunwoody of the Center for Women Policy Studies in Washington, D.C., found that many cases of abuse go unreported because emergency room staff typically do not ask women if their injuries are the result of abuse.[9]

At the command level, there may be deliberate underreporting due to the stigma associated with abuse. According to Dr. MacLennan, "Chiefs of staff may not wish to give the impression that service life brutalizes individuals or places great stress on families or that their service has more violence than another."[10]

Like their civilian sisters, many military wives do not report abuse, because, on some level, they feel they "deserved it" or because they are not even aware that they are being abused. Unless the abuse is frequent and severe, they feel it doesn't "count." Yet under the UCMJ (Uniform Code of Military Justice) as under most state laws, it is a crime not only to abuse one's wife, but to threaten to do so. Although UCMJ does not consider spousal rape or indecent assault with the intent to rape punishable offenses, charges for forcible sodomy can be brought against abusive husbands under military law.[11]

According to Sharon Sauter, MSW, Family Advocacy Officer for the Air Force, domestic violence programs for abused military wives have grown "tremendously" in the past five years. The problem today is not so much that services do not exist, but that military wives are still reluctant to report abuse or do not know where to start in seeking assistance. In addition, many wives still mistakenly believe that the violence will cease on its own, without outside intervention.

The old days, when military men could get by with almost murdering their wives, are gone. While abusers are not always apprehended, anti-battering laws are on the books and in many cases are enforced, especially when the battering involves child abuse or child sexual assault.[12] Commanders can be charged for failing to conduct an inquiry into a battered military wife's complaint.

In fact, there is such growing awareness of the problem that Commander Robert D. McCullah recently stated in *Wife Abuse in the Armed Forces* that the "stresses among military personnel can compromise our nation's defense posture."[13] In the West study, numerous military officers at a variety of bases voiced considerable concern about the detrimental effect of domestic violence on the serviceman's efficiency and on "morale and military readiness" in general.[14]

According to Chaplain E.A. Orlander, CHS, USN, who directed a successful batterer rehabilitation program at the Marine Corps Barrack at Camp Lejuene, North Carolina, "Marines who experience healthy nonviolent relationships at home are more likely to perform their greatest potential on the job."[15] Recent directives from the Commandant of the Marine Corps emphasize that spouse abuse is inconsistent with the high personal and professional standards of the Marines.[16]

In general, military wives, like Evelyn, have appeared less disconcerted and disappointed by their husbands' numbing and other symptoms of PTSD than nonmilitary wives because, as military wives, they had learned to expect less from marriage than other women.

Furthermore, during years of adapting to their husbands' many absences and the family's frequent relocations, many of the military wives had learned to become relatively emotionally self-sufficient. Often, the military wife's strengths and self-reliance make her more tolerant of emotional distance and lack of communication within her marriage, more accepting of her husband's alcohol or drug addiction or his sexual flings, as well as of his PTSD.

Kitty, for example, was born in a small town in Kentucky. Her high school sweetheart, William, decided to join the military rather than fight a futile battle against the poverty of Appalachia. When he found out that he was going to be sent to Vietnam, he and Kitty married immediately as part of the glamour of a soldier going off to war.

William never talked about his Vietnam experiences, but going overseas was a culture shock for him. He had never been outside Kentucky and was naive in many ways. Although his Vietnam experience eroded many of his illusions about patriotism and about becoming a John Wayne, he decided to make the military his life. His only other option, he felt, was to join the unemployment lines in his home town or settle for a low-paying, dead-end job like his father had.

As they traveled from base to base, Kitty was not only William's emotional support system, but his only tie to his past. There were only a few signs of PTSD until, some ten years after the war, William decided to quit the Army. He was "fed up" with taking orders and had developed an intense hatred for one of his commanding officers. However, when William left the military, he began to experience some of the symptoms of PTSD more frequently, especially the nightmares. Since the military provides a supportive structure for military values, often men who served in Vietnam do not experience PTSD symptoms until they leave the military.

All along Kitty had not expected much emotionally from William. When she became a military wife, her rural tradition of female self-reliance and passivity matched perfectly with the military's expectations for wives. When William became depressed, or abusive, Kitty did not go into shock. Growing up in an economically depressed area, she was used to unhappy, frustrated men, some of whom felt free to lash out at their wives. In her home town, for example, wife beating was almost accepted and, as in many rural areas, there were few resources for abused women.

"You just don't talk about it," was the rule. The same rule applied in the military. Consequently, when William sometimes hit her, Kitty thought that hitting was a "normal part of marriage" which she was powerless, or had no right, to stop.

Another taboo subject was mental illness or emotional trouble. These were not talked about in Kitty's home town, or on base. Even while William was in the military and not at the height of his PTSD suffering, Kitty had noticed a few signs of emotional problems. Yet neither she nor William dared to break the taboo and seek help. Whenever she brought the subject up, William would go to bed or for a long walk.

Today William is back home in Kentucky—alone. Kitty is in college in a nearby state, pursuing a career of her choice, a career which she had postponed many times due to the military and her husband's problems. She now suffers from the fatigue, loneliness, and other hardships common to struggling single mothers. Yet she is certain that she did not want to resign herself to the limitations of her small town in Kentucky, nor to the limitations of a marriage with a husband whose long periods of emotional numbing were peppered with angry outbursts.

Even though Kitty is now divorced, she comes to group to better understand, and accept, what happened to her high school sweetheart. She also wants to better understand, and accept, herself—all of herself, even her fears and insecurities. While some women have difficulty accepting their strengths, Kitty has the opposite problem, accepting her feelings of helplessness and powerlessness. Since she was taught—by both her upbringing and the military—to keep such feelings to herself, it has been difficult for her to accept that at times she feels vulnerable or overloaded. She is afraid of being thought "weak."

"I'm supposed to be strong all the time," she says. "In my home town, women were supposed to take anything—the cold, the heat, the poverty, and even abuse—without complaining. I found the same expectations in the military. I had to 'hang tough' no matter what and accept whatever my husband was, or did. Now I feel I don't have to accept everything that comes my way, especially any threats or physical abuse."

Like Kitty, all but one of the military wives who have attended group report physical abuse as part of their marriages. However, like Kitty, in most instances the abuse was intermittent and confined to a few, significant episodes. In a few cases, when the wife was in the military herself, she physically fought back.

Helen exemplifies the contradiction of a military wife who is a high-ranking officer in her own right, but who, at home is still "the wife." Yet Helen's submissive behavior at home, in contrast to her assertive behavior at work, is not truly a contradiction. As Del Martin explains in *Battered Women: Issues of Public Policy*, most women are "socialized to believe that their greatest achievement in life is marriage and motherhood and that failure of the marriage is the wife's personal failure."[17] A woman can easily hold a position of power and authority at work, but at home quickly resume the subordinate role for which she has been psychosocialized from a young age.

Helen is now head of a Triage unit. After Vietnam, her husband collapsed into an infantile dependent role. He gladly did the dishes while she went to work. Every now and then he would attempt to work, but the stress from the job, combined with his PTSD, was too much for him.

At home, Helen's husband is restless. He expects her to be there for him, when he wants her, leaving her little time for herself. Yet he is rarely concerned with her needs, or so it seems to Helen, except for those rare, but treasured moments, when it is obvious that he needs and cherishes her above all other human beings.

Helen resents her husband expecting her to be superwoman; to be able to handle the job, the home, the children, and him, with no breaks, and no complaints. But she also holds these expectations for herself and admits to being her own worst critic.

When Helen first came to group, she tried to help everyone else. She had done much reading on PTSD and spoke a strong feminist line. She was quick to tell other women not to "put up with it," and to put themselves, not their husbands and children, first for a change. She was also able to deeply feel the other women's anger and pain, but rarely acknowledged her own.

Helen had been a military wife before she decided to join the military herself. While her husband was in Vietnam (he served for two tours), she was busy advancing in rank. After Vietnam, her husband left the military, but he did not object to Helen continuing her military career. As both a military wife and a woman in a largely male dominated group, she was trained, and expected to be strong and independent, to hide her needs from others, especially her needs to be taken care of, to be protected, and to feel loved.

In her mind, as in the mind of many in the military, such needs were signs of "weakness" and cause for "shame." Furthermore, as a child, she had been punished for showing her feelings and dependency needs. In her heart of hearts, however, even though she was almost forty and considered herself quite liberated, she did want to lean on someone, "just a little bit." While she was extremely helpful and encouraging to the other women in group, taking their phone calls in the middle of the night, for example, Helen rarely called on the other women, or me, for support.

"If you can handle everything yourself, why do you come to group?" a group member once asked her.

Helen grudgingly admitted that she too, needed help, and that having to be strong all the time had made her bitter and hard. Yet she saw no alternative to being an "iron woman." The standards which she felt imposed on her by the military were now a part of herself. She was jealous of the women in group who could cry, feel sorry for themselves, and express fears of "going crazy" or "falling apart."

"I want to be a basket case too, but I can't allow myself any of that," she explained. "I rigidly put my nose to the grindstone, day after day. There's no softness in me, no vulnerability. I don't like what I've become, but it isn't all my fault. Circumstances, like being a military wife, a wife of a Vietnam combat vet, and a military officer, have forced me to be like this.

"If I act any differently, femininely I call it, I'll be mocked at work. Also, it puts too much pressure on my husband if I show him I have needs. He can't take it when I have needs. He's the only one allowed to have needs. Yet I know that inside me there's a little girl aching to be held, aching to play. But I can't let her out. She has a lot of tears too, but she's not allowed to cry."

For the most part Helen continued to be as unselfish in group as she was in her personal life, rarely taking any group time to discuss her concerns. Once, however, the group encouraged her to take some of her own advice: focus on herself and plan some ways of nurturing herself which were not dependent on her husband. The most she could come up with were to insist on not being woken up in the middle of the night to hear war stories about Vietnam and on going to the grocery store only once a week, not whenever her husband or children needed something. Helen also decided to take some vacations by herself and to reconnect with relatives and old friends. After over a year in group, Helen also made some progress in accepting her dependency needs and feelings of helplessness as inevitable aspects of being human, rather than signs of personal failure.

Helen decided to confront her husband about two instances of physical abuse from the past. While her husband was not generally abusive, nor did she particularly anticipate any more beatings, she made it clear that she had changed from the time he first assaulted her. Then she had accepted the abuse without comment, not even going to the hospital when she needed to because he felt it would have endangered his military career. But now he had to "listen up"-—should he ever lay a hand on her again, if he did not seek help immediately and stay in therapy until he learned to control his aggressiveness, she would be gone, taking her children and her paycheck with her.

Summary

Military Vietnam wives are often strangled by the expectation that they be silent heroines and unacknowledged pillars of strength. They also tend to suffer from isolation when they encounter disparagement of Vietnam veterans or a lack of understanding of PTSD within the military. If their husbands are alcoholic or abusive, their isolation may be extreme. Since drinking tends to be accepted in the military, the military wife must often bear the brunt of her husband's alcoholic behavior alone. Similarly, if she is being abused, she may feel she must endure this to protect her husband's image. In recent years, however, there has been an increase in services available to the abused military wife.

The military wife is used to managing the household, rearing the children, and coping with all the daily crises of living. Since these responsibilities are a part of her role as a military wife, when and if her husband does not take part in these tasks as a result of his PTSD, she may accept that as natural.

She may be accustomed to a marriage where her emotional needs are not always met. The frequent travel and other separations that are part of military life have often forced the military wife to meet her emotional needs by herself or deny them. This geographic instability also hinders her from establishing friendships and other roots and increases her dependence on her husband at the same time it prevents her husband from being physically present, much less emotionally available.

When this isolation is compounded by the emotional numbing that is part of PTSD, the military Vietnam wife may feel and actually be, exceptionally emotionally alone. If she has internalized the 'strong woman' norms demanded of military wives, she may be reluctant to admit to her loneliness or to any of her other emotional distresses. All wives of men with PTSD have a stressful existence. Military wives, however, bear an especially difficult burden.

Nine

Wives of Black and Hispanic Vietnam Veterans

Coping with PTSD is like coping with racism. You need a lot of faith and a lot of hope because it's a constant uphill battle. As the wife of a Black combat veteran, I know my husband is blighted with two ills—PTSD and an intense rage at the racism in our society—the racism which burned Black homes while he was burning Vietnamese ones fighting for America and the racism that kept him from getting a job when he got back to America.

When Graham got off the plane after serving two tours of duty in Vietnam and went out to celebrate with his buddies, he was refused service at the restaurant. The manager even gave him the finger. Graham's white buddies were ready to pounce on the manager but Graham wouldn't let them. At the next restaurant they went to, Graham was served dirty water in a greasy glass and a beer with spit in it.

I found out about these incidents years later. Like so many Vietnam veterans, my husband never talked about his experiences. I only heard about them when his nightmares got out of control and he had to seek help. I don't know why he didn't tell me sooner. Maybe he thought we had enough problems or maybe he was trying to protect me.

I, like many Black Vietnam wives, am also a child of the 50s. The 50s, for the most part, were better times *economically for Blacks. Many Black fathers were able to work two jobs. They were paid less than a white with one job, but with their wives' income, many Black families, like mine, lived comfortably. By Black pre-integration standards that is.*

Today, as a Black woman of the 80s, I expect and want financial and emotional security, just like a white woman. But PTSD has damaged my husband's ability to feel, and racism has destroyed his peace of mind. Unfortunately, when he's angry, his enemy no longer has a face or name. Since I'm the only one around, sometimes he blames me for the 'system' or for what somebody in the war did or didn't do. I can tell when he's angry because he totally shuts down and withdraws from me.

Like last week. Someone walked into my husband's office and asked to speak to the manager. When my husband said that he was the manager, the person said, 'No, I want to talk to the real manager.'

I asked my husband if he was upset by this incident. 'No, no, it's okay,' he said. But I know he's upset and hurt and doesn't know what or who to blame—the system or himself.

When the white women in group talk about their husbands, I understand because I feel that way too. In a lot of ways, our marriage problems are the same. Yet I'm different. As a Black woman, I have borne the brunt of both racism and sexism. My husband is different too. He had a double dose of rejection; first by the whites and second by the Blacks who thought he was a traitor for fighting the Vietnamese when he should have stayed home and fought for civil rights.

I'm also different in that I never expected a life of luxury. I expected to work both before and after marriage and childbirth. Having to work was a given, not a blessing, not a tragedy, just a given. For example, in college I was one of only eight Blacks on campus. I wanted to go to college to get a decent job. My friends—the white ones—had no intention of working after marriage. The only one who was serious about education as a means to a job was one girl whose widowed mother had had to work to support the family.

My conflict today is not accepting that I have to work, but harmonizing my independence and self-reliance with my marriage. The idea of female dependence, which has come out in the last twenty years, is something totally new to me. It was my family tradition and my church that instilled in me the ability and the willingness to work to improve my situation.

So here I am, trying to be a Black woman of the 80s with all these trends and at the same time struggling with Graham's PTSD. I know what my goal is. I want more sharing, financially, emotionally, and sexually, in my marriage.

Wife of a Black combat vet

Bessie Taylor had three sons, Ross, Mitchell, and Sam. Although she worked long hours for not much over the minimum wage, she considered herself fortunate. For her, changing sheets and sweeping floors at a class B hotel in East St. Louis, Missouri was one step above tilling her sharecropper parents' fields just outside Birmingham, Alabama.

Her husband, Gus, was a janitor. But Bessie knew her Gus was more than a janitor. During World War II, her Gus, like many Blacks, had served valiantly (in a segregated unit, however). Gus had wanted to make the military his life, but after he saw white soldiers being given preferential medical treatment on the battlefield and experiencing color prejudice in other ways, he decided to quit the military as soon as the war was over. Furthermore, during his military career, he was accused of not being a "real American" because he was Black and had slightly Oriental features. Gus was the frequent butt of racial jokes. In addition, he had never received his well-deserved, often promised promotion.[1]

However, Gus hid his bitterness and neither he, nor Bessie, was "anti-American" at all. In fact, they were very patriotic. While they didn't like racism, they accepted it as inevitable and raised their three sons to be God-fearing loyal citizens.

In 1959, when their oldest son, Ross, decided to pursue a career in the military, neither parent objected. The position of Blacks in the military had improved since World War II. Although racism was far from dead, in general, the military was now more integrated than ever before. Blacks were even being allowed into the Marine Corps.[2]

After the bombing of North Vietnam in 1965, Ross was sent to Vietnam. Every night Bessie Taylor prayed on her knees that her son would return alive. The entire congregation of her church prayed with her, for they all knew that at that time 25% of the American death toll in Vietnam was Black.[3] In contrast, young Blacks constituted only 11% of the American population.

Some claimed that this disproportionately high Black death rate was the result of Black soldiers, like Ross, who heroically volunteered for combat duty. Others, however, attributed the Black death toll to racism.[4] Both radical and not so radical Black groups claimed that "Blacks were being drafted for genocidal purposes. Just to get rid of...the Black male."[5] This message was echoed by Hanoi Helen, a North Vietnamese broadcaster who appealed to Black soldiers to go home because, in her view, the American involvement in Vietnam was a racist capitalist plot to eliminate Blacks.[6]

In 1965, the Black death rate was so high that the Pentagon purposely reduced the number of Black soldiers on the front line.[7] But this did not quell the Taylors' fear for Ross. When Mitchell wanted to follow in his brother's footsteps and enlist, the Taylors said "no!"

At that time as part of the war on poverty, the military was actively encouraging Blacks to join. In fact, during the mid-sixties, Blacks were being "massively recruited." For many young Black men, the military offered relatively fewer obstacles to economic and social advancement than other careers and occupations. Great numbers of Black youth "responded to the call."[8]

Despite his parents' objections, Mitchell desperately wanted to join the military, not only for economic reasons, but for patriotic ones. Even though Blacks had been mistreated in America, Mitchell loved America and believed in the cause of freedom and democracy. His parents agreed with him philosophically, but they still begged him not to join, especially since Ross had signed up for a second year in Vietnam.

Mitchell obeyed their wishes, made plans to marry, and began working in a print shop.

One month before the assassination of the Rev. Dr. Martin Luther King Jr., Ross Taylor was shot to death, not by the V.C., but by "friendly fire." The Taylors were not given this information, however. Instead they received a letter announcing their son's death as a hero.

Gus Taylor pulled his hair, cursed God, and burned the letter, along with his Bible and all his souvenirs from World War II. Bessie Taylor also pulled her hair, but she would not curse God. Instead she prayed to understand the "reason" for her son's death, which only further enraged her husband.

Meanwhile, Mitchell rushed down to the Marine recruiting office and signed up for combat duty in Vietnam. There was no stopping him now. Even if his parents continued to oppose him, he would go to Vietnam and kill as many "gooks" as he could find to avenge his brother's death. Also, being one of the first Black Marines seemed far more glamorous to Mitchell than pushing cartons in a print shop where he was often called "boy."

Mitchell quickly married his fiance, Sandra, and shortly thereafter, with his mother's Bible in his pocket, landed in Vietnam, unconsciously hoping to find his brother there, or at least, to discover more about how he had been killed. But the Vietnam which Mitchell encountered in late 1968 and early 1969 was not the same Vietnam as his brother had seen in 1965. Although the Black death toll was now reduced, it was still disproportionately high. As Wallace Terry, author of Bloods, points out, by 1969, career Black soldiers were being replaced by Black draftees many of whom were unwilling to adopt "Uncle Tom" roles. Due to the civil rights movement at home, especially after the assassination of Dr. Martin Luther King Jr., Black soldiers were more openly disgruntled about racism in the military than ever before. When they observed discrimination in positioning, medals, decorations, and promotions, many spoke out.[9]

As a result, they were often given "bad paper," that is, less than honorable discharges. In fact, "Blacks received a grossly disproportionate number of dishonorable or 'bad paper' discharges," which negatively affected their veteran's benefits and career opportunities upon return home.[10]

Furthermore, there were numerous racial incidents, not so much on the front lines, but in the rear.[11] As Dr. Allen, a Black psychiatrist explains, "Conflict was expressed through graffiti, segregation, fraggings, and fights. For many men it was as if there two wars—one against the enemy and the other against other Americans."[12]

Some racial incidents occurred during basic training when Black soldiers heard the Vietnamese people being ridiculed, belittled, and dehumanized as "gooks" who only deserved to be killed.[13] Some of the racial epithets and slurs used against the Vietnamese were strikingly familiar to those used against Blacks. The slogan, "The only good gook is a dead one," was all too similar to "The only good nigger is a dead one."

But Mitchell closed his ears to the voices of Black militancy. His goal was to avenge his brother's death. He jumped into combat with a ferocity which earned him much respect. In the jungles of Vietnam, Mitchell became close with many of his comrades, regardless of their race. He even became friends with a card-carrying member of the Klu Klux Klan, who changed his view of Blacks after seeing Mitchell risk his life to save a white comrade.

When Mitchell's unit encountered mutilated American bodies (both Black and white), they sometimes retaliated with the indiscriminate killing of civilians and livestock, other pointless destruction, the raping of Vietnamese women, and other violent acts. Although this violated Mitchell's religious upbringing, by now he was so psychically numb, that he ignored the Bible in his pocket. He joined in the violence without thought—until he and his unit reached a village where some of the peasants had fuller features and darker skin than other Vietnamese groups.

As Mitchell's buddies forced a peasant to unearth his hidden rice and other food supplies, Mitchell remembered how in Alabama the KKK had forced his grandmother to dig up some of her hidden produce and belongings. And when Mitchell's buddies began to rape the peasant's curly haired, full lipped daughter (who reminded Mitchell of his wife) and forced the weeping peasant to watch, Mitchell remembered that his grandparents were poor peasants too. Furthermore, he had heard stories of how Black men had had to endure the torture of watching their sisters, mothers, and wives be assaulted by marauding whites. "What if that was my mother, or my Sandra?" he thought.

"Come on, Mitchell. Join in. What's wrong with you? Are you a faggot?" his friends called.

Despite his new awareness, Mitchell did not have the strength to resist the group. But when the peasants were about to be shot, Mitchell urged his friends to go shoot some water buffalo instead.

Full of self-hate, Mitchell threw his mother's Bible down the village well, which had just been poisoned by the American troops. Shaking with anxiety, he wanted to scoop up some of the poisoned water and drink it. But in her last letter, Sandra had informed him that he was now the father of twin boys. Mitchell decided to live, not for himself, nor for Sandra, whom he doubted he could ever love again, but for his two boys, one of whom was named after his dead brother, Ross.

Sandra's letter had also stated that his brother, Sam, had recently been arrested for simply driving through an all-white neighborhood in suburban St. Louis, probably due to his participation in a civil rights rally. Furthermore, the home of one of Sandra's relatives had just been bombed.

Sitting at the well, frozen with pain, Mitchell began to ask himself the same questions many Black soldiers asked themselves: "What am I doing here? Why am I killing and hurting people who look more like me than the people who are hurting my relatives and friends back home?"[14]

As numerous studies have shown, compared to white Vietnam veterans, Black Vietnam veterans suffer not only from higher rates of PTSD, but tend to have endured postwar stress symptoms for longer periods of time since the war.[15] The significantly greater readjustment problems of Black Vietnam veterans can be attributed to the fact that they have had to deal with two stressors: first, the war, and secondly, racism, both in the military and back home. In addition, they have had to deal with the guilt and conflict inherent in the "gook identification" syndrome.[16]

According to psychologist Parsons, the "gook identification" syndrome is the "conscious and unconscious emotional identification by Black soldiers with the devalued, maligned, abused and helpless aspects of the Vietnamese people."[17] Even if the Black veteran did not participate in any combat or abusive violence against the Vietnamese, he often experienced a sense of shame and considerable confusion about the purpose and morality of the project he was involved with.

In general Blacks were less able to dehumanize the enemy than whites because the Vietnamese, like the Blacks, were not white, were poor, and were struggling for their independence. Black soldiers could also identify with the "tribulations, misery, and general suffering of the Vietnamese at the hands of a super power."[18] Research has found that Black soldiers were more likely to express positive or neutral feelings toward the Vietnamese than white soldiers, were more likely to oppose the war, and were more emotionally disturbed by abusive violence and atrocities committed against the Vietnamese than were whites.[19]

For example, during his tour of duty, Mitchell encountered barracks decorated with the Confederate flag and GIs from other units who called him "boy" or "nigger." He was tempted to fight these other soldiers, but remembering his goals, held back. After returning to the U.S., he also encountered the Confederate flag, this time behind the desk of the first employer from whom he sought work.

"I had been promised the job over the phone, but the minute the manager saw my face, he decided he didn't really need any more help right then," Mitchell explains.

As Mitchell went from one job interview to the next, encountering one subtle form of racism after another, he remembered some little boys he had seen in Vietnam. They would run from one GI to the next, trying to sell their mothers, or their sisters. Oh, how he used to laugh at them. "Animals, yellow animals," he secretly thought.

But now on the streets himself, almost begging for work, Mitchell felt that he was in the same position as those beggar boys. Mitchell's guilt about having hurt Vietnamese people was only compounded when a Black employer refused to hire him because he had gone off to Vietnam and "killed his own kind." At times Mitchell felt that admitting that he was a Vietnam vet was like building the very gallows on which he could be hung.

Nevertheless, according to General Westmoreland, and W. Terry, the service of Black troops in Vietnam was superior.[20] However, Black troops, like white troops, seldom received a hero's welcome and, like their white counterparts, they often returned home to families that did not want to hear about the war. In addition, some Black Vietnam veterans had to deal with the taunts and rejection of those Blacks who believed that Blacks who fought in Vietnam had betrayed their race by participating in a "white man's war," a war that was not only immoral, but illegal.

At the same time, employers were sometimes reluctant to hire the Black Vietnam veteran, not only for racial reasons, but because he had served in Vietnam and was therefore, potentially dangerous. To compound the problem, unemployment was higher in most areas than when the vet had left for Vietnam, especially if he had come from an economically deprived neighborhood. Studies completed in 1969 and 1970 showed that Black Vietnam vets had double the unemployment rate of white Vietnam veterans or earned substantially less.[21]

Terry concludes, "...What can be said about the dysfunction of Vietnam veterans in general can be doubled in its impact upon most Blacks; they hoped to come home to more than they had before;

they came back to less....The doors to the Great Society had been shut."[22]

Even before Mitchell returned from Vietnam and began to scream from nightmares, turning to alcohol in order to sleep, Sandra knew there was no such thing as a "handsome Black knight" who would whisk her away from the realities of life into a land of bliss. Although she was pumped with the same romantic mythology as the white women in the group—that the "right man" would fill her life with excitement and meet all of her needs, Sandra was also raised in a tradition where most of the women worked and often functioned as the major, if not the sole, support of the family, both emotionally and financially.

Throughout American history, for a variety of reasons, Black men often found it difficult, if not impossible, to find meaningful or productive work. Many could not find any work at all. The Black woman, however, could almost always find work in white people's houses or in other low-paying, dead-end jobs.

Black women, however, suffered from a "double jeopardy." They were both Black and female.[23] Like many women, they were often paid less than men for the same work or relegated to jobs without

1984 Median Earnings

Year Round Full-Time Workers

All women	14,780	All men	23,218
White women	14,904	White men	23,962
Black women	13,720	Black men	16,940

Table 1

any possibility of advancement. As late as 1984, the Women's Bureau of the U.S. Department of Labor reports: "As has been the case historically, women are still concentrated in low paying jobs. Thus, the average woman earns only 64 cents for every dollar earned by the average man when both work year round full time," with Black women earning less than white men, white women, or Black men.[24]

(See Table 1) Some three years later (1987), women advanced to making 68 cents for every dollar earned by a man, with female college graduates and male high school dropouts earning roughly the same annual salary.[25]

In sum, "despite their increasing educational attainment and their strong continued labor force experience, Black women are still more likely than white women to be unemployed, to be in low paying jobs, and to account for a larger proportion of the poor."[26]

Sandra's mother, for example, supported a husband and four children on the salary of a laundress. Although Sandra's father sought work, East St. Louis was an economically depressed area and he could only find work sporadically. Like many of her neighbors, Sandra's mother accepted her role as prime, and sometimes, sole support of the family and as emotional caretaker of the family. As research has shown, despite the Black woman's historical work role, she often seeks to fulfill her family role in a traditionally feminine manner.[27]

Sandra's mother maintained her courage and strength through her faith and involvement in the church, where she was somebody important, director of the choir, not "just a maid." She was not anti-male, but she taught all her daughters not to put their faith in men, but in themselves and in a spiritual being. She also warned her daughters to never give up all their money to a man, but keep some of their earnings for themselves.

Sandra was brought up in the church and she believed deeply. But she did not want to live her mother's life, struggling for every nickel and dime. In Mitchell she saw an ambition and determination which matched her own. When he asked her to marry him, she immediately agreed, even though she was only nineteen and had hopes of going to college. She never dreamt Mitchell would lose his ambition, as well as his faith, in Vietnam.

The arrival of twin sons destroyed her plans for schooling, but not her dream of social and economic advancement. While Mitchell was in Vietnam, she worked as a salesgirl, never expecting not to work just because she had babies. In group, Sandra, like the other Black women, never expressed the deep guilt which some of the white women have felt about leaving their children to work outside the home. While the Black women regarded their maternal role as primary and had some home-career conflicts, they were of a different order of magnitude than the conflicts of the white women. Somehow, the

Black women, probably due to their historical role as workers, experienced their work role as less "abnormal" or "deviant."

Sandra worked hard, caught on quickly, and, as a result of the increased opportunities made available to minorities in the early 70s, slowly advanced to a supervisory position. When the department store went so far as to open up their managerial training to Blacks, Sandra was the first to enroll and quickly rose to the position of manager of several departments.

But Sandra did not mention her vocational achievements to Mitchell. Nor did she tell him when she began to make more money than he. She kept part of her earnings in a secret account. She did not feel she was being deceptive: she simply did not want to insult Mitchell's masculinity.

During the civil rights movement, Sandra had been exposed to Black liberation ideology and other ideologies which analyzed how the Black man had been crippled, if not "castrated" by society.[28] Sometimes it was forgotten that the Black woman had also been persecuted and "castrated" and she was viewed as the "matriarch" who was also a "castrator of Black men."[29] Sandra did not want to fall into that category, especially since her husband had once implied that she was able to maintain her job only because she was "high yellow" and because she was willing to act subservient to whites.

True, Sandra did overlook some of the racial slurs that came her way. But she did so not out of meekness, but out of self-interest. Her goal was economic advancement and security. She wanted to move her family out of their roach-infested apartment in East St. Louis to something better. In Sandra's view, there was nothing to be gained by "acting touchy" and fighting a losing battle against the system.

Furthermore, in her case, the system had not treated her as harshly as it had her husband. She had been able to take advantage of some of the doors opened to Blacks in the 70s. In contrast, her husband, embittered by Vietnam, angrily refused to use his veteran's educational and medical benefits.

During the war, Mitchell was run over by an army jeep whose driver, high on drugs, had lost control of his vehicle. Mitchell's skull was fractured. He lay in a coma for several weeks. Upon reviving, he had lost much of his memory. Three years and seven operations later, Mitchell's memory and other mental abilities were restored. There was no evidence of the accident save for slight nervous tremors.

When he applied for compensation, the doctors were divided. Half attributed the tremors to his military experience; half, to his drinking. In addition, Mitchell's military records were burned in a St. Louis fire. After these experiences, Mitchell vowed never again to ask the government for help.

When Sandra wanted to leave the slums of East St. Louis, Mitchell objected. How could they afford a home across the river? Sandra lied. She told Mitchell that her mother had given her the down payment for the home. Mitchell knew it was a lie, but he did not contradict Sandra. He argued that, as man of the house, he didn't want any handouts from her family, just like he didn't want any handouts from the government. But Sandra felt they had to move for the sake of the children and Mitchell relented.

After recovering from his last operation, Mitchell worked full time but his career advancement was hampered by his depression. Even though he had a high I.Q., he could not think beyond showing up at work on time, doing what he had to do, then going home to drink and forget it all. Basically, Mitchell hated his job. He was acutely aware of every form of racial discrimination, both subtle or overt. In Sandra's view, he sometimes "imagined" discriminatory incidents or remarks and "made mountains out of molehills." In Mitchell's view, Sandra was naive.

Furthermore, Mitchell could not identify with those Blacks in his office whom he felt fit the stereotype of the Black male as "shiftless and lazy." He especially could not tolerate Blacks who had not been politicized through some major experience with discrimination and who saw him as "too serious," as "thinking too much," or as "living in the past." In addition, Mitchell felt avoided by both Blacks and whites. Mitchell felt that they were all afraid of him because they knew he was a combat vet.

A major issue in Sandra and Mitchell's marriage was money. Even though Mitchell's drinking was not yet interfering with his work performance, alcohol was becoming an increasingly large item on the family's budget. Mitchell drank alone, but he also drank at a local bar, where he liked to treat others, especially other Vietnam veterans. He also liked to send extravagant gifts to his parents and his brother Ross's widow.

Sandra smoldered at the bills, but said nothing. She knew that when he treated his war buddies or sent gifts to relatives, he felt powerful, like a "real man." "I can't take that away from him," she'd say in group, until the day she discovered that there wasn't enough money for the basic bills.

At this point, Sandra felt she had to take action, but she could not confront her husband. Although she obviously "wore the pants" in the family, and Mitchell would do whatever she wanted, she did not want to "castrate" him or "emasculate" him by restricting the amount of money he could spend on liquor or on gifts to his relatives.

As usual, whenever she felt "stuck," between her role as family caretaker and her role of submissive wife, she decided to pray about what to do. Sandra prayed about almost everything, especially Mitchell's healing. She was certain that if only she prayed hard enough, Mitchell would eventually seek treatment for his alcoholism and his PTSD. Meanwhile, she was doubling up on her church activities, not only for purposes of spiritual growth, but because the church helped fill many of her other needs. Although she rarely admitted it, Sandra was lonely. Mitchell left her alone much of the time and church helped fill her emotional and social needs, as well as her spiritual ones.

While some Black veterans emerged from their Vietnam experience with a renewed and deepened faith in God or a Higher Power, others, like Mitchell, became cynical and suffered from a deep spiritual despair.[30] Mitchell refused to attend church with Sandra, or with his mother. He never participated in grace at family meal time, nor would he tuck the children in bed because prayers were said, which greatly angered Sandra.

Eventually Mitchell stopped eating with the family and Sandra moved out of the bedroom. His screaming and sobbing during nightmares kept her up at night. Also, she did not like to be with him while he was drinking. While she rarely refused him sex, she did not want to put herself in a position where sex would be "automatic."

Sandra took her sons to church often, for religious purposes, but because also she felt that her sons would be exposed to many "strong" Black men there, men with a positive outlook on life. Mitchell objected. He did not want his sons to be "brainwashed." But this argument, like most others between Sandra and Mitchell, ended in a stalemate.

Sandra and Mitchell rarely talked. While Sandra was able to express her feelings, Mitchell could not relate to her on an emotional level. He could share with his mother, however, and with some of his female cousins. Sandra resented that he would not open to her and that she knew very little about her husband's Vietnam experience.

But she felt it would not be productive to press Mitchell or insist that he talk to her.

Although Sandra and Mitchell had little emotional communication, they did have frequent verbal conflicts over money and sex, with Mitchell wanting more sex and no limitations on his spending. But these conflicts masked the more complex psychological problems and power struggles between them.

Mitchell wanted to assert himself as head of the household. However, after seeing how women were treated in Vietnam, he did not want to bully his wife. Furthermore, he had utmost respect for Sandra. She had been faithful to him during his absence, had nursed him through his years of surgery, and had been a good wife and mother as well as an excellent provider.

Sandra also represented to him the spirituality which he had lost. Although Mitchell had given up on God, the second before he was hit by the jeep in Vietnam, he had prayed for help. Sandra told her church friends that it was a miracle that Mitchell had not been killed. But Mitchell reminded her that he had prayed for his brother Ross and Ross died anyway. So had many others died despite the prayers of their relatives. Actually, Mitchell didn't know what to believe about God. Yet a small part of him wished to regain his former faith. Hence he clung to Sandra and did not want to oppose her.

Sandra, on the other hand, was hesitant to leave Mitchell because she knew that Black women outnumbered Black men to such an extent that if she left Mitchell, she might never remarry or find another man. Yet, painful as it would be, she knew she could make it on her own, without one. Besides, Mitchell was but a "shadow" in her life anyway. In addition, she had tasted the power of self-determination. She was not only a successful mother, but a successful career woman. Her major problem was that while she was clearly "in charge" at home, she felt she had to act dependent and submissive for the sake of her husband's ego and her sons' developing masculine egos. If she "castrated" her husband, she would also be "castrating" her sons. Also, she did not want to see her husband go "down the tubes."

On the other hand, she felt morally responsible to protect her sons from their father's cynicism and negativity and the family's budget from the potentially ruinous effects of alcoholism.

Like many of the military wives who have attended group, Sandra did not have, or did not admit to having high or romantic expectations of marriage. She would often say that if only Mitchell gave up drinking, was willing to join in at least one family activity a week, and would talk to her, even about minor matters, she would be content. Deep emotional intimacy she could not imagine, much less hope for. Turning to Mitchell for emotional support also seemed like an impossibility.

While it is difficult to make generalities about such a diverse and currently socially mobile group as Black women, one consistent impression of the Black women who have sought help is their high level of functioning and capacity for work. Yet, in meeting Sandra and other extremely functional well balanced Black women, the psychological costs for all the coping they have been expected to do and have done are not readily apparent. Sandra, for example, came to group extremely skeptical. She didn't believe much in psychotherapy. Furthermore, she certainly didn't believe it was she that needed help, only Mitchell.

Much like her mother and Mitchell's mother, Sandra grew up submerging her own needs. Whenever feelings of helplessness or personal insecurity would arise within her, she would reject them. Such feelings were not acceptable and they would certainly not help her in her struggle for survival.

Like many of the Black women who have attended group, Sandra had great difficulty sharing her fears and stating her personal needs for attention, comfort, and support. She has never cried in group nor lost control of herself at home. While some of the white women openly weep in group and admit to having "hysterical fits" where they would "trash" their husbands' belongings, smash plates, or run around saying they are going to run away from home, so far no Black woman has behaved or reported behaving in such a manner.

Part of the Black woman's reluctance to share may be cultural. As psychologist Parsons explains, Blacks in therapy may show less emotion than whites because, during the centuries of slavery, as well as afterward, they learned to wear a mask.[31] This mask served an important purpose for it hid "from the white man the extent and intensity of their (the Blacks') feelings of frustration and the anger that went along with this."[32] In addition, in the days of slavery, the only possessions slave owners could not take from Blacks were their "inner feelings, thoughts, and beliefs." Therefore, "for many Blacks, sharing too much too soon with a therapist is not only culturally impossible but is an indication of a failure of family tradition, as well as a sign of mental disease."[33] For the Black Vietnam veteran, sharing is often "complicated" by the "additional mental burden of shame at having killed third world brothers and sisters in the war."[34]

For his wife, sharing personal problems in a predominantly white group run by a white therapist may also be extremely difficult. The Black woman may fear that she will be adversely judged by the others, including other Black women, or she may feel disloyal to her husband if she shares her marital problems with "whities."

For example, approximately one fourth of the black wives seen were in battering or prebattering relationships. But they took longer to share their situation with the group than white women in similar binds, because, as they stated, they did not want to perpetuate the stereotype of the Black man as a violence-prone individual. In addition, some were more reluctant to call the police than white women. While battered women frequently are reluctant to call the police, some Black women voiced an additional concern. They were hesitant to turn their husbands in to the authorities because they did not trust what would happen to a Black man in the hands of the police. Involving the police was, for some of the women, not only a violation of their loyalty toward their husbands, but toward their race.[35] In addition, some women felt the police would fail to protect them because of their color.

Some of the Black abused women, however, would head straight for the phone the minute their husbands would raise their fists. A number have been extremely assertive in obtaining protection orders and other legal help. However, more than the white women, Black women tended to fear entanglements with bureaucracies and authorities. When some of them left their husbands, they did so quietly, without involving attorneys, police, or mental health professionals.

In general, the Black women I have seen appear less conflicted about combining motherhood with work roles. They have tended to express less anxiety and guilt about pursuing careers or working outside the home. In addition, they seem to suffer less from "fear of success" than white women, who are often afraid of losing their femininity if they successfully compete in previously predominately male arenas. However some women, like Sandra, have difficulty in that they want to maintain their self-reliance and independence, while at the same time maintaining relationships with their husbands.

Although all the women who attend group need help in differentiating which of their problems are due to internal conflicts, which are due to their husbands' PTSD, and which are due to external realities, the Black woman can also examine the role of racism or racial conflicts in her life, and in the life of her husband. While not all of the woman's problems can be attributed to racial factors, some are. She may need to acknowledge how her life has been affected by social forces outside of herself.

While the black woman should feel free to discuss racial concerns, it cannot be assumed that all her concerns are racial. If she does not want to discuss any racial conflicts, she should not be pressured to do so. Perhaps she does not need, or want, help in this area. Furthermore, she may be uncomfortable discussing racial problems or differences if the group is predominantly non-Black.

She may also be hesitant to discuss racial matters, because at times she may be confused about the role of racism in her life, as well as in the life of her husband. "I don't want to be paranoid," said Doris, "But when my supervisor reprimands me, I'm never sure if his complaints are legitimate or if he's picking on me because I'm Black." Doris readily admits that sometimes she fails to complete all that is technically required of her. "But the books are never thrown at the whites or the Orientals in the office—only the Blacks."

In therapy, Doris has had the courage to take a good hard look at her behavior and identify the ways, both large and small, in which she may be contributing to tensions between her supervisor and herself. At the same time, however, she has finally mustered the courage to stand up to, rather than accept, certain racist and sexist practices and attitudes at the office.

Her husband, Fred, however, either forgets that many problems have racial, rather than personal origins and drowns himself in self-blame. Or he tends to blame almost all his problems on racism and forgets to look at himself. Either way, he is left feeling hopeless and powerless.

Doris's fiance died in Vietnam. She was still wearing black when she met Fred, soon after he returned from Vietnam. During their many years of marriage, Doris has spent countless hours trying to talk Fred out of his paralyzing fear that the "system" was "out to get him." While Doris does not deny the existence of racism, she feels that Fred has lost many job opportunities simply because his attitude communicates a considerable amount of underlying anger as well as a sense of defeatism. Doris does not accompany Fred on his interviews. However, she can tell that he is alienating prospective employers simply by the way he speaks and carries himself while talking on the phone with them.

Whenever she feels he might be receptive to her advice, she gently suggests that he might be setting himself up for failure by anticipating discrimination or other forms of rejection and tries to encourage him to think about what he might be doing to hurt his chances for success. She also tries to pass on some interview tips.

Sometimes Fred listens. Other times his smoldering anger at the racism he has encountered, both in the military and afterward, shifts onto Doris. He has never hit her, but he has verbally mocked her and accused her of "selling out."

"You have the wrong enemy!" she'll shout back, but Fred still resents that while he was in the rice paddies, Doris and other Black women were going to school or moving ahead in good paying jobs. In contrast, he feels that Vietnam has delayed his career development, not one year, but ten.

Upon his return from Vietnam, Fred tried to use his benefits to go to college. But the anti-veteran attitude of many college students drove him from school and into the police department. There he worked hard as a front line cop only to be repeatedly turned down for promotion. In his particular precinct, only Irish Catholics received promotions.

Fred quit in disgust and was unemployed for several years. As he struggled with depression and with doors closed to him because of his race and his status as a veteran, he tried to get compensation for a lower back problem he felt was war related. The government, however, was not in agreement and there were numerous phone calls and letters about his claim. Every time a letter arrived, Fred was certain the person writing was spying on him or "out to get him."

"It's only a form letter from someone behind a desk," Doris would point out. "Don't take everything so personally. Whoever wrote this letter doesn't even know you're Black."

But it was difficult for Fred not to personalize form letters or any other kind of interaction with a bureaucracy. The only persons he trusted were his mother and Doris.

Doris understood Fred's dependence on her but it exhausted her. She became weary of having to constantly reassure Fred that he was safe, but she never complained. She knew that Fred had had a particularly rough time in Vietnam, not only because he had served on the front lines, but because at one point he had been called upon to help quell rioting Black troops.

"I don't think he'll ever get over having to hurt some of the brothers. He was on both sides, but on no side, and both sides made threats on his life. Fred's greatest fear is that someday he'll accidentally run into someone from that part of his past."

When Doris first came to group, she was sad, not angry. Whenever Fred encountered yet another frustration or failure, she would wrap the black kerchief from her fiance's funeral around her hair and grieve. Fred, on the other hand, had difficulty feeling raw grief. At times it seemed as if Doris was doing his grieving for him. Every time, she would pull Fred through his disappointment. Then, when he was back on his feet, she would collapse into a short-term depression that caused her to miss a few days of work. She also developed insomnia, was easily startled, and began worrying that she too had PTSD.

At first Doris felt her only hope was to convince Fred to return to school. His GI benefits had expired, but she had been setting aside money and acquired a minority loan for him. With Doris's support and the help of several Vet Center counselors, Fred was able to complete some legal training. He is currently working for a firm which helps disadvantaged groups. He is productive and effective on the job and grateful to have found a constructive outlet for his anger and his pain.

Wives Of Hispanic Veterans

Like Black Vietnam veterans, Hispanic Vietnam veterans constitute a minority within a minority in the U.S. Also like the Black Vietnam veteran, the Hispanic Vietnam veteran often suffered from economic and educational disadvantages prior to the war, from the "gook identification syndrome" and various forms of discrimination during the war, and from economic and vocational distress following the war.[36] In Vietnam, writes Harrington in the National Hispanic PTSD Conference, "Hispanic veterans...suffered the highest ratio of casualties of any community in the nation. Hispanics were 7% of all troops and 20% of all killed. One of two Hispanics who went to Vietnam served in a combat unit. One out of every five Hispanics who went to Vietnam was KIA (Killed In Action). One of three was WIA (Wounded in Action). Discrimination against Hispanics began right with the recruitment process. For example, in New Mexico in 1970 Mexicans were 27% of the population, 69% of all draftees and 44% of all combat deaths."[37]

In addition, the Hispanic Vietnam veteran had to and may still currently be dealing with the stresses of the acculturation process.[38]

Meanwhile his wife, sister, and mother were earning and are still earning even less than Black women.[39]

According to Lillian Baragas, who works with Hispanic Vietnam wives, Hispanic help-seeking wives are often "very depressed" and have low self-esteem. "They believe their veteran's behavior is caused by something they're not doing and their roles as wives and partners are not being fulfilled."[40] Given the strong family and church orientation of Hispanic culture, women are often encouraged to be supportive of the veteran and strongly discouraged from seeking separation or divorce. At the same time, however, Baragas says, "Friends who don't understand PTSD are going to tell her she's crazy for staying with the veteran."[41]

Often Hispanic Vietnam wives, like their husbands, do not seek the help of mental health professionals or Vet Centers, seeking help first from their family and church. "Counseling carries negative connotations in Hispanic society," Baragas explains.[42] She has found that Hispanic women find it "difficult to self-disclose in group settings."[43] However, relatively structured educational programs on PTSD have helped Hispanic Vietnam wives understand that they are not the cause of their husband's distress.

Summary

Like their husbands, Black and Hispanic Vietnam wives suffer from a "double jeopardy." Whereas their husbands labored, and in many instances, continue to labor under the burden of discrimination because they are nonwhite as well as Vietnam veterans, the wives are subject to the dual oppression of sexism and racism.

National statistics show that on the average, Black and Hispanic women earn less than white women. In addition, Black and Hispanic Vietnam wives are living with men whose PTSD tends to be more severe and of longer duration than that of white veterans. For many Black and Hispanic vets, PTSD is intensified by the "gook identification syndrome." Their PTSD is exacerbated by multiple experiences with racial or ethnic discrimination both before, and after, the war. In general these veterans have greater difficulty finding jobs than their white counterparts. Furthermore, a number of Black veterans suffered from rejection not only from the white community, but from those members of the Black community that saw them as "traitors" for fighting a white man's war.

In contrast, Vietnam veterans of native American Indian origin sometimes came from tribes that were able to separate the war from the warrior. Such vets were given honor and homage upon their return. Their reentry into society was facilitated by tribal reentry ceremonies. Yet even those native American Indian vets who were greeted and treated like honorable heroes by their tribes were not oblivious to the fact that in society at large, they were scorned and not respected. (Until recently, at least.)

While there is little information available about Indian Vietnam wives, clinical experience and the Vet Center study reveal that Black and Hispanic wives suffer from the same depression, isolation, and frustrations as white Vietnam wives. Yet Black wives appear less conflicted about their role as a major source of emotional and economic support for their families. They do, however, feel that they want and deserve the same economic security and emotional and sexual fulfillment in their marriages as their white sisters.

Ten

PTSD and Children

When Dad left (for Vietnam) I was not told too much why he had to leave and what he was going to be doing....I cried terribly when he left, and emptiness and fear flooded my body and mind.

My father came home with a hearing impairment.... His resentment today toward his deafness is still eating him up inside, because it has gradually gotten worse over the years.

He had changed a great deal when he got home. His nightmares and diving in the bushes from his fear from the war were a few things I heard and saw. His drinking got a lot worse, and so did his anger. Violence entered our house for the first time roughly a year later from his return from 'Nam. He physically abused me and the rest of the family. Verbal abuse was almost all the time. I never, never knew what to expect....Him being so unpredictable aroused a tremendous amount of paranoia in my daily living.

It seemed like he had his own war he was fighting inside himself, and with the effect of alcohol he couldn't control his unbelievable rage that would explode in front of anybody.

My resentment toward my mother grew also. I felt she didn't care for us kids or else she would protect us from this insane man. It was terrible, horrid fear in her eyes and face when Dad would lash out and attack us as if we were the enemy.

A lot of bitterness, hatred, anger, resentment, and absolutely no pity for him was all I felt for quite a few years. I felt I was trapped in a vicious circle of fear with *no way out and no one around to understand me and talk with. I became an extremist for destruction and hate and blame toward myself. I held myself responsible for my father's behavior, because I felt I was unacceptable and hated in his eyes.*

For over ten years it never dawned on me my father's behavior might be caused by what he went through in Vietnam.

I was ashamed of myself and felt extremely guilty for all the years of condemning my father to hell when he was already in a living hell of guilt, remorse, and hatred toward himself.

I can assure you I have been deeply affected directly from the war in Vietnam. I couldn't be excused from it because it came home with Dad and lived in our house for a good portion of my life.

Today though, I am trying to learn and understand the destruction the war placed on our combat vets and Vietnam era vets. It tears me up inside to see their unmistakable misery within. I have seen it with my own eyes with my Dad.

I will never forget the craziness and insane behavior from both myself and my father in the past. But my awareness and acceptance is the biggest asset I have today. I am working on all those feelings I have suppressed for several years and to me, this is the best thing I can do for myself. To keep trying and keep loving him for who he is and where he's been, and to understand it was not me who should be responsible any longer for his behavior.

Kid of a vet[1]

"Birth reminds me of death," writes Harry, a brain surgeon who served in Vietnam. "When I first saw the shriveled mass that was my newborn daughter, I felt pangs, thinking about how all the guys that died in Vietnam were once little babies like that. Some of them died like that that—as shriveled masses.

"As much as I hate to admit it, right there, in the delivery room, I decided not to love my daughter. What if she would get sick and die on me, or betray me in some other way? I simply could not handle it.

"It makes me wonder what it's all about, why we struggle so hard in this life, only to die in the end. Sometimes I wonder why I bother to live at all."

As Harry's last statement reveals, he is severely depressed and, at times, suicidal. More than once, he has had to ask his wife, Nelda, to lock up the firearms he brought home from Vietnam in a safety vault and hide the key from him. Even though Harry never shot anyone, nor was shot at, he, like many medical professionals who served during the war, suffers from many of the classical symptoms of PTSD, especially survivor guilt.[2]

Yet Harry finds it difficult to admit that he suffered any psychological effects from the war. During his medical training, he was taught to "develop a high degree of clinical detachment."[3] Such emotional detachment, he learned, was absolutely necessary in order to make the "right medical decisions," but it also served to harden him to his own emotional reactions to the war. In addition, Harry is reluctant to admit to having emotional problems because he is afraid of losing his colleagues' "respect, or worse (his) job or practice."[4]

If it weren't for Nelda's insistence, Harry would not have had the courage to come to a Vet Center for help. Although therapy was helping him with his depression, Nelda did not see much improvement in Harry's attitude toward their three children.

While the literature suggests that many Vietnam veterans are extremely capable and involved fathers, the overwhelming majority of wives seen at the Vet Center describe their husbands as emotionally withdrawn from the children and assuming little, if any, responsibility for the children's physical care or emotional development.[5] In addition, some wives complain that their husbands are excessively demanding, critical, or controlling of the children, treating the children as if they were privates in barracks.[6] In one home, for example, children were required to salute the father. In the Vet Center study, some 73% of Vet Centers counselors polled report that vets with PTSD tend to withdraw from their children and some 80% report that vets with PTSD tend to be overcritical of their children.

Perhaps it is primarily women whose husbands are not actively involved with their children who seek help. Nelda's complaint, "I'm a married single parent," has been echoed by almost every mother who has attended group. This does not mean that their husbands do not love their children, but rather that their PTSD interferes with their desire to be good fathers.

In this era of changing sex roles, many men seek to become more involved with their children and many mothers, even stay-at-home mothers, expect their husbands to spend quality time with the children, as well as to assume more of the physical childcare duties. But this change in attitude toward traditional sex roles does not seem to have affected the majority of Vietnam veteran families seen so far. Almost always the majority of the childcare seems to be relegated solely to the mother.

Candice Williams, who has worked with hundreds of Vietnam veterans and conducted women's support groups, explains that "In Vietnam veteran families, there is often overattachment to culturally stereotyped roles," despite the "tremendous role changes (which) have occurred in the family during the past decade."[7]

For Nelda, as for most of the mothers, the image of the "liberated couple" where husband and wife happily and equally share the housework and the childcare is an impossible dream. Nelda would be grateful if Harry would just show the children some fatherly love and stop criticizing them "just for being children"—for making noises, not being on time, acting contrary at meals, balking while dressing, or whatever. Although Nelda works outside the home and could certainly use Harry's help with some of the routine household and childcare chores, her heart's desire is not to have Harry change diapers or fix lunches. Rather she prays for the day when Harry will stop destroying the children's self-esteem with his critical comments and unrealistic expectations.

"Harry doesn't think a two-year-old can understand when he says negative things about her, but she does. And he doesn't think his children miss him, but they do. Even though he hurts their feelings by not showing up at their games and school plays, they love him anyway.

"He's their father and they need him. They need strokes from Daddy, as well as from Mommy."

There is nothing closer to most women's hearts than their children. Among almost all of the wives and girlfriends of Vietnam veterans I have counseled, their children are their prime concern, in most cases overriding their worry for their husbands or for themselves. When a child is hurting, that child's pain, usually becomes the mother's major focus of attention and the dominant topic of group discussion or individual therapy.

Even the incarcerated Vietnam wives I have worked with, women convicted of crimes, such as murder, attempted murder, or theft, women who are "street smart" and heavily invested in presenting a tough "macha" image to the world, would almost always break down, or at least ask for help, when sharing about their children.

Like many other Vietnam wives seen at the Vet Center, Nelda feels her children's pain. She even feels it when they aren't feeling it, but denying it instead. In an attempt to help her children, Nelda tries to compensate for her husband's absences and other deficiencies as a parent by giving her children extra attention and love. But she is tired of being her children's emotional "bandaid" and, furthermore, she fears, and realistically so, that all her love and extra efforts cannot undo Harry's emotional damage to the children. "Do you know how I feel when I see my son giving up on a school project because his father has called him 'dumb' or 'lazy'?" No matter how hard she tries to convince Harry Jr. that he can succeed at a certain school project, he has internalized his father's low image of him to such an alarming extent that he gives up almost immediately.

While Nelda is enraged at the destruction of her son's self-esteem, she is also "sick and tired" of being accused of being a "bad mother."

"Here's me, doing everything, and here's my husband, the critic. Why am I to blame every time the children misbehave or have a problem at school?" Nelda often asks with disgust. Even though she knows her husband's accusations are not true, she, like her son, has adopted her husband's low image of her. On some level, she sees herself as an inadequate mother, even though every piece of objective evidence points otherwise.

As Harry and Nelda's story illustrates, the major problems experienced by children in homes afflicted with PTSD are emotional. If the veteran's PTSD expresses itself in irritability, outbursts of temper, frequent flashbacks, or erratic behavior, the children are often frightened and anxious, not knowing what to expect next. "I've got to be home all the time to keep the children from falling apart in case he (the veteran) falls apart," explains Beth, mother of three. "Only when he goes on camping trips, do the kids and I get a break."

While younger children learn to go to their rooms when Daddy goes "off," older children may leave for the evening. Or, they may stay home and try to help their father. "Even if I leave home for the weekend, I take my father with me in my mind," explains Beth's oldest son, Tom, age 14, who is more troubled by his father's crying spells and negative attitude toward life than by his father's anger.

In Tom's home, as in other homes, the veteran's dramatic emotions and mood swings, or his severe depression, usually determine the emotional climate of the home. Aware of their father's volatility and emotional sensitivities, Tom and his sisters have learned, like their mother, to "walk on eggshells." As frequently occurs in Vietnam homes, the children are not told why their father is so troubled, or so distant. As a result they often blame themselves for their father's unhappiness or his withdrawal from them.

A Vet Center counselor who has worked with children explains: "In the majority of these troubled families, the children have been given little explanation for their father's difficulties and the stresses of family life. Inevitably they attribute much of the blame and responsibility to themselves, just as do the children of divorcing, alcoholic, and otherwise troubled parents. The patterns of communication among family members are often very sparse so that there is little opportunity to acquire a more accurate or differentiated explanation. Indeed, the child's sense of responsibility may be heightened by the frequent exhortations of 'Be quiet. Be good. Don't upset your father.' Thus, these children may grow up feeling alienated from their fathers, responsible for the difficulties in the family, and isolated from community supports." [8]

In Tom's home, however, the father has recounted his traumatic experiences in Vietnam so frequently that, by now, Tom is bored with his father's war stories. "I can't stand hearing about it anymore!" Tom sometimes shouts. "Forget the past, Dad! Live in the present!"

But Tom's father can't "forget the past" and such outbursts on Tom's part engender unresolvable father-son disputes, which leave the veteran father feeling misunderstood and unloved by his own family and Tom feeling guilty for further upsetting his father and for not having suffered as much as his father did. Although Tom wants to help his father, he feels helpless to do so. Yet Tom often willingly restricts his activities in order to be with his father. At the same time, he resents the burden his father's emotional pain and problems have imposed on his life.

While Tom has never been rejected by his peers or neighbors, in some communities children have been ostracized for having a Vietnam veteran father, especially if their father has committed an antisocial act in the community, has emotionally regressed, or had flashbacks in public. In other cases, children may be seen as "different" because their father has adopted an unusual or nonconforming life style or form of dress. In families where there are frequent moves, the child's educational progress and friendships may be disrupted. [9]

The psychological problems experienced by children of Vietnam veterans as a direct result of the veteran's PTSD generally occur in one of seven different family settings:

1. Families such as Harry and Nelda's, in which the mother functions as a virtual single parent due to the veteran's emotional conflicts or withdrawal;
2. Families in which the mother is so chronically stressed or depressed that she turns to one of the children for excessive emotional support;
3. Families in which there is "secondary traumatization"—where one or more of the children overidentifies with the veteran, exhibits some of the father's symptoms (or other symptoms), or attempts to "rescue" the veteran;[10]
4. Families in which there is an overprotectiveness of and overvaluation of the children by the veteran;
5. Families in which there is physical, as well as emotional, abuse of the mother or the children;
6. Families in which there is alcohol/drug abuse as well as PTSD;
7. Families in which the woman has children from a former marriage.

These categories of families are not mutually exclusive, as will be shown by using some of the same families to illustrate different family problems. Furthermore, the children, like their mothers, tend to suffer from self-blame, low self-esteem, difficulty expressing anger and aggression, and conflicts in establishing themselves as unique individuals apart from the family system. According to the Vet Center study, some 82% of the counselors polled indicated low self-esteem to be a problem in children of Vietnam veterans suffering from PTSD. Approximately 56% of the counselors polled noted that children tend to feel responsible for the veteran's emotional well-being.

While some homes are characterized by close attachments among family members, in other homes there is considerable emotional distance and anger. The children may respond to their parents' anger with anger of their own, or with various forms of emotional distancing. They may turn up the stereo when Dad or Mom begins to yell. Or perhaps they simply plug themselves into the T.V. set using headphones. According to Ellen Salom, who has conducted groups for children at a Vet Center in Philadelphia, when children are asked to draw pictures of their homes, they sometimes depict homes where each family member is in a separate room.[11] Such pictures suggest a high degree of emotional alienation and lack of communication in the family. On the other hand, in other families there is solid bonding, although usually it is the mother and children who form a tight subunit in the family which excludes the veteran.

Many of the psychological patterns found among children of traumatized Vietnam veterans are similar to those found among children of World War II veterans with PTSD and among children of the survivors of the Nazi concentration camps.[12] In his study of World War II veterans with PTSD, for example, Rosenheck found veterans reluctant to discuss their war experiences with their children. "This reluctance," writes Rosenheck, "derived from embarrassment and guilt about acts of brutality they had committed as well as from the fear that they would become upset while discussing specific incidents. They were also afraid that unpleasant details would frighten and alienate their children."[13]

Not much research has been completed on the children of PTSD afflicted Vietnam veterans. Clinical reports are also scarce. Therefore, this chapter does not necessarily apply to all help-seeking Vietnam veteran families and certainly not to all children of those many Vietnam veterans who do not suffer from severe cases of PTSD or who are somehow able to contain their PTSD in such a manner so as to not affect their families.

This chapter is based on:

1. The reports of mothers who have attended the Vet Center group;
2. Collaborative work with child psychologists and other counselors who have worked with the children directly;
3. The results of a national survey of Vet Center counselors regarding the effects of PTSD on children; and
4. Existing articles on children of Vietnam veterans with PTSD, adult children of World War II veterans with PTSD, children of holocaust victims, and adult children of alcoholics.

The Effects Of Distancing On Children

While veterans complain about not feeling emotionally closer to their children, their children often exhibit various symptoms in response to their father's lack of emotional involvement with them. True, the father's intention in distancing himself from his child may not be a rejection of the child. Yet children tend to view their father's alienation as rejection. If, in addition, there is name calling or other forms of emotional abuse, the child may become convinced that he or she is not loved or accepted by their father. In some cases, when a veteran calls his child "lazy" or some other negative label, he may think he is teaching the child the right values, like the value of work. However, children usually experience such name calling as humiliating. It makes them feel that they are not good enough for their father.

The child's reactions to the father's emotional distancing appear to be age-related. Among pre-schoolers, there may be increased separation anxiety, evidenced by increased clinging to the mother, increased fearfulness, and even increased aggressive behavior. "Whenever Harry walks into the room, Donna starts screaming," explains Nelda. "She won't let him feed her either." Then Nelda is blamed for not teaching the children to love their father. Mothers of slightly older preschool children have reported increased temper tantrums following their father's absences from the home, as well as decreased interest in playing with other children.

Between the ages of four and seven, children's understanding of the world is egocentric.[14] In their view, the world revolves about their needs and they believe that their thoughts and wishes can actually cause external events. Hence they easily blame themselves for their father's alienation, anger, or depression. Even if the child were to be given some education about Vietnam, the child would have difficulty digesting and comprehending such information. At this age, children still tend to believe that they are the major cause of all the activity around them. Furthermore, "In times of stress," notes Suhr, "even adolescent or older children can revert to (such) egocentric modes of thinking..."[15]

By the time children have reached the ages of seven or eight, their capacity for concrete reasoning has increased.[16] Now they are able to see cause and effect more clearly. Yet, since they are usually not told about the impact of Vietnam on their father, they may still personalize the father's alienation. In some cases, they feel great sadness and actively grieve for him. Nelda's middle child, Joleen, age 7, actually pined when her father failed to keep his promise to watch a certain T.V. show with her. Other mothers have noted depression in their children, a lack of interest in social activities, and much keeping to themselves in their rooms. "Daddy doesn't play with me because he doesn't like me," some children have frankly said with tears in their eyes.

At the age of seven or eight, children may also become involved in loyalty conflicts between the parents. A child may side with the mother, or with the veteran. It is not uncommon for children who side with the veteran to also join with him in any denial of his PTSD, alcoholism, or other problems. Since some children tend to idealize their parents, they may find it hard to admit that one of their parents has a serious problem. In several cases, the Vietnam wife's attempts to encourage her husband to seek professional help have met with resistance not only from the veteran, but from his "ally," one of the children.

"Why are you trying to send my Daddy away to a hospital? He's not sick," children have told their mothers. Some have even threatened to run away from home if the mother carries out her plans. Children who ally with the veteran often blame their mother for their father's PTSD symptoms and other unhappiness. Or they may think she is trying to take the father away from them by pushing him to seek inpatient treatment. They may also fear that once father leaves, he may never return. Or that someday their mother may send them away, as she did their father. These fears can usually be alleviated by careful explanations of what treatment involves and visiting the treatment facility with the children (if permissible).

According to the Vet Center study, some 42% of counselors polled found that children have ambivalent feelings toward the mother. "They're downright negative," writes one counselor. Another, however, notes that some children cling to the mother. In his study of World War II veterans with PTSD, Rosenheck found similar patterns. Some children sided with their mother and admired her efforts to help the father. Other children were highly critical of the mother for not being supportive enough of the veteran.[17]

At the age of seven or eight, children may not only begin to take sides, but, if there is much quarreling in the home, like children of divorcing parents, they may come to "distrust parents who are modeling painful, vicious behaviors."[18] Unable to trust either parent, the child feels insecure and may evidence not only depression, but rebellion at both parents' commands.

At the same time, like his mother, the child may have learned to be quiet. Among children of Nazi holocaust survivors, the same inhibition of angry feelings has been found.[19] These children have often kept their angry feelings to themselves because they did not want to cause additional suffering to their obviously already suffering parent(s). In a parallel manner, some children from Vietnam homes do not want to upset their already obviously upset father or their overburdened mother. In addition, the child may have been severely punished for aggressive or defiant behavior by the father. Given military training and background, some vets equate anger with disrespect and tolerate little "disobedience" from their children.

When Children Repress Anger

Children may also stifle their anger because of their natural dependency on their parents. Generally, it is difficult for most persons to be angry at those on whom they are emotionally or financially dependent, for if the anger is expressed, there is a high risk of alienating the person whose love and attention or support is so desperately needed.

Children's repressed anger can eventually emerge in the form of: self-mutilation, suicidal thoughts, and sudden outbursts of aggression. According to the Vet Center study, aggressive behavior on the part of children is far more common than self-mutilation. Some 76% of the counselors polled indicated that they had observed aggressiveness to be a problem among children of Vietnam veterans suffering from PTSD whereas only 10% found evidence of self-mutilation. Among the children whose mothers have attended group, self-mutilation, suicidal thoughts, and angry displays of temper have occurred primarily among sons, rather than daughters. In one case, a ten-year-old son habitually scraped his legs with razor blades, not enough to injure himself, but enough to leave noticeable marks. In another instance, a child scratched his head to such an extent that he became partially bald. Other examples of self-mutilation include head banging, self-burning, skin pinching, hair pulling, and extreme fingernail biting.

In most cases, such self-mutilation is a way of coping with emotional pain, rather than a way to control the parents through guilt or active attempts at suicide.[20] Generally the children are ashamed of their actions and commit them in private. Typically the self-mutilation represents repressed anger or a form of grieving or pining for the father.

Suicidal depressions are another result of repressed anger, with several children contemplating suicide as a means of making their Dads "sorry" for "not loving" them or for "not doing things" with them or as a means of escaping the arguing and other forms of unhappiness at home.

In contrast to children who internalize their anger in the form of self-mutilation, depression, or suicidal thoughts, are those who externalize their anger by fighting relentlessly with their siblings or peers at school or who destroy property at home. In some cases, the child blames the mother for his or her aggression. "You made my Dad sick!" or "Why can't you make Dad better?" tormented sons have cried out as they smash tables, walls, or stereo sets. In other instances, otherwise "perfect" daughters have been found tearing drapes off windows or smashing windows, saying "I hate you! I hate you, Mom," blaming the mother for all of the family's problems.

Another distressing development for the Vietnam wife is when her children learn to use emotional withdrawal as a means of punishing her or manipulating her into giving in to their desires. One wife, the mother of a teenager, feels that her son has learned to wall her out whenever he is displeased with her rules. "My son was not a problem when he was young, but now whenever things don't go his way, or he doesn't like the family rules, he threatens to abandon me or totally tunes me out. I couldn't understand where this behavior came from, since it wasn't evident in his younger years, until it suddenly dawned on me that he's treating me exactly the way his father treats me."

In other instances, anger stemming from the family situation is displaced onto Orientals, specifically Vietnamese refugees. According to the Vet Center study, however, only 13% of the counselors polled found hatred of Orientals, specifically Vietnamese persons, to be a problem among children. While the child may have learned to hate Orientals from the father, Orientals provide a relatively safe target for the hostility which the child feels toward his father or mother, but does not feel safe to express. While no violence against Orientals has been reported, several children have verbally harassed Vietnamese refugees and relish telling anti-Vietnamese or "gook" jokes.

For example, Brian, age 11, was referred for psychological testing because his academic problems seemed to reflect an emotional problem rather than a lack of ability. His grades began to decline after the second grade and he became more hostile and aggressive with his classmates. He refused to sit near Oriental children, and got into fights with children when he felt they were "wrong." Right and wrong were big issues in his family since his father, a former combat vet, had become very sensitive to issues of justice and fairness as the result of his Vietnam experience.

Brian would also pull pranks and then lie about his behavior. When Brian's father returned from Vietnam, he was easily startled by sudden noises and often felt anxious around strangers. In a parallel manner, Brian became frightened by the ringing of the school bell, and suspicious of strangers, even the psychological examiner sent by the school.

Despite his anxiety about strangers, Brian worked well with the examiner. He worked hard on the intellectual puzzles the examiner gave him until he was asked to put together puzzles of humans and animals. The cut up pieces reminded him of the gore in his father's war stories and he was unable to concentrate on this part of the testing. He also showed signs of anxiety when asked to define words like "knife" or to deal with words and concepts having to do with aggression. Whenever questions or pictures about vehicles came up, Brian exhibited an extreme fear that the vehicles would be blown up or crash, as his father had described occurred in Vietnam when vehicles were booby trapped or set with explosives.

When Brian had trouble with a test, he expressed fear that the examiner would "yell" at him, as apparently his parents did when he brought home poor marks. Even when he was assured he would have a second chance at certain items, he did not appear to believe the examiner and would give up.

As a result of the testing, it was recommended that Brian receive special educational services, as well as individual and family therapy. He was placed in a special classroom environment where he received more individualized attention. There was less expected of him there than in a regular classroom and he, consequently, experienced many more academic successes than in his regular classroom. Over time he became more self-confident and was less aggressive toward other students.

Counseling with a child psychologist also helped Brian separate his father's war realities from the reality of his own everyday life. Although Brian had trouble opening up to the therapist, eventually he revealed that much of his mental life was spent fantasizing about his father's experiences in Vietnam. Often his conceptions of what his father had experienced were severe distortions of what his father had shared with him. Some of Brian's ideas had become confused with movies and television programs about war.

In family therapy sessions with his father, Brian got a clearer picture of his father's war experiences, which enabled him to focus more on reality. Brian also needed many assurances that his father was no longer in danger, as he had been in Vietnam, and that the dangers his father had gone through did not exist in their particular neighborhood. The therapist and Brian's mother had reassured him many times but once his father said the same things, those reassurances became more effective.

The family therapy sessions also revealed that, in part, Brian was doing poorly in school in order to get his father's attention. Even being yelled at was better than being ignored. When it became clear to Brian that his father was willing to give him attention in other ways, Brian's school performance and emotional state improved.

The most significant breakthrough in family therapy occurred when Brian was finally able to articulate his anger at his father. Ever since he was a small child, Brian had been unable to show anger toward his father because he didn't want to aggravate and upset him, and because he feared his father's physical strength.

Even though Brian's father had never hit either Brian or Brian's mother, he had destroyed property. Once when he was angry at his wife, he smashed the glass door at the entrance to their apartment building.

"Don't you know we might get evicted for that?" Brian's mother shouted.

"Don't you raise your voice at me, woman. I'm the man in the house," Brian's father shouted back.

"But the property manager is going to make trouble for us."

"I can handle that puny runt. Remember, I've stood up to armed men."

"But what if a child had been standing near you and had gotten hurt by the flying glass?"

"Then it would have been the kid's fault for being there, not mine."

Brian's father's last words were probably said in anger. Most likely he had forgotten he ever said them. But Brian did not forget—not the words, and not the smashed door. He was afraid that if he made one wrong move at home, he would become the object of his father's powerful fist. Consequently, he acted out his aggressive feelings at school. Even the teachers and the principal seemed safer than his father. At home he was afraid to stand up for himself, even when he felt his father was being unjust.

For example, Brian's father suffered frequent fears about his family's safety. Whenever a family member went out, they were required to call home upon arrival at their destination. Sometimes after getting to a friend's house, Brian would quickly call home. "Hi, Dad. I'm okay, Dad. Bye, Dad."

Sometimes his father interpreted his brevity as a sign of disrespect. Other times he felt his son was hanging up on him. In therapy, he was able to tell of an incident in Vietnam when a command control operator had muttered some information to him quickly, almost inaudibly, then hung up on him. This left him with incomplete information and as a result he was not able to save some wounded Americans from the Viet Cong. As a result, he was intolerant of mistakes in his family as well as himself and "hyper" whenever somebody spoke to him on the phone quickly or inaudibly.

As a result of that session, Brian learned how to talk to his father when he was in a hurry. "Don't get hyper, Dad, but I'm talking fast because I don't have much time to play with my friends unless I get started right now. If there's something really important you want to talk about, I'll stay on the line. But if you just want to talk about the usual stuff, I'd rather wait until later."

In the presence of a third party—the therapist—Brian was able to speak directly to his father about things that were bothering him. The more he was able to do that, the less need he had to act out his anger in school.

This presentation of the various reactions children have to their father's PTSD and the descriptions of other troubled children to follow in this chapter are not intended to present a picture of *all* children of Vietnam veterans with PTSD as suffering from severe or irrevocable psychological damage. Simply put, some children can cope better than others.

While some children are severely emotionally hurt by the situations in their homes, other children display great strength and develop an advanced degree of emotional maturity and objectivity as a result of the stress. Furthermore, even those children who have been emotionally hurt by PTSD and related problems can, with proper intervention, be helped considerably.

Why The Veteran Distances From His Children

In Harry's case, as in the case of other Vietnam veterans with PTSD (especially combat vets), the roots of his emotional withdrawal and ambivalent feelings toward his children are usually much deeper and more complex than simple male chauvinism, sheer insensitivity, or outright cruelty. In fact, philosophically, some vets truly believe in women's liberation and men's liberation, and very much want to be active, emotionally responsive fathers. Yet on a day-to-day basis, they find themselves extremely annoyed and impatient with their children.

According to the Vet Center study, approximately 85% of the counselors polled indicated that vets with PTSD have a low tolerance for children's noise and games. Some 51% indicated that vets with PTSD have special difficulty tolerating the "terrible twos" and some 79% have trouble with adolescent or preadolescent rebellion against parental authority. Of course, even non-PTSD afflicted parents may have problems with these stages of childhood development. However, in the case of the Vietnam vet, authority issues developed as a result of his Vietnam involvement may exacerbate his own unresolved issues and make rearing his own children an especially stressful experience.

"In all honesty, I'd rather be alone," confesses Harry, who also feels very guilty about his limited ability to tolerate his children. Similarly a veteran treated by Haley (who has worked with many Vietnam veterans) feels guilty for snapping at his wife and children "for every little thing."[21] In fact, this veteran considered himself "'...a poor excuse for a father' when his three-year-old asked why he looked so sad and yelled all the time."[22]

Parenting requires an enormous amount of energy, energy which some PTSD afflicted veterans lack due to depression or preoccupation with their war experiences. In this, they are like some of the survivors of the Nazi concentration camps, who, due to their focus on their traumatic experiences in the camps and their subsequent demoralization, have been found to lack the energy to parent.[23]

Vets with severe cases of PTSD or who are in inpatient treatment programs often feel they cannot handle the stresses of childrearing while simultaneously trying to recover from PTSD. According to Haley, who has seen this in her work with veterans, "Fatherhood may overtax the veteran's ability to resolve a trauma. Any point during the child's development can impinge upon the veteran's depression, withdrawal or conflicts." [24] As a result, the vet may allocate the job of parenting to his wife, not realizing that his very physical or emotional absence from the home is the source of many of his wife's difficulties with their children.

In some cases, the trauma of combat or specific injuries have caused irrevocable physiological damage to the veteran's nervous system.[25] Even without physiological damage, however, PTSD afflicted veterans often evidence the startle response to sudden noises and movements. Children may be strictly warned by their mothers not to surprise their father by jumping on him or in any manner approaching him from behind. The edginess some vets feel around others, especially children, can be seen as an exaggerated startle response.[26]

Combat memories also play a role in the veteran's ambivalent feelings toward his children. As a result of combat experiences, some PTSD afflicted veterans respond negatively to their children's aggressive play or to their children when they approach the ages of children they killed or saw killed in Vietnam.[27] One vet's PTSD lay dormant, until his son became nine, the exact age of a young boy he inadvertently killed during the war.

This type of reaction is not atypical, even among noncombat veterans.[28] Harry, like other medical personnel, often treated Vietnamese children. When his daughter turned two, he had to flee from her birthday party, remembering a two-year-old Vietnamese girl whose life he had failed to save. Some vets may not even want to have children as a result of their war experiences. For example, Harrington and Jay, therapists who conduct groups for Vietnam veterans, cite the case of Tony, "who had seen a friend knifed in front of his eyes. The friend, a corpsman, was treating a Vietnamese family of mother, father, grandmother, and infant that had been detained for questioning. When the corpsman turned from the father, the mother grabbed the corpsman's knife and stuck it through his back. In the instant it took the woman to stab the corpsman, Tony shot the entire family with automatic fire, including the infant. Ten years later, in group therapy, Tony, whose wife thought his bitterness and displays of indifference were reflections of her inadequacies, admitted that he would not have children because of his belief that a man who could react so quickly and so violently was not fit to become a father."[29]

Sometimes the veteran's memories, not just of children killed in Vietnam, but of any kind of person killed in Vietnam, are activated by simply watching children play. Haley cites an example of a veteran who had "never thought of the Viet Cong as people, as parents with children or as people who would be parents someday," until he watched his own children at play.[30] Often it is the birth of a child which makes the vet realize that, after all, the Viet Cong were not just "gooks," but human beings too.

In addition, since children in Vietnam were often used to carry hand grenades and other explosives or were used as ploys to trap vets, the vet may have learned to fear children. In a few isolated instances, children have not only been physically abused, but actually killed by their veteran father or stepfather because he allegedly mistook them for or responded to them as if they were booby trapped or otherwise attacking Vietnamese children.

If, in addition, the veteran actually killed children in Vietnam, his difficulties in relating to children, especially his own, are obvious. "Veterans who...feared or killed women and children during combat may find it difficult to make the transition to the roles of husband, protector, and nurturing parent," writes Haley.[31] In addition, Veteran's Administration psychiatrist Glover has found that some vets who killed women and children in Vietnam suffer from auditory hallucinations which "manifest themselves as the anguished cries of women and children killed by the veteran. At times the vet may see the face of a Vietnamese woman or child while he is relating to a family member."[32]

Another source of the veteran's ambivalence and anger toward his children, which most vets admit is irrational, is that in protecting and guiding their own children, they are reminded of times they felt unprotected, or were misguided, in Vietnam. "I'm jealous of my own kids," admits Harry, who, through therapy, has realized that when he feels restrictive or punitive toward his children he is often angry about not being protected (parented) in Vietnam. "Why didn't someone tell me about Vietnam before I went? Why was I such a fool as to enlist?" he often asks.

Harry went to Vietnam thinking he would help to save lives as doctors did in World War II—in safely placed hospitals in demilitarized zones. He was totally unprepared for rocket and other attacks on his hospital, as well as for the volume of casualties and the horrible types of disfiguring injuries caused by guerilla warfare tactics. Furthermore, medical school had not taught Harry how to decide who would be helped to live vs. who would have to be allowed to die, decisions which he was forced to make due to limited medical supplies and services.

Harry's children receive the best medical care, but Harry cannot take them to the doctor's. Just walking into a pediatrician's office fills him with an irrational rage. He can't help but compare the excellent care his children receive for relatively minor medical problems with what he saw in Vietnam: not only young Americans, but young Vietnamese children dying of napalm and various forms of hideous, deforming injuries. In addition, when Harry observes his children's innocence he is reminded of the innocence he lost in Vietnam. Since this is painful for him, he often avoids his children.

Military experience can also carry over into the veteran's attitude toward child discipline. Approximately 40% of the Vet Center counselors polled indicated that the Vietnam vet with PTSD tends to underdiscipline his children. However, an almost equal number reported that vets with PTSD tend to overdiscipline. In some cases, vets expect strict obedience from their children, treating their children as if they were small soldiers. For example, Tom and his two sisters must be constantly "on guard" or "at attention" when their father is at home. But the minute Dad leaves, the children become extremely unruly and undisciplined, taking out all their rebellious feelings and repressed anger at being "ordered around" on their mother, and on one another. Then their mother, Beth, is berated by her husband for not being able to "control" the children. Yet she feels powerless to counteract her children's normal reaction to being overregulated by their father.

Beth, like many Vietnam wives, sometimes hides her children's misbehavior from her husband. She fears that her husband might overly punish the children or call them derogatory names. Sometimes Beth becomes trapped, however, for example, when one of the children imitates the father by "trashing" a piece of furniture. "If Dad can do it, why can't I?" Under such circumstances, Beth must either quickly replace the broken furniture and cover up the expenditure with a lie, or else turn her children over to her husband for disciplinary measures.

In some homes, the veteran's need to control the children is disguised as a form of discipline. "My husband watches every move Tom makes," explains Beth, "He actually counts how many times Tom goes to the refrigerator. If Tom goes too often, my husband jumps all over him."

In some instances, the vet enforces certain home rules with great vigor, but seems relatively unconcerned when the children have disciplinary difficulties in school. According to Vet Center counselor

Salom, such inconsistences in discipline are not uncommon and create confusion for the child who may often fail to understand different levels of "right and wrong."[33]

Still other veterans are not disciplinarians at all, but may become exceptionally harsh in response to their children's aggressiveness. When vets see their children being cruel to a pet or to a new baby, it may "reawaken (for them) the painful effects of combat aggression and sadism."[34] If a vet committed atrocities in Vietnam, he may react by being superstrict with his children, especially his sons, and may not allow even normal aggressiveness. Some vets even feel that their sadism and aggressiveness is being "passed on" to their children genetically.

Mother's Helper

In homes where the mother is exceptionally stressed, as well as lonely, she may, in desperation, turn to one of her children for excessive emotional or other forms of support. Generally, women more often turn to daughters than sons for help with housework, childcare, for example, which, in turn, sets the stage for talking and emotional sharing.

Harry and Nelda's family is typical of this excessive use of a child for emotional support. Nelda had a fourth child, whose birth precipitated a panic attack in Harry, who found himself having flashbacks and periods of being unable to concentrate during surgery. He resigned from his position as a surgeon at a major urban hospital and found a job writing medical reports. However, the pay was less and since his depression had worsened, he was unable to stay focused on intellectual tasks, despite his brilliance. As a result, Nelda had to help him with his report writing, even though she had also had to assume a full-time job to make up for Harry's lower salary. Meanwhile, her fourth child was still an infant.

"It started when I found Mom crying in the kitchen, saying 'God help me. I can't do it all. I just can't do it all.'" says Joleen.

"'I'll help you Mommy,' I said, and from that day on I helped with all the dishwashing and dinner preparation and clean up. I felt proud to be able to help my Mom, and when the new baby got old enough for me to hold, I took over being Mom to him too.

"I didn't mind not being able to watch T.V. after school, but I did mind having to quit Girl Scouts. But Mom needed me more and more and I had to help her so she could help Daddy so our family wouldn't be poor and have to move."

However, it was not Nelda's turning to Joleen for household help that was destructive, but rather Nelda's sharing of her marital secrets and emotional pain with her daughter. As Nelda instructed her daughter in certain chores, or as they did them together, Nelda would often graphically describe to Joleen how Harry verbally denigrated her and how disappointed she was with her marriage. She also warned Joleen never to marry a Vietnam veteran, or any kind of veteran.

At the age of seven, Joleen was unprepared to hear her mother's "secrets" about her father. Yet Joleen also felt privileged that her mother would turn to her. Since her father was usually emotionally distant from her and had often disappointed her, Joleen quickly sided with her mother. Yet, as any child, she still wanted—needed—to believe that her father was a good man.

Surely her Daddy wasn't that bad. And if he was so horrible, didn't that make her, as his daughter, horrible too? Also, Joleen felt disloyal listening to her mother talk against her father, But how, at age seven, could she tell her poor victimized Mommy to stop?

As a child, Joleen had few defenses against her mother's feelings. She was easily overpowered by them and they became a part of her personality. Instead of developing along her own lines and having her own feelings, Joleen took on her mother's personality and emotions. Joleen became "enmeshed" with her mother.

For example, she would feel her mother's pain and sorrow as if they were her own and intuitively knew when her mother would be sad or unhappy. Often she would spend her allowance to buy her mother perfume or flowers saying, "Someday Daddy will love you again and buy you presents. Meanwhile, you have me."

Starved for love and affection, Nelda accepted the gifts. By the age of ten, Joleen was not only buying her mother gifts, but giving her mother pep talks and advice on how to handle her husband and the other children. She could not imagine life without her mother and processed life through her mother's eyes. Furthermore, she dared not to be different from her mother, lest her mother "crumble."

Needless to say, Joleen's peer relationships suffered. In addition, at the age of eleven or twelve, when children normally begin to separate from their parents, Joleen's natural separation process was stunted.

When Joleen, at age thirteen, developed an ulcer, Nelda went for help. "I know it wasn't fair of me to put Joleen between her father and myself," Nelda told the group. "But before this group, I had no one to turn to. My parents were far away and the only women I knew were the wives of other doctors. I couldn't talk to them because it would have ruined Harry's reputation. Besides, they would have never understood. All of their husbands were successful and none were having problems like Harry. Of course, none of their husbands had served in Vietnam either.

"I was so alone and afraid. Without Joleen I might have never been able to keep my sanity. And I needed her, I really needed her help. But I should have never had her take emotional care of me."

In order to reverse the dangerous trend which had begun in Joleen, Nelda ceased talking to her about her marital problems, asked Harry and Harry Jr. to assume some of Joleen's chores, even if they did balk at doing "women's work," and put Joleen in therapy.

According to Joleen's therapist, Joleen suffered from depression, as well as nightmares due to repressed anger and fears surrounding her enmeshment with her mother. In one recurring nightmare, her mother's hairbrush and one of her father's guns from Vietnam fly together from one room of the house to another, sometimes clashing into one another, sometimes chasing Joleen, and sometimes destroying furniture along the way. The hairbrush was interpreted as symbolizing her mother's anger, the gun, her father's. The dream shows that Joleen was afraid of her parents' arguing—as symbolized by the hairbrush and knife clashing into one another and destroying property—as well as her mother and father's individual anger toward her—as symbolized by both the hairbrush and the knife chasing Joleen. Joleen sincerely felt that if she did not help and comfort mother enough, mother would be mad. On the other hand, by sympathizing with her mother, Joleen was afraid of incurring the wrath of her father.

In another dream, Joleen envisioned herself as a mummy glued to her mother's leg. She asked her mother to release her, but her mother said "no." This dream depicts the symbiotic nature of the mother-daughter relationship and Joleen's desire to be her own person, not a mummy attached to her mother. It also represents Joleen's awareness that if she remained an obedient "mother's helper" and caretaker, she would never become an individual. Instead she would remain a reflection of her mother's emotions and problems.

Joleen's progress in therapy was impeded by her brother Harry's teenage rebellion. Harry Jr. was now not only daring to talk back to his father, but deliberately defying his many rules, not completing his chores or homework, staying out late, or whatever. He even wanted to date an Oriental girl! There were numerous father-son disputes, with Nelda threatening to commit suicide unless Harry and Harry Jr., came to terms.

Joleen was tempted to enter the fights as family peacemaker and to give her mother emotional support. In addition, she wanted to be an even more obedient and passive child in the family in order to compensate for her brother's rebellion. Joleen's therapist, however, advised her to detach from the family disputes as much as possible. Although Joleen could not help but have an emotional reaction to the family turmoil, she could stay in her room while the others argued. Also, Joleen was encouraged to continue being assertive about her need for time off from household duties in order to participate in some sports and social activities for herself.

Depression and conflicts such as Joleen's are not unique to Vietnam veteran families. In many families in which the mother is overwrought, or dysfunctional, it is not uncommon for one of the daughters to become a "little adult" or to take emotional care of the mother, or father. The resulting depression has also been observed among daughters of refugee camp survivors.[35]

Secondary Traumatization

One type of family which is considered dysfunctional is the enmeshed family. Joleen and her mother illustrate a case of mother-daughter enmeshment. Such enmeshment can also occur when one of the children becomes traumatized by the veteran's war experiences. This process, called "secondary traumatization," has been found not only among children of Vietnam veterans, but also among children of World War II veterans with PTSD, and among children of the survivors of the Nazi Holocaust.[36]

In secondary traumatization, the child, in some manner, relives his father's traumatic war experiences or becomes obsessed with the war-related issues which trouble and concern the veteran. The child may even manifest symptoms similar to the veteran's. The child may have nightmares about Vietnam, or combat, or worry a great deal about death and injury. Vet Center counselors report that, in some cases, children as young as three or four years old, have learned to imitate their fathers and hide under their beds when an airplane or helicopter flies overhead. Whether or not these children actually experience fear or are simply imitating Daddy is not known.

In families of World War II veterans where there was secondary traumatization, Rosenheck also found that "for some of the veteran's offspring, their father was, by far, the most important person in their lives. It is as if they were constantly together, constantly embroiled in a shared emotional cauldron. For these children, life seems to have been a series of anticipation of, and reactions to, their father's moods, impulses, and obsessions."[37]

In another study, Rosenheck cites the case of Alan, the ten-year-old son of a Vietnam combat vet who, although he did not have nightmares, had great difficulty sleeping because he "worried about being killed or kidnapped. His main fear was that he, his father, or both would be shot 'like in the war.' In many of his (Alan's) fantasies, it was as if he was living in one of his father's flashbacks rather than in his own reality."[38]In the Vet Center study, about 65% of the counselors polled observed symptoms similar to the veteran's in his children. This does not mean that 65% of the children of Vietnam veterans evidence symptoms similar to their father's, but rather that 65% of the counselors said that they had witnessed this phenomenon in some children of vets.

I have observed only one child evidencing secondary traumatization, Ben. Like the ten-year-old described by Rosenheck, Ben was obsessed with power and violence. He was constantly playing war games, reading war comics, and only wanted war toys for Christmas. It was impossible to have a conversation with Ben without his mentioning Vietnam and his father's various heroic feats. Despite his superior I.Q., he had trouble concentrating in school and was in frequent fights. His participation in sports was intense, and, he admitted, a way to prove to his father that he was as strong and brave as any Vietnam veteran. Ben would also attack his sisters, and the neighbors, with plastic swords, hurling anti-Vietnamese epithets.

Children who suffer from secondary traumatization may or may not assume a "rescuer" role in relation to their fathers. The "rescuer role" may be assumed by another child in the family who takes it upon himself to help make the father "happy."[39] Ben did assume the "rescuer" role and, when he wasn't playing sports or war games, spent an inordinate amount of time with his father, who was not only his father, but his best, if not only, friend.

At the age of fourteen, however, Ben, due to the natural changes of adolescence, began to want to separate from his father. Also, he became interested in girls, most of whom frowned on his interest in violence. Yet Ben felt guilty about experiencing the normal adolescent process of separating and becoming an individual, as if in growing up he was abandoning his father.

At the same time, Ben's father was experiencing his son's growing up—and away—as yet another loss, rekindling feelings of betrayal and abandonment associated with his war experience. In an effort to hold on to his son (who had been not only a son, but an admiring companion), Ben's father began to impose unnecessary restrictions on Ben's activities and to criticize Ben for minor imperfections, leading to further conflict between father and son, and more guilt on Ben's part.

Ben's father needed counseling to see that punishments and remarks were not bringing his son closer to him, but driving him farther away. Ben's father needed to be told repeatedly by his therapist, as well as by his friends who were parents, that losing children in their own lives is a normal part of parenthood, not a personal rejection.

Yet it still felt like a rejection to Ben's father and, for a while, he considered emotionally divorcing himself from his son and not interacting with him at all. "You don't have to disappear from your son's life. You only have to recede gradually," his therapist advised him.

"Your son still needs you and will continue to need you for the rest of your life. You are no longer in the forefront of his life as you were when he was younger, but this doesn't mean he doesn't love you. You need to learn to let go a little bit at a time."

The therapist's advice sounded easy, but Ben's father had difficulty tolerating the wrenching pain involved with allowing his son to develop his own interests and activities. Losing people is hard for anyone, but especially for Vietnam vets because they have already experienced many losses and because it threatens their sense of control. It highlights their powerlessness over other people, even their own children.

Yet this veteran was able to see that by not being so demanding of his son's attention, and by not creating friction over minor matters, that Ben talked with him more and showed him more respect. The ultimate compliment came, when after a week of watching what he said, Ben's father heard Ben say, "Gee, Dad, you haven't bugged me for a whole week. That makes me feel real good. Like I have a real Dad."

On a day-to-day basis, however, it was usually difficult for Ben's father not to be jealous when his son rushed through dinner and then left to be with his friends. The pain of realizing that his son was growing up, and in small but real ways, progressively leaving him, filled him with anger and despair.

"What my son is doing is all so normal," he told his therapist. "Why can't I adjust?"

"Turn the situation around and look at the positive. Isn't your son's growth beautiful? Didn't you play a part in producing such a mentally and physically healthy child? Would you really want your son to have no friends and be glued to you all the time? What if all your son did was hang around with you? Then you really would have a problem."

There were still times when Ben's father had trouble accepting that his son was growing up. But with help, he was able to accept feelings of loss as part of living and to relate to his son in a more constructive manner.

When The Veteran Overprotects And Overvalues His Children

While withdrawal from both wife and children is the most common pattern, there are instances where a veteran is able to maintain closeness with one or more of his children, but not his wife.[40] Even if a veteran is not particularly emotionally close to his children, however, he may still be extremely protective of them, triple checking their seat belts, carefully screening their friends and activities, or, in general, restricting their mobility.[41]

In addition to overprotection of children, overvaluation of children may occur. Overvaluing a child does not mean loving a child "too much," for there are no real bounds to parental love. Rather overvaluing a child means that the child becomes the parent's major, if only, reason for living or that the child functions as a symbol or as a form of restitution for what the parent has lost.[42] This results in tremendous pressure on the child to fulfill the parent's need for a purpose in life or to achieve goals which the parent was unable to fulfill due to the war.

For example, a vet who lost his arm in Vietnam deeply desired that his son become a musician, which had been his career choice prior to his war injury. He gave his son music lessons, took him to concerts, and in many other ways encouraged his son to develop his musical talents. Upon reaching adolescence, however, the son abandoned his interest in music. Initially the veteran argued with him. Yet he eventually realized that he could not force his son into a musical career. As a result, the vet had to once again suffer his grief about his lost arm and musical career, a sorrow which the hope that his son would be a musician had eased substantially for many years.

Issues surrounding grief become more prominent as the veteran approaches midlife and wants to leave a legacy to the next generation. If his children, whom he values so much, turn out different than he hoped or, for some reason, fail to idealize him as a parent, the veteran's resulting despair may be great.[43]

For Vietnam veterans, a child's birth may symbolize the rebirth of a dead buddy, or of a dead Vietnamese girlfriend.[44] Even if the child does not have a symbolic identity for the veteran, the child may provide the veteran with his only real reason for living. Harry, for example, for all his ambivalence toward his children, has frequently stated (both in group and in front of his family) that if it weren't for his children, he would have killed himself long ago. With his professional skills and ambitions at a standstill due to PTSD, and with his marriage now devoid of love and passion, without his children there "would be no point in living."

When Harry became suicidal, he pasted pictures of his children on his car dashboard so as to resist his temptation to drive his car off the road. His children, particularly Joleen and Harry Jr., were aware of the pictures and experienced their importance to their father as a awesome sense of responsibility for his well-being, and for his very life. As a result, Joleen and Harry Jr. became extremely anxious about not pleasing their father. If they were delayed somewhere, they were frantic about finding a phone to let him know they were safe; otherwise they were afraid he would think the worst and try to kill himself. On the surface the children's anxiety was not apparent. It manifested itself in a decreased ability to enjoy themselves, and a mental preoccupation with their father's well-being.

Even after Harry's suicidal periods became less frequent and less intense, his children showed considerable concern for him and felt it was their role to help take care of him. When Nelda would mention wanting to leave Harry, the children would protest. "You can't do that. Daddy will kill himself."

Today, however, some five years after Harry's last serious suicidal depression, Harry Jr. seems relatively free of excess concern about his father. Joleen, however, still worries about him and sometimes restricts her activities so that she can stay home and protect her father from himself. Even though she has been repeatedly told by her therapist, her mother, and Harry himself that he is no longer actively suicidal and that she is not responsible for his well-being, the old notion that she must protect her father still exists in her mind.

Violence In The Family

Mark was referred for psychological testing due to poor school performance. He was also in frequent fights with his schoolmates and enjoyed disrupting the classroom. Talking with Mark revealed that his father began to beat him, and his mother, soon after returning from Vietnam. Despite his above average I.Q., Mark often could not concentrate on his schoolwork because he never knew in what condition he would find his mother after school, or whether he would be abused himself. His aggression toward his peers and teachers was, to some extent, a displacement of his angry feelings toward his father, whom he was too small and weak to oppose.

When Mark was told that punching his peers and knocking them to the ground was "wrong," he was surprised. He felt that hitting was "okay." He had learned that violence was permissible from his father, who felt it was every man's "right" to beat his wife, or girlfriend. Furthermore, usually the police supported Mark's father in this notion. When Mark's mother would call for help, sometimes the police would not even come. While the traditional police policy of "no arrest, get out fast, protect yourself," is slowly on its way out in some areas, it was still in effect in Mark's middle class suburban neighborhood where, despite the new antibattering legislation, men could get by with almost murdering their wives.

One factor in the police's attitude may have been the fact that the largest percentage of police fatalities (some 23%) and some 40% of police injuries occur while intervening in family disputes. Training bulletins in some police departments explicitly warn officers of the danger to their lives if they arrest husbands who are apt to turn on police to save face.[45] Among the police in Mark's neighborhood, it was well-known that Mark's father was a former combat Marine. Perhaps this awareness contributed to their avoidance of Mark's mother's calls and to their usually blaming the abuse on her. Other

Vietnam wives whose husbands' fighting skills are known in the community have had similar problems with police response.

The root of Mark's father's violence was his low self-esteem. Even though he left Vietnam decorated as a "hero" and was now the manager of an electronics communication firm, Mark's father did not feel like a "hero" at all. He expended much of his psychic energy hiding his self-doubts, not only from others, but from himself as well. Battering was his means of coping not only with his present life frustrations, but with many of his unresolved feelings about Vietnam.

Family violence is often multigenerational—it tends to be passed down from one generation to the next.[46] Therefore, it followed that Mark would pattern himself after his father and use hitting and other forms of physical aggression as a means of feeling important, of coping with daily living, and of dealing with feelings. For example, if Mark felt slighted by another child, he would instantly hit the child rather than feel the pain of being rejected. Or, if a teacher gave Mark a low grade, she could expect to be insulted, or to have her property vandalized.

While Mark admired his powerful father, Mark also hated him. When Mark was in kindergarten, Mark used to pray that his father would get drunk and pass out. That way he would not have to feel helpless and impotent as he heard his mother scream. Many times Mark tried to protect his mother—only to be slammed against the wall and further emasculated by his father's taunts of "punk," "wimp," or "sissy."

In many abusive homes, often one child is singled out to be abused and he or she becomes the family's battered child. But in Mark's home, both Mark and his younger brother were beaten. The sisters were spared. Research shows that while girl children are more often the recipients of sexual assault within the family, boy children are more often the targets of severe physical battering.[47] "Boys are tough they can 'take it.' Girls can't," the thinking goes. Often the physical battering of boys is rationalized as a means of preparing them for the rigors of manhood.

Ostensibly in order to "toughen up" his sons, Mark's father did not allow them to cry or show pain. If they did they were beaten even harder. On some level, Mark felt responsible for his own abuse. If only he was more lovable, smarter, or better then his father would not beat him so.

Psychological testing revealed that Mark's chronic internal guilt and poor self-image, began at the age of four, in his mother's kitchen. There Mark saw his father cut his mother's arms three times as a "punishment" for Mark's poor table manners. Obviously Mark's table manners were but a pretext for the abuse. However, given the egocentric thinking of children, after this incident, Mark began to take responsibility for the parental fights and kept trying to "be perfect" in hopes of keeping battering incidents to a minimum.

Mark harbored considerable hostility toward his father. Yet, he also loved him very much. After all, his father was not an inhuman monster, but an individual with many strengths and admirable qualities. Mark's father could be exceptionally charming, loving, and playful. When not being brutish, he would take Mark and his brother on camping trips and overseas vacations and lavish them with the special attention every child craves from his father.

Furthermore, the three stage battering cycle which applied between Mark's father and mother also applied between Mark and his father. Battering tends to occur in a three stage cycle. During stage one—the tension rising stage—tensions rise between the couple, leading to stage two—the acute battering incident. Following the violence, however, comes stage three—the honeymoon stage—where the abuser repents and promises never again to hurt the woman he so loves. Usually this stage is accompanied by a profusion of gifts and ardent lovemaking, during which the woman's hopes for love and romance are renewed. Therefore, she forgives, and stays.

While this pattern of arguing and making up is common to many relationships, the distinctive feature of the battering cycle is that it involves what psychologist Lenore Walker calls a "sense of overkill."[48] The batterer is extreme, not only in his physical cruelty, but in his loving repentant behavior. Mark's father, for example, once tried to cut off his wife's hair, while also punching her. When she tried to phone the police, he ripped the phone off the wall. She finally escaped to her bedroom, where she locked herself up for twelve hours and contemplated suicide. When her husband returned from work that evening, he gave her a twelve-stone ruby ring, which he had purchased for her in Thailand during R&R and had been saving to give to her at "just the right moment." He begged his wife's forgiveness. This time he was truly sorry. Surely it would never happen again. Just to prove it, he would go to church on Sunday.

This honeymoon period lasted three weeks. After the next incident, Mark's father came home with a goldplated hairbrush—and a bouquet of orchids.

The same battering cycle applied between Mark and his father, who would come home with carloads of gifts for his sons following particularly severe beatings. Other times he took them out to dinner or to a ball game, shared "top-secret" Vietnam war stories with them, or in other ways was the most wonderful father imaginable. During these brief times, Mark's spirits soared. His dreams of having a "real father," were kindled and he was determined to be the "best boy" imaginable so his father would continue to love him. But when his father would become abusive again, as he always would, Mark's self-confidence would crash.

Starved for his father's affection and approval, Mark was determined to join the Marines when he came of age. There he would volunteer for the most difficult assignments. Mark hoped that our country would be involved in another Vietnam war by then, so he could prove his manhood to his father, as well as to himself. Meanwhile he would content himself with wearing Vietnam combat fatigues and harassing the Vietnamese clerks at the local drugstore.

Although Mark presented a "tough" bully image, in reality, he was frightened not only of the world, but of the "monsters" on his insides. He had panic attacks which he never shared with anyone. In the course of therapy, it was discovered that the "monsters" he feared were his own feelings, specifically his murderous, vengeful impulses, not only toward his father, but toward his mother as well.

Mark saw his mother as a victim, but he valued "strength" and despised his mother for being "weak." Fundamentally, he was furious with her for accepting the abuse *and* for failing to protect him from the father. It did not help that Mark's father often blamed his wife for his abusiveness. "I'm only hitting you because your mother did...," or "Your mother makes me hit you." Sometimes Mark's father would even claim that his wife had beaten herself up, even though Mark himself had witnessed the beating.

Mark did not know what to believe, his eyes or his father's lies. In addition, he was exposed to so much verbal denigration of his mother by his father that he lost most of his respect for his mother despite his love for her.

Mark also resented his mother when she put his father first, as she often had to, to keep the peace, and consequently had little time for him. In general, depending on the level of abuse, battered Vietnam wives often struggle to fulfill their maternal role. They usually have to spend so much of their time placating the veteran, avoiding beatings, or recovering from them, they sometimes have little energy left over for nurturing their children. At times, they may even wish they were childless so they could "run away from home" with ease.

Mark's mother was a very dedicated mother. Yet, on some level, she resented Mark, as she did all her children, for it was her very dedication to them which prevented her from leaving her abusive veteran. On one occasion, unforgettable to Mark, she communicated the depth of her resentment.

Once, when Mark was six, his father came home drunk. That night the acute battering incident lasted six hours. Listening to his mother's cries and troubled by fantasies of hurting his father, Mark could not sleep.

The next morning, Mark's father left for work, cursing his wife and blaming her for "making" him drink and causing the beating. If she were not such an inept dumb-dumb, he would not have to "discipline" her to keep the family "in order."

As soon as his father slammed the door, Mark felt sick to his stomach. When his mother stooped to help him, she winced with pain.

Three of her ribs were broken. But she was not going for medical treatment. She was forbidden to go to the family doctor. If she kept showing up at his office with injuries, he might become suspicious. Usually Mark's mother, like many abused women, went to the hospital emergency room.[49] Treatment was more impersonal there and lies, such as, "I fell off a ladder," were more readily believed. But Mark's father had to approve first.

Weeping over the toilet bowl, Mark's mother removed the twelve-stone ruby ring from her finger and threw it down the toilet.

Mark was horrified. "Dad will kill you for that."

She just glared at him, grabbed the goldplated hairbrush and tried to flush it down the toilet too.

"Stop, Mom!"

"You stop!" she growled back. "I wish I could flush you down the toilet. You, your brother, and all your sisters and Vietnam too. If it weren't for you kids and that...war, I'd have been out of here long ago. Now I'm trapped, a slave in my own home."

The woman then became hysterical. "Don't you ever cross me, Mark. Or I'll whip you with this hairbrush."

Mark's mother never used the goldplated hairbrush, or any other physical force, on her children. Other parents, however, have used hairbrushes and other "weapons" on their children, sometimes with deep, long-term effects.

To date, there are no formal studies of children from abusive Vietnam veteran homes. In general, our knowledge of children from violent homes is limited. Preliminary studies, however, show that these children often do not achieve at their grade level and evidence various emotional immaturities.[50] Some of these children cling to stuffed animals, their blankets, or to other security symbols long after their peers have abandoned such objects. In school, they may have reading or math problems, even though they do not have a learning disability. Mark's brother, for example, also performed below-average in school. In fact, he was considered almost "mentally retarded" by school officials until psychological testing revealed that he had an average I.Q. His school performance was stymied by the violence at home, which rendered him passive, rather than aggressive like Mark. Like his brother, this child was also involved in school fights, but of a different nature. He did not attack other children. Rather, whenever he saw other children fighting, he would intervene to help protect the weaker one.

According to Walker, in a paper presented to the American Psychological Association, existing studies also show that a disproportionate number of children from violent homes become runaways, alcoholics, drug addicts, prostitutes, and pimps. For many, life on the streets seems more benevolent than life at home, where the two people they love and need the most are tearing each other apart.[51] Some children side with the victim (the mother); others identify with the aggressor (the father) and eventually come to imitate him by abusing the mother and perhaps other family members as well. Most children, however, feel some loyalty toward both parents and become split down the middle emotionally. They also tend to have ambivalent feelings toward both parents loving them, yet also hating them for all the fighting. "If they really loved me, they wouldn't fight," explains Mark.

Like combat vets, children from violent homes can learn to "tune out" and deny the violence. They can just continue watching T.V. or listening to the radio. Even when their mother emerges black and blue, or bleeding, they may act as if "nothing happened." As they grow older, these children may turn to alcohol, food, or drugs as a way of furthering the pattern of denial and emotional numbing.[52]

Vietnam veterans who were also battered as children sometimes have two sets of PTSD: one from the Vietnam war and another from their childhood. They have flashbacks not only about the Viet Cong, but about their angry fathers. After issues regarding Vietnam are dealt with, vets who were battered as children often need to examine yet another level of trauma—that of being abused by a parent.

According to the Vet Center study, some 10% of Vietnam wives seen, report that their husband is physically abusive to one or more of their children. This does not mean that 10% of Vietnam veterans are child abusers, but rather that at the Vet Centers polled, counselors found approximately 10% of wives seeking help complaining about this problem. Child abuse is a widespread social problem affecting all social groups, not just Vietnam veterans with PTSD. In 1985, for example, there were 1,928,000 reported cases of child abuse and neglect. Some 40%-43% of these cases were substantiated.[53] Other surveys, however, suggest that the actual rates of physical abuse of children are higher than official reports show.[54] A recent report found that in 1986, approximately 1,300 children were killed by their parents. This represents a 23% increase from 1985.[55]

Studies of family violence show that once violence is introduced into a home, it not only escalates over time but has the potential of spreading to more than one family member. While there is no in-depth study specifically on the dynamics of family violence in Vietnam veteran homes, it can only be assumed that the phenomenon observed in other homes where there is physical abuse of the wife may also hold true in violent PTSD afflicted homes. Further research, however, would be needed to clarify this point.

In general, however, it has been found that there is a greater probability that children will be injured in a home where there is wife abuse, than in a home where the mother is not being violated. In homes where there is physical abuse of the mother, the children may be injured:
1. Simply because they are in the way;
2. Because they, like Mark, try to protect their mother; or
3. Because their mother uses them as a shield against the veteran.

Furthermore, if a veteran is in the hitting habit, when his wife is not available as a victim, he may extend his violence to his children.

When child abuse occurs in a Vietnam home, it is more likely to be committed by the veteran than by his wife. According to the Vet Center study, only approximately 3% of help-seeking Vietnam wives report having abused their children. This finding supports my observation that the majority of the women who have attended the Vet Center group have proven to be extremely dedicated mothers. They work hard to provide their children not only with the necessities of life, but also with needed psychotherapy, medical attention, or educational help. Most of the mothers who are single now continually put their children's needs above their own. Free evenings are not spent at parties or the spa, but driving children to therapy, doctor's appointments, or to Al-A-Teen meetings.

Yet there have been instances where women have been under so much stress for such an extended period of time that they have succumbed to physically assaulting one of their children. Some of the incidents *did* border on child abuse. In each case, the assault was a one-time occurrence, reflecting the woman's extreme state of physical and psychological exhaustion. In addition, each assault also involved displaced anger toward the veteran. Afraid to talk back to, or confront, her husband for fear that he would strike her or "go crazy" some other way, the woman would discharge her frustrations and pent up anger toward her veteran on a relatively safe, available target—her child.

Needless to say, the guilt and loss of self-esteem experienced by the mother who has hurt her child are enormous, in some instances precipitating a suicide attempt on her part. Her guilt also usually prevents her from giving herself much-needed rest or "time-out" from her many duties, both inside and outside the home, or from seeking help.

It cannot be overemphasized that no woman who has attended group thus far could be classified as a child abuser and that those who have committed even a single act of physical child abuse number less than 4%. Almost all of them function as their children's major caretaker, emotional support system, and protector from the veteran's indifference and inconsistencies toward his children or his emotional or physical abuse of them.

Yet among the battered Vietnam wives, there have been instances where the woman has put her husband before her children, sometimes due to her real fear of her husband, but sometimes due to her intense psychological attachment to him. In several cases, adolescent and even preadolescent children of battered Vietnam wives have run away from home to avoid being beaten by their veteran father. In other instances, children have run away from home to protest the beating of their mother, even though they themselves were not abused.

In cases where the abused Vietnam wife has allowed her child to be abused in order to appease her batterer, the knowledge that she has sacrificed her child to her veteran's anger diminishes her already low self-esteem and confirms her batterer's image of herself as a worthless person and "no good" mother. Hence when her child leaves her or verbally chastises her, she feels she "deserves it" and increasingly sinks into a state of helpless passivity and personal despair. While the beating of one of her children has often precipitated the battered woman's flight from her home, some abused Vietnam wives have not had the economic means to escape. Or, their self-esteem has become so eroded that they lack the will and self-confidence to make the break.

Children And Alcoholism

"I grew up in a little Vietnam," says a child of an alcoholic. "I didn't know why I was there. I didn't really know who the enemy was."[56]

Like children from violent homes, children from alcoholic homes also suffer from living in the emotional crossfire between the parents. Often they learn to suppress their feelings—especially their anger— and their emotional needs. Many erroneously feel that they are the cause of their father's drinking. Girls especially may adopt a caretaker role toward the alcoholic, or toward the mother.

Also like children from violent homes, children from alcoholic homes frequently suffer from low self-esteem and guilt. With approximately 90% of child abuse cases involving alcohol, children of alcoholic homes may also develop some of the symptoms of PTSD.[57]

These patterns, however, are common to many alcoholic homes, not only to homes where there is both PTSD and alcoholism. Yet, when the alcoholic also has PTSD, these patterns become intensified for there are now two powerful forces which keep children emotionally stifled and feeling guilty about their father's condition. For example, Lisa's father is a vet who became addicted to alcohol only after his tour of duty and who used alcohol in order to deal with his PTSD. While he was drinking, there was no clue that Vietnam haunted his present life. Before he joined AA, all Lisa had to worry about was whether or not her father would be too drunk to help her with her homework or drive her to her piano lessons.

After her father joined AA, however, his PTSD clearly emerged. Before, he was waking up in the middle of the night to drink. Now he was waking up to search out Viet Cong. In both situations, Lisa felt protective of her father but it was more embarrassing for her to have a father who thought himself in the jungles than one who drank too much. At least alcoholism was something her friends had heard of. Alcoholism was "bad" but it wasn't "crazy," like PTSD. Who had heard of PTSD?

Stepchildren

Some Vietnam veterans are jealous of their children. The birth of a child and the many demands of parenting (especially during the early years) usually divert the wife's attention away from the veteran to her child. Young children interrupt not only lovemaking, but the quiet and privacy which the PTSD afflicted veteran might feel he needs in order to recover from his war experiences.

If a vet has cause to resent his own children, how much more so those of another man? While no research has yet been completed on stepchildren of Vietnam veterans, in my experience some of the most severe cases of child abuse have occurred in families where there are stepchildren. In each instance, however, the veteran was not in treatment or was attending therapy irregularly.

While child abuse has certainly not occurred in each family where there are stepchildren, the majority of women with children from former marriages report that their vet frequently resents the time and money they spend on these children. Such jealousy, however, is not uncommon among blended families. In a few extreme cases, the veteran insisted that the wife send her children by her former marriage to their father or to another relative.

Helping Children Cope With PTSD

Based on his studies of children of World War II veterans and Vietnam veterans with PTSD, Rosenheck suggests that children who are extensively and repeatedly exposed to detailed descriptions of their father's traumatic war experiences are more likely to develop secondary traumatization than children who are given little or no information about their father's war experiences.[58] He notes that secondary traumatization did not occur in those World War II families where the father deliberately kept his war experiences a secret so as not to negatively affect his children.

This finding, however, should not imply that Vietnam cannot be openly discussed in the family. There is a profound difference between excessively exposing a child to descriptions of traumatic events and giving that child certain basic information about the nature of the Vietnam war and the potentially devastating effect of war on the human psyche. Furthermore, children from homes in which there are "no talk" rules often hunger to understand their father. In addition, if they are educated about PTSD and its effects on the family, they are less likely to blame themselves for their father's problems. They will also feel less alienated from him.

While it is difficult, if not impossible, for young children to understand the nature of their father's war experiences, or to comprehend the meaning of these experiences to their father, even children as young as 4 or 5 can understand some of the father's basic feelings about his war experiences. While a young child will certainly not profit from gory descriptions of combat, he or she usually can understand sadness or anger. "Daddy is sad (or mad) because somebody he loved died (or, got lost, or got sick) in the war." Perhaps an analogy could be made between the father's feelings and the child's feelings upon having a bike stolen or watching a pet die.

In addition, mothers can acknowledge to their children when their father is behaving unusually or inappropriately. While the mother need not denigrate or ridicule her husband, she can make factual statements about his behavior which help the child to understand. A mother can say, "In the war, Daddy learned that noises meant danger. That is why he jumps when you drop something." Or, "In the war, Daddy learned to be afraid of strangers and new places. That is why he likes to sit near the door." Or, "Daddy walks around the house at night because he can't stop thinking about sad and scary things that happened in the war."

Often children, especially young children, cannot identify their feelings, especially when they are having several emotions at the same time. A mother can help her children become in touch with their various emotions by asking, "How do you feel when Daddy and Mommy argue so much?" or, "when Daddy drinks so much?" or "when Daddy makes a hole in the wall?"

If the children cannot articulate their feelings, the mother can suggest feelings to them. She can say, "If I was a little girl (or boy) and my Mommy and Daddy argued, I would be scared that they would start hitting each other and forget about taking care of me. I would be mad at them too. I would also be mixed up because I wouldn't know who was right and who was wrong. I would want both of them to be right because they are my Mom and Dad. I would want to stop the fight but I would feel sad because I wouldn't know how to make them stop. Do you ever feel any of these ways?"

Instead of pretending that her husband's absence or sudden departure from the home "doesn't matter" or "shouldn't" be talked about, a mother can acknowledge the reality of the father's absence and say, "When Daddy leaves like that, I worry about him. I wonder if he is safe and am scared that he might be hurt. But I'm also mad at him for leaving without saying where he is going. Sometimes I get so mad at him I wish he would never come back. But then I'm sorry for thinking like that. It sounds funny, but I can be mad at him and love him at the same time too. Do you ever feel like me?" or "How do you feel when Daddy is gone?"

Or, "When Daddy yells at me, I feel scared and angry. I feel as if it was my fault that he yelled even though I know it wasn't."

Depending on the particular family situation, a mother can encourage her children to share their feelings about their family life with her and with their father, if she judges her husband as being able to tolerate and accept the children's honesty. In addition, unacceptable behavior must not be denied or minimized. If there is violence in the home, it is important that it be stated that violence is wrong, and dangerous. Similarly, if the veteran has an alcohol or drug problem, it is important that the problem be acknowledged.

Regardless of their ages, children need to be told repeatedly that they are not the cause of their father's or their mother's turmoil. According to Salom, who has conducted groups for adolescent children of Vietnam veterans, adolescents can profit greatly from direct instruction about PTSD and its potential effects on family life.[59] In her groups, children are given lectures and shown films about Vietnam and encouraged to identify the particular symptoms their father exhibits. The ways in which their father's specific symptoms affects them and what they can do to cope are also discussed.

Salom also assists children in seeing that they probably have little to do with the veteran's emotions or actions, but that, nevertheless, there are ways in which they can deal with their father's behavior. Children also receive help in recognizing "what they can control and what they cannot, what they are and are not responsible for."[60] In addition, children are assisted in developing their self-esteem. To date, an estimated 14% of Vet Centers offer programs for children.

Self-mutilating children, depressed or suicidal children, or children who manifest other psychological symptoms need help beyond a Vet Center children's group. A private psychologist, psychiatrist, or social worker must be consulted since most Vet Centers do not employ child specialists.

In addition, physical or sexual abuse of children cannot be tolerated. The children's physical safety must be a top priority, regardless of the circumstances. Either the abuser, or the children, must be removed from the home and appropriate help sought for each. Child abuse is not only a moral offense, but a crime. All states have mandatory child abuse reporting laws for professionals and others who come into contact with children. In some states, however, the mandatory child abuse reporting laws apply to all persons, including other family members. Therefore, a mother may be in violation of the child abuse laws of her state if she permits her children to be abused without reporting the abuser.

Summary

In homes where the veteran suffers from PTSD, the children are affected. Low self-esteem and self-blame for their father's unhappiness are the two most common problems seen so far. Some children will show symptoms similar to the father's.

If the vet tends to withdraw from his children because he cannot handle the pressures of parenting, or because he had bad combat experiences with children, the children tend to feel unwanted, unloved, and inadequate. In some cases, they blame the mother for their father's PTSD and in other cases, they cling excessively to her.

Vietnam wives often feel as if they are "single parents" with the burden of their children's emotional and physical well-being on their shoulders. They often try to compensate for their husband's distancing behavior, alcoholism, or violence by being "supermothers."

In some homes, the financial and emotional pressures on the parents sometimes lead to child abuse, either by the veteran or his wife. More common than physical abuse is verbal criticism of the children. While some vets distance themselves and avoid disciplining their children, others are deeply involved in excessively critical reviews of their children's behavior. In many instances, the Vietnam wife is a buffer between her children and her husband and finds herself unappreciated and misunderstood by both sides.

Children from PTSD afflicted homes often suffer from mixed feelings about their parents and mixed loyalties. Their feelings of being "different" because of their father's PTSD is only compounded if he is also an alcoholic or violent. As a Vet Center counselor who works with these children suggests, "It is quite possible that the future will see self-help groups for Adult Children of Vietnam Veterans similar to contemporary groups for Adult Children of Alcoholics."

Eleven

Suicide and the Vietnam Veteran Family

I was crazy about him. He was crazy about me. But why we were so attracted to each other, I'll probably never understand. I am beginning to understand, however, why Joel killed himself.

I met Joel about seven years after he got out of the service. His face was all scarred, but it wasn't just from Vietnam. It was from his youth in the slums of New Orleans too. Because of his childhood and Vietnam, he looked tough, but he was really very kind. He just didn't believe in himself, no matter what I said or did. He didn't believe in my love for him either.

For no particular reason, one day he woke up and said he was leaving me. He had to head up north where he could be free.

I thought there was something wrong with me, but I never asked. In those days, I never asked men questions, I just accepted what they said.

For a year and a half I wrote him in Wisconsin, where he was working on a farm. The first few months, he'd send me a postcard once a month. Then the postcards started getting shorter and shorter and fewer and fewer. When I called for his birthday, he refused the call. Then my letters started coming back to me unopened.

I gave up then and started dating other men. Eventually I married. About a month later, I received a letter from Joel's landlady. Joel had committed himself to a psychiatric hospital, then escaped his ward, and threw himself in front of a bus.

The landlady had seen my letters. No one else wrote Joel. She thought I would want to know.

My first reaction was to blame myself. Was it something I had said or done? Could I have possibly prevented this? Was it my fault for marrying another man?

But Joel hadn't even known I was engaged, much less married. And after all, he had rejected me, not the other way around. But still, I felt guilty.

Bits and pieces of our conversations came back to me. Sometimes he'd make jokes about 'Nam...about how his first day there he saw some guy blow his brains out and what color the brains were...about some village and some mother and child...about seeing heads mounted in the sand...about how even living in the slums hadn't prepared him for Vietnam. But he was always so funny about it that nobody realized he had a problem, not even him.

After the news of his death, I went to a counselor. She told me to detach from the situation—not to blame myself and to try not to let Joel's suicide upset me and my new marriage. But how can you detach from someone you loved? From someone you've slept with and given yourself to in so many ways?

At least if I could have attended his funeral, I could have mourned him. But I couldn't go and there was nowhere else to mourn him either until I came to group. To so many people, Joel was just a 'shiftless, crazy' Vietnam vet. But I know there was more to him than that and that his death was something more than one guy's failure to cope.

> Joel's girlfriend, Brenda,
> now a volunteer at a Vietnam
> Veteran Outreach Center

On June first, when Harry (the brain surgeon we met in Chapter 10) mentioned suicide, Nelda went into denial. His statement of suicidal intent raised her anxiety level to such a degree that she shoved it out of her awareness. When Harry made subsequent remarks about wishing to die in a car accident or hoping that God would take him away, Nelda would tremble. She didn't know what to say and felt helpless. "Come off it," "Stop joking," or "Let's talk about something pleasant," she would say, or in other ways dismiss Harry's remarks.

Yet she was uneasy. Recent newspaper articles on suicide had warned that *all* suicidal statements should be taken seriously. Nelda had also read that the "person who most frequently commits suicide in the U.S. is a white Protestant male in his 40s or 50s on a downwardly mobile social course, who has suffered a severe interpersonal loss in a relationship with wife or girlfriend, and who has used a gun to kill himself."[1] Physicians were also reported to have high suicide rates.[2]

While Harry did not have a gun and still had a marriage, he was a white Protestant physician approaching 40 and definitely on a downwardly mobile, social and occupational course. Nelda had cause for concern. However, the possibility that her husband would actually kill himself was so threatening to her, she preferred to hope that if Harry's suicidal wishes were not talked about they would magically disappear.

In addition, although Nelda would dare not admit it to herself, Harry's suicidal statements made her furious. How dare he talk about suicide! Didn't she have enough to deal with—children, job, a financial crisis, and PTSD—without him becoming suicidal too? After all, Harry was supposed to be the "man" in the family, and now he was falling apart on her.

"You'll feel better after you eat breakfast," Nelda would tell Harry when he'd wake up saying he was profoundly sad to still be alive.

On October first, Harry announced to Nelda that if things didn't get better, he would kill himself on New Year's Eve. There were other signs also: Harry stopped attending group at the Vet Center and, although he had always been withdrawn from the family, he was now more withdrawn than ever. Sometimes he would spend the entire weekend in his bedroom, Also, he had little, if any, interest in sex.

It was Harry's brother, John, however, who finally shattered Nelda's denial. Harry had given John a birthday present in advance, saying he would probably not be alive for his brother's birthday. He had also asked John to help take care of Nelda and the children after he killed himself with an overdose of certain medications. Since Harry was a physician, he could easily obtain any medications he wanted and knew perfectly well how many pills to take, and in what combinations, to die.

Nelda went into shock. She was finally facing the reality of Harry's suicide threats. Despite her anger at Harry, she did love him. She also felt guilty. Hadn't she been a good wife? Where had she failed him? Why hadn't she picked up on the obvious signs before? She was angry too. Didn't he want to live—for her?

"No, no, it can't be true," she sobbed in group. "But it is true. What do I do now?"

Nelda's first step was to talk to Harry openly about his suicidal plans and to contact his therapist at the local Vet Center. In cases of *impending* suicide—not vague suicidal wishes or suicidal thoughts——therapists sometimes decide to break the bonds of confidentiality and inform family members that their loved one is planning to kill themselves. In a like manner, if a Vietnam wife determines that her husband shows definite signs of suicidal intent, she should not hesitate to call her husband's therapist, his minister, or other authorities. Depending on the circumstances, she may even decide to inform her husband's family, friends, or other persons whom she feels could be helpful.

Also, the Vietnam wife need not hide her actions from her husband. Nelda told Harry, "I don't care whether you object or not, I'm letting your therapist and your parents know. You can go kill yourself if you want to, but you're going to have to fight us first."

In some cases, if the veteran is capable of violence or extreme paranoia, the actions suggested above may not be advisable. It is strongly suggested that the Vietnam wife discuss the particulars of her situation with a qualified mental health professional, perhaps at a local Vet Center.

In general, suicidal persons usually welcome such actions— and the subsequent attention. In many cases, they want someone else to take over. If they were 100% intent on killing themselves, they would have already done so. Instead, they chose to live and send out signals to others, hoping that someone would take care of them, give them hope, and affirm the worth of living.

Like Nelda, the Vietnam wife whose husband has been or is suicidal, or who has suicidal periods, lives under immense pressure. Even more than other wives, she refrains from expressing her anger and is careful about her speech and behavior toward her husband. In addition, she often searches for ways to minimize the stresses in her husband's life so as to avert a possible tragedy. Nelda, for example, found herself carefully monitoring not only her own actions, but those of her children. "Don't do that! Don't do this!," she'd say.

"We can't let Daddy feel bad." She also tried to make life easier for Harry by not pressuring him to attend certain social and family functions. At first she was willing to go alone, despite the embarrassment. Eventually, however, she stopped going at all and became reclusive— like Harry. Only after Harry had made noticeable progress in his therapy and began to socialize again, did Nelda realize how detrimental the isolation had been to her mental health.

Even after the acute suicidal crisis has subsided, the Vietnam wife needs to be aware that suicide can occur several weeks or months after her husband appears calmer and more elevated in mood. Sometimes the veteran's seeming improvement is the result of his inner decision to commit suicide at some future time and thereby terminate what he perceives as an unbearably painful or hopeless existence.[3]

The veteran's suicidal state, or statements, can also spill over to his children, conveying to them the message that life is not worth living. In several instances, children of veterans who have threatened or attempted suicide have threatened or attempted suicide themselves, children as young as thirteen.

This association between parental suicidal behavior and suicidal behavior in children is not unique to Vietnam veterans. As research has shown, suicide in the family is a significant risk factor for suicide in the other family members. In fact, it used to be believed that suicide was hereditary.[4] Although the genetic basis for suicide has not been scientifically substantiated, when a father commits suicide, or even talks about it, he provides a suicidal model for his child. Also, the child can acquire a sense of hopelessness and powerlessness. "If Father, who is bigger and stronger than me, a warrior even, cannot handle life, how can I, who am so much smaller and less experienced, ever hope to do so?"

In some cases, the veteran's threats of suicide may seem manipulative in that they occur in some predictable fashion—on a monthly basis, when his wife disagrees with him, when she refuses him sex, or whatever. After several such threats, sometimes wives begin to laugh. "There he goes again—talking suicide—just to get me to do what he wants." Despite their laughter, however, the women are afraid. "My worst fear," says one wife, "is that someday I'll come home from work and find that he's shot himself with one of his 'Nam guns."

This woman's husband has threatened suicide at least a dozen times. Although she has learned not to panic at every suicide note, she knows enough about suicidal behavior not to be led into a false sense of complacency. Just because her husband has made several suicidal gestures, as well as a few unsuccessful attempts, does not mean that he lacks the potential to complete a suicide. Even if he is a "manipulator," someday, somewhere, given the right amount of stress, he may, in fact, self-destruct.[5] According to some researchers, approximately one tenth of those who threaten suicide actually do follow through to completion.[6] Furthermore, some 35%-40% of suicide completers have been found to have made previous suicide attempts.[7] Some researchers contend that 80% of completers had at least one prior suicide attempt.[8]

In several instances, vets have threatened suicide upon learning of their wife's or girlfriend's decision to separate. The woman is often confused, not knowing whether the threat is serious or merely a means of coercing her into staying. "He might just be trying to scare me, but I also believe that if I leave, he might do it," says Susan, whose husband, with few friends and no support system, is at a high risk for suicide. In addition, he has suffered from depression ever since Vietnam and has refused to have children due to possible contamination from Agent Orange. Since he is also dissatisfied with his job, should Susan leave, he feels he has nothing to live for. To compound the problem, he has amassed a variety of medications, not only from his tour of duty in Vietnam, but from subsequent hospitalizations for war injuries. These medications are hidden throughout the home, along with at least two weapons, one from Vietnam and one purchased since.

Susan decided to stay with her husband until he sought help. When she suggested therapy, she expected him to resist the idea. But he did not. Like many suicidal persons, male and female, young and old, Susan's husband was ambivalent about whether to live or die and was looking for someone else to save him.

After he made noticeable progress in therapy and began to develop a support system, Susan left, confident that should her husband become suicidal again he would have a therapist and friends to lean on. Susan, however, is an exception. In my experience, more typically, the unhappily married Vietnam wife whose husband has threatened suicide feels compelled to stay in a marriage she no longer desires in order to preserve her husband's life. Even though she may be miserable, she does not want the guilt of her husband's death on her conscience. If there are children in the family and the veteran has stated to her, in front of the children, "If you leave me, I'll kill myself," or has made an overt suicide attempt, the pressure on the woman to stay is obvious.

"If you divorce Daddy, he'll die," or "Don't let my Daddy die," children have told their already guilt-ridden mothers, in some instances foreclosing the possibility that the woman will pursue separation or divorce. Even though the veteran's suicidal behavior is the veteran's responsibility, not his wife's, some wives have been told by the veteran's parents, siblings or war buddies, "If you leave and he kills himself, it'll be all your fault."

Among the physically abused Vietnam wives who have attended group, a pattern has been noted. Upon deciding to leave her abuser, the battered Vietnam wife typically reports that he has threatened to either kill her, or himself. In some cases, the veteran actually does make a suicidal gesture, or attempt. In my experience, however, to date, no abusive veteran has clearly committed suicide under the circumstance of his wife's departure or statement of intent to leave. Some abusers have, however, checked themselves into psychiatric units at V.A. or other hospitals. Still others have gone to live with their mothers or other relatives, where they have sunk into deep depressions, often asking the woman to come back in order to "save" them.

Despite the guilt heaped upon them by the veteran's suicidal messages or behavior, some women have nevertheless managed to leave abusive or otherwise undesirable marriages.

Suicide is the ninth leading cause of death in the U.S. among the general population.[9] In general, there are 10-12 suicides per 100,000 Americans per year.[10] There are no statistics on suicide among wives and children of Vietnam veterans and the statistics on suicide among Vietnam veterans themselves are presently an area of considerable debate. While in 1975 the Public Health Service Center found that the suicide rate among Vietnam veterans was 23% higher than among other veterans in the same age group, the studies that exist on suicide among Vietnam veterans are not only few in number, but highly controversial in nature.[11]

In some instances, the suicide is masked. For example, one-car collisions and other vehicular accidents may sometimes be deemed as suicidal. However, it is impossible to interview the victim to determine whether the cause of death was a driving error or a sincere wish to die. The same problem arises regarding certain poisonings or drug overdoses. Were they accidental or suicidal? Along these lines, alcohol and drug abuse, as well as other forms of self-destructive behavior, can be seen as mini-suicides, which, for some individuals, ultimately lead to death. Such deaths, however, are typically not included in suicide statistics.

In the case of the Vietnam veteran, the question arises as to whether veterans who pursue life-threatening vocations or avocations are motivated, in part, by suicidal wishes. For example, is the veteran who works in law enforcement or on dangerous construction, suicidal or not? What about veterans who volunteer to handle contaminated radioactive wastes or ask to be assigned to the most risky tasks on their particular job?

Similarly, if the veteran's hobbies include boating in shark-infested waters when he cannot swim, wine-tasting, gourmet cooking or cake-baking when he is diabetic, sky diving, or high speed motorcycle racing, is the veteran consciously, or unconsciously, seeking death? While he may not be overtly suicidal, his life style may lead to death. Such a death, however, will not be recorded as a suicide.

Similarly, if a vet provokes another person—his wife, the police, a drunken or armed stranger or attacker, or a violent known enemy—into killing him, his death will probably be listed as murder, not suicide. As Wolfgang noted in his famous study of spouse murders, some murders are "victim-precipitated." In these murders the victim is a "direct positive precipitator in the crime."[12] "This does not mean that the victim merely quarrelled with or insulted the offender. It means that the victim was the first to use physical force, to show and use a weapon, or to strike a blow."[13]

"A lot of things Ted did made me feel he wanted to die," explains Elaine. "Yet he always laughed at men, especially Vietnam vets, who killed themselves. 'Sissies,' he always called them. Just to prove he wasn't a 'wimp' he'd drive fast down icy hills and eat wild mushrooms without checking to see if they were poisonous."

The biggest risk Ted took was standing up to two muggers. "I gave them my purse immediately," said Elaine, "But Ted refused to give up his wallet. When they pounced on him, I was certain it was the end."

Luckily a police car passed by just at the right moment. But there was no police car in Elaine's kitchen when Ted threatened to scald her with boiling water. This threat climaxed a Memorial Day weekend of physical abuse and threats on the life of Elaine's mother, whom Ted was certain was trying to convince Elaine to leave him.

Elaine tried to calm him down but he only punched her harder and began to boil water. "You ungrateful bitch," he shouted. "I'm going to scar your face so that nobody else will ever want you. That way, you'll never leave me." At this point, Elaine grabbed a kitchen knife and killed him.

Elaine's story illustrates what Wolfgang found to be true in his study of mate slayings: that a "higher proportion of husbands than wives provoked their mates into killing them, that is, first struck their mates and changed the level of social interaction from that of verbalizing to assaulting."[14] On the basis of his findings, Wolfgang theorizes that men who view suicide as "unmasculine" or "passive," but who nevertheless harbor serious suicidal wishes, may achieve their death wish not by killing themselves directly, but by placing themselves in dangerous situations where they invite another person's attack.[15]

For example, the Vietnam wives incarcerated for the murder or attempted murder of their veteran describe their husbands as "begging to die." In one instance the veteran beat his wife with the butt of a rifle to the point where she required hospitalization. He not only refused to take her to the hospital, but handed her the rifle and dared her to shoot him. "I saw plenty of death in Vietnam. I'm not afraid to die," he said.

She vowed to take him up on his dare should he hit her again. When he tried to attack her with a broken dish, she shot him. Was his death homicidal, suicidal, or both?

To date, only two major studies on suicide among Vietnam veterans have been completed. A third large-scale study is currently underway. The first, completed by Hearst, et. al., examined death records of California and Pennsylvania men involved in the lottery draft system between 1974-1983.[16] On the basis of their results, these researchers concluded that motor vehicle accident and suicide rates were higher among those who served in Vietnam than among those who did not.

The second and more recent study, which sampled several thousand vets and nonvets, found that "total mortality among Vietnam veterans was 17% higher than for other veterans." The excess deaths occurred "mainly in the first five years after discharge...and...involved primarily motor vehicle accidents, suicide, homicide, and accidental poisonings."[17]

There are several factors which may put the PTSD afflicted veteran at special risk for suicide:
1. His depression or alcohol or drug abuse;
2. His social isolation;

3. His familiarity with (and often possession of) firearms or other weapons; and
4. The hopelessness which he may experience as part of his PTSD.

Among some PTSD afflicted veterans, there may also be a mind set which views violence, even violence toward himself, as a viable solution to life's problems.

The Vietnam wife must be alert to signals, not only from her husband, but from her son or daughter, that suicide is on their minds. She must also take seriously any wishes on her part to end her own life.

Most suicides do not happen without warning. The suicidal veteran, like other suicidal persons, will often give clues regarding his intentions.[18] The Vietnam wife must not think, "No, it could never happen in my family," as if suicide was a moral disgrace or a phenomenon limited to the mentally deranged or the lower socioeconomic classes. In the U.S. suicide occurs proportionally among all levels of society, among the well-educated, as well as the uneducated, and among mentally healthy persons who are, nevertheless, extremely unhappy.[19]

For example, Richard came from a high achieving family. His father, an immigrant, had worked two jobs during the depression, rising from dishwasher to restaurant owner in less than ten years. While Richard's father prided himself on being the best gourmet chef in Pittsburgh, he wanted more for his children than that.

"I want you all to be professors, doctors, lawyers," he repeatedly told his children, echoing the words of countless immigrants before him. Richard's siblings did what their father wanted; they became doctors, lawyers, and teachers. Richard, however, dropped out of college to go to Vietnam.

His parents' feelings were mixed. In their country of origin, only desperate people joined the military. Richard's grandfathers had dressed as girls in order to avoid conscription. On the other hand, Richard's parents shared their son's patriotic fervor. By serving his country, Richard was making the entire family "real" Americans. They were certain that if only Richard returned alive, he would resume his plans to become a famous biologist.

In Vietnam Richard was given the job of pulling bodies out of rivers and trying to identify them. Some of the bodies were decomposing or half eaten by fish. Some were American, others were Vietnamese. Often he had to salvage bodies from "no man's land" areas also, where he was constantly subject to attack.

When Richard returned home, he was given a hero's welcome by his ethnic community. Yet he did not feel like a hero. Sure, he had been shot at many times, but he had never valiantly saved lives or conquered the enemy. Why, he hadn't even had the courage to stand up for himself whenever he was falsely blamed for errors in the body counts.

Under pressure from his parents, Richard went back to the University of Pittsburgh but his heart wasn't in it. A depression was growing in him which he did not want to face. He was also starting to experience flashbacks. For example, whenever his class had to go to a river or lake to obtain plant specimens, Richard saw arms, legs, and dismembered bodies in the water. In his dreams, these arms and legs reached out to him.

"Just forget about it. You'll snap out of it soon," he would tell himself in the mornings. But he did not snap out of it and began using alcohol in order to cope. He also married April, the girl next door, hoping that marriage might help solve his problem.

But neither April's beauty, nor her love could stop his nightmares. Nor did sex cure his insomnia. Yet Richard continued to suffer in silence. Like his father, he felt that seeking help outside the family was a disgrace and that "real" men solved their problems on their own.

By the time Richard finished graduate school, he was not only a father, but a weekend drinker. He functioned fine during the week, but on weekends his life belonged to the bottle. All during graduate school, April attributed Richard's drinking and his emotional withdrawal to the pressures of his studies. Once he began working, however, she blamed his drinking on his authoritarian section chief, Dr. G.

Richard was one of the research firm's most brilliant biologists. Although Dr. G. was often critical of Richard, he also valued Richard highly and assigned him to top priority experiments. With the help of alcohol, Richard was able to veil his war memories and work diligently on all his assignments. One time, though, he made a serious mistake. He forgot to set the correct temperature on a certain specimen and ruined the experiment. Unfortunately, the experiment was part of a million dollar project.

Richard was willing to duplicate the experiment by working overtime without pay, but Dr. G wouldn't hear of it. For some reason,

Dr. G. became rigidly irrational and chose to use this incident to try to get Richard fired. He even went so far as to examine Richard's college records and, on the grounds of some minor technicality, tried to prove that Richard did not really have a graduate degree.

Richard fantasized about burning down Dr. G.'s home and other such aggressive acts. His alternate fantasy was of suicide. April had never seen her husband so angry or so depressed. Sometimes when he read newspaper accounts of murder/suicides, he would say, "That's the way out—I'll kill him, then myself." These words were so horrifying to April that she refused to really hear them.

The path Richard eventually chose, however, was not aggressive at all; he simply resigned from his job. He was afraid that if he tried to stand up for himself and lost, the sense of failure would be too bitter. He also feared that, in revenge, he might attack Dr. G., set explosives to his home, or do something else of a very violent nature. Rather than risk failure, or an act of aggression, Richard quelled his anger with alcohol and gave up. He felt he did not have the patience to go through the formal procedures and investigations which would have been necessary for him to save his job. In leaving without a fight, however, Richard confirmed his Vietnam view of himself as a weak, inept coward.

He then began working in his father's restaurant. "It should be a snap," he thought. The pressures, however, came to feel enormous, which only deepened his sense of inadequacy.

Among other problems, Richard had great difficulty managing the personnel beneath him. While he did not want to be authoritarian like some of his military commanders (and like Dr. G.), he could not tolerate "insubordination" either. Furthermore, the food in boiling pots sometimes reminded him of the bodies in the rivers in Vietnam and working with fish gave him migraines. The intense heat in the kitchen didn't help either.

His drinking increased, as did his absences from home. April began to wonder if Richard was cheating on her and hired a private detective to follow him. But Richard was not visiting other women, only the local bars and the local Vietnam memorial. Sometimes he sat by the memorial for hours.

By now Richard wasn't just a weekend drinker, but a full-fledged, everyday, alcoholic. His sexual interest and abilities waned, leaving April with virtually no contact with him at all. She resorted to masturbation, which she tried to keep a secret from him. Once he caught her.

"He didn't say much," April related. "But I knew that it destroyed him.

"I thought of saying, 'Well, isn't this better than me having an affair?' but thank God, I didn't. Then he asked me how long I had been doing it. I lied to spare his feelings, but he knew I was lying. After that, he hardly ever touched me."

Next Richard quit his restaurant job and floated from one odd job to the next. April was now almost totally emotionally and sexually abandoned. And financially insecure as well. Feeling as if she no longer had a husband, she moved in with her parents.

"I can't live without you. I need you. You are my whole life," Richard pleaded. Yet when she would phone him, he usually wouldn't talk with her.

April was disgusted but she was willing to consider returning to Richard, provided he mend his ways.

Richard, however, felt there was no hope for him. He turned over all his assets to his wife, then left town to go work as a cab driver in Scranton. Once in a while he would drive to Pittsburgh to see his parents and son, but basically he was detached from his entire family. Each time he returned, he was more withdrawn and more depressed.

When his brother, a successful lawyer, received yet another big promotion, Richard didn't even attend the family's celebration party. In fact, the last time Richard visited Pittsburgh was to go to his son's birthday party. He hadn't wanted to attend, but his favorite cousin talked him into it. All during the party, Richard sat in the corner, staring into space, saying nothing. Every now and then, he would mutter, "I wish I didn't have a son so I wouldn't have to leave him behind."

Nobody, not even April, picked up the clues. Even when Richard mailed the rest of his belongings to April and other members of his family, nobody suspected the depth of his misery.

Within weeks, Richard mailed a suicide note to his mother, then drove his cab into the Susquehanna river.

As Richard's story illustrates, suicide is not restricted to any particular social class. In fact, there is no one type of suicidal veteran, or Vietnam wife, or teenager, or child. However, the following characteristics have been found to correlate with suicide:

1. A family history of suicide or depression, or, a recent suicide of a friend, relative, or war buddy;
2. A prior suicide attempt;

3. Lack of strong affiliative bonds to another person or group of persons—feelings of not belonging to anyone or to any human group;
4. Social isolation: lack of a support system or inability to use available supports;
5. Alcohol or drug usage;
6. Reckless behavior;
7. Conflicts with authority (for vets, conflicts with employers, the law, or with government agencies; for teens, expulsion from school for example);
8. Depression, with possible irritability or agitation;
9. Feelings of being trapped, stuck, or sinful;
10. Feelings of hopelessness, helplessness, worthlessness, or humiliation;
11. Suppressed rage or free-floating hostility; or
12. Negative thinking: negative view of past, present and future, black and white thinking, irrational beliefs.[20]

Signals that suicide is possible include:

1. Announcements of suicidal thoughts or intentions, such as, "I'm going to kill myself," "I won't be here for Christmas," "You won't have to worry about me anymore," "This might be the last time you see me," or "This is my last day."
2. Suicidal writings or drawings, notes written as if already dead.
3. Termination behaviors: giving away prized possessions, writing a will, cleaning up unfinished business, saying goodbye to friends and relatives, purchasing a burial plot, writing one's own eulogy, designing one's tombstone, purchasing a one-way ticket to a potential suicide location, for example.
4. Noticeable withdrawal from family or friends or from previously attended therapy.
5. Any dramatic change in mood or emotional state.
6. Changes in eating habits (significant weight gain or weight loss).
7. Changes in sleeping habits (increased sleeping, fitful sleep, insomnia).
8. Loss of interest in friends and formerly pleasurable activities, like sex, music, or sports.
9. Difficulties with concentration.
10. Recent interpersonal loss (death in the family, rejection by a significant other).
11. Increased alcohol or drug usage.
12. Decreased functioning at work (or in school).

13. Preoccupation with fanatical or cult material.
14. Outbursts of violent or rebellious behavior (especially if out of character).
15. Psychomotor retardation: slumped posture, slow movements, repetitious behavior and statements.
16. Any evidence of loss of touch with reality.
17. Excessive or inappropriate guilt.[21]

While the Vietnam wife should not try to assess her husband's suicidal potential on her own, she needs to be aware of the factors which increase the likelihood of suicide and share information about her husband's suicidal intentions with an appropriate mental health professional, clergyman, or other authority like the police.

Upon the mere mention of the word "suicide" or upon the emergence of any of the suicidal indicators listed above, the veteran should be encouraged to seek professional help. Even if he is only thinking suicidal thoughts and has no definite plan, his suicidal thoughts need to be openly discussed. If the vet is already in treatment, he needs to be encouraged to share his suicidal thoughts with his therapist. Left unaired, the negative thoughts can feed upon themselves and develop into a full-blown suicide crisis.

In general, the probability of suicide is increased if the veteran has a well-thought-out, definite plan for killing himself rather than a vague wish to die. For example, the veteran who says he is planning to kill himself with an overdose of pills, but does not know what pills he would take (or in what quantities) and does not have a specific date established for his suicide is probably less likely to kill himself than the veteran who has spent two weeks in the library researching various types of medication, has already purchased the pills, and has a definite date in mind. Similarly, the veteran who says he will shoot himself, but does not own a gun and has no plans to purchase a gun, is less likely to kill himself than the veteran who has one or more guns at his immediate disposal and who spends much of his spare time at rifle ranges.

This does not mean that the vet who talks about suicide but does not have a plan is not capable of suicide. He is, and his suicidal wishes need to be acknowledged and openly discussed.

A sign that suicide is imminent is if the vet feels *compelled* to act on his impulse to self-destruct.[22] Statements such as, "I'm afraid to be alone," or, "I don't know if I can stop myself," or "There's a voice in my head that says, 'Do it! Do it, now!'" or "Hide the rat poison. I'm afraid I'll take some," warrant an immediate response. Even if the veteran has several powerful deterrents to his suicidal plans, such as a strong commitment to his job, family, or certain friends or strong religious beliefs against suicide, if he is evidencing *any* signs that he is unable to control his impulses, he should not be left alone. He may need hospitalization, or at least, the intervention of a therapist or clergyperson. If the veteran states that God, voices, or some force outside himself is "ordering him" to kill himself, psychiatric hospitalization is almost always needed.

Another important clue that suicide is imminent is if the veteran, after having communicated in some way that he is planning to kill himself, is unable to talk to anyone about his suicidal wishes or plans. As long as he can talk about his suicidal feelings and maintain an emotional connection with at least one person, whether it be his wife, a relative, a friend, or a therapist, there is hope.

Basically, the Vietnam wife can ask her husband the following questions:

Do you want to kill yourself?

Do you have a plan?

What is your plan?

On a scale of one to twenty, what is the probability you will put your plan into effect? Or, How much do you want to die? How much do you want to live?

Do you have a particular date in mind?

Do you feel you *must* kill yourself?

Do you feel there is someone trying to kill you? (For vets with paranoid tendencies.)

Is there someone, or something, telling you to kill yourself? (For vets with histories of psychoses or paranoia.)

Are you willing to give me the pills, the gun, the keys to the car (or whatever is the designated means of suicide)?

Can you promise me you won't kill yourself until you talk to (a therapist, the family doctor, a clergyman, or some other trained professional)?[23]

The veteran's responses to these questions can help the Vietnam wife identify the possibility that her husband might hurt himself. If he has a plan and a date, is unwilling to relinquish the means of self-destruction, or is unable to commit to not killing himself for a short period of time, the wife must not hesitate to act. In addition to any observable signs or disturbing answers to the above questions, the Vietnam wife must also trust her own gut reaction.

If, for *any* reason, she feels that her husband might possibly hurt himself or is not in control of himself, she must attempt to get control over whatever the veteran has identified as his means of self-destruction and seek outside help, *immediately*. She can call the local Vet Center, Veteran's Administration Medical Center, as well as any local suicide crisis hot line for help. The police or rescue squad could also be called for information and assistance. In an emergency, the suicidal Vietnam veteran can also be taken to the emergency room of any local hospital offering psychiatric care.

If there are signs of impending suicide and the wife must leave, a relative, family friend, or neighbor can be called to be home with the veteran. While some vets have welcomed the protective presence of another human being, others have yelled at their wives that they don't need "babysitters." Similarly, in situations where suicide seems imminent and the wife insists on finding help, sometimes the vet resists her efforts.

When the wife meets with such resistance, she can firmly say, "I am afraid. You just indicated to me that you are thinking about killing yourself. I care about you too much to take the chance that you might act on your impulse. Even if the chances of your killing yourself are one in a million, you mean too much for me to give you the opportunity to end your life. I would rather be safe than sorry."

In several instances, when the wife has been firm about initiating responsible action, the veteran has not only agreed to let a relative or friend be with him, but consented to go for help. In other instances, however, the veteran's resistance has only escalated. Some vets have even become extremely hostile or verbally abusive toward their wives. Yet, it is not uncommon for some suicidal persons (whether they be Vietnam veterans or not) to become angry or abusive at the very persons from whom they are seeking help. Many times, the hostility a suicidal person displays toward his or her helper is a reflection of the anger he or she harbors toward some other person.

The wife should not take her husband's anger personally, nor allow it to deter her from protecting her husband from his own impulses. However, if her husband begins to threaten violence— whether toward himself, toward her, or toward someone else—the woman must reconsider her strategy.

In my experience, there have been several instances where suicidal veterans have seriously threatened to kill themselves if their wives dared to call for help. In a few dramatic cases, vets have barricaded themselves in their homes, with their wives and children and, sometimes, with one or more weapons. "If you call the police, I'll kill myself first," or "If the police come, I'll fire at them and let them kill me," or "Anyone you call near this house, even if it's my sister, is history! I don't care if I go to jail. There's no reason to live anymore anyway."

Other vets have threatened to jump into their cars and speed to certain death if their wives so much as touched the phone. Some wives have not even been allowed to *talk* to the veteran, or to be in the same room with him. In one case the veteran threatened to harm his wife should she attempt to call for help.

More typically, however, when the veteran is resistant to help, the wife is cowed into not calling for outside assistance by his anger or threats to divorce her or otherwise abandon her or hurt her.

Although it is not generally advisable for the Vietnam wife to try to handle the suicidal veteran on her own, in some instances she may be forced to do so. Even though she is not a trained therapist, there may be times she needs to act like one. Through her talking, she might buy time and convince her husband to seek help and give life a chance.

She can discuss the subject of suicide with her husband directly. Many wives are afraid to mention the subject, thinking that this might precipitate a suicide attempt. However, generally, suicidal persons experience great relief when afforded the opportunity to talk openly about their suicidal thoughts. Often they have not shared their suicidal feelings with others for fear of disapproval and rejection.

The suicidal veteran needs to be told, "When you say you want to kill yourself, I believe you," not "Oh, you can't mean it," or, "You'll get over it soon enough," or "Nothing is that bad." The latter responses can convey to the veteran one or more of the following messages:

1. Suicide is so socially unacceptable or morally repugnant to me, I don't want to discuss it.
2. There's something wrong with you if you are talking that way.
3. You aren't entitled to feel that bad.
4. I'm sick and tired of hearing you complain.
5. I don't care enough about you to listen.

Most wives do care, however, deeply so. Yet even they, at least initially, may shrug off their husband's suicidal statements and discourage him from sharing freely. The subject of suicide may create considerable anxiety in the Vietnam wife. She may have a great fear of death, or she may be struggling with her own suicidal thoughts. Furthermore, she may feel inadequate to handle the situation. "I can't cope with this suicide talk. Therefore, it can't be true," she may wish. Or perhaps she feels she cannot discuss the topic of suicide without blurting out, "And what's supposed to happen to me and the kids if you go kill yourself?"

Some Vietnam wives, assume that if their husband is in treatment at a Vet Center, then there is no risk of suicide. This is not the case. True, suicidal feelings do sometimes force vets to seek help initially. However, being in individual or group therapy does not necessarily eliminate the veteran's negative thinking and sense of hopelessness. While suicidal thoughts and plans are often discussed in therapy, in some cases, it is to his wife or another family member, rather than to his therapist or therapy group, that the veteran first reveals his suicidal desires.

Furthermore, even after a vet has received help with and success-fully overcome an acute suicidal crisis or protracted suicidal period, suicidal thoughts *can* return, for being in therapy does not spare the veteran (or anyone else) from life's agonies. Although it is not true that once a person is suicidal, he is suicidal forever, if the veteran's response to pain, frustration, or to life's many dilemmas was suicidal at one point in time, he may respond in like manner once again, at some future time.[24]

The Vietnam wife with a suicidal husband often finds herself men-tally preparing for the possibility by thinking about the family's finan-cial situation. She wonders if she will need to go back to work or find a higher paying job. She also thinks about such things as childcare, transportation, and bills. Yet she cannot discuss her needs, or her plans, with her husband lest she reinforce his suicidal feel-ings. Furthermore, she usually hesitates to concretely pursue any jobs or training programs for fear of arousing his suspicions. Special problems come up when the Vietnam wife has no training and must go back to school before she can find work. She may be reluctant to go through the admissions procedures, pay the fees, and commit herself to a job program unless her husband actually does kill him-self, by which time she may be too late to get the training she needs.

"At least if I knew when he was going to do it, I could make plans," one wife explains, half-jokingly. "But I'm in limbo. I'm also stuck at home. Sometimes I feel I just can't do anything." Like other wives of suicidal veterans, this wife suffers from an extreme form of social isolation. She fears leaving her husband alone. Even if he insists that she go out alone, she stays home—just in case. Her children's social lives are also restricted. In essence, the family's entire life has slowly become tied up with the veteran's problems.

This wife, like others, also serves as the buffer between her husband and the world. She explains to relatives why he cannot be stressed or why he cannot attend family functions. At the same time, she feels guilty about talking about her husband's problems with others. "He would kill me if he knew I told his mother why he doesn't come to visit. But what am I supposed to do? She can tell when I'm lying."

The possibility of a husband committing suicide can create both anger and alienation, as well as emotional exhaustion. Yet there may be times when the wife is called upon to ignore her anger, and help pull her husband through not one, but several, suicide crises. For example, when Nelda managed to shove Harry back into therapy, she thought she was finished acting as his counselor, but there were still many times when she had to help him deal with his suicidal feelings. In these discussions, she used the same approach and many of the same arguments against suicide as she did the first time, when she convinced Harry to flush his pills down the toilet.

The first step Nelda took in talking to her husband was to ask "Why do you want to kill yourself?" or "What has changed in your life that you now want to die?"

While a suicidal condition is the result of many factors, not just one incident, there may be a single incident or a future imagined event or stress which precipitates a suicidal crisis. It is not the incident itself, but the meaning of the incident, which creates the overwhelming pain. In talking to a suicidal veteran, or to any other suicidal person, it is important not to mock their reasons for wanting to commit suicide, regardless of how insignificant the reasons might seem. It is also important to probe beneath the specific incident, to discover its meaning to the individual.

For example, Harry's suicidal crisis was precipitated by his chief at work calling him "stupid," and making derogatory statements about his work performance. Instead of saying, "There you go again, overreacting to everything as usual," or "That's a dumb reason for wanting to commit suicide," Nelda empathized: "For someone like you, Harry, whose identity is so wrapped up in his work and in being intelligent, being called stupid must have been a devastating experience." Nelda then tried to move Harry away from the specific incident to the general issues which the incident symbolized. For

Harry, his chief's remarks had highlighted the fact that ever since Vietnam, he had begun to lose confidence in his professional abilities. All of his life, being called "stupid" was one of his greatest fears. Now he had been called that by a man whom he respected.

Harry also felt like a failure as a husband and father. He knew he was not meeting his family's emotional needs. He also felt guilty because, due to his change in job status from a practicing surgeon to a medical report writer, Nelda had to work. He was certain that Nelda greatly resented him and was now staying with him only out of duty, not out of love.

He was also positive that his daughter Joleen's depression was all his fault and that Harry Jr., his pride and joy, was now rebelling against him at every turn because he was an inadequate father. Caught in the negative thinking which characterizes depressed persons, Harry was positive that Joleen would never improve, that he would never again be close to Harry Jr., that he and Nelda could never recapture their old romance.

Last, but not least, the derogatory comments made by Harry's superior at work had reminded Harry of all the times he had failed to save lives or felt incompetent in Vietnam.

"But killing yourself now won't bring back the dead," Nelda shouted. "And would those boys you saw die want you to kill yourself—or would they want you to go on and live and do something positive in this world? Can you decide to go on living—for them?"

"I'm crazy, I'm crazy, I don't deserve to live," Harry replied.

"You're not crazy! You're a victim of trauma. Stop beating yourself up! You can't help it. You were caught in a war situation where there were limited medical supplies and personnel, but an abundance of confusion, and exhaustion."

The same logic can be applied in talking to the suicidal combat vet, who may be chastising himself for his cowardice or mistakes (perceived or real) in Vietnam. If a vet is truly remorseful, he can be told that the best way he can make it up to those who are gone is to go on living and make a contribution to surviving Vietnam veterans, or to society in general. However, if he kills himself, he will only be throwing away his intelligence, insight, or whatever other talents or skills he might have.

If the veteran has a belief in a higher being or God, the Vietnam wife is lucky. She can then use all the theological arguments against suicide and stress to the veteran that God's plan for him does not include self-destruction.

Harry, however, hated God. Yet Nelda was still able to tell him that his life had a purpose.

"The reasons for your existence may not be clear to you at the moment, Harry," she said, "And they may not become apparent to you for quite some time, but you are here on this earth for a reason. In the past, you've helped a lot of people as a surgeon. Even in Vietnam, you saved lives, although you tend to remember only those who died on your table. Even if you never get better, just writing those medical reports, serves a purpose.

"I know you wanted to be a famous doctor, Harry, but you don't have to be famous to matter to me, or the kids. We love you. If you kill yourself, we'll be devastated."

"I'm a mess, Nelda, and frankly, those kids would be better off without me. Harry Jr. wishes me dead all the time!"

"He doesn't mean it, Harry, and even a messed up father is better than no father at all. If you think you're a bad father now, I say that if you kill yourself, you really will be a bad father. Even if you have the most legitimate reasons in the world for ending your life, our kids won't understand. All they'll know is that Daddy didn't care enough about them to stay alive. If you kill yourself, their emotional problems won't get better, they'll only get worse because they'll feel abandoned—and betrayed—by you."

Nelda then began to list Harry's various strengths and talents, in a sincere, not superficial, manner. At first, Harry did not want to listen, for he did not quite believe that there was much positive about him. Yet, it did him good to hear Nelda enumerate the various times he had shown kindness and love to others, integrity on the job, and other qualities.

"You're so down on yourself, you feel worthless," Nelda continued. "But you're important to lots of people besides me and the kids." Nelda then listed these people one by one.

In his depressed state, Harry needed to be reminded that he mattered to others, that if he died, he would be missed. Furthermore he would be teaching his children that life was not worth living.

"Well, that's the truth. Life isn't worth living." Harry insisted.

It would have made no sense for Nelda to argue with Harry that life could be joyous, unless she also empathized with his pain and depression.

"I know life seems black to you now, Harry, and with good reason. I wish I could say that I truly understand, but I can't. I never went to Vietnam, have never struggled with PTSD, or been demoted on my job, or had many of the problems you've had which have led you to feel so terrible.

"Perhaps if I were you, right now, I'd want to kill myself too. But I also know that feelings aren't facts and that very few situations are utterly hopeless. This is not to say that what you went through in Vietnam wasn't horrible, horrible beyond belief. Part of your suicidal feeling has to do with your rage and sense of powerlessness over events in Vietnam. But part is also due to feeling powerless over your life today."

With a good therapist, Nelda suggested, Harry could make changes in his life in the present that would make his life more fulfilling and bearable.

"No situation is hopeless," Nelda kept repeating, "not even your PTSD. You could get more therapy, antidepressant medication, and other help. You could even go to a PTSD inpatient program. There's no reason for you to feel so bad all the time."

"Nothing can help," Harry insisted.

"That's your depression talking, not you! How do you know nothing can help unless you try? You walked out of therapy before you even finished dealing with your feelings. Give therapy another try. If it doesn't help after a few weeks or months, you can always kill yourself later."

"We can't afford any more help for me," Harry replied.

"What's cheaper, therapy bills or funeral expenses?" A typical funeral, Nelda estimated, cost at least $4,000, the price of about a year's worth of private sessions. Furthermore, if Harry killed himself Nelda was certain she would get so depressed she would have to go to therapy at least twice a week, for at least ten years, which would cost about $80,000. The children would probably have to all go for therapy too. "So you see," Nelda concluded, "it's really cheaper for you to get help. Besides, the Vet Center is free."

Nelda then pointed out that right now, Harry was evaluating everything in terms of mistakes made in the past and problems coming up in the future. Also, as part of his depression, he was negatively projecting into the future. "How do you know Joleen isn't going to get better? She's already made progress. And how do you know that, a year from now, Harry Jr. and you won't be closer than you are today?

"A year from now, two years from now, you might even be doing surgery again. Who do you think you are, Harry, to predict the future, some kind of God?"

Despite Nelda's eloquence, Harry kept insisting that life was hopeless and not worth living. Furthermore, he would greatly appreciate it if Nelda would keep her Pollyanna logic to herself. His feelings were not a matter of logic, life was not a matter of logic. No words could talk him out of his misery.

"Even the Jews in the Nazi concentration camps and prisoners of war in Vietnam, Korea, and World War II wanted to live," Nelda said. "Sure, some of them died from giving up, but some of them carried on, hoping against hope, that they would survive."

"Fools! They should have all committed suicide," Harry retorted.

"Life is hard," Nelda replied. "No one is happy all the time. Most of us live for moments, a few brief moments when we feel at peace with ourselves, when we see something beautiful, or when we feel close to someone. Some of those prisoners kept on living just to see a bird or the sun in the morning, or to show a small kindness to a fellow prisoner.

"I'm not bringing up the concentration camp victims to make you feel guilty, Harry, or to make you feel like you have no right to feel miserable. But your situation, as terrible as it is, isn't as hopeless as theirs."

Nelda then brought in examples of how friends of theirs, immigrants from Lithuania, had endured various struggles and persecutions. "They could have given up, many times, but they didn't. We all have an urge to live, Harry, you too, even though it's buried under your depression right now. A part of you does want to die, but a part of you wants to live also, or else you would have already killed yourself."

Nelda then also drew examples from some of Harry's Vietnam veteran friends, some of whom were missing arms and legs. "Would you tell your quadriplegic friend, to go die because he lost all his limbs?"

Just as Nelda needed to address Harry's hopelessness, she needed to address his black and white thinking and irrational beliefs. For example, just because Harry and Harry Jr. were arguing, did not mean that they were enemies or that Harry Jr. didn't love him anymore. Harry Jr. was going through the typical adolescent process of separation from the parents. His rebelliousness would not last forever. Also, just because she and Harry were having marital problems, didn't mean she didn't love him.

"Are you angry at me, Harry?" Nelda asked. "They say that sometimes people kill themselves out of suppressed rage, as a form of vengeance on others. If you're angry at me, say so. I'd rather you yell at me and throw things all around the house than kill yourself."

Yes, Harry was angry at Nelda, but he was even angrier at one of his colleagues, in whom he had confided about his post-Vietnam psychological problems. Harry was certain that this colleague had informed the chief of the department about his PTSD, which had resulted in the chief's derogatory comments. Furthermore, this betrayal had activated for Harry all his feelings of betrayal surrounding his Vietnam experience.

"Maybe you think that if you kill yourself, you'll be punishing this so-called friend of yours," Nelda said. "Do you picture him at your funeral, overcome with remorse for how he mistreated you? Maybe he *will* drip with guilt, but I guarantee you, a week later, he'll be at a party having a wonderful time, and not think about you at all.

"Do you think that if you kill yourself, you'll be getting back at me and the kids for the ways we've let you down? If you kill yourself, we certainly will be sorry for all the times we hurt your feelings or were mad at you. We'll miss you a lot too.

"But we will go on to enjoy whatever there is that's enjoyable in this life. If you kill yourself, the main person you'll be hurting is yourself."

If the veteran is seeking vengeance on "the system" through his suicide, he needs to be reminded that the "system" will not be harmed one bit by his death. In fact, if he kills himself, he is letting the "system" win. While his death might create some commotion and perhaps, even some guilt, on the part of officials, the commotion and the guilt will be temporary. If the vet has tremendous rage toward the "system," he is better off learning how to channel that rage into positive action than in destroying himself.

Basically, the suicidal veteran needs to be told that suicide is not a rational solution to his problems. As Burns points out, "suicide is unnecessary," as there are many other ways of solving problems.[25] The veteran can also be asked to identify his reasons for living. These deterrents to suicide can be mentioned to him as often as needed.

He can also be asked to go back in time and remember when he felt loved, competent, successful, and needed. However, the severely depressed veteran may have great difficulty remembering this. He may become even more depressed realizing that he can't even remember what happiness and self-satisfaction ever felt like. At this point, it is important to assure him that, although it may be a struggle, he can and will get better.

If he fears he is "insane" or "crazy" because he has suicidal thoughts, he needs to be assured that many persons have suicidal thoughts, even supposedly "normal" persons. In time, and with help, the thoughts can lessen in frequency and intensity. The veteran can eventually learn to cope with his other symptoms. In sum, the suicidal vet needs to see his depression and hopelessness, as well as his other symptoms, as parts of his psychological stress disorder, not as permanent features of his personality. He can also be helped to look forward to a future where he has a greater sense of mastery over himself, and his environment, and where life will not be as painful.

In talking to her suicidal husband, the Vietnam wife should not limit herself to the suggestions presented in this chapter. She should not hesitate to use whatever arguments she feels would be encouraging to her husband and to ask those who know and love him for help. Even if her husband is in treatment, she should not hesitate to speak up. In our culture, there tends to be an overreliance on professionals. Women often feel inadequate in approaching their suicidal husband. Yet, a woman may have much wisdom and can support her husband on a day-to-day basis with a depth of heart and commitment which far exceeds what may be found in a therapist's office. Furthermore, she should discard any ideas presented in this chapter which she feels would not be effective with her particular husband.

Suicidal Thoughts In Children

Not only the Vietnam veteran, but his wife or child, can become suicidal. A number of children have not only talked about suicide, but have made suicide attempts, usually requiring subsequent hospitalization. In each case so far, the child, or teen, gave one or more clear warning signs.

Upon recognizing one or more of the suicide warning signs listed in this chapter, in either herself or her child, the Vietnam wife should seek professional help as soon as possible. Young children are in special danger because they are not always aware of how final their actions can be. Also they, like teenagers, tend to be more impulsive than adults, hence even more attention needs to be given to any indication that suicide is on their minds. Children and teens are also more likely to view life's problems as permanent, rather than temporary. They may react intensely to events which, to adults, may seem "trivial." For instance, a teenage boy may want to kill himself because his girlfriend began to date another boy; a teenage girl, because she binged and gained three pounds.

However, it is strongly recommended that a child's or adolescent's concerns, regardless of how insignificant they may seem, not be dismissed as "trivial." They must be talked about. Just as wives have hoped that their husband's suicidal intentions would disappear if they were not talked about, they have also hoped that their children's talk of suicide would also magically go away if left undiscussed.

This is not the case. The Vietnam wife needs to address the subject of suicide as openly with her child or teen as she would with her husband. Some of the suggestions offered in this chapter for questioning and talking to the suicidal veteran can also be used with appropriate modifications in approaching the suicidal young person.

In asking her child questions about his or her plans to commit suicide, the Vietnam wife need not fear that she will spark a suicide attempt. In fact, her inquiry and concern may save her child's life, especially if she can convince her child to talk to someone; the family physician, a therapist, a minister, or a counselor. She should not allow her fears of not saying or doing the "right thing" or her guilt about the fact that her child has expressed suicidal wishes paralyze her from speaking to her child from her heart.

Even if her child is in therapy, she cannot necessarily rely on the therapist to detect all the signs and to provide all the support and action the child needs. In a few instances, mothers did inform therapists or school officials about their child's suicidal intentions, and these authorities either did nothing, minimized the possibility of suicide, or indicated that the child's suicidal state was not their responsibility, but the responsibility of some other professional or authority.

Ultimately, it is up to the parents to provide proper care for their suicidal child and to support that child in the absence of responsible outside help and even when the child is in therapy. After all, no professional cares as much about the child as his mother. The Vietnam wife must communicate her love in as many ways as she knows how and let her child know that she is behind him or her 100%—for example, by being available to listen any time of the day or night. The child can also be told that even more help is available—inpatient hospitalization, intensive outpatient psychotherapy, medication.

If the family has financial difficulties and the child might feel guilty about the cost of therapy or other such help, the mother can stress that such help is a necessity, not a luxury. "You don't know how sad it makes me to see you so unhappy that you want to die. No amount of money is important compared to having you safe and happy," a mother told a suicidal daughter who was greatly concerned about the cost of her therapy. The daughter needed to be told that her life was worth more than any amount of money.

In addition, the Vietnam wife can give her child the phone number of the local suicide crisis center or hotline or other resources and urge him or her to use any of these resources in case of an emergency. She can also post these numbers, along with phone numbers of concerned relatives and friends, near the phone. As an added precaution, she can remove firearms or dangerous medications from the home, or keep them under lock and key. If the child becomes overtly suicidal, he or she can be hospitalized involuntarily.

Suicidal Thoughts In The Vietnam Wife

The Vietnam wife must also attend to her own suicidal impulses. When her thoughts begin to shift from simply thinking about suicide to planning the date and fantasizing about the funeral, she should run for help. Even if she is not serious about committing suicide, reoccurring or persistent suicidal thoughts betray a profound despair or sorrow or a suppressed rage which merit professional consultation. If she becomes too afraid of herself, hospitalization may be necessary.

A number of women who have attended group have contemplated suicide. A few have made suicide attempts. However, no woman has actually killed herself. Most of the women who have contemplated suicide have been prevented from carrying out their plans primarily due to a deep sense of responsibility and dedication to their children.

In the cases observed, two types of women have contemplated or attempted suicide: battered or formerly battered women and women sexually abused as children. Not all the abused women or incest survivors were suicidal, however, only those married to an abusive veteran who was not in treatment or who was in treatment only sporadically, dropping in and out of treatment programs as he desired.

Among all the suicidal women, three dynamics were present:
1. An active self hate;
2. Suppressed or only partially recognized anger toward at least one, usually more than one, abusive male; and

3. Feelings of psychological bondage to an emotionally ungiving, and often outright emotionally abusive, veteran.

The suicidal, battered and formerly battered women hated themselves for allowing themselves to be abused by their husbands or for permitting their veterans to abuse their children. They felt they were "crazy" or that there was something inherently "wrong" with them because they had chosen to marry or had been sexually or emotionally attracted to an abusive man. Some of the women were almost entirely out of touch with their anger toward their abusers, denying that they had any anger at all. Some were aware of their anger toward their batterer, but had never fully expressed it, or felt confused because they still had loving feelings toward him.

Like the battered woman, women who were incest survivors also had feelings of worthlessness and self-condemnation. Some had never dealt with their incest experience or had dealt with it incompletely, or only superficially.

Based on my observations, in combination with the frustrations of marriage to a PTSD afflicted Vietnam veteran who has not benefitted from treatment, the Vietnam wife who is also an incest survivor or a battered or formerly battered woman, may be at high risk for suicide. In a recent study, some 84% of female incest survivors had attempted suicide.[26] The suicide rate for battered women is also abnormally high.[27]

Summary

The Vietnam wife whose husband is at a high risk for suicide is living under immense pressure. On some level she may feel that she is both the source of, and the solution to, her husband's suicidal wishes. On another level, even if she knows she is guiltless, she may still feel responsible for her husband's death wish, or at the very least for preventing him from actually killing himself.

Once the veteran has talked of suicide, the wife typically watches her speech and behavior and trains her children to do the same. She also may take on additional responsibilities to try to make things as easy for her husband as possible.

In some cases, the Vietnam wife may sense that her husband's threats are manipulative. Yet even if so, she may hesitate to confront him or to leave him for fear that he will actually carry out his threat.

This threat of suicide casts a blanket of fear and guilt over the entire family. Not only the wife but the children are deeply affected. By listening to their father, children can get the idea that self-destruction is a viable solution to the problems of living. Or they may learn to feel that life is not worth living at all.

The Vietnam wife must be always alert to suicidal thoughts in her husband, her children, and herself. If she sees any signs, she must get help immediately. She should speak words of love, hope, and understanding straight from her heart and use any argument possible to keep her loved one alive. She must also be alert to any death wishes in herself and get any emotional, spiritual, or therapeutic help necessary to assist her.

Twelve

"I Believe In Love"
The Hope of Therapy

Before my husband began PTSD therapy, neither of us knew what was wrong with him. He blamed society for all his problems and I blamed him for all of mine. It took a year of individual and group therapy for him to unload his war stories and come to accept himself for what he did or didn't do during Vietnam. Then came the even bigger job of trying to live life with all its ups and downs.

When we were having our rough times, my parents and friends kept urging me to leave him. But I had faith in him and felt that counseling could help. And it has. We still have problems, though. PTSD counseling hasn't gotten rid of my husband's old-fashioned ideas about the woman's role or given me back the years I spent emotionally and financially supporting a man whose inner life was one raging storm after another. Counseling hasn't even gotten rid of all Stu's symptoms. But it has made them much more manageable.

Stu still gets depressed, and angry, but not as often and not for so long. His nightmares are almost gone and so is all that hate he was carrying around. We even talk now. Before all we did was yell at each other. Believe it or not, now we make "appointments" to talk about things. If we find we can't communicate at home, we make a marriage counseling appointment at the Vet Center for a 'marriage tune-up.'

By attending a woman's group at the center, I've learned not to take it personally when Stu goes off. I *just go and do something else. I've also learned not to blame my husband for all my problems. I have issues with my parents and things in my past that have nothing to do with him and I have to work them out myself.*

But Stu had to get help and get on his feet before I felt free to take a look at myself. When he was into his depressions and his drinking, I didn't have the luxury of taking care of my emotional needs.

He's much better now, but that doesn't mean I am. I still don't feel comfortable asserting myself, though I'm not as afraid as I used to be. I still panic when I go against what other people want me to do. After all those years of being a people pleaser and doing everything for everybody else, it's hard to shift gears.

As a result of his therapy, Stu doesn't need me as much as he used to. I'm glad but it leaves me at a loss. Frankly, I'm so used to one crisis after another that sometimes I don't know how to handle all this peace. I also don't know what to do with all the resentments I've built up over the years.

I find it impossible to forget some of my grievances. Yet I don't want to ruin the progress Stu and I have made by making a big deal about things that happened years ago.

The miracle is that, despite everything, the love we had long ago isn't all gone. Don't ask me why or how, but it survived. There must be something strong between us, otherwise we would have been history a long time ago.

Wife of a combat vet

Today popular songs often call love an illusion and many books are devoted to finding pathologies in love relationships. Often a woman's dedication to her husband, or lover, is described as a "love addiction" or as an expression of one or more of her "neurotic needs." Nevertheless, somehow, somewhere, despite all the disappointments and strains, many of the Vietnam wives who have attended group still "believe in love."

"Why would I put up with him if I didn't love him?" more than one woman has stated. "I know he has a bad case of PTSD, but how often do you fall in love?" asks Rita.

Despite her love, however, Rita, like many of the wives, seriously questions whether she can continue to remain in a marriage which is often not functional for her. Her major hope is that therapy will make the continuation of her marriage possible.

When Rita first came to group, she came looking for ways to help her husband. Although she wished her husband would seek counseling, secretly, she hoped to heal him herself. Wasn't her love and understanding enough? Hadn't she read numerous books on Vietnam and PTSD? And, as the adult child of an alcoholic, wasn't she an expert caretaker? The problem was, however, that her husband would not open up to her. In his view, her desire to be helpful was "intrusive." "You can't understand. You weren't there," was his standard reply to her carefully worded questions.

Rita's next hope was that medication would help free her husband of his PTSD. In recent years, a number of psychiatric drugs have proven effective in relieving some of the symptoms of PTSD—anxiety, depression, and paranoia, and in suppressing REM stage dreams and the startle response.[1] There is no one drug which has been used for all vets with PTSD.[2] Since PTSD expresses itself differently in each veteran and since some veterans suffer from problems in addition to PTSD, medication is usually aimed at the symptoms which are most disabling to him.

While drugs are useful, drugs do not treat PTSD, but only the symptoms associated with PTSD.[3] By reducing the severity of the symptoms, medication can increase the veteran's ability to function and his ability to deal with the roots of his PTSD.

However, sometimes psychotropic medication can interfere with therapy.[4] Furthermore, medication must be taken as prescribed and monitored often. In some cases, vets are noncompliant, taking medication only when they "feel bad" and refusing to return for medication check-ups. Other complications arise if the veteran is suicidal or if he is abusing alcohol or drugs.[5] Medication alone is not the total answer. While a useful adjunct to therapy, medication should never be used as a substitute for therapy.

Vietnam veterans with PTSD are not all the same. Some have psychological stressors in addition to their PTSD. Because there are so many things to consider, therapy must always be individualized. We can make some generalizations, however.

In order for a veteran to overcome the paralyzing and destructive effects of his war experiences, he needs to reconsider his Vietnam experience on three levels: 1. the cognitive or mental, 2. the emotional, and 3. the moral or spiritual. Group therapy with other Vietnam veterans, led by a qualified, caring therapist knowledgeable about PTSD and the nature of the Vietnam war, is often recommended.[6]

Being in group helps the veteran emerge from his social isolation and allows him to practice his often rusty social skills. The group can help resocialize the veteran, while simultaneously providing him with a community of support, as well as with a realistic perspective on his war experiences. He may also receive honest and valuable feedback about himself, feedback which he might be willing to accept only from persons who "were there."

For some vets, war experiences are only partially remembered. For others, they are almost totally repressed. The veteran's traumatic memories are not repressed because he is, or was, "neurotic," but because, by definition, a trauma is an event which so overwhelms an individual that he cannot accept it as happening to him.

In order for healing to begin, the Vietnam veteran needs to "uncover the trauma."[7] The specific events which were traumatic to him need to be brought out of repression and into his conscious awareness, then shared in group or individual therapy. There he can be helped to understand the meaning of these events in his life. Often these events involve incidents where the veteran's action, or inaction, led to the injury or death of another human being.[8]

In most cases, combat was the setting for such traumatic events, but there were other sites also. For example, like many medics and other medical personnel, some rear support personnel with PTSD feel that their errors in judgement (real or perceived) may have cost American or Vietnamese civilian lives. Similarly, some technical repair troops have suffered because they felt responsible for certain machinery breakdowns, which resulted in casualties.

While there are veterans who have killed and felt no guilt, in many cases, the veteran's memories are "distorted in the direction of unreasonable guilt."[9,10] Such veterans often fail to acknowledge how the complex and ambiguous nature of combat or of the entire war situation may have contributed to their behavior. The therapist and other veterans can help the vet evaluate the incident more objectively and relieve him of "long held guilt."[11]

In group, the vet may come to realize that perhaps he was not such a coward after all, or perhaps his friends would have been killed anyway. If indeed his cowardice or viciousness resulted in an irreversible tragedy, the vet must feel the pain of his guilt directly, rather than run from it. With the help of the group, he can try to learn to forgive himself. "The message is..." writes Williams, that many veterans "...did the best job in the situation that could have been done considering the circumstances and the resources available in the situation."[12]

After reformulating the trauma mentally, the next step toward healing involves feeling the feelings associated with the traumatic event(s), as well as with other war events, feelings which were not felt at the time the event(s) occurred. Repressed grief and repressed anger are usually the two major emotions which emerge. As the veteran's rage rises to the surface, he can be helped in learning how to direct the powerful energy of his rage into constructive, rather than destructive, channels. Often at this point, the veteran may begin to make associations between past and present and see how his war experiences and his reactions to them have negatively influenced his life and relationships since the war. He may also come to appreciate any positive aspects of his military experience.

For some vets, recovery from PTSD necessitates a spiritual or moral healing, as well as an emotional one. Spiritually, some vets seek absolution for their actions.

For some vets, group therapy is the route to self-forgiveness. For others, the assistance of a clergyman or minister is needed. The need for absolution may also result in the veteran becoming involved in various "survivor missions," (such as helping other Vietnam veterans or Vietnamese refugees) or in other charitable works.[13]

Many wives have been extremely tolerant of the time, energy, and money their recovering husbands have devoted to helping fellow veterans or other persons in need. As they see their husbands break out of their isolation, they rejoice. However, wives also feel resentful when their husbands seem to be giving more time and love to others than to their marriages and children.

In sum, therapy can help reduce the veteran's sense of guilt, teach him how to control his anger, and enable him to become aware of his various emotions and to be able to express them more effectively. Furthermore, therapy, especially group therapy, can help reduce the stigma associated with being a Vietnam veteran, build the veteran's pride in his honorable and dutiful actions, remove his "fear of mental illness," and help him "clarify (his) identity" and values.[14] This applies only to groups conducted by qualified therapists, not to informal or unstructured groups where veterans might be confronted in a destructive, rather than a constructive, manner.

If a veteran is abusing drugs or alcohol it is important for the therapist to determine if the veteran is a chronic substance abuser or if he is using drugs or alcohol as a form of self-medication for the symptoms of PTSD.[15]

If a veteran is given a primary diagnosis of alcohol or drug abuse with a secondary diagnosis of PTSD, usually it will be recommended, if not required, that he complete an alcohol or drug rehabilitation program before entering counseling for PTSD. If the veteran's primary diagnosis is PTSD and his secondary diagnosis is substance abuse, he will usually be asked to refrain from drinking or drugging for the duration of the therapy. Simply put, a veteran needs to be sober (or clean) before he can deal with his Vietnam issues.[16]

In the past, PTSD was largely unrecognized by the mental health community. Even today, despite the large numbers of "competent research projects that validate PTSD," some psychiatrists, psychologists, and social workers still "doubt the validity of PTSD or consider it a very rare phenomenon."[18] Instead, they look to "predisposing factors" to account for the veteran's problems, almost totally ignoring or minimizing the trauma of war.[1] As a result many vets with PTSD were, and in some instances, still are, misdiagnosed as being neurotic, psychotic, or having various character disorders.[19]

Today, however, an opposite danger may also exist. As Jelinek and Williams (both veteran therapists) point out, with increased recognition of PTSD, it is possible that therapists, especially veteran therapists "see PTSD in every veteran...and... elevate the importance of that disorder and minimize or neglect additional psychopathology."[20]

Furthermore, while perhaps *too* many veterans with PTSD have been misdiagnosed as being character disordered or psychotic, there are veterans with PTSD who are also character disordered, schizophrenic, paranoid, or who have personality problems beyond PTSD.[21] In many instances, previous personality problems or traumas only served to complicate and intensify the veteran's reaction to the Vietnam war.

These vets need help *both* with PTSD *and* their other problems. They can be helped. However, the full range of their problems must be acknowledged.

Wives are often disappointed when therapy doesn't "fix" their husbands as rapidly as they desire. Women who have waited ten or fifteen years for their husbands to finally seek help often are dismayed to discover that the healing process can be painfully slow. Children, too, may be anxious for their father to improve. It takes a long time—usually at least a year. Depending on the individual, it may take even longer. Furthermore, healing requires that the veteran attend sessions regularly, not sporadically or only when in crisis, as is the pattern with some vets.

Family members need to remember that the war occurred many years ago. Meanwhile, their veteran has been practicing certain coping mechanisms for many years. His coping mechanisms may be firmly entrenched. Considerable time may be needed for healing to occur.

Family members sometimes hope that after their veteran undergoes therapy they will never hear the word "Vietnam" again or that they will no longer have to be saddened by the veteran's sadness or plagued by his negativity or bitterness. While therapy can help restore a man to his pre-Vietnam level of functioning, no therapy can remove Vietnam from the veteran's memory. Just as rape victims cannot "forget" the rape, or battered women, their abuse, Vietnam will be with some veterans until the day they die.

That the trauma of war can leave permanent physical and psychological scars has been well-documented.[22] The veteran's sadness, anger, or other feelings about the war are bound to return. Being well, for the Vietnam veteran, lies not in "feeling better all the time," or in "never thinking or hurting about Vietnam again," but rather in being reintegrated into society and in being able to function in a family or career.[23] For the veteran, as for any human being, therapy cannot promise the absence of pain, or rage, but only a closer emotional connectedness to oneself and others.

Nevertheless, with help, the veteran can grow past much of his Vietnam experience and learn to put more energy into his present life. While he may still suffer from intrusive thoughts, they will be less frequent and, hopefully, less intense. Similarly, there may still be periods of numbing, rage, or grief. But these periods will be shorter in duration, better understood, and less feared by the veteran and his wife.[24] Rita explains:

> It took three years of therapy: his therapy, my therapy, couples therapy—the works—for our relationship to improve. Frankly, I never thought our marriage would make it. But today, he's less angry. That's a miracle. Also, when he gets angry about Vietnam, he can now say, 'Rita,

*I'm having a PTSD attack. Leave me alone.' That's a
miracle too.*

*But even if he doesn't warn me, I've learned to walk
out of the room and not take his anger or coolness so
personally. The woman's group helped me with that.*

While Rita's husband can never forget Vietnam, he, like many vets
who have sought help, has experienced considerable relief from some
of the symptoms of PTSD. In addition, he is able to deal with reality
more constructively, is more flexible, and has found "creative and
constructive outlets" for his anger, and his pain.[25] For example, he
is now a Big Brother to an inner city youth and is actively involved
in an anti-smoking campaign in his community.

While wives can usually understand why therapy for PTSD can
take time, it may still be difficult for them to wait for their husband's
healing to manifest itself. Many a wife has held back expressing her
grievances toward her husband while he was in therapy for fear of
overloading him. "He can't deal with me and Vietnam." Some of
these women have also been advised by their husband's therapist to
not bring up marital problems until their husband has resolved many
of his Vietnam issues.

In cases where the veteran's PTSD is so severe that the veteran
is severely regressed, almost totally noncommunicative, or extremely rigid or violent, the wife's decision to refrain from voicing her
various concerns may be prudent. On the other hand, she cannot
be silent forever, nor can she always wait until her husband is substantially healed to discuss certain matters. Often there are issues,
especially regarding children, which cannot wait. Furthermore, an
improved relationship with his wife and children and an increased
capacity to deal with present realities are a part of the veteran's recovery. The veteran cannot be protected forever from knowledge about
how his behavior is stressing his family.

For example, Marsha had to confront her husband, Kevin, about
certain issues because she had to make a decision about their son's
school placement. He was achieving beyond his grade level and had
been recommended for the gifted and talented program. However,
for him to be part of this program he would have to be bussed to a
school far from his home and in a less desirable neighborhood.

Marsha knew that Kevin had many fears about vehicular accidents
and crime. When he was seven, one of his friends had died in a
school bus accident. Once, before entering PTSD therapy, he had

had an anxiety attack and had nearly run into a school bus himself. Several car accidents, combined with his Vietnam experience, intensified his concerns about his family's safety.

Usually Marsha didn't bring up problems that might make Kevin "hyper" but on this issue she needed to get Kevin's views. Also, if their son was to be enrolled, she needed Kevin's written consent. When she brought the subject up, Kevin refused to deal with it.

"Don't pressure me. You know I can't take pressure. Let me get more counseling under my belt before bringing up things like that."

"But if we don't make up our minds, our son is going to lose his chance," Marsha reminded him.

"It'll have to wait."

"But we can't wait."

"I said, it'll have to wait."

A few days later, Marsha brought the subject up again. Kevin still refused to discuss the issue saying he had to get himself together first. Marsha pressed the issue and Kevin accused her of being willing to endanger their son's life. Marsha, in turn, accused Kevin of letting his "irrational fears" stunt their child's development. Then Kevin started on Marsha's weight and Marsha let loose on the subject of how Kevin and his "stupid war" had not only made her fat but a nervous wreck.

As the argument escalated, the original subject of discussion was lost. Marsha forgot to mention her own fears about bussing and Kevin forgot about his pride in his son's abilities and his deep desire to help the child do well.

Meanwhile, the child, who was supposed to be sleeping, tried to stop the fight. "Don't fight because of me. I don't want to go to that new school anyhow. All I want to do is grow up and be a soldier like Daddy and get wounded in a war."

"See what you've done! You've warped his mind," shrieked Marsha.

Kevin yelled back and the argument finally ended with Kevin frozen in anger for days.

At a total loss, Marsha went to Kevin's counselor and asked for his assistance. He suggested an "emergency" couples counseling session limited to the school issue only. During the session, Kevin and Marsha were able to give up the arguing and look at the school problem objectively. They found out that they basically agreed. They wanted every advantage for their son but were afraid of the bussing and the poor neighborhood.

The counselor suggested that they look at programs in other counties. Perhaps even move to an area with a gifted and talented program nearer home. Or they could make arrangements to drive their son to school or have a cab take him.

As Marsha's case illustrates, a consultation with the veteran's therapist may be needed to help a woman decide whether or not to confront her husband, and on what issues and to assist her in resolving certain issues which cannot wait. In this regard, couples counseling may also be helpful. However, couples counseling is usually advised only after the veteran has made noticeable progress in his PTSD treatment.

When vets are in treatment, their wives or girlfriends often find it helpful to attend a woman's support group. There they can air grievances which they sometimes feel they must keep to themselves at home. If a woman decides to remain silent on all but the most urgent matters until her husband has achieved a certain level of recovery, her decision needs to be respected. She can, however, commit to the group, and to herself, that she will speak up at some future point in time.

If a woman cannot wait, however, the group can give her encouragement and support for her decision, as well as help in prioritizing her marital concerns so as to not bombard her vet with all her complaints at once.

Most of the Vietnam wives who have attended group have exercised tremendous patience in waiting for their husbands to reach the point where they can tolerate, and profit from, feedback from a woman. Wives have also endured their husband's therapeutic process where, in many cases, "it gets worse before it gets better." As Rita explains to newcomers:

> When your husband goes into therapy, you think, 'Hurrah! The problems are finally over with.' Well, guess what? There are more nightmares, more holes in the wall, more anger at you.
>
> In therapy all the feelings your husband has bottled up for years start coming out, in group of course, but on you too. My husband even started drinking more— blaming it all on me, as usual. It got so bad, I started wondering why I ever begged him to go for help in the first place.

> *Then, when the group started teaching him how to be assertive, rather than passive or aggressive, which were his usual styles, I got mad. Here I was, holding in everything for years and not being assertive so he wouldn't get upset and quit therapy, and here he was, practicing his group's assertiveness training on me. Then, when I objected, he accused me of undercutting his therapy.*
>
> *Now things have evened out between us. Thanks to the woman's group, I've learned how to be more assertive too and, thanks to the men's group, my husband can take it. But it took us three years of counseling, not to mention a lot of yelling and a lot of tears and heartache on my part.*
>
> *But it was worth it. At least I have a marriage now. Before I had nothing.*

Not just wives, but clinicians have noted that therapy may bring about increased thinking and dreaming about Vietnam, as well as more emotionality.[26] If the therapy is working, many of the veteran's long-buried emotions and memories will begin to surface. As they surface, the veteran will experience more inner turmoil, more restlessness, and more pain. Experiencing these feelings may make him temporarily "inefficient" in terms of work and more vulnerable, psychologically. In some cases, as a defense against his increased feelings of personal vulnerability, the veteran may become more hostile, or domineering, toward his wife and others.

While the wife need not tolerate violence, she can expect her husband to be not only angrier, but sadder, and perhaps, more openly afraid. She may need to assure him frequently that he is not "falling apart" and that the feelings, although intense, will not destroy him. Neither will they last forever. The vet may also need to be reminded that although feeling his feelings can be a very painful and disorienting process, in the long run he will only be strengthened by facing his feelings rather running from them.

Rita's husband, for example, sat in group for six months before he shared his Vietnam experiences. "That night," Rita says, "he went out drinking. The next night, he cried on my lap all night long, just like a baby. Then he cried for almost a whole week afterward too. He couldn't even go to work.

"'Am I going crazy?' he'd ask me.

"'No, honey, you're just feeling your pain.'"

Rita's husband is a well paid, highly functional professional. His PTSD never expressed itself in job problems. Rather, his major difficulty was depression and an inability to relate to others. Upon starting group, he became more depressed, but eventually he began the grieving process. He needed to go through the grieving process not just once, but several times, before he could free himself of certain memories.

As a result, he is now closer to his wife, can read bedtime stories to his children without becoming excessively annoyed, and is even able to take Rita on vacations without criticizing her.

While Rita was overjoyed at her husband's progress, at first she didn't know how to act around him. "I'm not used to him being normal." It was a new feeling for her not to have to think four times before she said something to him. Furthermore, although she felt relieved that her husband was finally able to participate more in family life, she felt somewhat disoriented giving up her old role of managing almost everything all by herself. Also, she was somewhat frightened of the demands her husband might make of her emotionally and sexually.

> When my husband finished therapy, it was like starting all over again, not only in terms of renegotiating who was going to do what, but in terms of our entire relationship.
>
> After Vietnam, my husband and I got into this pattern where he shut me out and I, in my own way, shut him out too. I learned to not expect much from him emotionally and sometimes even when he did want to be close, I rejected him. I guess I was angry at having to be the stable one while he was allowed to be moody and unpredictable.
>
> Our entire relationship became centered around money and the children. We stopped going out and having fun together, like we used to, before Vietnam. We even forgot how to talk to each other like man and wife, or even like friends. All our talk was about the house and the kids, me complaining about him, or him, about me.
>
> Now he wants to have a 'real' relationship with me. But I've forgotten how to be relaxed around him. I'm a

whiz at anticipating his moods and appeasing him, but now he wants to know me as an individual.

What a joke! After all these years of functioning, functioning, functioning, am I still an individual? Somewhere, in the midst of just trying to survive and keep the family, and myself from going under, I lost myself.

It's been five years since I've read a book. I haven't done anything else interesting either. Is my husband now going to find me boring? Now that he's better, will he still want me?

Like Rita, other wives sometimes voice feelings of personal insecurity as they watch their husbands become stronger. Since their previous relationships with their husbands were often based on being their caretakers, the women fear that they will be abandoned now that they are not so intensely needed. In my experience, however, very few veterans have abandoned their wives following successful treatment for PTSD. The women who have been deserted are those whose husbands did not seek help or who came for help only intermittently.

According to the Vet Center study, 91% of the counselors polled indicate that help-seeking Vietnam wives often complain of feeling as if they have lost their personal identity in constantly responding to the veteran's needs and the many family crises. In some instances, the veteran's recovery poses an identity crisis for his wife, who must now deal with herself and her own feelings, which in the past were put "on hold" because of her husband's PTSD. As Candice Williams notes, "Total sacrifice of the woman is characteristic in dysfunctional combat veteran family systems..."[27] One of the group members, Marsha, was typical of wives who face this kind of identity crisis.

I was a girl when I married. Now I sometimes feel like I'm an old lady, even though I have yet to hit the big '4-0'. My husband is fine, or almost fine, but I'm not, even though everybody expects me to be. Worse, I expect me to be. But just because he's got his PTSD under fair control doesn't mean that I'm over my pain and anger.

Nowadays I even get hugs without asking for them. You'd think I'd be overjoyed. But I keep remembering

*all the times I was dying for a little love and never got
a crumb.*

*Sometimes I think about telling my husband how I
feel, but I don't want to ruin the progress he's made by
bring up all my past resentments. Yet he senses my feelings and asks me why I'm so cold.*

I never know what to say.

*'Don't dare look back,' I tell myself. 'If you start
thinking about all you sacrificed for him, you'll start
putting holes in the wall and tearing up the furniture
like he used to.'*

*Usually I try to cast out my resentments as soon as
they crop up, but it doesn't always work. I guess all those
years of supporting him before therapy and then during
the stress of therapy have drained me. Sometimes I feel
a great emptiness and hollowness inside, as if I've lost
all my blood and have no more strength or love to give.*

*I want to get back to who I was before Vietnam came
into my life. In my head, I know there's a wonderful
future out there for me, but there's this bitter, angry
woman standing in my way. That's me. She's a tired
woman too, who has spoiled not only her husband, but
her children, and her in-laws too.*

*I'm in a rut and I know it, but I can't seem to get
out of it. My husband isn't stopping me as much as he
used to, although he still gets in my way. My main
problem is that I don't know where to begin. There's got
to be more to life than working and having a family.
But what?*

Marsha is in the midst of her own midlife crisis. Sometimes she
thinks about taking a course or pursuing a hobby but it seems like
too much effort for her. Yet she knows that doing something small,
just for herself, is the first step toward getting more satisfaction out
of life.

She also suffers from what she calls "PTSD or Vietnam wife burnout." After having spent years focussed on her husband and his
postwar problems, she is at a loss in establishing goals for herself.
While her husband's progress has freed her somewhat, she is hindered
in taking a look at herself by the emotional and physical exhaustion
accumulated over the years. Or perhaps depression has eroded her

ability to concentrate and her self-confidence to such a degree that she now doubts she will be able to complete any project she starts.

In some cases, the Vietnam wife is impeded in her development by a husband who, although he has made substantial progress, is still reluctant to assume major responsibilities with the children or the housework. Even though the Vietnam wife in this situation may no longer have to deal with constant crises, she will still have little time and energy to pursue her individual goals aside from earning a living and taking care of a family.

It is often suggested to Vietnam wives that they begin where they left off—that they examine their pre-Vietnam or premarital years and try to remember things which used to spark their interest. They also need encouragement in asking for what they need from their husbands. One wife remembered that she had enjoyed painting before her marriage. She has since taken an art course and is thinking about starting a small handpainted card business. It all began, however, with her signing up for a two hour art workshop which she almost didn't go to because her fifteen-year-old son needed a last-minute ride to a basketball game.

Gathering together all her assertive skills, she told her son that in the future he would have to give her advance notice about his games or find his own ride. In addition, she insisted that, this time, her husband do the chauffeuring. After years of feeling as if she was living in her husband's shadow, and the shadow of the Vietnam war, it was now time for her. What's more, she felt she had earned it.

Getting Help

Today there are 189 Vet Centers throughout the U.S. The location of the nearest Vet Center can be found in the back of the book. Vet Centers offer individual and group therapy for Vietnam veterans, as well as vocational guidance, financial assistance information, and help in obtaining veteran's benefits. Some have food relief and clothing programs and most have groups for wives or girlfriends. In addition, some Vet Centers have group programs for children. Most offer free educational materials and information sessions aimed at helping veterans and their families understand PTSD.

Help is also available at our nation's Veteran's Administration Medical Centers. Often individual, group, and marriage counseling can be obtained through the psychiatry, psychology, or social work services, or through the medical center's outpatient mental hygiene clinic. In addition, 28 V.A. hospitals sponsor PTSD inpatient units. Inquiry about these PTSD units, as well as about help in the private sector, can be made at Vet Centers.

A veteran may be reluctant to seek help because it violates his sense of masculinity or his vow to have as little to do with the government as possible. Or perhaps he learned to mistrust mental health professionals, as he did clergymen, because of certain negative experiences with such professionals during the war. During the war, some vets saw psychiatrists, psychologists, and other mental health professionals as being in collusion with the military.[28] Or perhaps the veteran avoids therapy because he fears he will be misdiagnosed or misunderstood.

A veteran may also feel embarrassed to admit to "still being bothered" by events which occurred some years ago. Perhaps he feels he should be over Vietnam by now and wonders if he is "abnormal" for still thinking or dreaming about the war. Or perhaps he envisions therapy as a form of entrapment.

Some vets do seek help on their own, but others are shoved into treatment by wives or other family members, or by employers.

Perhaps the most frequently asked question by wives is, "How do I get my husband into treatment?"

Each woman is an expert on her own husband. Often she, more than anyone else, knows which approach will be most effective with him. In general, reluctant vets need to be told, either by their wives, another family member, or another veteran, that having PTSD is not shameful or unmanly and that seeking help is an act of courage and honesty, not a sign of weakness. The vet can also be reminded that other veterans have sought help and benefitted immensely.

As Williams points out, some vets feel they do not deserve treatment because their problems are not as severe as those of other veterans; because they were not as seriously wounded as others; or because they did not see as much combat.[29] In such cases, the vet needs to be reminded that trauma is trauma and that PTSD is a normal human response to extraordinary stress. Even American civilians who were in Vietnam developed PTSD.

If the veteran has a negative attitude toward the V.A. or the Vet Center program, he can be encouraged to give the V.A. and the Vet Centers a chance. Most Vet Centers are staffed primarily by Vietnam veterans, individuals who truly understand. What does he have to lose by attending a few sessions? If he does not benefit, he can always quit.

Generally, telling a veteran that he is "crazy" and listing his character defects will not motivate him to seek help. Empathy works far better. Rita, for example, was able to convince her husband to go to a Vet Center by saying, "Haven't you suffered enough? Don't you deserve a little help? You're always complaining about how the government ripped you off. Well, here's a way the government can pay you back."

Harrington, who conducts groups for Vietnam veterans in twelve, two-hour sessions, tells resistant vets, "You owe yourself 24 hours of help—that's one day out of your life. Is that too much for all the suffering you've been through?"[30]

Williams asks, "What good has it done keeping all this inside of yourself for so long? You might want to try something else, such as sharing with men who have had similar experiences and can understand."[31] Other arguments that might be used are "You're paying for these services, you might well use them," or "How do you know it won't help until you've tried it?"

A woman can let her husband know that help is available by giving him the phone number of the Vet Center and Vet Center literature about PTSD. She can also indicate her willingness to be supportive. However, many women fear, and justifiably so, that if they push too hard, their husbands will become even more resistant to the idea of treatment. Some women dare not mention the idea to their husbands, knowing that the idea will be immediately rejected if it comes from them. In desperation, some women have called the Vet Center asking for a Vietnam veteran who has undergone therapy to please come by the home posing as a repairman and "casually" mention treatment to her husband.

While Vet Centers cannot provide such services, vets who have undergone therapy are often willing to talk to veterans who are hesitant about seeking help. Often another veteran, or a concerned relative or family friend, may be able to discuss the need for therapy with a veteran more effectively than his wife.

In some circumstances, however, the woman does not have the luxury of waiting for her husband to seek treatment. When her husband becomes so regressed, so violent, so self-destructive, or so disoriented from reality that he cannot take care of himself or becomes a danger to himself or others, the woman may need to explore the possibility of strongly urging him to seek help and, in certain extreme circumstances, of committing him against his will. Veteran's Administration Medical Centers do not accept involuntary patients, however they may have information on state or country committal procedures. Such information may also be available at local courthouses or police stations.

In some communities, emergency crisis teams are available to come to the home to evaluate the veteran. If these crisis teams include policemen, the veteran must be informed in advance that police are coming and that they are coming to help him, not assault him. Also, the crisis team needs to be advised that they are dealing with a Vietnam veteran whose anxiety level may be aroused by seeing uniformed personnel.

Some women feel guilty about calling in rescue squads or literally driving their husbands to Vet Centers or alcohol or drug treatment centers for help. They feel they are "wrong" or doing their husband a "disservice." However, when a man is severely impaired by PTSD, alcoholism, or a drug addiction, the woman is not "betraying him," but saving his life by forcing him to seek help. When the husband is unable to think and act rationally, he must no longer be seen as head of the household, but as a family member who needs help. The woman must take control of the situation, as she would if her husband were a child who needed help. The first step can be to contact the nearest Vet Center or Veteran's Administration Medical Center or a community service agency.

Summary

PTSD therapy involves:
1. Helping the veteran uncover the specific events in the war which he has been attempting to deny or which he has been unable to accept;
2. Supporting him as he feels the feelings associated with these traumatic events;
3. Helping him acquire a greater understanding of how his war experiences have affected his life in the present; and
4. Helping the veteran find constructive uses for his Vietnam experience.

Recovery from PTSD does not mean a total disappearance of symptoms, but rather a reduction in their frequency and intensity. Once the symptoms are under control, the veteran will be able to enjoy a more satisfying life. Most likely he will think about Vietnam many times but his war experiences will no longer paralyze him or be the focus of his mental and emotional life. As he puts the war in perspective, he learns that he is not alone in his feelings. He will move from hopelessness and helplessness toward an attitude of gratitude that he is alive and can be useful to his family and society.

The therapeutic process, however, may take many months and can be temporarily disruptive not only to the veteran, but to his wife who can expect to witness some of the veteran's previously suppressed emotions. Furthermore, PTSD therapy does not necessarily solve all of the veteran's problems. Nor does it automatically heal his marriage. Usually, both the veteran and his wife need to learn how to stop scapegoating each other and improve their communication skills. Couples counseling is often useful to help them discuss problems left unresolved due to the veteran's PTSD and issues involving parenting, division of labor in the home, and other such concerns. Couples counseling is most beneficial, however, when the veteran is psychologically ready to deal with marital problems and when the therapist is sex fair.

One of the most common feelings experienced by Vietnam wives who have nursed their husbands first through PTSD and then through PTSD therapy is the feeling of "burnout." Once the vet is finally on the path to recovery, his wife may find herself aware of many months and years of stored up anger and resentment. She must then deal with the dilemma of what to do with this built up pile of grievances. On the one hand, she may want to confront her husband directly. On the other hand, she may want to enjoy the vet's improved emotional state and to keep the family peace.

In many cases, the veteran's emotional progress frees the Vietnam wife to focus on her own goals. However, if her vet still adheres to traditional views of the woman's role or is unwilling to consistently assume various childcare or housekeeping functions, the vet may continue to pose a formidable obstacle to her personal development. Even when the veteran is supportive, the Vietnam wife may experience difficulties grappling with the challenge of establishing her own identity and interests. In many cases, emotional and physical fatigue, as well as years of focusing on the veteran rather than herself, have depleted the woman's emotional, intellectual, and creative resources. Often a recuperation period is necessary before the woman can begin working on her own issues.

As a result of counseling, many couples have renewed their commitment to one another and can relate to each other on a deep and meaningful level. Not only in their marriage, but in their personal lives, they are able to make positive use of the frustrations, pain, and anger they experienced in the past.

Thirteen

Stay or Go?

Should I stay or should I go? The question haunts me. I keep praying for the right answer, but no answer seems right. I don't want to end my marriage; I just want to stop hurting so much.

Some days I make a definite decision to go. But when I think of my children, pangs of guilt seize me. 'What will happen to them if I leave? Won't they hate me for taking them away from their father and disrupting the only life they've ever known? Doesn't divorce damage children emotionally? Can't I stick it out for their sakes?'

On the other hand, I feel I am doing myself, and my children no favor by staying in a marriage where I am so miserable. But isn't some of that unhappiness my fault? Maybe I just expect too much.

I'm in a rut and I know it. The rut feels hellish at times, but at least it's familiar. All my life I've been taught that a woman needs a man and that she can't possibly survive in the cold, cruel world without one.

If I leave my husband, who will I have? I now feel so unattractive and undesirable as a woman that I can't conceive of any other man ever wanting me. Isn't it better to have my husband than to have no one at all?

Sometimes when I sleep with him, I feel both love and hate, and I can't tell which is stronger. When I see his missing toes and fingers, my feelings are all mixed up. I pity him and want to take care of him, yet a growing part of me is tired of all that. I want more—for me.

I'm stuck in indecision. Hopefully in the next year or two, I'll finally make a choice. I'm really scared though, for this may well be the most difficult choice of my whole life. But at least I'm willing to deal with

*my options, rather than run from them the way I
used to.*

Wife of a veteran

Some women come to the Vet Center with their minds already
made up—they are leaving their veteran tomorrow. For example,
Trudy came to the Vet Center only once and then only because her
husband had pleaded with her to find out more about PTSD and
the Vietnam war before saying goodbye.

But Trudy wasn't interested in hearing any more about Vietnam
or PTSD She had heard enough already. "I'm Vietnamed out," she
said. "Now I want out."

She was not interested in couples counseling or in the woman's
group either. She felt her husband's problems were deeper than Vietnam and she was tired of his using Vietnam as an excuse. He had
been in PTSD counseling for three years now, but, according to
Trudy, nothing had changed. True, his nightmares and other
symptoms had diminished and he had given up alcohol. But he still
was unable to give her the emotional warmth and closeness she
desired. Therefore, she was leaving—the sooner the better.

In contrast to Trudy, most of the women who come to the Vet
Center are in a state of confusion about whether to stay with their
veteran or not. Fran has been thinking of leaving her husband for
four years. Her first statement to the group was, "I've thought about
it and thought about it. But I still can't make up my mind."

Like some of the other women, Fran vacillates between wanting
to make her marriage work and feeling exhausted. "I've tried and
tried with him, with no success. I feel like giving up. Yet I just can't
say, 'The heck with him,' either. Many times I ask myself, 'Do I still
love him?' only to come up with the sorry conclusion that after ten
years of marriage, I honestly don't know."

While Fran no longer hopes for a storybook romance with her husband, in the back of her mind she fantasizes that someday he will
reduce his verbal abuses, stay sober, and show her more affection
and appreciation. Yet Jerry, who served two tours of duty in Vietnam, has never sought help. In fact, whenever Fran suggests that he
might do well to drop by the Vet Center or attend an A.A. meeting,
he laughs. In his view, the marital problems are all Fran's fault.

When Fran decided to join the woman's group, Jerry rejoiced. He
thought the woman's group would help Fran be more understanding
toward him, help "straighten her out," and turn her into a better

wife and mother. Jerry was dismayed when he realized that while Fran did learn about PTSD in group, she also learned that she had options other than staying in a marriage which did not meet her needs. Furthermore, she was not responsible for his PTSD or his alcoholism. Although Fran came to acknowledge that she had brought several of her own problems into the marriage, she also came to realize that she was not 95% to blame for the marital difficulties, which was her belief in the early years of her marriage.

When Fran began to be more assertive at home, Jerry wanted her to quit the woman's group. But Fran was no longer taking orders from him, like she used to. She had hardened her heart toward Jerry's negative comments and various accusations. Today when he chastises or criticizes her, she no longer shudders with fear, guilt, or shame. She doesn't even become defensive. Instead, she stares at him blankly, calls a friend, or simply leaves the room. "You're full of baloney," she might even say.

Nevertheless, years of being blamed and criticized have served to erode Fran's self-esteem and to demoralize and immobilize her to the point where she has difficulty taking action in many spheres of her life. For instance, she has abandoned some of her career interests and hobbies, as well as some of her friendships, not only because Jerry was, and is, so often jealous of such involvements, but because she is too fatigued and too preoccupied with the state of her marriage to invest her energies elsewhere.

Years of living with criticism and rejection have also resulted in Fran's feeling unattractive as a woman, even though she is a graceful, lovely woman. "If I leave him, will I be able to find another man?" she wonders. Even if she could, she feels too worn out to start all over again with a new man. "This is my second marriage," she explains. "I really want to make it work this time. Besides, by now, I'm used to Jerry. It isn't great with him, but at least I know what to expect. There's a certain security in that. On the other hand, I don't want to spend the rest of my life like this either."

Many times Fran has planned to leave Jerry, then she changes her mind. She then berates herself for staying in a marriage where she feels emotionally deprived while at the same time physically and emotionally overextended. Fran frequently states that the main reason she stays with Jerry is for her children, whom she feels would be "devastated" by a marital breakup. Furthermore, it is difficult to leave a man with whom one has shared many years.

Also, Fran is confused about who her husband truly is. In her view, he has at least two different personalities. "There's the PTSD Jerry and the non-PTSD Jerry. The sober Jerry and the drinking one. If he was all bad all the time, it would be easy to make up my mind. But he can be so charming, so loving, so sensitive, so good when he's good. It gives me hope."

What Fran is reluctant to admit, however, either to herself or to the group, is the extent to which she has become emotionally dependent on Jerry. Fran is not alone with this problem. Many of the wives who have attended group are, for a variety of reasons, emotionally dependent on their husbands. In some cases, this emotional dependence is the result of the social isolation and restrictions which the veteran has imposed or required. For Jerry's sake, Fran severed many important family and social ties, depriving herself of many sources of feedback and positive regard. Consequently, over the years, Fran's self-esteem has become closely tied to Jerry's reactions and views of her.

Jerry is also her only source of affection since, by now, Fran has become distant from her parents, her siblings, and many of her former friends. Should Fran leave Jerry, she does not feel she would have a family or social network to turn to for support. She is afraid she would find herself literally almost entirely alone in the world. Although she could turn to certain persons for help, after having minimized her relationships with these persons for so many years, she is hesitant to do so.

Not all Vietnam wives are as socially isolated as Fran, Yet, in my experience, those who are generally find it more difficult to leave their veteran when the relationship deteriorates than those wives who have a supportive extended family or a network of friends.

The irony is that prior to meeting Jerry, Fran, like many wives, was a very independent woman, managing both her personal and work life on her own. In fact, Fran is certain that one reason Jerry was drawn to her initially was because she was so self-sufficient and autonomous. "But he's destroyed the very qualities in me which attracted him in the first place," she sadly admits.

Other Vietnam wives have the same lament. However, unlike Fran, some women have not even embraced the possibility of ending their marriage with their veteran. This is especially the case with women who have strong religious convictions or moral scruples against divorce. Yet even these women begin to consider the idea of separation or divorce once they reach the breaking point of endurance.

In my experience, only a small percentage of women have active-ly pursued a separation or divorce. This observation is inconsistent with statistics which show a relatively high divorce rate for Vietnam veterans, at least upon initial return from Vietnam and as late as 1979. According to the President's Commission on Mental Health (1978), "approximately 38% of the marriages of Vietnam veterans broke up within six months of their return from Southeast Asia."[1] Furthermore, a study published in 1979 notes that "the divorce rate for Vietnam veterans is higher than for the general population."[2] Clinical experience has shown that "nonmarital relationships involv-ing...veterans have shown the same trend toward instability."[3]

Perhaps this inconsistency between the relatively high divorce rates for Vietnam veterans and the tendency of women in group to stay with their marriages can be explained by the possibility that women on the brink of divorce or separation are not generally those who seek couples counseling or other help at a Vet Center. Rather, coun-seling programs and Vet Centers may attract women who are still seeking ways of improving or saving their relationships with their veteran. Furthermore, Vietnam wives in the process of divorce may be furious with their veteran and may want to divest themselves of everything and anything having to do with him, including Vietnam. Therefore, they are not likely to appear at the Vet Center inquiring about PTSD.

Vietnam wives who stay in marriages which are extremely stress-ful and painful for them, stay for a variety of reasons. They fear the loneliness, the financial hardship, or the stigma associated with being separated or divorced. Many women interpret divorce as an admis-sion that they have "failed" at marriage. While both men and women tend to experience a sense of failure and shame upon the breakup of their marriage, research has shown that these feelings are deeper and tend to persist for a longer period of time in women.[4] The Viet-nam wife may also stay with her veteran because she feels sorry for him. She may pity him because he has PTSD, war injuries, or other scars from the war. Or perhaps he had a physically or sexually abusive childhood.

On a very personal level, the Vietnam wife may experience the collective guilt many Americans have regarding the U.S. involvement in Vietnam and the subsequent shunning of Vietnam veterans. Most likely she is well-aware that her veteran has felt profoundly betrayed, and abandoned, by the U.S. government, by U.S. society, and, in some instances, by his family and community as well. She may have stood in long lines and made many phone calls to help her veteran obtain certain financial or medical benefits. Or perhaps she has spent hours waiting with him at doctors' offices or educating his family, her family, their neighbors, and their clergy about PTSD in hopes of creating a more understanding and sympathetic environment for him and for their children.

Consequently she may have difficulty even contemplating leaving the veteran because, on some level, she does not want to add to his feeling of being betrayed and abandoned by deserting him also. This is especially the case when the veteran has war related medical problems or when he has begun counseling for PTSD. Some Vietnam wives want to wait and see if their husband is going to recover from his back condition (or his skin condition, or his Agent Orange tumors, or some other condition acquired in Vietnam) before they decide to leave him. Others want to see if counseling will help.

Yet even these women sometimes angrily say, "I don't feel sorry for him anymore. The only person I feel sorry for is me!" and vehemently announce that they no longer want to be "living sacrifices" for men, who, for a host of reasons, may be not only trampling on their affections, but squandering their money on alcohol, drugs, or, in few cases, other women.

The sense of guilt which the Vietnam wife might feel about leaving her veteran is compounded in those cases where the Vietnam veteran is exceptionally emotionally or financially dependent on her and where she is aware of that dependency. "He has nobody but me. What will happen to him if I go?" women say. Or "I don't love him like I used to, but I don't want to see him crack up or on the streets either." Some women fear the veteran will commit suicide if they leave.

Rose, Daniel's third wife, greatly fears what would happen to Daniel should she leave. Daniel lost many friends in Vietnam. Upon returning from the war, he found that his wife had taken a lover. She promptly divorced him, taking with her their infant son. Six months later, she and the infant were killed in an automobile accident. Almost immediately, Daniel married another woman who, after five years of marriage, also became adulterous and fled the state with their young child.

Rose does not think her husband can handle another loss, which he would interpret as yet another betrayal. Although Daniel has never been violent with Rose and has never even threatened to hurt her, Rose senses the tremendous amount of rage he harbors within, and, his intense loneliness. "He says I'm the only one he trusts in the world. His whole life revolves around me and our three daughters." she says. "I'm afraid of what would happen to him—and possibly to me—if I go."

For Rose, as for a few others, the sense of fear and guilt about leaving the veteran is combined with feelings of fear and guilt regarding prior experiences of disappointing a father or father figure. For example, Rose's father greatly disapproved of her marriage to Daniel due to religious differences. Soon after the wedding, Rose's father had a heart attack. The entire family blamed Rose. Despite the irrationality of their accusation, Rose believed she had caused, or at least significantly contributed to, her father's illness. Now, thoughts of leaving her husband bring to the surface all of Rose's old fears surrounding "deserting" her father at the time of her marriage to Daniel.

Today Rose is in crisis. Daniel wants to move to an isolated rural area. As a result of his experiences in Vietnam, he has a low tolerance for noise, and for other people, except Rose and the girls. Rose, however, likes city life, and other people.

"Just because you want to be a hermit, doesn't mean the kids and I have to go be hermits too," she argues in marriage counseling. Yet Daniel is certain that living in the country would eliminate his depression. Perhaps he would be less grouchy and more affectionate to Rose if they moved.

Rose, however, feels she would literally "die" all alone on a mountain top, with just Daniel and the children. Yet, if Daniel insists on moving, she will follow. "If it'll help him, I can't say no," she says. "After all he's been through in Vietnam and since, he deserves to spend the rest of the years the way he wants."

Other couples are like Rose and Daniel, with the veteran wanting to relocate to a relatively secluded area and his wife not wanting to give up her present life style. Not all wives are like Rose, however. Many refuse to relocate. Sometimes the veteran leaves his wife in favor of living in an isolated locale. Other times the couple becomes stalemated on the issue.

"If you loved me enough, you would do what is best for me," the veteran may say. On the other hand, his wife may feel that what the veteran perceives as being best for him would be a form of emotional and intellectual death for her, and detrimental to their children.

Some wives, like Rose, feel they must go along with their husbands in order to prove their loyalty and dedication. However, for many of them, this sense of loyalty coexists with a host of fears about venturing forth into the world as a woman alone. Some of these fears stem from the woman's personal insecurities. Some, however, stem from having learned, as children, that women are "too weak" to make it on their own, without a man to protect and support them. Traditionally, society has also taught many women to seek love and approval from men, rather than from themselves, or from other women. Unless she has had a nontraditional upbringing, the Vietnam wife may not be able to feel like a worthwhile, competent person without male approval or companionship.

Women are also taught that if they are "good" they will be rewarded by having a strong man to love and support them. Consequently many women are "often ill-prepared, psychologically or educationally to sustain themselves without a husband." Furthermore, most women have few role models for independent living. Making the break may mean "an incredibly complex and difficult journey into territory that has never been mapped for them by society or by other women in their families or social groups."[5] Or, if the woman has already undergone a separation or divorce prior to her relationship with the veteran, she may remember the hurt, anxiety, and stress involved and may not want to re-experience such pain ever again.

Last, but not least, some Vietnam wives stay because, on some level, they feel responsible for their husband's condition. Even though "C-C-C," (you didn't Cause it, you can't Control it, you can't Cure it, referring to the veteran's PTSD) is continually emphasized in group, some women have not overcome the cultural conditioning which has taught them, as women, to take responsibility for the peace and harmony of the family and for their husband's emotional and physical well-being. They still hope that if only they change or improve themselves enough, that their husband's PTSD, and other sources of marital unhappiness will significantly diminish.

In a few cases, this cultural conditioning has been reinforced by certain religious ideas, such as that the husband is the God-ordained head of the household to whom the woman should always be submissive and subservient. Along these lines, some women feel that their marital problems are "trials" sent by God which they must suffer and endure. A few even feel that their husband's objectionable behavior is God's punishment to them for certain sins and that their husband's abusiveness is God's means of chastising them and developing their moral character.

While some women are trapped by sex role conditioning, or by various religious ideologies, others are trapped by sheer economics. Leaving would mean financial hardship, if not outright destitution. Some women have handed over their property to their husbands, allowing them to retain the family's assets in their names only, or have otherwise lost control of their property. Some women were coerced into surrendering their property through violence; others, through the veteran's pleading and cajoling. In several instances, however, women relinquished control of their assets as a matter of course, simply because they were brought up in an era where the man, not the woman, was supposed to take care of the finances. They unthinkingly "gave" their houses, their bank accounts, and other material possessions to their husband, in good faith, not realizing that someday they might want to separate.

Vietnam wives in such financial situations would have to begin their new lives with practically nothing. Or they may even be unable to consider a new life because they cannot afford an attorney or legal costs. Lack of funds is a crucial problem in instances where the veteran has threatened to contest the divorce, to keep most of the marital property for himself, or to fight for custody of the children. The Vietnam wife who does not have the economic power to fight for her rights in court may decide to stay rather than lose her children or her assets.

Financial reasons for staying are especially prevalent among Vietnam wives who are being physically abused. A common pattern in homes where there is wife abuse is for the abuser to have tight control over the family's finances, even if the wife is an outside wage earner.[6] In addition, should the abused Vietnam wife decide to leave, she will have to contend with police or legal systems which are only beginning to respond to the needs of battered women. Often, abused Vietnam wives have been discouraged from seeking a formal separation or divorce because of the lengthy and complicated legal procedures involved in domestic violence cases. These women are especially discouraged:

1. When they are called names or not believed by police or by various court officials;
2. When they are blamed for the abuse;
3. When they are required to produce evidence or eyewitnesses for abuses which have largely occurred behind closed doors; or
4. When they are considered "just another battered woman" who is cluttering up the court dockets and who will probably "kiss

and make up" with her batterer after filing for a divorce anyway.

Nevertheless, due to recent legislation and improved attitudes toward abused women, many forms of legal and police protection and help are available to battered women today which were not available ten years ago. Numerous legal and police obstacles can still exist, however, significantly impeding the woman's attempt to obtain an equitable separation or divorce.[7] If the legal and financial obstacles are too great, then she may give up trying to obtain her independence and decide to stay with her abuser instead.

She will be especially tempted to stay if her husband has threatened to retaliate against her, their children, or other family members should she leave. Under such circumstances, the woman may reason that it is safer for her to stay at home. As Schechter, author of "The Future of the Battered Woman's Movement," points out, "So it does not surprise me that battered women sometimes choose to stay with their abusers and know where they are, rather than wait to be hunted down. The illusion of control that comes from knowing where he is can be easier to live with than the more explicit terror of uncertainty."

For some battered Vietnam wives, ending their marriages has necessitated disguising their identity and fleeing to other states. The costs, however, have been high. Not only have these women had to leave their jobs, their communities, their families, and their familiar surroundings, but they have had to uproot their children, interrupt their schooling, disrupt their friendships, and in other ways significantly alter their lives.

Not all women can have such courage and fortitude. Furthermore, during the "honeymoon" stage of the battering cycle, the abuser can be so loving and repentant that it is easy for the woman to forgive him "one more time" and to give the relationship yet another chance.

"How many of his problems are due to Vietnam and PTSD and how many are due to his basic personality, his family background, or other factors?" women ask. They also wonder about their own role in the relationship difficulties: "Who's to blame? Him, me, Vietnam, the U.S. government, my childhood, his childhood, or what?" Younger women or women who do not yet have children, that is, women who have less time and energy invested in their veteran and who can thus more easily envision a future without him, especially want answers to these questions. Often they say, "If I could be sure that most of his problems have to do with Vietnam, I'd stay with him until he finishes therapy. But if his problems are deeper than that, I want out now, while I'm still young and without children."

While some women urgently want answers, there are no simple replies to their questions. In most cases, understanding the dynamics of a relationship and predicting its future is a far more complex matter than simply assigning blame to one partner, to the government, or to society at large. Furthermore, the concept of PTSD was only officially accepted in 1980 and is still being researched and in the process of being understood.

In addition, it is being increasingly recognized that a veteran can be suffering from other psychological syndromes in addition to PTSD. This area is still being explored and debated by researchers and therapists. Once again, there are no clear lines of demarcation between veterans who suffer "only" from PTSD and those who suffer from PTSD in addition to other problems. However, some rough guidelines do exist.

Some possible differences between the veteran who uses alcohol as a form of self-medication for PTSD and the veteran who is truly a problem drinker, or an alcoholic, have already been discussed. In addition, there are some ways to differentiate between a veteran who suffers primarily from PTSD and one who suffers primarily from a character disorder in addition to PTSD.

The primarily PTSD afflicted veteran is characterized by excessive self-blame and survivor guilt. As Newman says in *PTSD: A Handbook for Clinicians*, veterans with a primary diagnosis of PTSD are aware of their maladaptive behavior, "generally accept responsibility for (it) and are genuinely distressed by it. Although they view their PTSD symptoms as irrational, they tend to blame themselves for being the way they are."[9] In contrast, the primarily character-disordered veteran uses PTSD to justify his actions and may use his disorder to take advantage of others.

The PTSD afflicted veteran's major fear is "loss of control," that is, being overwhelmed by pain, helplessness, or rage. Even though he may have infrequent outbursts of temper, in general much of his psychic energy is directed toward controlling his aggressive impulses. When his internal tensions mount to the bursting point, however, his internal controls may fail him and he may erupt. Subsequently, he usually experiences remorse over his outburst and may expend even more energy trying to suppress his aggressiveness. Hence, he may become increasingly socially and emotionally withdrawn following an angry outburst.

In contrast, the character-disordered veteran expresses his anger, not only more frequently than the primarily PTSD afflicted veteran, but with little remorse.

A final difference is that the primarily PTSD afflicted veteran often has a strong aversion to social contact and may be excessively withdrawn. In contrast, the primarily character-disordered veteran may fear being alone.[10]

Vietnam wives whose husbands were alcoholic, drug addicted, or violent prior to the war, whose husbands show definite signs of being character-disordered in addition to having PTSD, and whose husbands are determined never ever to seek help have a much clearer picture of their veteran's psychological state than women whose husbands pursue therapy or alcohol or drug rehabilitation inconsistently, or who seem to be involved in a therapeutic program only halfheartedly. According to some of the wives, their husbands seek some form of counseling only when in crisis or only when so depressed or distraught that they absolutely must talk to someone.

"But the minute he feels better, he starts canceling his appointments and says he doesn't need help anymore," says Carol, whose husband has been in and out of therapy for many months. Like many women who are married or involved with veterans who display this pattern of attendance at counseling sessions, Carol has postponed deciding about whether to stay with her husband or leave him because she hopes that if her husband would only follow through on his counseling program, he might overcome his PTSD and be able to give more to the marriage.

"He's always so much better after he sees his counselor," says Carol. "In fact, for one or two weeks afterward, he's wonderful to me. Then he starts to crash again. When he hits bottom, he goes running back to the Vet Center.

"I keep telling him that he should keep all his appointments and go for counseling even when he feels good. He says he doesn't want to take up some other guy's time. But I think that's just an excuse.

"If I knew that it would always be like this, some good times, followed by more bad times, I'd probably pack my bags tomorrow. But when I see how well he does, even after just a one hour session, I can't help but hope that if he really stuck with the counseling, our marriage would be a good one."

"Tell him you'll leave him if he doesn't stick with the counseling," another Vietnam wife suggests to Carol. Women frequently make this suggestion to one another. Some women, however, are unable to present such ultimatums to their husbands, primarily because they are not prepared to follow through. They are not willing to actually leave should the veteran fail to pursue a counseling or alcohol or drug rehabilitation program.

Some women do insist that the veteran get help—or else lose them. The results have been mixed. Some veterans have sought help and benefitted greatly.

Most vets can recover. Recovery, however, depends on the degree of exposure to combat: the greater the exposure to death, the greater the therapeutic task before the veteran. In some cases, recovery is limited. The veteran is able to take care of himself and his family. He is able to keep a job and abstain from substance abuse, but he still functions emotionally as if he were in Vietnam, to one degree or another.

His wife is then faced with the dilemma of whether or not to accept this degree of progress as enough. "I hate to leave him now that he's finally standing on his own two feet. He's come so far and had to work so hard to get where he is. But I had hoped for more." Yet this wife is the envy of wives whose husbands have not yet reached this degree of recovery and of wives who are still trying to figure out the veteran's reasons for going into counseling and whether or not there will be any permanent changes as a result of that counseling.

Veronica, for example, wonders if her husband is sincere about dealing with his PTSD or other problems or if he is only "pretending" to be interested in therapy, or in improving, in order to prevent her from leaving.

> I don't know what to think. This is the second time I've insisted he seek help. The first time he went to group for two months, then quit. During that time, he'd cancel appointments a lot, but when I'd remind him that I would leave unless he went back to counseling, he'd keep a couple of appointments, then stop going again.
>
> This time he's not only attending his Vet Center group regularly, but also is going to his A.A. meetings twice a week.
>
> Yet I'm scared. Is he only doing this to get me to stay? And, once he knows that I'm not going to leave him, will he go back to his old ways?

Veronica, like many wives, is in emotional limbo, waiting to see what the outcome of her husband's present involvement in therapeutic programs will be. Other wives have already separated from their veterans, but are willing to return upon signs of marked improvement in specific areas. However, like Veronica, they wonder if their veteran is only faking good behavior in order to get them back or not. They very much want to believe that their husband is sincere and that his progress is real and permanent.

Some questions a Vietnam wife might ask in order to assess her husband's progress are as follows:

1. Does he attend sessions or A.A. or N.A. meetings regularly?

    Regular attendance is a positive sign. However, it is not a guarantee that the veteran is truly working on himself.

2. What is his attitude toward his counseling? Has he been able to establish a trusting relationship with his therapist, counselor, or group leader? If he is in group, has he been able to identify with, and make friends with, some of the other veterans? Or, is he almost always negative and contemptuous of the counseling program, the therapist, or the other veterans?

    If the veteran is able to maintain an open-minded, trusting attitude toward treatment and is able to emerge from his social and emotional isolation by forming some sort of emotional bond, either with the therapist, or with the other veterans in group, this is a another positive sign. Recovery from PTSD does not mean forgetting about Vietnam as much as it means being reintegrated into society and being able to emotionally connect and trust others again. For some vets, this process begins in group or individual therapy when the veteran forms ties with the therapist or other group members.

3. Are there any consistent signs of positive change, either in behavior or in attitude, however small?

    The important word here is "consistent." Most people can display good behavior for a short time but the changes need to be long lasting and able to endure the inevitable stresses in life.

    As stated in Chapter 11, changes in the veteran due to treatment may not be evident for many months. It is possible for some veterans to attend individual or group therapy, A.A. meetings, or other treatment programs for six to eight months without any dramatic signs of change. Yet there may be small indications that the veteran is coming to understand and accept himself, and, to blame others less. There may be less anger displayed at others, increased contemplativeness, as well as increased emotional pain. Certain activities—overworking, compulsive sex, compulsive exercising, gambling—which may have served "escapist" functions may diminish in frequency, although they might not disappear entirely.

In addition, the veteran may seem more discontented and confused about who he is, what he feels, and what he wants out of life after going into treatment. These, however, can be positive, not negative signs. Increased inner turmoil and self-questioning suggest that the veteran may be beginning to deal with some of the deep issues and long buried feelings underlying his symptoms. In fact, if a person is in treatment and does not show some signs of increased anxiety, emotional pain, or confusion, this may be an indication that he is not taking the therapy seriously or not working hard in therapy. Almost always, personal growth entails some degree of emotional pain and periods of self-questioning and self-doubt.

4. Is he beginning to assume responsibility for his moods, his emotions, and his behavior or is he still blaming others?

The veteran who is showing increased awareness of his PTSD or who is making progress in therapy will have increased recognition of his emotional, physical, or other needs and have less need to blame others. He may say, "Something happened today at work which reminded me about Vietnam. I didn't think it would bother me, but apparently it did. That makes me feel like not being with you and the kids tonight. Usually I would start a fight with you just so I could get to be alone. But maybe this time I can just tell you that I need to be by myself."

Or, he may say, "You picked a terrible time to ask me for help. I feel awful, but it's not your fault. I'm just really angry tonight about.... Maybe I'll feel better in a few hours."

5. If the veteran previously could not talk about Vietnam, is he now able to discuss some aspects of experience, at least in part? Or, if the veteran was previously obsessed with Vietnam, has his preoccupation with Vietnam lessened somewhat?

A "yes" to any of these questions indicates some movement toward resolving Vietnam issues. One wife, for example, was certain that her husband was making progress when he was able to see cooked rice without becoming upset. Rice was a forbidden food in their home due to its association with Vietnam. Talk about Vietnam was also forbidden.

"How long do I wait and how many signs of change do I have to see before I can be sure that he is really going to improve, and stay improved?" women often ask. Once again, there are no pat answers to such questions. In all cases, these questions must be addressed on an individual basis, taking into account the full complexity of the veteran's personality and the entire family system.

In some cases, veterans have shown remarkable improvement over a short period of time. They have given up alcohol or drugs, or battering, or some other problem behavior almost entirely after just a few weeks of help. Upon seeing such changes, some women are tempted to give up their skepticism about the future of their marriage, or, if they have already left, they may be tempted to return.

Mary's husband, Les, suffered from both PTSD and alcoholism. With the aid of her in-laws, but at considerable financial expense to herself, Mary shoved her husband into a private alcohol rehabilitation program. He left treatment with the best of intentions, but resumed drinking almost immediately.

"The next time he hits bottom, I'm not going to be around," Mary vowed to the group. That night she gave Les her final ultimatum: Get help or get out!

Les admitted himself to the alcohol ward at the local Veteran's Administration Medical Center and promised to attend group therapy at the local Vet Center after completing alcohol treatment. After discharge, he wanted to come back home. Just to prove he was sincere, he attended follow-up sessions at the hospital and A.A. meetings faithfully. He even got a sponsor and brought gifts when he visited. When he thanked Mary for all she had sacrificed for him and showered love and attention on their nine-year-old daughter, Mary's heart melted—almost.

Mary could see the happiness in her daughter's eyes when her Daddy was around. Yet Mary did not want to open her heart to Les, only to have it broken again. More importantly, she did not want to give their daughter, Merle, any false hopes. At ten, Merle was well over 140 pounds. According to the child's therapist, Merle was using excess food to cope with her feelings, especially her anger and her grief. She was angry with both parents for arguing, but she was especially angry at her father for his inconsistencies and failures to keep his word with her. Time after time she had waited for him to show up as he had promised and time after time he didn't come. Despite all her disappointments, she missed him and ate to hide her feelings of abandonment.

Even though Les had disappointed the family many times, this time it appeared he was truly turning over a new leaf. He had stayed sober for over six weeks. When Merle pleaded with her mother to Les return, Mary couldn't say no.

The family then went on a wonderful vacation. Mary felt as if she were on her second honeymoon and Merle lost ten pounds. Within months, however, Les stopped attending A.A. meetings. In addition, he failed to pursue PTSD therapy as he had promised. Apparently when he gave up drinking, his PTSD symptoms began to manifest themselves more forcefully and he turned again to alcohol for relief.

As before, Les began to stay away from home and make promises to his daughter that he didn't keep. Merle's weight skyrocketed.

Mary grieved for her own disappointment, but she grieved even more for her daughter. "How can you explain this to a child? Now she's not only lost faith in her father, but in me for telling her that her Daddy was 'okay' or almost okay."

Not only for herself, but for her children, it has always proven important for the Vietnam wife to wait a significant period of time to make sure the vet has really changed. A "pink cloud" phenomenon often accompanies entering treatment. Individuals often show drastic initial improvements and excitedly announce that their problems are finally over. Yet for this initial alleviation of symptoms and rush of good feelings to become permanent usually requires some close self-examination and emotional work.

It is at this point—the point of confrontation of previously hidden feelings and conflicts—that many persons quit treatment despite the initial positive results and their initial surge of enthusiasm. Therefore, it is prudent for a woman to assume an observer role when her husband first enters treatment and to see if he is willing to do the hard work which self-knowledge and personal growth entails.

The decision-making process is even more complex and more difficult for two special groups of Vietnam wives: those who are obese and those who were sexually or physically abused as children. Often the obese wife feels trapped in her marriage by her weight. "As fat as I am, what other man would want me?"

While the obese Vietnam wife feels "ugly" on the outside, the wife who was sexually or physically abused by a parent or caretaker as a child may feel "ugly" on the inside, especially if she has yet to deal with her childhood experiences. The low self-esteem which usually results from having been abused, combined with other factors associated with the abuse, often serve to keep the formerly abused Vietnam wife in her marriage.

"How can I leave Ralph? His love was the first love I ever knew," explains Phyllis who was physically battered by both parents and sexually molested not only by her father, but by her brother too. Thrown out of her home at eighteen, she met Ralph, who was on his way to Vietnam. When he returned, they married. At the time, Ralph's PTSD was dormant. He was supportive of Phyllis, not only financially, but emotionally.

Later, when his PTSD began to manifest itself, when Phyllis was ill, sometimes Ralph would ignore her. But many times he was helpful and protective, fulfilling Phyllis's deep wish to finally have someone take care of her.

As a child she had had no parent to lean on and very little nurturing. In fact her parents leaned on her. While it is difficult to make a general statement about such a diverse group as abusive parents, usually they have been found to be emotionally immature and unreliable in meeting their family responsibilities. They are also often impulsive, have a low frustration level tolerance and act out their frustrations and needs through verbal and physical abuse or sexual molestation of their children. They have also been found to be overdemanding, highly critical, and often extremely punishing of the child who does not fulfill their expectations.[11]

The child is forced to meet the parent's needs, not the other way around. In essence, the child becomes the abusive parent's caretaker as well as the parent's victim.[12] In cases of incest, for example, the daughter is sometimes expected to fulfill the father's emotional *and* sexual needs.[13]

As a result, the Vietnam wife who, like Phyllis, comes from an abusive past may find her husband's mood swings, his impulsive or unpredictable behavior, his low frustration level tolerance, and his periods of irresponsibility familiar. Due to her background, she is used to living with an adult who can be emotionally immature, overly demanding, excessively critical, abusive and at the same time, emotionally dependent on her. She has also had many years of practice at being a caretaker.

Therefore, she may be more tolerant of her husband's verbal or physical assaults and his excessive emotional and financial dependence on her. She is also more liable to accept the social isolation and other restrictions her husband may place on her.

The Vietnam wife may stay in the marriage because, compared to other Vietnam wives, she may be more tolerant of her husband's ambivalence toward her. A common complaint of Vietnam wives is that they receive double messages from their husbands. "I need you...stay away." While some women get furious at receiving both rejection and affection from the same man, the Vietnam wife who was abused as a child may be more accepting of this behavior. In her past, she may have lived with such double messages and the experience of receiving both pain and love from the same person on a daily basis.

On the other hand, if the Vietnam wife is sufficiently aware of what went on in her childhood, she may be infuriated at having to once again live with double messages and be considerably less tolerant of her husband's mixed messages than other wives. In addition, when she is angry at her husband, she may be experiencing double anger: first, anger toward her husband and second, anger toward the parent who gave her double messages in the past. At times she may confuse who she is really angry at. Phyllis explains, "Sometimes when I think about leaving my husband, I wonder if I really want to leave him or whether I am really trying to leave my father. It's not fair to put the anger I have toward my parents onto my husband but sometimes that's what I do." Because of her past, it is often difficult for Phyllis and wives like her to form an objective picture of her husband and his PTSD and to view him as separate from other persons in her life.

Mental health professionals who work with Vietnam wives need to inquire about any history of childhood abuse and help the Vietnam wife who is a child abuse or incest survivor identify how her past experiences are influencing her marriage, and her decision to stay with or leave, her veteran. If the Vietnam wife has yet to deal with being victimized as a child, therapy oriented toward helping her understand and resolve her traumatization by a qualified mental health professional is recommended.

Theoretically mental health professionals are supposed to be entirely objective, neither encouraging a couple to stay together, nor to split apart. Yet, in reality, sometimes the counselor's personal beliefs about marriage and the family may emerge. Responsible therapists need to be aware of their values and attempt not to force their beliefs on their clients.

Vietnam wives in the process of deciding whether to stay or go should not allow themselves to be unduly influenced by the therapist's biases, or by the therapist's own marital status. For example, the therapist may be married, divorced, or single. Yet the marital status which is right for the therapist may not be right for the Vietnam wife. Furthermore, if the Vietnam wife senses that the therapist is trying to push her either into staying with the veteran or into leaving him, she should ask the therapist to adopt a more neutral attitude.

Some wives report being told by therapists to "leave immediately," or to "go home and give more." Candice Williams, in *Post Traumatic Stress Disorders of the Vietnam Veteran*, cites an instance of a "woman who was crying out for help...a well-meaning counselor told her she should be more patient and show greater compassion and understanding for her veteran husband. However, this woman was on the verge of collapse. She had given and given and had nothing left. Yet she was supposed to give more. The woman had no way out: there was no recognition that she had her own problems. Following intervention through the woman's group, she was able to see herself as important. Rather than focusing on her failure to keep her husband, she was better able to take care of herself. As a result, she was better able to give support of a positive nature."[14]

Almost every Vietnam wife has many options other than staying with her veteran. If she does not recognize her options, she may feel trapped. This feeling of entrapment is dangerous. It can lead not only to extreme emotional numbing, depression, or a general sense of paralysis and desperation about life, but to suicidal thoughts or suicide attempts, or to eating disorders, substance abuse, phobias, and a host of other things.

It is important for every Vietnam wife, even if she wants to stay with her veteran, to recognize her options. Even women who are firmly committed to their marriages need to affirm that they are with their veteran by choice and that, should the relationship substantially deteriorate or become unendurable for other reasons, they have a way out other than suicide or numbing.

"I would never leave my husband," one wife says, "But it's good to know that I could, if I wanted to. This makes me take responsibility for myself in the marriage. Until now I've been using numbing as my way of coping. But I also realize that numbing is a way of punishing him too. The only problem is that my numbing affects my children, and, where does it stop? Already I've been turning down invitations and avoiding my friends. Maybe someday I'll be almost totally isolated if this keeps up.

"Now that I realize that I'm not bound to my husband, like a serf to a lord, I have to take some action on myself."

Often I ask women to write a list of all their fears; both their emotional fears and their financial fears about both staying with the veteran and about leaving him. While a paper and pencil exercise may seem like a superficial means of dealing with such a profound issue as the fate of one's love relationship, often listing emotions and fears on paper can be helpful. At the very least, it can be a starting point to clearer thinking, the beginning of examining options other than accepting things the way they are.

With her list in hand, the Vietnam wife can match her fears with reality. For example, if she carefully assesses her finances and writes out a budget, she may realize that she can make it on her own, without the veteran's financial support. Of course, this may mean forsaking certain luxuries. For some women, financial discomfort may be a small price to pay for freedom from excessive criticism, physical abuse, or other forms of bondage.

Some women are willing to accept the reduced standard of living which might accompany a separation or divorce for themselves, but they are reluctant to deprive their children of the material advantages to which they are accustomed. Yet children will not crumble without certain luxuries, and, it may be more important for mother to make the break and begin to take control of her life than for the children to have a new T.V. set or an annual vacation.

Nevertheless, as previously mentioned, there are some women who, for a variety of reasons, are, or feel, literally trapped into their marriages by financial pressures, threats of violence, or whatever. Even in some of these cases, the constraints are temporary. With sufficient brainstorming and research, and with the help of others, the woman may be able to see a way out. Even if she cannot separate for a year or two years, or even for four years, she can make long-range plans to leave, if, and only if, this is her choice.

The Vietnam wife may also be surprised to discover that she has more financial options than she previously realized. Perhaps there is a family member or friend who can loan her the money she needs to start a new life. Perhaps she can even overcome her pride and ask for help, realizing that even if she has been alienated from certain friends or family members, these persons may still care about her and would be glad to be of assistance.

In addition, some women are shortsighted, looking at only their immediate assets or their immediate salaries. They tend to forget that in the years, or even the months to come, they may be promoted or able to find better jobs. Furthermore, there is always the possibility of resuming one's education or job training and of searching out scholarships and loans to do so. All these possibilities entail hard work, of course, as well as the risks of trying something new. This can be extremely frightening to women, especially if their self-confidence has been eroded in their marriage. Women's centers and returning women's programs at local universities or colleges can help women, not only with vocational and educational planning, but by providing support services for women who are suffering a crisis of confidence.

Many women feel that the only options they have are either staying with the veteran and accepting things the way they are or leaving him entirely. In reality, however, a woman has several other choices. The Vietnam wife can negotiate for a trial separation, or she can make her staying contingent on the veteran seeking help for PTSD or any substance abuse problem. She can also require that the veteran not only attend therapy but that he show noticeable improvement in some areas or be drug or alcohol free for a certain length of time before she commits the rest of her life to him. In cases where the veteran has been physically abusive, the woman can make the continuation of the relationship contingent on the vet seeking help for his battering and on the end of violence in the home.

If the Vietnam wife is making the continuation of the relationship contingent on certain changes on the part of the veteran, she needs to clarify for herself as specifically as possible what changes she is requiring. For example, she needs to ask herself, "What behaviors will I tolerate and which ones are totally unacceptable to me?"

Some wives want their husband to stop drinking entirely. Others, however, would be content if the drinking binges were reduced to twice a month, rather than being weekly occurrences. Still others have indicated a willingness to stay with the veteran if he would only switch from hard liquor to beer or from hard drugs to marijuana. Other wives will tolerate no form of alcohol, but can tolerate marijuana smoking, providing the veteran does not smoke himself into a semi-coma.

A major area of confusion is the issue of "slips." While some men manage to maintain almost perfect abstinence from alcohol or drugs after joining a substance abuse program, it is not uncommon even for the best intentioned man to "slip" back on occasion. However, these slips do not necessary mean that the veteran is in total irreversible relapse, or that he is not in recovery.

Only the Vietnam wife can decide how many slips she will tolerate. However, for a greater understanding of her husband's slips, she may want to discuss his behavior with his therapist or a qualified counselor. There are several questions she needs to consider.

Does her husband admit to the slips, or does he try to hide them? After a slip, does he attempt to resume his efforts to get help? Over time, are the slips shorter in duration, involving less and less of the particular substance being abused? Or, do the slips get longer every time, involving larger and larger quantities of alcohol or drugs?

Other desired changes may pertain to household and childcare responsibilities. The Vietnam wife who wants her veteran to be more active in these areas needs to spell out her expectations as specifically and concretely as possible. For example, does she want her husband to take over certain chores entirely? Is she expecting him to take care of the children a certain number of hours a week so she can have some time for herself?

Perhaps she is seeking a change in attitude instead. Many wives have stated that they don't care if their husband never scrubs a toilet bowl or takes the children out on the weekend. What they want is for him to be less irritable around the children and to show some interest in their activities and homework.

Other wives would be content with even less. Some women feel that their marriages would be tolerable if only the veteran could bring in a reliable income, however small, if he could stop "trashing" the house or if, in other ways, he could "turn off his volcano."

The woman who is trying to decide whether she should stay or go can also set a time limit for herself. The "deadline" needs to be flexible, however. For example, a woman may decide to make up her mind after a year's trial separation. However, if after the year is past, the woman is still not certain, she has every right to extend her deadline. In fact, the deadline can be extended as often as is necessary for the woman to gather the information she needs about her veteran and for her to sort our her feelings about him.

Many women pressure themselves to make up their minds quickly, often chastising themselves for being "wishy washy," that is, wanting to leave their husband one day and being madly in love with or forgiving toward him the next. A standard joke in the group is "I was going to leave him on Saturday, but..."

The "but" usually begins a description of how, upon learning of his wife's intention to leave, the veteran became his most romantic, sexual, giving, and loving self and how, in displaying his strengths and many good qualities, convinced his wife to stay. It is the veteran who puts the woman on such an emotional yo-yo, yet it is the woman who berates herself for not being able to make up her mind and for having such strong conflicting feelings toward the same man.

Women who are ambivalent need to give themselves credit for taking the time and emotional energy to consider the future of their relationship seriously and for not acting impulsively. The Vietnam wife needs to appreciate that her decision is a very complex one, involving consideration of many factors. She may need many months, or even years, to come to a decision which is right for her. She needs to give herself permission to take as much time as she needs to decide.

There is no shame in waiting to be relatively sure that all the tender feelings are gone, or in waiting to be relatively certain that the veteran will never change. On the other hand, once the love affair is over, or, the veteran's behavior becomes totally unacceptable, there is no shame in her making a definite and quick decision to leave or to make him leave.

For example, Marcia's husband had been through both outpatient PTSD therapy and an inpatient alcohol treatment program. For many months afterward, he was not only sober but free from nightmares. After he began working, however, he began smoking marijuana, arguing to Marcia that compared to alcohol, the drug was relatively harmless. The marijuana led to some light drinking which turned into heaving drinking.

When Marcia filed for divorce, her husband begged for another chance. He was on a waiting list to be admitted to a Veteran's Administration Medical Center inpatient PTSD program. Couldn't Marcia wait until he had completed this program before she made her final decision?

"He's already eaten up three years of my life," Marcia told the group. "I'm afraid that if I don't get out now, I'll never get out. Maybe I'm wrong. Maybe this time he's really going to get better. But I just can't take the chance."

In making her decision, the Vietnam wife needs to be assured that there are seldom any "right" or "wrong" answers. Neither is there any way she can predict the future. A veteran may show all the signs of making significant changes and then, a few years later, revert to his old self-destructive patterns. On the other hand, some veterans have shunned treatment and all forms of help, only to conquer many of their symptoms on their own and to become extremely dedicated, supportive husbands.

In a few cases, veterans have pressured their wives to move to another city or town, or to a rural area, thinking that a geographical change, or a more isolated environment, would effect a personality change or help them give up alcohol or drugs. Generally, "geographical cures" do not work. However, in a few cases, they did. The veteran not only gave up his addiction, but also made significant progress in other areas of life.

Both the path of staying and the path of leaving are fraught, not only with risks, but with pain. For the wife who decides to stay with her veteran, even if he does not meet her needs, there is pain in realizing that she is settling for much less than what she hoped for in a love relationship. Her pain is increased when she compares herself with women who have dissolved unfulfilling relationships, women whom she tends to perceive as stronger, braver, and more self-loving than herself. On the other hand, the wife who decides to leave may deluge herself with the "what if's." "What if I had waited just a little longer?" "What if it was just his job pressures, his mother's death, not his personality, that caused the problems?"

Furthermore, many women, even women who are almost totally alienated from their veteran at the time of separation, may experience a sense of loss when they finally end the relationship. Along with the relief of being "finally free," there may also be mourning for the positive aspects of the relationship and, at the very least, for the broken dreams and hopes. Furthermore, if there are children involved, the woman may become aware of her children's pain at the marital breakup and their grieving at being separated from the father.

A common fear of Vietnam wives is that divorce is mentally unhealthy for children. Undoubtedly children suffer anger, grief, and pain when a divorce occurs. However, this does not mean that children will suffer irrevocable emotional scars. Children are often resilient and may, ultimately, find it easier to cope with the break up of the family than to live in a household full of tension and unhappiness, or with a depressed mother. In addition, a marital break up does not mean that the children will not continue to have a relationship with their father. Especially in this age of joint custody, there are many flexible custody arrangements available to divorcing couples and children of divorce are no longer the oddity they were some ten to twenty years ago.

On the other hand, the stress of a divorce on children should not be minimized. Some may need outside professional help during the transition period.

In a few cases, Vietnam wives have sought a separation or divorce, not because the veteran failed to seek help with his PTSD or because he was reluctant to make certain changes, but because they realized that even if the veteran totally recovered from his war experiences and met all their "requirements," they no longer loved him. "He did beautifully in his PTSD group and he's making every effort to do what I want him to do, but—and I don't know why—the love is gone." Some of these women realize that they married the veteran for "the wrong reasons." Perhaps they married young, unthinkingly, due to social or family pressures to be married before a certain age. Other wives have simply discovered that their needs, at age 40 or 45, are quite different from their needs at 19, 20, or 24 when they first married.

Whether or not a Vietnam wife decides to stay with her husband or to leave him, it is important that she attempt to consciously focus on her own needs and her personal goals for her life. Simply leaving the veteran will not guarantee that she will develop herself in the future. In her next relationship, she may continue to defer to her partner and neglect herself. The Vietnam wife who decides to stay with her veteran, or who feels trapped in her marriage, for one reason or the other, needs to seek as many ways of taking care of herself within the constraints of her marriage as possible.

She can attempt to put into her life as much emotional support and self-expression as possible. While she may not be able to change the veteran, or to change her marital status, she may be able to pursue activities or friendships which bring her at least some measure of joy and fulfillment. Or she may begin to work on some of her own problem areas. For example, several women who struggle with obesity, bulimia, or anorexia-nervosa, have decided to stay married. Yet they have committed themselves to obtaining help for their eating disorders, by consulting a nutritionist, by participating in eating disorders counseling, or by beginning an exercise program.

A number of wives have felt that much of their discontent with their marriage was their "fault" in that they were overextending themselves as the veteran's caretaker. They hoped that the marriage could be saved if they began to allocate more of their energies for themselves and if the veteran could tolerate their personal growth. Some wives began to refuse to make appointments for the veteran, stopped paying his debts, or running his errands, and set limits on the amount of "therapy" and comforting they would give him when he was depressed about Vietnam or other issues. The ways in which these women focussed on themselves were manifold. Some took up swimming or other sports. Others resumed certain hobbies or went back to school. Some simply hired babysitters so they could have time to themselves. In cases where the veteran was excessively threatened or otherwise could not tolerate the woman's self-development, or, where the woman outgrew the veteran emotionally or intellectually, the marriages sometimes dissolved.

While some women leave their marriages with sufficient alimony, property, or child support so that they do not have to struggle financially, and have children who adjust beautifully and instantly to the changes in the family, this has not been the reality for any of the Vietnam wives I have seen. For most of the women, separation or divorce has necessitated a host of adjustments: financial, emotional, social, and sexual.

Even though the Vietnam wife may have been an outside wage earner and felt like a single parent while married, the veteran usually provided some financial help, as well as some help with such things as the children, the housework, the car, and the finances. There is now a qualitative difference in her feeling of being "responsible for everything." She now knows, in a new way, that the entire burden of the home, the family's finances, and the children's needs are on her, and on her alone. Unless, of course, the veteran continues to provide help or one of the children is an adult who can offer a substantial financial or emotional contribution.

In most cases, however, the separated or divorced Vietnam wife has even more multiple roles to contend with than she did before. While she is now released from the time-consuming, energy-absorbing role of wife, she may not have that much more time for herself because she now may have to work harder to meet her bills. She may find herself having to work full time, instead of part time, or taking on a part-time job, in addition to a full-time job. Or, if she was a homemaker prior to the separation or divorce, she may find herself thrust into the world of work, which in itself, requires numerous adjustments. Furthermore, she may be competing in the labor force with single persons and with men who generally have more time and energy to devote to their careers.

304 | VIETNAM WIVES

In addition, if she is a mother, the separated or divorced Vietnam wife also has to deal with her children's reaction to the family breakup. The reaction of a child is a highly individual matter, depending not only on the age of the child, but on his or her relationship to each parent, and the availability of emotional supports. While children may adjust eventually, they do not necessarily do so immediately. Almost always there is anger at one parent, or perhaps at both, as well as fear of abandonment, and the discomfort of having to adjust to a lower standard of living. Some children may withdraw, become aggressive, develop psychosomatic problems, or become depressed.

It is not uncommon, for example, for previously quiet children to suddenly erupt with emotion several months after the family breakup. If the veteran and his wife engaged in emotional numbing as a defense during their marriage, one or more of their children may have learned to do likewise. Or perhaps the child learned to be quiet during any parental arguments, feeling that being quiet and repressing his or her own emotions was the safest thing to do. After the separation or divorce, however, children may feel more free to express their feelings.

Children need to be encouraged to talk. Supportive counseling, or at least access to a caring friend, family member, or minister, may be needed. Children often need assurance that their feelings of pain, anger, fear, and confusion are normal to children in the midst of a family breakup or that they are simply undergoing the grieving process—for the family life that was and for the idealized family life that never will be.

For example, at first Jo-Allison's daughter hated her mother for "making Daddy leave" and said so frequently. Jo-Allison's son, however, said nothing. But, at age 10, he began to wet the bed. Meanwhile Jo-Allison was trying to learn how to fix cars and broken water heaters in order to save on repair bills and, in other ways, was adjusting to the massive strains of being a single parent. She was also coping with her own sense of bereavement at losing her previously major societal role: that of wife. It was hard for her to deal with her children's anger, grief, and their many emotional needs, which were intensified by the divorce, while at the same time coping with her own emotional pain.

Understandably, she felt overwhelmed. Yet she often berated herself for not being able to handle everything at once, even though she was doing the work of at least two people.

It's hard, it's just too hard. It was hard living with Albert and his moods; with a man who, although he had a good heart, was simply not there for me emotionally, financially, sexually, or spiritually. But divorce is no picnic either.

It's painful to be all alone, to have only myself to lean on, and not to have a buffer between me and the world. I never realized how vulnerable a woman could feel without a man beside her.

But still, I'm not sorry I left. Albert never abused me, but our marriage was going nowhere and I was going downhill—fast. I was just too lonely in that marriage.

But it's lonely outside of marriage too. Whenever I see couples walk by hand in hand, it hurts, it hurts bad.

And I'm so sensitive now. At work, my feelings get hurt so easily. I even worry about what my friends think of me. Maybe it's because I don't have someone at home who loves me.

Even with his PTSD, Albert, in his own way, loved me. He really did, even though he couldn't show it very often. Sure my kids and my Mom love me, but it's not the same, not like a man loving you.

What if I get sick or hurt in a car accident? Who will take care of me?

Albert could never take my being ill. When I had my miscarriage, I had to drive myself to the hospital. But at least he was there, somewhere, and I knew he'd come around to help me eventually.

Now there's no one to help me—with anything. It's all on me—the house, the kids, the car, the bills, and the stupid water heater too. I know I used to manage almost everything when I was married, so it really isn't that different. But it sure feels different. At least Albert was around, sometimes. And he did help, a little, and even that little bit helped.

I get very anxious sometimes, and afraid, even when there's nothing to be anxious or afraid about. Maybe it's just this sense that now I'm all alone in the world and that I, and only I, am responsible for the future of my life and for my own happiness. Before there was always

Albert to blame for my misery, and to take up my time.
But now he's gone.

Jo-Allison wishes that she had more self-assurance and self-confidence and frequently says she hates herself for not being "stronger" or "more definite." Not only does she fail to give herself credit for all the strengths she does have, but she fails to appreciate that the process of reformulating a personal identity and life goals after a divorce is difficult, painful, and frightening for both men and women, but especially for women who have spent years taking care of their husbands and children and not themselves.

While Jo-Allison's loneliness is real, it is also an expression of many of her unresolved feelings toward Albert, specifically her anger, if not rage, at his frequent rejections of her. Her loneliness lessened somewhat after she commenced the grieving process, which entailed the five stages of grief—denial, anger, bargaining, depression, and acceptance or forgiveness. Her feelings did not progress in cookbook fashion from one step to the other. Sometimes, she went back and forth between stages and sometimes she was at several stages simultaneously. Beginning to resolve the grieving, however, helped free her to go on to meet new men and to engage in new activities. Yet her mourning continued over several years, as old memories about her marriage were released from repression into conscious awareness.

In addition to dealing with her own grieving process and her children's reactions to the divorce, Jo-Allison had to contend with the reactions of her ex-husband's family. Her ex-mother-in-law, for example, frequently chastises Jo-Allison for "deserting" her deserving son.

"My mother-in-law and I used to be so close, but now she calls me names in front of my own children," Jo-Allison says. "Yet, I don't forbid my children from seeing her because I know they need all the emotional support and sense of family they can get."

Despite the problems with her ex-mother-in-law, Jo-Allison considers herself fortunate in that she has considerable emotional and even some financial support from her own parents. Hence she tends to feel less alone and vulnerable than women whose parents are dead, rejecting, or otherwise unavailable. However, the increased contact with her mother and other members of her family after the divorce did bring to the surface some of Jo-Allison's unresolved issues with her family. "Here I was, dealing with all my feelings about separating from my husband, while at the same time having to deal with all the feelings my Mom and Dad had. I truly thought I was going nuts," Jo-Allison explains.

Another problem was that one of Jo-Allison's cousins felt she was a "sinner" for "breaking up a happy home." "It was never a happy home," Jo-Allison tried to explain, but her cousin was not interested in listening. Like Jo-Allison, many separated and divorced Vietnam wives are surprised, and hurt, to discover that they become the object of criticism and speculation by women in their families or in their circle of friends. These women do not approve of divorce or secretly desire to divorce their own husbands, but are too afraid to do so. Special problems arise when the Vietnam wife's mother or father are against divorce or when they remind her, "I told you so." In addition, the divorced or separated Vietnam wife may be perceived as a sexual threat, by both single and married women. As a result, she may feel alienated from, and actually be excluded from, certain natural sources of support.

In general, separation and divorce tend to be easiest, both financially and emotionally, for women who are childless. The Vietnam wife who has no children can make a relatively clean break from her veteran. Not only does she never have to see him again unless she chooses to, but she is free to relocate, to move back to her hometown, or near her relatives. The Vietnam wife who is a mother, however, may be constrained by court injunction or by the needs of her children to see their father to remain in a certain geographical area.

In addition, she may find herself embroiled in a prolonged, expensive, and, perhaps, humiliating custody battle where she is accused of being a poor mother or of having been an inadequate wife. There may be social service and other investigations by mental health professionals who are less than sympathetic, who know little, or nothing, about PTSD, or who have a "blame-the-mother" orientation. Furthermore, considerable mudslinging can occur during court proceedings, which only compounds the Vietnam wife's loss of self-esteem at being divorced and which only exacerbates any bitterness she may harbor toward her veteran.

One wife explains, "After all those years I cared for my husband, nursed his war injuries, put up with his moods—and his relatives—had sex with him when I didn't want to, he tears me down in court and accuses me of things I never did.

"The lies, the accusations—they cut me in half. Is this my thanks? Being degraded in a courtroom in front of strangers by the man to whom I gave so much of my life!"

Wives who have to undergo prolonged and degrading court proceedings sometimes develop panic attacks, rage reactions, or certain phobic reactions—like the dry heaves or vomiting. They are understandably intimidated by the court proceedings and, consequently, are easily tempted to "give in" to the opposition and surrender certain rights rather than have to endure any more legal, financial, and emotional pressures. It is highly recommended that the Vietnam wife who finds herself in the midst of difficult court proceedings give herself permission to lean on others and to borrow their courage and strength. If possible, she needs to try to stand firm in requesting the child support and other financial help to which she and her children are entitled, and in requesting the type of visitation schedule or custody arrangements which she feels are in the best interest of her children.

In general, only a handful of Vietnam veterans have been vindictive or have dragged their former wives and children through prolonged court procedures. Some vets have settled quietly and generously. Others have left town and made few, or only intermittent, attempts to see their children. In such cases, the child usually feels abandoned and goes into mourning for the lost parent. The child may even idealize the lost parent and may, like Jo-Allison's daughter, become angry at the mother for leaving the father. It has often been difficult for Vietnam wives who have their own feelings of being abandoned by the veteran to become the object of their child's anger, while at the same time trying to help their child with his or her grieving process.

While many women have been successful in obtaining child support in legal proceedings, very few have received any alimony. Furthermore there are sometimes problems receiving the child support on schedule or in the full amount. In some cases, the ex-husband desires special favors in return for his prompt and full payment—meals, a place to stay, affection, extra visitation, even sex. Some Vietnam wives have had to expend considerable energy setting limits on their former husbands and defending themselves against the veteran's attempts to get them to act, once again, like wives or caretakers.

The Vietnam wife who is a mother may never be totally free of the veteran and may need continued support in handling the many times she must come into contact with him or otherwise have to deal with him. There may be problems when he picks up the children for visitation. He may engage in verbal or physical abuse, or perhaps attempt to manipulate her.

However, even if the veteran is a saint when he comes for the children, his sheer physical presence can arouse in the woman all the old feelings, both the love and the anger, and put her in a state of excruciating pain. Many women feel that once they are separated or divorced, they will no longer have any tender feelings toward their former spouse. This is not the case. It is perfectly normal for a woman to still have love feelings toward her former husband, even if she feels she can no longer live with him or even if she is enraged at him. One cannot love a man for years and then suddenly and completely kill all the loving feelings.

Lest the above description of the transition period seem too negative and grim, it must be emphasized that the transition period does not last forever. The woman, like her children, can slowly make all the necessary adjustments. However, the process can be extremely difficult and taxing.

Nevertheless, out of the pain and the sadness, a new woman can be born who will—eventually—be able to enjoy her freedom and autonomy. She can spend her free time and her money as she chooses without having to account to anyone. While there may always be loneliness, the fear of growing old alone, and sexual frustration, there are the opportunities which being alone can bring in terms of friendships, creative pursuits, or other interests.

It is highly recommended that the separated or divorced Vietnam wife who does not have a natural or already established support system avail herself of the services of a therapist or otherwise establish a support system for herself. Even though she may feel she does not have the time for friendships or a support group, she needs to be kind to herself and not try to handle all the adjustments all alone, without some form of support.

There are books which contain many positive suggestions for coping with separation and loss, and with living alone. However, while taking some of the positive actions suggested in these books can be helpful, no amount of action or self-will can eliminate the suffering which is part of the mourning process. Neither is the process of letting go ever total or complete, especially if the marriage has been a long one. Some wives dream of their husbands years after the divorce. This does not mean that these women are neurotically "clinging to the past," but rather, that the effects of having been deeply attached to a man, of having slept with him and sacrificed hundreds of times can never be 100% eliminated. Just as the Vietnam veteran cannot simply "forget about" Vietnam, the Vietnam wife may not be able to "forget about" a man she cared deeply about at one time in her life. Neither can a former Vietnam wife forget the trauma *she* experienced—the abuse, fear, and embarrassment.

Hence, the Vietnam wife must be prepared for reoccurring, and sometimes unexpected times of sadness, anger, and pain regarding the breakup of her marriage. She should not immediately assume that these feelings are signs of "wallowing in the past." They may be legitimate feelings of mourning.

In addition, the Vietnam wife who is embarking on a new life as a woman alone must also be prepared for times of self-doubt, insecurity, fear, and tension. Once again, these are not indications that she is "not strong," or "overly dependent," or that she has a Wendy, a Cinderella or some other complex. These moments are inevitable when leaving the security of the old role of wife and forging a new identity in a society that is just beginning to accept single and divorced women as "normal" and complete human beings.

Summary

For many Vietnam wives, the issue of whether to stay or go is fraught with indecision. Even if the Vietnam wife is unhappy, after having invested so heavily in her marriage, she may be reluctant to give up on her veteran, especially if he has yet to seek help or if he has serious war injuries. The woman's fear of the unknown and of loneliness also play a role, as do any fears surrounding the emotional and financial hardships involved in being on her own.

The Vietnam wife may also wonder if her decision will result in negative psychological effects for her husband and children. If her husband is suicidal or extremely dependent on her, she may worry that he will significantly deteriorate without her. If he has been violent, she may fear that he will be destructive either to her or her children.

Some women want to leave but cannot afford to do so financially. Others are—or feel—trapped by their obesity or some other source of personal inadequacy. Women who were abused as children are often influenced to stay by patterns learned as children.

The Vietnam wife who is seriously considering the possibility of a separation or divorce should take as long as she needs to make a decision and feel free to change her mind as often as she needs to.

In making her decision, she should try for the most objective possible picture of her husband's condition and its effect on her and their children. She needs to keep in mind that, untreated, PTSD, alcoholism, and drug addiction usually get worse. If she decides to stay with a veteran who refuses help, she should try to build a support system for herself so that her husband's problems do not overwhelm her.

Both staying with the veteran, and leaving him, can involve risk and pain. Only the Vietnam wife herself can decide which path to choose.

Epilogue

The fighting in Vietnam may be over, but the war still lives, not only in the hearts and minds of Vietnam veterans and their families, but in the consciousness of our nation. Our papers are filled with accounts of commemorative services for the Tet offensive and other highlights of the Vietnam war. In Washington, D.C., controversies about the design of The Wall abound and in other locales more and more memorials to Vietnam veterans are being or have been erected. Meanwhile our television and movie screens are flooded with a variety of films about the war.

We frequently read news accounts of the return of the remains of American MIA's and of Hanoi's recent efforts to present a *new* Vietnam image, more open to the world and wanting improved relations with the U.S. "Vietnam wants to forget the past, let bygones be bygones," says Vietnam's Communist Party General Secretary Nguyen Van Linh. "We want to push back that bitter past. We don't want to remember it. We just want to look ahead so we can have good relationships." [1]

Perhaps certain Vietnamese officials want to forget the war, for their own political and economic purposes, but how easily can the PTSD afflicted, Agent Orange contaminated, or handicapped Vietnam veteran or his wife forget? So far, our government has refused Hanoi's requests for economic assistance, but there is still talk of the U.S. sending foreign aid to Vietnam. [2]

One can only wonder how Vietnam veterans will react if someday soon our government decides to trade with, financially assist, or otherwise help its former enemy. Those Vietnam veterans who feel they have failed to receive full compensation for their war injuries or other readjustment difficulties may feel even more embittered and betrayed. Their wives may feel the same way.

Some vets proudly refuse to seek government help, but others are still waiting for their compensation claims to be processed. In addition, since the war some vets have developed new physical and psychological problems which they feel are war-related.

For example, Anna's husband, Tony, left Vietnam with a red spot on his chest. Like many vets who served in the field, Tony suffered from rashes during his tour of duty. Yet in his case, as in others, the rashes were quickly treated with available ointments and were not noted on the record. Today, a horrible rash covers Tony's arms and feet. Due to the lack of documentation, however, Tony does not know if he can prove that his rash is war-related.

Tony freely admits that his rash is exacerbated by his PTSD or other stresses. For example, whenever he sees war movies or has problems at home or at work, his rash flares up. Yet he feels that the physicial origin of the rash, as well as the origin of his mental stress, lie in his war experiences and that therefore he should be compensated. When he takes time off work to receive medical treatment or to process compensation papers, his wife must work overtime to make ends meet. Both she and Tony become enraged when they read in the papers that Vietnamese officials are toning down the anti-American propaganda and talking about "two hundred years of friendship and only ten years of war." [3]

In a few years, Tony and Anna's sons, like the sons and daughters of other Vietnam families, will be military age. To what extent will the vet, or his wife, promote or oppose their son's or daughter's participation in the military? While some Vietnam veterans and Vietnam wives are firm supporters of the military, others are totally against it. Still others feel that their support of the military is dependent on the nature of the military's current invovlement. "If our country was invaded or there was another Hitler on the scene, I would gladly send my son to go die for his country," explains one wife. But she would never ever encourage her boy to go fight for another Vietnam.

Her husband, a much decorated war hero and an extremely patriotic individual, agrees with her completely. They, like other Americans, are concerned that some of the current conflicts in Central America and elsewhere may evolve into "new Vietnams" and that our country will once again be embroiled in the moral crisis and political and military controversies which fractured our nation during the 60s.

This book is but a peek into the lives of a limited group of PTSD afflicted Vietnam veterans and their families. Since PTSD has only recently been recognized as a significant psychological disorder and researchers are still in the process of gathering information about how trauma can affect an individual, our knowledge of the full impact of PTSD is limited. Consequently, it is difficult to make any accurate, long-range predictions about how PTSD may affect Vietnam families in the future. The completion of the National Vietnam

Veteran Readjustment Study, however, will undoubtedly enhance our pool of information.

Even without research results, however, Vet Center counselors anticipate that the problems of some PTSD afflicted Vietnam families will not disappear overnight. In some cases, the problems will simply continue, but in other cases, they will only escalate over time, especially if the vet has medical problems or has PTSD but has not sought assistance.

Yet even vets who have received readjustment counseling may continue to suffer. Tony, for example, still sees the faces of men who died in Vietnam. "I have a Ph.D. in psychology and have been through two years of PTSD therapy, but I still can't get over this thing." Like many vets who have undergone therapy, Tony feels that therapy has helped him to better understand and get a handle on his PTSD, but there are still times when the numbing overcomes him, or when he breaks down in tears. As Tony's case illustrates, trauma victims may never make the trauma go away. What they can do, however, is to enlarge their capacity to deal with the trauma.

"I can only deal with so much stress," Tony explains. "Vietnam raped my mind, and my heart. If today I'm having trouble coping with my job, which is only a job, how am I going to handle it when something big happens, like somebody in my family dies or one of my children becomes terminally ill?"

To date, we have no data on whether or not PTSD afflicted Vietnam veterans, like Tony, who experienced trauma and major losses in their late adolescence or early adulthood, will be more, or less, able to cope with the many personal losses that attend midlife and aging. The midlife crisis and the inevitable physical and psychological changes associated with growing older are difficult for most persons to accept. However, they may pose special challenges for both the veteran with PTSD and his wife.

The new wounds may reawaken the old ones. Or, if the vet has never allowed himself to feel, then the indisputable losses of midlife (the departure of children, the loss of a youthful appearance, the loss of certain career and social oportunities) and the even more obvious losses of aging (decreased physical abilities, increased medical problems, the death of friends) may shatter the vet's denial and force him to deal not only with his present life situation, but with his Vietnam memories as well.

Midlife and aging may also be especially difficult for vets who suffer from war injuries. In some cases, growing older may put stress on the war injuries, creating increased physical pain or other medical complications. The vet's physical and mental health will especially suffer if he develops a new medical condition like diabetes, lower back pain, or heart disease.

Even though the Vietnam wife does not have PTSD and war injuries, the midlife and aging years may be especially difficult for her too. It is at midlife that she may fully come to appreciate the heavy dues she has paid for keeping her marriage together. "Where's the reward?" she may ask. In some cases, she may have neglected herself, physically, emotionally, or spiritually, and is now paying the price for her lack of self-care. For example, she may have delayed seeking medical or psychological assistance, putting her husband's and children's needs before her own. She may have also postponed developing her career, her avocational interests, and certain friendships in order to serve her family.

While she may be proud of having been a faithful and dedicated wife and mother, her self-appreciation may be colored by sadness and grief regarding the opportunities she missed during her younger years due to her husband's PTSD and her family's pressing needs. She may also experience jealousy and anger toward women who appear to have had easier lives.

The Vietnam wife's attempts to accept her life are not helped by the fact that our society holds a double standard of aging—one for men and one for women. While many prejudices and misconceptions surround the aging process for both sexes, as a group, women have been found to suffer more depression, anxiety, and role confusion than men when they begin to lose their youthful appearances or in other ways show that they are indeed aging.[4]

Traditionally, physical beauty has been one of the major sources of women's personal power and sense of self-esteem. In contrast, men have derived their sense of power and self-worth more from job and career achievements. Hence aging is more of a stigma for women than for men and can result in self-rejection, a major identity crisis, or a flare-up of any pre-existing psychological problems. If, in addition, the Vietnam wife is obese, her feelings of valuelessness may be enormous, especially if she does not have a strong appreciation of her emotional and spiritual strengths.

For those Vietnam wives who are mothers, the aging process is especially painful because it includes the slow demise and eventual termination of the mother role. As women of the 50s, most Vietnam wives were socialized to make their children their chief concern. In fact, some Vietnam wives have spent years functioning as virtual single parents, overextending themselves time and time again for the sake of their children's well-being.

However, as children naturally begin to separate, society expects women to suddenly drop the mother role. The lessening of the mother role, culiminating in the "empty nest," represents a difficult transition for most women, but especially for the Vietnam wife who has often made her children the focus of her life.

As both the Vietnam wife and her husband approach the end of their lives, they will need more than ever to feel that their lives had meaning and purpose. In order to avoid stagnation and despair about their mortality, they will need to find sources of strength from within themselves and new directions in life and to extend themselves to others. This will be difficult, however, if the veteran is still emotionally "stuck" in Vietnam and his wife, emotionally trapped in an extreme caretaker role, or, alternatively, in a multitude of unresolved resentments toward her husband.

Another danger is that, over time, the vet and his wife may to one degree or another, succumb to the "learned helplessness syndrome," or the tendency of human beings to generalize defeat in one area of life to other areas of their life. For example, if the vet feels "defeated" in overcoming his PTSD or like a failure because he has not achieved vocationally or financially to the extent of his peers who did not go to Vietnam, his sense of failure regarding his work role may "spill over" into his evaluation of himself as a father, husband, or son.

Similarly, the Vietnam wife may allow her feelings about her wife role to generalize to her other roles. For example, it is not uncommon for the Vietnam wife to feel deficient as a wife. Even though she may be an excellent wife by many people's standards, because she is not receiving validation, encouragement, or sexual or emotional fulfillment from her husband, she may conclude that she has "failed" in her role as wife. She may allow this negative self-evaluation of her wife role to "spill over" into her view of herself as a worker, mother, or other areas of life where she may be obviously quite competent and successful. Her sense of failure will only be exacerbated if her children, to one degree or another, have made her the scapegoat for the family's problems or have imitated their father's patterns of emotional withdrawal or noncommunicativeness.

Both the Vietnam wife and her husband and children can be helped by realizing that, for most people, life is not a progression from one success to the other, one pleasure to the next. Even though the media often presents "normal" life as being relatively pain-free, the reality is that most humans do suffer various failures, disappointments, and emotional heartaches on this earth. Even in our relatively affluent country, the stress-free existence so frequently portrayed on T.V., is, for many people, a myth.

Time does not heal all wounds and the vet who wants to be whole and have a positive outlook on life must usually fight for his psychological well-being. Those vets who have sought help are fortunate. At least they have been exposed to the tools by which they can achieve some measure of inner peace and cope with the stresses of life. In contrast stand vets who have never sought help. According to dozens of Vet Center counselors, there are thousands of vets who suffer from PTSD who have yet to avail themselves of the services of a therapist or counselor. Since these men have been living with their PTSD without help for so many years, their defenses, their social isolation, and any maladaptive behaviors resulting from the PTSD are by now well-engrained and, consequently, more resistant to change. If these vets ever seek help, the healing process may not only be longer, but harder for them than for those who sought help when they were younger. If they do not seek help, they may continue in a life style which promotes the denial of emotion. In some cases, this will entail alcohol and drug abuse. In other cases, there may be no addictive illness, but the vet may push away his wife and children and ultimately lose his family.

A not unfamiliar story is that of the high-achieving vet with no external signs of stress. Not wanting to be identified as a "vet with problems," he not only shows no signs of emotional distress, but becomes a financial or intellectual success. Perhaps he works 12-14 hours a day and is admired by his colleagues. But he is alienated from his family and, over time, his family emotionally divorces him or develops a life style without him. Or perhaps his wife actually leaves with the children. When the vet eventually kills himself or simply just disappears, Vietnam may never be suspected as having played a role because he never talked about Vietnam or acted as if Vietnam ever troubled him. Even if he does not commit suicide directly, but indirectly, through alcohol or drugs, Vietnam may still never be suspected.

According to some Vet Center counselors, some vets never seek help at Vet Centers, but attempt a form of self-therapy by frequenting Vietnam veteran memorials or engrossing themselves in books and films about Vietnam. Some frequent these memorials at night—so nobody can see them. Still other vets are affected unknowingly. Because they function at work or are able to maintain relationships at home, they are unaware of the impact of PTSD on their lives.

When the vet has a severe and untreated case of PTSD, his wife may slowly abandon all hope and retreat into social isolation and depression, just like her husband. Some Vietnam wives tenatively plan to stay with their husbands only until their children graduate high school or college. At that point, if their marriages have not improved, they may divorce.

And what of the children? At this point, we have more questions than answers. Based on our knowledge of adult children of alcoholics, as well as limited information about some children from PTSD afflicted families, we can surmise that some children may be plagued by low self-esteem and difficulties with anger and intimacy. "Don't talk, don't feel, don't trust," the message often given in alcoholic homes, has been found in some Vietnam homes. In addition, a childhood atmosphere of emotional repression in combination with family tensions and stress is usually implicated in the later development of depression or alcoholism, drug addiction, eating disorders or other means of dealing with conflicting and unacceptable feelings.

Furthermore, the child growing up in a home stressed by PTSD (especially untreated PTSD) may have as a role model for being a husband or wife, a relationship characterized by emotional withdrawal and anger on the part of not just one, but both parents. Later in life, when that child becomes an adolescent or adult and attempts to establish meaningful relationships with others, he or she may have difficulties. If the parents do not demonstrate good communication or have inadequate means of resolving their conflicts, the child may have to learn basic communication or assertiveness skills as an adult. If, in addition, there is physical abuse in the home, the child's problems will only be multipled.

Another set of problems attend those families where the vet, and perhaps, one of his children suffers from Agent Orange contamination or where such contamination is suspected. Although the vet may attempt to hide his skin tumors or other evidences of the chemical exposure, children cannot always be totally protected from their father's condition. Children in such homes often wonder when, and if, their father is going to die and, if they too will die or have physical effects from the chemical. They also wonder if their children too, might bear the scars of Agent Orange.

On the other hand, in those instances where the veteran has been able to accept his pain and grow from it, his loving feelings toward his wife and children are usually intensified. In such homes the vet takes pride in his work, but is not a workaholic. His family life is a priority and there is good communication, not only between him and his wife, but between him and his children, not only about the matters of daily living, but about deeper issues also. Children as young as seven or eight can become sensitized to a wide range of human emotions and attuned to the issues of war, poverty, and other political and social controversies. Their development has been helped, not hurt, by realizing that life entails losses and pain and that overseas events can affect their lives on a daily basis.

Hopefully this book has not promoted any simplistic or stereotypic thinking about Vietnam veterans and their families. As I have repeatedly stressed, each Vietnam veteran, wife, and child is unique. Our knowledge of trauma and its effects on survivors and their families is only beginning to unfold and I view my observations as preliminary and limited in nature. I offer them in hopes of assuring those who are troubled that they are not alone and that help is available.

The next section outlines some suggestions for seeking help, not only for PTSD, but for the problems associated with PTSD, such as alcoholism, drug addiction, and obesity. The Resource Guide provides listings of Vietnam Veteran Outreach Centers, Veteran's Administration Medical Centers, and other sources of assistance.

Coping Techniques for the Vietnam Wife

Coping With Anger And Depression

Your high levels of stress and the many demands on your physical and emotional energies can easily cause you to become overwrought and overextended, leading to anger. Most of the Vietnam wives I have worked with have harbored considerable anger, not only toward their husbands, but toward themselves and their life in general. However, out of concern for their husband's psychological state or for their children's emotional well-being, they have often kept their anger bottled up inside.

Yet repressed anger can cause as many difficulties for you as for your husband. For example, in some cases repressed anger has contributed to the development of an alcohol, drug, or, more commonly, an eating problem, usually compulsive overeating. In other cases, repressed anger has played a role in perpetuating certain physical symptoms, ranging from chronic headaches and backaches to hyperventilation, hypertension, asthma, chest pains, and sugar diabetes. These medical conditions may be related to psychological factors, such as the repression of anger or high levels of stress and anxiety. In many instances, medical symptoms were relieved when the woman was able to vocalize her anger and then go on to make concrete changes in her life. Within months, blood pressure and sugar levels dropped, chest pains abated, asthma attacks decreased in frequency, and headaches and backaches almost disappeared.

One of the most common results of suppressed anger is depression. There are three theories on depression: that depression is anger turned inward; that depression results from negative self-evaluations; and that depression stems from lack of reinforcement from the environment. In your case, all three theories may apply. Not only may you be stifling your anger at your husband, but at the same time, you may be judging yourself as a failure due to the unhappiness in your home.

You may be experiencing your anger as depression and pain. Some of the classic symptoms of depression are excessive or inappropriate guilt, tearfulness or crying, indecision, insomnia or hypersomnia (sleeping too much), low energy level or fatigue, and feelings of inadequacy and low self-esteem. Other symptoms are noticeable changes in weight or in eating habits, social withdrawal, loss of interest or enjoyment in pleasurable activities, and an inability to respond with apparent pleasure to praise or rewards.

If you are experiencing some of these symptoms, you may want to seek individual or group counseling. In counseling you can explore the possibility that repressed anger may be contributing to your depression. It is critical that you recognize and deal with your anger directly, rather than indirectly, constructively, rather than destructively. If you are unaware of your anger, you may find yourself displacing that anger onto yourself. Or you may find yourself lashing out at your children or inappropriately attacking your husband.

Acknowledging anger may be an extremely difficult task for you. In order for you to feel angry, you must get past the idea that you are responsible for your husband's and children's well-being. To be angry implies that you have rights—that you are entitled to a certain amount of respect and consideration from others. Women's liberation aside, when push comes to shove, you may still put men's rights ahead of women's rights and feel that your husband's happiness is more important than your own.

You may have special difficulty feeling angry if your anger is mixed in with guilt over any inappropriate or sarcastic remarks you might have made to your husband. Guilt over having been verbally vicious may inhibit your awareness of your true anger. In general, most of the Vietnam wives I have seen have tended to express anger toward their husbands primarily only under four conditions:

1. When they were certain that they were almost 100% "right" on a certain issue. If they were only 90% "right," they tended to deny the anger.
2. When their partner's behavior was injuring one of the children, either emotionally or physically.
3. When they found themselves displacing the anger they harbored toward their husbands onto their children in the form of extreme irritability, excessive scolding, or even verbal or physical abuse.
4. When they found themselves at an emotional, financial, or physical breaking point.

You need to give yourself permission to appreciate, rather than deny or minimize, the burden which your husband's PTSD or other readjustment difficulties have imposed upon you and your family. You also need to acknowledge the full range of feelings you might have about your husband's problems. In individual or group therapy, or in a twelve-step program such as Al-Anon or Nar-Anon, you can learn:

1. That it is perfectly possible (and perfectly normal) to feel both anger and compassion toward your husband at the same time;
2. That you are entitled to some happiness despite the enormity of your husband's pain;
3. That you are not responsible for your husband's angry responses, unless, perhaps, you deliberately provoked a fight or made cutting comments.

The concept of "detaching with love," borrowed from Al-Anon is useful for many Vietnam wives. Detaching from the troubled veteran does not mean that you become coldly indifferent toward him, but rather that you no longer take responsibility for his distress, or his recovery. Detachment does not mean that you will not share in his sufferings, for such sharing is essential to marital intimacy. Rather it means that, to the best of your ability, you do not allow the veteran's behavior to control your actions, your mood, or self-esteem. You can, for example, understand and be empathic toward your husband's PTSD, but do your best to not be victimized by it.

While the concept of detachment is easy to grasp philosophically, it is usually difficult to practice on a daily basis. Since most of us do not wear earplugs, blindfolds, or coats of armor at home, it is usually hard for us to be immune to our husbands' mood or behavior. However, the more you can detach from taking responsibility for your husband's problems and the more you can focus on your own emotions and life goals, the more manageable your life can become. Your stress and anger levels will also be reduced.

Individual or group counseling or other supports may be needed, however, to help you identify your personal needs and see your needs as being as important as the needs of your husband and children. You also need to learn how to meet more of your needs yourself, without relying on your husband, who may be emotionally unavailable to you. For some Vietnam wives, this may mean reducing work loads, scheduling recreational activities, returning to school or to long abandoned personal projects.

Pursuing personal objectives, however, usually requires setting limits on giving to others. Most of the Vietnam wives I have seen have had considerable difficulty setting such limits and sticking to them. You need to see that limit setting and pursuing personal objectives is neither "selfish," nor incompatible with being a responsible, caring wife and mother. If you sacrifice yourself totally for your husband or children, you may end up resentful or extremely depressed and perhaps endanger your physical health as well.

Since many Vietnam wives fear their anger, I emphasize that anger is a normal human emotion. Most people, for example, become angry several times a day. Anger is especially inevitable in intimate relationships, particularly when one partner is troubled. Extreme or persistent anger is also a signal that some basic needs are not being met and that change is needed. In that light, anger can be positive. Being angry can tell you that something is wrong and needs to be changed.

All your years of stored up anger need not be dealt with all at once. You can express your anger to your therapist, to other group members, or to your husband or other family members in small, manageable doses.

Acknowledging your anger does not necessarily mean that you have to act on it. All you have to do is feel it. You can decide later what to do about your anger, if anything. Some wives fear that admitting to anger will lead to separation or divorce. In fact, the opposite is true. It is the long-term repression of anger on the part of either you or your husband which more often leads to the end of your marriage or to suicidal thoughts or suicide attempts. If you find yourself thinking about suicide, especially if you are making specific plans to kill yourself, you need to seek professional help immediately.

Couples Communication And Couples Counseling

Most Vietnam wives prefer to select one or two issues to discuss with their husbands at a time, rather than overwhelm him with numerous grievances. This might be a good approach for you to follow too. It is a good idea to wait until the appropriate time and place to approach your husband. For example, it is not generally advisable to approach him when he has been drinking or is exhausted, on the anniversary of the death date of a buddy, or after some difficulty at work. Some wives have found it helpful to make "appointments" with their husbands for such discussions, letting their husbands help choose the time and place. On the other hand, don't keep waiting indefinitely for that "perfect" time, place, or emotional mood. At some point, you may have to actually sit down and discuss things with your husband even if conditions are not exactly "right."

If you are worried about how to handle this discussion, you can practice in group or in individual therapy. You can rehearse your statements to your husband while the other women in group or the therapist pretend to be your husband. Then you will be prepared for his possible resistance, his guilt evoking responses, his angry retorts, or his indifference. When you start this discussion, remember to pay attention to your body language too. You can say "I'm angry" in a firm, calm voice, with your eyes looking right at your partner, not on the floor or the wall. A major problem for some of the women has been that they smile or laugh while discussing their hurts or angers, undercutting the seriousness of their communications. Don't do it. Keep in mind that you are an adult with the right to express your views and have them heard as the legitimate concerns of an adult.

You can communicate anger without hysterics or assaults on your husband's personality. If you find yourself becoming physically or psychologically abusive toward your husband, you can excuse yourself and postpone the discussion for a later time.

Couples counseling is often a useful forum for airing grievances and finding areas of agreement. A problem which can easily arise, however, is that the session becomes dominated by the veteran's unresolved war issues. Vietnam wives have reported politely listening to their husbands and the male therapist talk about Vietnam for practically the entire session. They have great difficulty interrupting, especially if their husband begins to weep or is in obvious pain or if the male therapist is a Vietnam veteran himself, which is often the case at Vet Centers. When this happens, the session can sometimes end without your issues being addressed at all.

Therapists, especially male therapists, can help you with this problem by giving you the opportunity (and permission) to voice your concerns. Otherwise, the counseling sessions may make you feel that your concerns are less important than your husband's. If you feel that way, tell the therapist and insist that something be done so that you feel that you have time to discuss the things bothering you.

No one party, male or female, should be allowed to dominate the session. The presence of a female therapist, provided she does not have negative attitudes toward women, often helps a wife be more assertive and feel less defensive about presenting her needs and issues.

Couples counseling is available at many Vet Centers and VA Medical Centers, as well as with private therapists. Wherever you seek help, be sure that the therapist will help both your husband *and* you.

Help In Selecting A Therapist

The following books and pamphlets offer guidelines to women in selecting therapists:

Women and Psychotherapy, A Consumer Handbook, National Coalition for Women's Mental Health. Send a self-addressed, stamped envelope and $5.00 to the National Coalition for Women's Mental Health, Women's Studies Program, Arizona State University, Tempe, AZ, 85287.

Choosing a Psychotherapist: A Consumer's Guide to Mental Health Treatment, S.C. Fisch, Waterford, MI, Minerva Press, 6653 Andersonville Road, Waterford, MI. Send a self-addressed, stamped envelope and $1.00.

Woman's Guide to Therapy, Friedman, S.; Gams, L.; Gottlieb, N.; Nesselson, C.; Prentice-Hall, 200 Old Toppen Road, Old Toppen, NJ 07656.

"If Sex Enters Into the Psychotherapy Relationship," Order Dept., American Psychological Association, Box 2710, Hyattsville, MD 20784.

You can also contact any of the following organizations to inquire if a listing of feminist or sex fair therapists has been compiled: local women's centers, rape crises or women's medical centers, local chapters of NOW (National Organization of Women), local hospitals, mental health centers, university counseling centers, or university women's studies programs.

The Association for Women in Psychology compiles a list of feminist counselors. Write: Feminist Therapist Roster, Association for Women in Psychology, 1200 17th St. NW, Washington, D.C. 20036.

Many psychologists—both men and women—call themselves "feminist" or "nonsexist" but you need to decide for yourself if they actually are. Remember that just because a therapist is a woman does not automatically make her a nonsexist therapist. You do not have to choose a woman therapist. There are many male therapists who are committed to nonsexist treatment and provide excellent counseling. In general, though, it takes a lot of effort for a man to be nonsexist and truly understand the influence of sex role stereotyping on a woman.

I would suggest that you interview potential therapists very carefully and make your decision based on how they relate to you, what they say, and their actions. You need to make an emotional match with your therapist. You must feel that you can trust him/her to guide you, to listen to you, and to be concerned about the things that concern you. If you have some special experiences that you need help with, such as incest, battering, or drug abuse, you will want to find out what view the prospective therapist takes. If the therapist believes that a young girl is "provocative" and partially responsible for an incestuous relationship, then this is not the right therapist for you.

The purpose of therapy is to help build an individual's strengths and bring out his or her inherent goodness, not to highlight his or her inadequacies. While problem areas are not to be ignored in therapy and there may be times in which confrontation in therapy is helpful, this is an art and should not be done by using negative sounding labels. In some instances, Vietnam wives report being openly called "crazy" by their therapist or having had various diagnoses thrown in their faces. "You have a borderline personality (or a schizoid one, a hysterical one, a narcissistic one, a passive aggressive one, an overly dependent one)" women have been told both kindly and unkindly.

In one case, the wife was told by her therapist that she was a "masochist" for having married a "crazy" Vietnam veteran and even more of a "masochist" for deciding to stay with him. The therapist also felt that this wife had "preborderline personality," as well as an "addiction to destructive relationships," and repeatedly reminded the wife of her "neurotic tendencies."

This did not encourage the wife to examine her patterns of relating to men. The wife just accepted her therapist's view of her as "sick." She concluded that she might as well keep her life as it was and give up any ideas of ever changing her marriage. After all, she probably deserved the treatment she was getting from her husband and certainly no other man would ever want her.

In group, it was necessary to help this Vietnam wife identify her therapist's negative view of her and help her get rid of the idea that she was a "hopeless case." The problem was made worse by the fact that her husband had also established himself as a "judge" of her personality.

This wife, like many women, needed help in freeing herself from outside authority figures. In our society, therapists are seen as authority figures and can have tremendous power over people, especially people who are vulnerable because they are in great emotional pain. If a therapist comes to a conclusion, even one that contradicts what a woman knows about herself, the woman may believe the therapist over her own self-knowledge. That is what happened to this wife.

A feminist view of this particular wife's problems would acknowledge that, to some extent, her low self-esteem, anxiety attacks, and crying spells were the logical results of the strains of being a full-time worker, having three children, and living with a man marred by PTSD. This does not mean that all her problems are due to these stresses, but that in counseling Vietnam wives, these stresses have to be taken into account.

A basic premise in feminist therapy is that every woman is an expert on her own life. The therapist's role is not to tell the woman what to do, but to help her get in touch with her past experiences and her true feelings about herself and her life so that she can make her own decisions.

You should not hesitate to confront your therapist if he/she uses psychologically degrading labels or if you leave your sessions feeling more defeated than ever, taking with you not greater self-understanding, but more negative feelings about yourself.

Therapists, male or female, who devalue women or any of women's roles in society or who use their position of authority to:
1. Control their clients;
2. Advance their careers at the client's expense; or
3. Use their position as a therapist to vent personal frustrations and ambivalence about the female sex role identity. A therapist of this type is to be avoided.

Also to be avoided are therapists who rigidly adhere to the idea that, consciously or unconsciously, you have chosen an emotionally distant veteran due to some need or another on your part. Such therapists may then insist that you are perpetuating your husband's PTSD by unconsciously or subtly discouraging his recovery due to your own need to keep your husband emotionally distant and emotionally dependent on you. Such an attitude blames you for your husband's problems and implies that you have somehow brought most of your problems upon yourself.

Blaming someone for his or her own pain seldom motivates that person to examine his or herself and make any concrete changes in his or her life. Especially in the case of women, a blaming attitude on the part of the therapist usually reinforces the woman's low self-esteem and sense of powerlessness and hinders, rather than helps, her ability to clearly assess her self, her marriage, or any other personal difficulties.

Women's Groups

You can participate in a woman's group in addition to individual therapy or participate in group only, depending on your needs. According to the Vet Center study, some 79% of the Vet Centers polled offer support groups for wives or girlfriends of Vietnam Veterans. Some of these groups run anywhere from eight to twenty-four weeks after which a new group is begun. Other groups are open-ended in that they terminate after the leader and the group decide that sufficient progress has been made. While almost all groups offer education about PTSD, some groups are more structured than others. Some allow the members to choose the topics of discussion, while in others, the topics are almost always leader-selected. Some groups are conducted by female therapists or volunteers; others by male therapists. Some groups have leaders of both sexes.

For more specific information about the closest Vietnam wives support group, contact the local Vietnam Veteran's Outreach Center. According to the Vet Center study, some Vet Centers also offer workshops and groups for children. There is a list of Vet Centers in the Resource Guide at the back of this book.

Some of the Vietnam wives who have come to group report being told by previous counselors to "go home and give more." They were hesitant to join a woman's group at a Vet Center because they feared the Vet Center staff would be rigidly pro-veteran and would chastise them for their discontents with their marriages. Women also voiced fears about being pressured to stay married to the veteran and be supportive of him at all costs. "I heard these women's groups are bandaid operations," one wife stated. "We come here once a week to feel better, but never go on to make any changes in our marriages, or our lives."

A viable woman's support group, however, needs to be more than a bandaid operation. It needs to be a forum where there is an open sharing of a full range of feelings, from love to hate and where positive changes can be made. The prime purpose of the group needs to be the promotion of your emotional and physical well-being, regardless of the outcome of your marriage.

Competent women's groups leaders do not pressure you to stay with your veteran, or to leave him, but rather help you identify your feelings, and your options. The group, as well as the leaders, can offer you a variety of perspectives on your situation and a supportive context in which you can make your own decisions about your life, not only with regard to your marriage, but with regard to your children, your career, and other matters.

A wide variety of women's groups can also be found through community service organizations or through private therapists. However, these groups are usually not focussed on PTSD-related marital issues. Some of these groups have a general focus on women's issues. Other have more specific concerns: coping with sexual harassment, coping with midlife, or whatever. Unlike Vet Center groups, however, these groups usually have a fee.

Listings of women's groups can usually be found at local libraries, in local papers, or through local social work, psychological/ psychiatric clinics, or local mental health bureaus. In addition, in some areas there are private therapists with expertise in PTSD who offer couples counseling or couples group work for PTSD afflicted families.

Coping With Multiple Roles

You can reduce your stress level by appreciating, examining, and making some concrete changes in your multiple role life style. The first step involves examining early sex role messages and myths and their effect on you. The "shoulds" which you typically carry with you are often the source of intense and recurrent guilt feelings as you try to make your own choices. Typically a woman has grown up learning about women in the most stereotyped, traditionally "feminine," ways. Her image of what a woman ought to be, how she ought to feel, and what she ought to want often clashes with how she experiences herself and what reality demands of her, resulting in feelings of being "not O.K."

Typically, over time, the Vietnam wife finds herself doing more and more. The expectations for her personal capacity seem to increase as the tasks increase. Yet the recognition of the strengths necessary to perform the tasks tend to fade. Frequently, your self-esteem diminishes as you and others start to take your efforts for granted. Then you need to focus (or be focussed by a therapist or counselor) on what you are accomplishing and on appreciating your positive qualities. I have provided you with several exercises to help you acknowledge your strengths.

In the midst of her profusion of activities, the working Vietnam wife tends to neglect herself. Among the women I have worked with, many have tended to postpone not only activities which are emotionally or spiritually fulfilling to themselves, but needed medical attention. The woman needs to "mother herself" as readily as she would (and probably has, numerous times) for her veteran or their children. "You wouldn't think twice about spending the money (or time) on your husband (or child), would you?" I point out. "Why do you think you deserve less?"

The importance of learning self-nurturing is critical. While you need to seek and gain external support, you must also be able to give to yourself. Quite often people who accomplish a great deal often come to be taken for granted and are not congratulated as often as they may need to be. Therefore, you need to learn to congratulate yourself, as well as to make time for activities which you enjoy which do not involve taking care of somebody else or completing tasks. Some wives have found great solace in ceramics, music, sewing, writing, or other activities.

Most of the Vietnam wives I have counseled attempt to maintain their traditional roles intact. They often accept all family and domestic responsibilities as though they were full-time homemakers. Redefining roles in human rather than sex role terms is a vital part of the counseling process through which the woman (and possibly her partner or family) come to see home care as a family matter. "Mothering" does not have to include laundering; "fathering" does not have to exclude it. Family care needs to be seen as a responsibility to be shared by all adult partners in the home.

In addition, outside support services can be utilized. You need to find and utilize support services such as child care, houseworkers, and tutoring.

You may also want to re-examine your career choice and job options. Traditionally, schools and counselors have not educated girls for careers. The assumptions about a woman's place have resulted in limited options being made available to women in their working lives. While visions of job or career choices have definitely expanded and are continuing to expand, the majority of women still work in traditionally feminine occupations. There may be career and educational options available to you now that were not available years ago. Some wives have sought out assertiveness training workshops, communication skills training, or specialized help in making educational and vocational decisions. You might want to explore doing the same kinds of things.

In group, women have found it useful to ask themselves what their career goals and job preferences would be (a) if they were not married to a PTSD afflicted veteran or to a drug addicted or alcoholic PTSD afflicted veteran; (b) if they were not married at all; or (c) if they did not have children. Separating your career goals from your family identity helps you select a new career goal.

Many a marriage has been saved by the wife forging ahead toward her goal, even in some small manner. In several cases, had the woman not pursued one of her vocational ambitions, she would have been strongly tempted to abandon her marriage. The sense of achievement, self-regard, and self-respect these women acquired by pursuing one of their own goals gave them the strength to cope with husbands who had little to offer emotionally because of their PTSD.

The specific exercises listed below are based on the experiences Dr. Brenda Alpert Sigall and I used in developing programs for multiple role women at the University of Maryland Counseling Center and the Washington, D.C. Veteran's Administration Medical Center.

The *Shoulds* Exercise

Think of all the *shoulds* you learned regarding your role as a woman (in general) or as a wife, mother, daughter, worker, professional woman (in particular). On a piece of paper draw three columns. In the first column, list as many *shoulds* as you can remember. Include those *shoulds* you heard as you were growing up as well as those which you hear now: from your parents, husband, children, neighbors, friends, employees, and the media.

In the second column, list the source of the should—where you learned it or who taught it to you. In the third column, describe what happened to you in the past when you did not live up to this particular *should*. For example, were you verbally chastised, rejected, hit, made to feel ashamed, or what?

Review your list, then ask yourself, How did it feel to list the *shoulds?* Which *shoulds* do you desire to keep? to alter? to discard? Do you see the *shoulds* as goals to be striven for or as measures of self-worth?

Other questions to be considered are: What happens inside you when you do not live up to the expectations of the *shoulds?* What do you say to yourself? How do you feel? How does this compare to what other people say to you?

What makes you feel "okay" when you diverge from the shoulds? What makes you feel "not okay" when you diverge? What can you do to help yourself feel better when you digress from the *shoulds?*

Writing Your Own Script: Tailoring Superwoman To Yourself

Almost every woman has an image of superwoman—the "ideal" woman who is all things to all people at all times with no wear and tear on the self and with a constant smile and loving heart to boot.

Brainstorm a list of adjectives describing the cultural ideal or stereotype of this super or "perfect" woman. Then brainstorm a list of personal costs and costs to others which attend the ideal image or the striving toward this ideal. For instance I always think of the ideal woman as perfectly dressed. Some of the costs of this could be money, time to take care of the clothes, do the necessary shopping, or whatever. The costs to others could include less money to spend on things for them.

Now write your own script, not a superwoman script, for one of your roles. (This exercise can be completed for additional roles also.)

Junk Vs. Joy

Another version of "Writing Your Own Script," is the "Junk vs. Joy" exercise.

Think about what is truly important about being a mother, wife, or worker. Which of your qualities do you really want to share with your family? Your co-workers? What activities are really necessary in each role?

For example, what is it to be a Mom? Is there a difference between being loving and baking cupcakes? When do the cupcakes get in the way of the loving?

The point of this exercise is to identify the junk vs. the joy of the roles in order to have more of the joy and less of the junk. On a piece of paper, draw a line dividing the paper in half. One side of the paper is labeled "joy," the other "junk." Underneath, list the junk vs. the joy of your various roles as a woman.

The Little Nothings I Do List.

In a sexist society, work and tasks which are allocated to women—for example, housework, childrearing, managing social events—are often considered inferior work, unimportant work, or "no work." The credit for this exercise goes to a Vietnam wife who worked part time and was constantly being accused, on the days when she did not work outside the home, of "doing nothing" in her traditional roles of homemaker, wife, chauffeur, and facilitator of her successful husband's numerous projects.

The problem began when she started to believe that she was "doing nothing" on her days "off" even though she was a very busy person and always short on time. For many years she believed that she was "doing nothing" until one day she got very smart. When her husband said, "Why can't you do this for me? You've had nothing to do all day," she decided to make a list of "all the little nothings I do."

Instructions: Make a list of all the "little nothings" you do, the essential tasks you perform to keep the house or human system you live in flowing, for which you get little or no credit, and which are virtually unrecognized by praise or money. You may be amazed at the number of things you actually *do* and how much time it takes to get them all done.

Personal Goals Vs. Cultural Expectations

We rarely take the time to think about what kind of person we want to be in relation to others (our partner, mate, child, or colleague). Too often we try to meet the cultural stereotype for the role instead of being the person we want to be and can truly be.

Pick one person—your husband, a child, a parent, or a colleague—and think about what kind of person you want to be in relation to that person. Think about it quietly and alone for a while. Then try to think of things you can do to get you closer to being that person.

Visualizing Yourself As A Success

This exercise encourages thinking of yourself as a person who is capable and competent of learning new skills. It is especially helpful for women who often tend to see themselves as incapable of succeeding at something new.

Relax for a few minutes, then close your eyes.

1. Visualize a particular specific aspect of your work life in which you feel inadequate or incompetent. Pick a definite and concrete instance in which you have not succeeded thus far and in which you feel you may never succeed (3-4 minutes).
2. Now visualize yourself as succeeding in this particular task (3-4 minutes).

Consider what steps you would need to take to make your success fantasy a reality and make a commitment to begin.

Give Yourself A Medal

For the next five minutes, get into yourself. Relax. Pretend you would like to give yourself a medal. What would it be for and what would be inscribed upon it?

Now write a two or three sentence statement about this medal.

Now write a two to three sentence statement about the process of giving yourself a medal. Was it difficult or easy to give yourself a medal or otherwise see your admirable qualities? Have you ever done it before? If you told other people about your medal, what would they think?

Acknowledging Your Strengths

This exercise format is the same as the "Medals" exercise above, except that you are asked to list five to ten of your strengths. Although this exercise seems very simple, it has usually proven extremely effective in helping women to acknowledge their strengths.

A variation of this exercise is to list five to ten accomplishments. Women tend to remember incomplete tasks and ways in which they have not lived up to some ideal image of womanhood. This would help you focus on some of the things you have finished and done well.

Combine, Combine, Combine

Time is the working woman's scarcest commodity. In this exercise, list all chores and activities both at home and at work by the week (not the day). Then review the lists to see if there are any ways in which responsibilities or activities can be possibly combined so as to save time.

An important condition in combining activities is that combining the activities not interfere with the quality of the outcome. For example, sit ups can be performed and nails painted while watching T.V. Necessary phone calls can be made while cooking or cleaning up in the kitchen. But activities cannot be combined if one of the tasks requires all your concentration.

The second part of this exercise involves routing driving so that you do not make a series of separate trips, but plan stops and chores to be time-efficient.

Coping With Eating Disorders

Regardless of how oppressive or unrewarding your life situation may be, you must take responsibility for your eating disorder rather than blame it on your husband, children, or some other outside factor. Usually some form of food abuse has been a lifelong pattern for a woman, beginning before her marriage, although perhaps worsened by stresses in the marriage. Over half the obese and bulimic Vietnam wives I have seen were victims of child sexual abuse or child sexual assault. Compulsive overeating or bulimia were their admitted means of coping with their rage, self-hate, and sense of powerlessness at being abused by a parent.

Usually the obese or bulimic Vietnam wife needs—and deserves —help beyond the latest diet published in a woman's magazine. Her first step toward recovery involves consulting a medical doctor or dietician to obtain a nutritionally sound food plan. Strange as it may sound, dieting is fattening. Excessive dieting reduces the basal metabolic rate and calories are burned more slowly. Secondly, dieting leads to binging.

You need a food plan for living which meets your nutritional needs, not a crash diet. However, you need more than just a good diet. If losing weight and keeping it off was simply a matter of finding the "right diet," then every person who desired to be thin would achieve his or her goal.

You also need a form of individual or group therapy which addresses the emotional issues underlying your excessive eating (or bulimia). For the compulsive overeater or bulimic, losing weight usually requires dealing with feelings which she finds unacceptable (anger, rage, and sexual desire) or extremely painful (sorrow and disappointment). You must also learn to develop a sense of self-worth that is based on more than cosmetic external appearance and includes a deeply internalized sense of self-respect and personal integrity.

Losing weight also requires that you learn to love yourself, all of yourself, including your fat or bulimic self. You must learn to see your eating disordered self not as "bad" or "immoral," but as a representation of your emotional needs for more love and support.

Compulsive overeating and bulimia are cunning, baffling, and often lifelong problems. You will need a tremendous amount of support and encouragement in learning how to face life without the crutch of excess food. I recommend that you find a therapist knowledgeable about eating disorders or get involved in a self-help group, such as Overeater's Anonymous. The therapy should help you identify your feelings and help you with diet management and other behavioral techniques for weight control.

You should have a complete medical examination, especially if you are bulimic. Women with bulimia need to have their iron and potassium levels checked regularly. Bulimia often results in an abnormally low potassium concentration as well as electrolyte imbalance. Physical check-ups are especially essential when you suffer general ill health as a result of your eating disorder.

An exercise program is also a good idea. Not only can it help you lose weight but it can be a means of expressing pent up frustrations and anger.

About O.A. (Overeaters Anonymous)

O.A. is not a diet or calories club. It is a twelve-step program similar to A.A. (Alcoholics Anonymous) and N.A. (Narcotics Anonymous) which views compulsive overeating (and bulimia) as a living problem, rather than as just a food or weight problem. The focus of O.A. is not on weight loss alone, but on emotional and spiritual recovery as well.

There are more than 7,000 O.A. meetings taking place throughout the world every week. Members do not sign up for meetings. They simply attend as often as they feel the need. Many attend meetings more than once a week, especially during times of stress. There are no coercive techniques, no dues or fees, and no humiliating "weigh-ins."

In addition to meetings, the O.A. program offers members the advantage of sponsors—supportive individuals who achieved some measurable degree of recovery from their compulsive overeating or bulimia—who are willing to help other overeaters or bulimics cope with their feelings and their life difficulties without the buffer of excess food.

Like A.A. and N.A., O.A. is an anonymous program. Members reveal their first names only.

O.A. is not a substitute for psychotherapy. In fact, O.A. encourages the use of medical doctors, dieticians, and knowledgeable psychotherapists. O.A., however, provides a readily available support group for those who desire to stop eating compulsively and not abuse themselves with food. In many areas, special meetings are oriented toward bulimics.

So far, O.A. boasts a comparable, if not higher, recovery rate for compulsive overeaters as compared to commercial weight loss programs and weight loss programs conducted by mental health professionals. If recovery is defined as long-term maintenance, not just losing excess weight but keeping it off for two years, the recovery rate for O.A. is close to 22%. The recovery rate for commercial and mental health administered weight loss programs and all other therapies combined is usually much lower.

O.A. can be found in most major metropolitan cities, as well as in some outlying areas. For further information contact O.A. World Service Office, 2190 190th Street, Torrance, CA 90504.

The following national organizations provide information regarding bulimia and anorexia.

National Anorexia Aid Society
Box 29461
Columbus, OH, 43229
phone 614/436–1112.

American Anorexia/Bulimia Association
133 Cedar Lane
Teaneck, NJ, 07666
phone 201/836–1800.

Center for the Study of Anorexia and Bulimia
1 West 91st St.
New York, NY, 10024
phone 212/595–3449.

ANAD—National Association of Anorexia Nervosa and Associated Disorders
P. O. Box 271
Highland Park, IL, 60035
phone 312/831–3438.

Suggested Readings

Overeaters Anonymous, Overeaters Anonymous, Inc., Torrance, CA, 1980, available from OA World Service, 2190 190th St., Torrance, CA 90504.

The Nutritional Ages of Women: A Lifelong Guide to Eating Right for Health, Beauty and Well-Being, by Patricia Long, MacMillan Publishing Co., New York, 1986.

Fat is a Family Affair, by Judith Hollis, Harper and Row, San Francisco, 1985.

Feeding The Hungry Heart, The Experience of Compulsive Overeating, Indianapolis, IN, Bobbs-Merrill, 1982.

Pamphlets available from Hazelden Press, Educational Materials, Box 176, Pleasant Valley Road, Center City, MN, 55012-0176 or call toll free 800/328-9000.

"Think Before You Eat"

"Sexuality and Compulsive Eating"

"Enough is a Feast"

"Learn about Eating Disorders"

"Anorexia"

"Bulimia: The Binge Eating and Purging Syndrome"

"Please Don't Give Me Chocolates"

"What is OA?"

"Killing Ourselves with Kindness"

"Accepting Powerlessness"

Hope for Compulsive Overeaters (Cassettes)

These are some of the ways you can start to take better care of yourself. I urge you to take that first step. Call a Vet Center, contact O.A., reach out in whatever way you can. You can get better control of your life, but only you can take that step. Many Vietnam wives have and so can you.

Summary Of Vet Center Study Results

The Vet Center survey is based on the perceptions of Vet Center counselors who have reported clinical work with from 53,699 to 63,135 Vietnam veterans and from 11,619 to 15,033 Vietnam wives. These counselors represent 100 of the existing 189 Vet Centers, or approximately 53% of all Vet Centers in the United States. The responses of 19 Vet Centers however, were excluded either (a) because they did not have and never had a woman's support group or (b) because the counselor who completed the questionnaire had limited experience with Vietnam wives or girlfriends—had counseled less than 40 Vietnam wives or Vietnam veterans. (Table 1)

In general, the results of the Vet Center study confirm the author's observations of the effect of PTSD on family life. In some areas, such as marital, sexual, and emotional intimacy, the effects of PTSD appear to be rather clearcut. For example, the overwhelming majority of responding Vet Center counselors throughout the nation, over 90%, agreed that twelve of the most common problems reported by Vietnam wives (or girlfriends of Vietnam veterans) include:[1]

1. Coping with the veteran's hypersensitivity—his tendency to overreact to the woman's statements and behaviors and to interpret them as insulting to him: 96%;
2. Coping with the veteran's emotional numbing—his tendency to shut off emotionally; to be reluctant, or unable, to share on a deep emotional level; and to in other ways withdraw from her or others: 97.5%;
3. Loneliness and social isolation stemming from the vet's expectation that she make him the focus of her life and his jealousy of her activities outside the home and her relationships with others, even with other women, members of her family, or her own children: 94%;
4. Coping with the veteran's verbal abuse: 91%;
5. Fearing to speak to the veteran: 91%;
6. Feeling confused about which problems are Vietnam related and which are not: 95.1%;

7. Feeling overwhelmed at having total or almost total responsibility for the emotional or financial stability of the household: 94%;
8. Feeling responsible for healing the veteran through her love and nurturance; or, the opposite, feeling that the vet's problems are his alone and do not involve her in the least: 94%;
9. Self-doubts created by the veteran's emotional instability or the family's financial problems: 94%;
10. Feeling as if she has lost her identity in constantly responding to the veteran's needs and many family crises: 91%;
11. Feeling as if she has lost control of her own life and is no longer able to identify or pursue her own goals: 95%; and
12. Coping with the veteran's outbursts of anger, such as destruction of family property: 95%. (Table 2)

Another common problem among Vietnam wives, observed by 84% of the polled counselors, was self-blame for the veteran's depressions, his rage reactions, or his wide flucuations in mood. (Table 2)

In addition, over 85% of the surveyed counselors found that vets with PTSD often experience periods of sexual dysfunction and sexual disinterest and have greater difficulty disclosing themselves and expressing themselves with their wives or girlfriends than non-PTSD afflicted vets. However, only 67% indicated that vets with PTSD often desire sex on demand. (Table 3)

A majority of the surveyed Vet Centers agreed that in the face of a loss in the family—the illness, injury, or death of a family member, vets tend to withdraw (93%) and suffer an increase in their PTSD symptoms. (89%) Counselors, however, were evenly split regarding whether or not the veteran is helpful and protective under such circumstances. Approximately forty percent of the counselors report that the vet is helpful and protective in times of family emergency; the other forty percent, however, report that he is not. (Table 4) Similarly, in the author's experience, some vets have been found to be exceptionally supportive of their wives and families during times of family crisis. On the other hand, other wives describe being abandoned, both emotionally and physically, by their husbands during their times of greatest need.

The responding Vet Center counselors are also in disagreement about whether Vietnam veterans with PTSD tend to overdiscipline or avoid disciplining their children. There is more consensus that vets tend to withdraw from their children (73%), tend to be overcritical of their children (80%), have a low tolerance for children's noises and games, especially war games (85%). About one-half of the responding Vet Centers report that veterans have special difficulty with the "terrible-two's" (the defiance and experimentalness which many two-year-old children display), and 79% report that vets have difficulty tolerating their adolescent or preadolescent child's rebellion against parental authority. (Table 5)

In addition, from 69%-83% of Vet Center counselors report the following psychological or behavior problems in children of Vietnam veterans suffering from PTSD:
1. Low self-esteem (83%);
2. Aggressiveness (77%);
3. Developmental difficulties in school (79%); and
4. Impaired social relationships (69%).
Other problems manifested by children include:
1. Self-mutilation (10%);
2. Feeling responsible for the veteran's emotional well-being (57%);
3. Hatred of Orientals, especially Vietnamese persons (14%);
4. Nightmares, daydreams, or other forms of preoccupation with events which were traumatic to the veteran (22%);
5. Symptoms similar to those of the veteran (65%);
6. Preoccupation with power and death (28%); and
7. Ambivalent feelings towards the mother (42%). (Table 6)

As many counselors, as well as the author, stress, it is difficult to make gross generalities about such a diverse population as PTSD afflicted Vietnam veterans who seek help at Vet Centers. While certain marital patterns and patterns of relating to children may exist in these Vietnam veteran families, this does not mean that these patterns exist in all, or even most, Vietnam veteran homes. The Vet Center study data is also limited by the fact that on certain items, substantial numbers of Vet Center counselors did not reply and that the survey is based on the responses of counselors at only 53% of existing Vet Centers. (Table 1)

Furthermore, while at a few Vet Centers, the questions were discussed by the entire Vet Center staff, in most instances, responses to the questionnaire reflect the observations of only one particular Vet Center counselor, not necessarily the combined opinion of the entire Vet Center staff or the opinion of the most knowledgeable or experienced Vet Center counselor. However, in defense of the Vet Center study results, it must be noted that in over 95% of cases, it was either the team leader or the present leader of the woman's support group, both of whom can be assumed to have knowledge of the effects of PTSD on family life, who completed the questionnaire. In addition, the responses of counselors who have counseled less than forty Vietnam wives were not considered in the study.

Nevertheless, survey results are always debatable on many grounds. This is especially the case with data on violence in the home. In general, there tends to be an underreporting of these problems since family members are often reluctant or ashamed to admit to the violence or are in denial. Furthermore, in the case of child abuse, clients, whether male or female, may be hesitant to admit to their crime due to shame, guilt, or fear of being turned in to the authorities, as is required by child abuse reporting laws. An additional problem is that some counselors fail to inquire about violence in the home because they fear humiliating the client or are unaware of the prevalence of the problem of domestic violence in our society.

In the author's experience, one-fourth of Vietnam wives seen can be considered battered women. As a result, their lives have become organized around avoiding or trying to control their husband's anger. These women are also battered in that their husbands exert control over them via psychological humiliation and manipulation,, social isolation, economic deprivation, as well as through threats of harm to family members or friends.

According to the Vet Center study (Table 7), however, approximately 25% of Vietnam wives seeking help complain of physical abuse. This 25% figure, however, is similar to, if not less than, rates for wife abuse found in other nationwide studies, which cite figures ranging from 28% to 50%.[2,3]

A greater discrepancy exists between the national rate of child abuse (1.5%) and the average rate of child abuse reported by Vet Center counselors for Vietnam veterans (11.4%) and for Vietnam wives (3%) (Table 8).[4] However, both the child abuse and wife abuse figures must be interpreted with great caution since counselors were asked about family violence in the Vietnam home only in the most general manner, not in behavioral terms. Definitions of wife abuse and child abuse may vary from one counselor to another. For example, some counselors consider as battered only those women who are beaten severely enough to require hospitalization or medical treatment, whereas other counselors consider as battered any woman who is controlled by her husband's violence or threats of violence, regardless of the frequency or severity of the beatings.

Similarly, some counselors consider occasional beatings or severe disciplinary means as child abuse. Others include in their statistics only children so obviously or severely beaten by their mother or father that outside intervention was required. In addition, it is possible that some counselors do not keep accurate records of domestic violence cases. Furthermore, it may be that wives of vets who batter children are more likely to seek help at Vet Centers than wives of vets who are not abusive. Hence, the relatively high rate of child abuse found in the Vet Center study may not be at all representative of the actual rate of child abuse in the Vietnam veteran population. In this study, any statistics on family violence are tentative at best.

Lastly, according to this study, approximately 20% of Vietnam wives seen at the responding Vet Centers were significantly overweight—at least 50 pounds overweight or double their ideal weight. (Table 9)

Table 1

The Vet Center Survey

The Vet Center survey is based on the perceptions of Vet Center counselors who have reported clinical work with from 53,699 to 63,135 Vietnam veterans and from 11,619 to 15,033 Vietnam wives. These counselors represent 100 of the existing 189 Vet Centers, or approximately 53% of all Vet Centers in the United States. The responses of 19 Vet Centers however, were excluded either (a) because they did not have and never had a woman's support group or (b) because the counselor who completed the questionnaire had limited experience with Vietnam wives or girlfriends —had counseled less than 40 Vietnam wives or Vietnam veterans.

Total Vet Centers responding to the questionnaire: 100

No. Vet Centers which currently have a woman's group: 79

No. Vet Centers which currently do not have a woman's   21
    group:

No. Vet Centers which have had a woman's group in the past: 6

Total No. Vet Centers having woman's group in   85
    past or present:

No. Vet Centers with counselors who have counseled   8
    less than 40 vets or vet wives:

Total no. Vet Centers being considered in study   81
    (Total No. Vet centers ever having woman's group with counselors who have counseled at least forty wives):

Table 2

Common Problems of Vietnam Wives

Listed below are some of the common problems reported by wives and girlfriends of PTSD afflicted Vietnam veterans who have attended my group.[1] Please indicate with a check mark in the indicated space if wives and girlfriends of PTSD afflicted veterans who have reported similar problems: 81 responses considered.

a. Coping with the veteran's hypersensitivity, i.e., his tendency to overreact to the woman's statements and behaviors and to interpret them as insulting to him. — 78 true 96% of total

b. Coping with the veteran's emotional numbing, i.e., his tendency to "shut off" emotionally; to be reluctant, or unable, to share on a deep emotional level; and to in other ways withdraw from her and others. — 79 true 98% of total

c. Loneliness and social isolation stemming from the vet's expectation that make she him the focus of her life and his jealousy of her activities outside the home and her relationships with others, even with other women, members of her family, or her own children. — 76 true 94% of total

d. Coping with the veteran's verbal abuse. — 74 true 91% of total

e. Fearing to speak to the veteran. — 74 true 91% of total

f. Feeling confused about which problems are Vietnam related and which are not. — 77 true 95% of total

g. Feeling overwhelmed at having total or almost total responsibility for the emotional or financial stability of the household. — 76 true 94% of total / 2 sometimes, not regularly 2% of total

h. Self-blame for the veteran's depres-   68 true 84% of total
   sions, his rage reactions, or his wide
   fluctations in mood.   5 sometimes,
                                              not regularly 6% of total

i. Feeling responsible for healing the   76 true 94% of total
   veteran through her love and nur-
   turance; or, the opposite, feeling that
   the vet's problems are his alone and do
   not involve her in the least.

j. Self-doubts created by the veteran's emo-   76 true 94% of total
   tional instability or the family's finan-
   cial problems.

k. Feeling as if she has lost her identity in   74 true 91% of total
   constantly responding to the veteran's
   needs and many family crises.

l. Feeling as if she has lost control of her   77 true 95% of total
   own life and is no longer able to iden-
   tify or pursue her own goals.

m.Coping with the veteran's outburst of   77 true 95% of total
   angers, for example, destruction of fami-
   ly property.

Table 3

PTSD and Marital, Sexual, and Emotional Intimacy

The following questions concern the effects of PTSD on marital sexual intimacy. 81 responses considered.

a. Vets with PTSD often experience periods of sexual dysfunction and sexual disinterest. True or false?

70 true 86% of total

5 false 6% of total

6 varies or don't know or no reply 7% of total

Additional Comments: "Not valid as blanket statement, not a symptom of PTSD, but seen with depression." "But so do my depressives, schizophrenics, and other clients." "No trend."

b. Vets with PTSD often desire sex on demand. True or false?

54 true 67% of total

16 false 20% of total

11 no reply or don't know or both 13% of total

c. Vets with PTSD have greater difficulty disclosing themselves and expressing themselves with their wives or girlfriends than non-PTSD afflicted combat vets? True or false?

71 true 88% of total

5 true 6% of total

5 no reply or not sure 6% of total

Table 4

Reactions to Losses in the Family

The following questions concern the reaction of PTSD afflicted veterans to a loss in the family, for example, the illness, injury, or death of another family member. 81 responses considered.

a. Under such circumstances, does the vet   75 true 92.5% of total
tend to withdraw? True or false

2 false 2.5% of total

4 no reply or sometimes yes,
sometimes no 5% of total

Additional Comments: "Aggression is another response; depends on predisposing factors."

b. Under such circumstances, do his   72 true 89% of total
symptoms increase? True or false?

2 false 2% of total

7 no reply or sometimes 9% of total

c. Under such circumstances, is the vet   32 true 40% of total
helpful and protective? True or false?

32 false 40% of total

17 no reply or both
or sometimes 20% of total

Table 5

The PTSD Afflicted Veteran's Relationship to His Children

The following questions concern the relationship of the PTSD afflicted veteran with his children. The literature describes a variety of reactions the PTSD afflicted veteran might have to his children. In your experience, do any of the following generalities ring true? 81 responses considered.

a. Vets with PTSD tend to withdraw from their children. True or false?

59 true 73% of total

14 false 17% of total

8 no reply or both or varies 10% of total

b. Vets with PTSD tend to be overcritical of their children. True or false?

65 true 80% of total

7 false 9% of total

9 both or no reply or sometimes 5% of total

c. Vets with PTSD either avoid disciplining their child, or over-discipline the child. True or false?

69 true 85% of total

8 false 10% of total

4 no reply or sometimes or varies 11% of total

d. If (c) is true in your experience, which pattern seems more prevalent: avoiding disciplining the child or over-disciplining the child?

27 avoiding disciplining
39.1% of total
(69 responses considered)

28 overdisciplining 40.5% of total
(69 responses considered)

14 both or no reply 20.2% of total
(69 responses considered)

e. Vets with PTSD have a low tolerance for children's noises and games, especially war games. True or false?

69 true 85% of total

4 false 5% of total

8 no reply or sometimes or varies
10% of total

f. Vets with PTSD have special difficulty tolerating the "terrible-two's," (the defiance and experimentalness which many two-year-old children display). True or false?

41 true 51% of total

15 false 18% of total

25 no reply or varies 31% of total

Additional Comments: "Every parent has trouble with the terrible twos."

g. Vets with PTSD have special difficulty tolerating their adolescent or preadolescent child's rebellion against parental authority. True or false?

64 true 79% of total

8 false 10% of total

9 no reply or not sure or other response 11% of total

Table 6

Psychological Problems Observed in Children of Vietnam Veterans with PTSD

Have you observed any of the following psychological or behavior problems in children of Vietnam veterans suffering from PTSD? If so, please indicate with a check mark in the space provided. 81 responses considered.

a. low self esteem	67 true 82.7% of total
b. self-mutilation	8 true 9.8 or 10% of total
c. aggressiveness	62 true 76.5% of total
d. symptoms similar to those of the veteran	53 true 65% of total
e. feeling responsible for the veteran's emotional well-being	46 true 56.7% of total
f. hatred of Orientals, especially Vietnamese persons	11 true 13.5% of total
g. nightmares, daydreams, or other forms of preoccupation with events which were traumatic to the veteran	18 true 22% of total
h. preoccupation with power and death	23 true 28.3% of total
i. developmental difficulties in school	64 true 79% of total
j. impaired social relationships	56 true 69% of total
k. ambivalent feelings towards the mother	34 true 42% of total

Additional Comments: "Attitudes toward mothers are downright negative." "No ambivalent feelings toward the mother noted—in fact, if anything, clinging to the mother."

Table 7

Wife Abuse

Have any of the wives of vets reported physical abuse?* If so, approximately what percentage of women seen at your center report this problem?

8 no reply

73 Vet Centers responding

25.38% average for 73 Vet Centers
with data on wife abuse

National average: Strauss, 1977a, 1977b[2]   at least 28% Walker, 1979[3]   50%

* The Vet Center survey failed to use a severity of violence scale such as has been used by previous researchers, for example, Strauss, in assessing domestic violence. Such a scale would have differentiated between throwing something at spouse; pushing, grabbing, or shoving spouse; slapping the spouse; kicking, biting or hitting with the fist; hitting or trying to hit with an object or weapon; being beaten by a spouse, being threatened with a knife or gun; or having used a knife or gun. Had such a scale been used, the results would have been more accurate.

Table 8

Child Abuse

a. Have any of the wives of vets reported child abuse by the veteran? If so, approximately what percentage of women seen at your center report this problem?

11 no reply

70 Vet Centers responding

average 11.4%

b. Have any of the wives of vets reported that they abuse their children? If so, approximately what percentage of women seen at your center report this problem?

12 no reply

69 Vet Centers responding

average 3.3%

Estimated national average of child abuse: 1.5% of children physically abused by parents or caretakers (NCCAN, 1983)[4]

Table 9

Obesity and the Vietnam Wife

In the author's experience, approximately one fifth of the women who have attended the Vet Center woman's group at the Silver Spring Vet Center have been significantly overweight, That is, at least 50 pounds overweight or double their ideal weight. In your experience, approximately what percentage of the wives who have come for help to your Vet Center have been significantly overweight?

9 no reply

72 Vet Centers responding

19.8% or 20% average of Vietnam wives wives with obesity problem.

Resource Guide

Where To Get Help For Wife Abuse

In The Military

Family Advocacy officers or representatives exist on every Army, Navy, Air Force, Marine Corps and Coast Guard installation. They can usually be contacted directly or through a family service or family support center. Abused wives may also contact the chaplain, the medical department, the Staff Judge Advocate, the social worker, the nearest Woman's Advocacy office (if available), their husband's commanding officer, or anyone in his chain of command.

Help can also be obtained from civilian sources, such as courts, service agencies, churches, battered women's shelters or state chapters of the National Coalition Against Domestic Violence. (The address is listed in the next paragraph.) Even wives living on bases under exclusive federal jurisdiction may seek help from civilian resources.

More information about the military legal system and available resources for abused military wives can be obtained from The Center for Women Policy Studies, 2000 P. St., N.W., Suite 508, Washington, D.C. 20036 (or call 202/872-1770); from the National Coalition Against Domestic Violence, P.O. Box 15127, Washington, D.C. 20003-0127 (or call 202/293-8860); or from the Military Family Resource Center, 4015 Wilson Blvd., Suite 903, Arlington, VA 22203-5190 (or call 202/696-4555 or toll free at 800/336-4592.)

Abused Air Force wives may call Ms. Sharon Sauter, MSW, Family Advocacy Officer for the Air Force directly at 202/767-5532. Navy wives can call the Navy Family Service Center at 202/433-6150, or Ms. Holly Pertmer, MSW, Social Work Service, Bethesda Naval Hospital, Bethesda, MD, phone number 301/295-1719. Marine Corps wives may also call Ms. Pertmer or other counselors at the Social Work Service at Bethesda Naval Hospital. Coast Guard wives may call Mr. Ralph Biase, MSW, at the Coast Guard Family Advocacy Service, phone number 202/267-2246 or 202/267-2237, and Army wives may call Ms. Brenda Hollis, MSW, at 202/696-3510 or 202/696-3511 or 202/696-3512.

Civilian Wives

You can get help from the courts, from the police, and through local organizations. Check your yellow pages telephone book or call your local police station. In many areas there are battered women's shelters that can also help.

Fact sheets and listings of books and articles on wife abuse can be obtained from the Center for Women Policy Studies, Suite 508, 2000 P. St. N.W., Washington, D.C., 20036; the National Coalition Against Domestic Violence, P.O. Box 15127, Washington, DC 20003-0127 Suite 305, Washington, D.C. 20037, 202/293–8860; (or call 202/293–8860); or the Southern California Coalition on Battered Women, Box 5036, Santa Monica, CA 90405.

Where To Get Help For Child Abuse

Parents Anonymous is a self-help group for parents who batter their children. Chapters exist throughout the U.S. For more information or the location of the nearest chapter, contact National Office of Parent's Anonymous, 6733 South Sepulveda Blvd. Suite 2701, Los Angeles, CA 90045; Toll Free: 800/421–0353 or 213/410–9732.

Parents United is a self-help group for all family members affected by sexual abuse. For more information, contact Parents United, Inc., P.O. Box 952, San Jose, California 95102, 408/280–5055 or the toll free referral line 800/422–4453.

For more information and free literature on child abuse contact the National Center on Child Abuse and Nelgect (NCCAN) P.O. Box 1182, Washington, D.C. 20013, or call 202/245–2856.

The following organizations can also offer help and assistance:

National Child Abuse and Neglect Clinical Resource Center
University of Colorado Health Sciences Center
1205 Oneida Street
Denver, CO 80220
phone: 303/321–3963

National Resource Center on Child Abuse and Neglect
American Association for Protecting Children
9725 East Hampton Avenue
Denver, CO 80231
phone: 303/695–0811

National Legal Resource Center for Child Welfare
American Bar Association
1800 M St., NW
Washington, D.C. 20036
phone: 202/331–2250

Help For Problems With Alcohol Or Drug Abuse

Information about A.A., Al-Anon, ADCIO, N.A., and Nar-A-Non meetings can be obtained from the local telephone directory, local library, at local A.A. or N.A. meetings, or by writing Al-Anon at Al-Anon Family Group Headquarters, Inc., P.O. Box 86, Midtown Station, New York, NY 10018-0862, 212/302-7240; Narcotics Anonymous World Service Office, Inc., P.O. Box 9999, 16155 Wyandotte Street, Van Nuys, CA 91406, 818/780-3951; and Nar-A-Non at Family Group Headquarters, P.O. Box 2562, Palos Verdes Estates, CA 90274, 213/547-5800.

Numerous books, pamphlets on alcoholism and drug addiction, both for the addicted individual and his or her family, are available from Hazelden, Educational Materials, Box 176, Pleasant Valley Road, Center City, MN 55012-0176. Toll free: 800/328-9000. A catalogue can be requested.

A.A. literature includes *Alcoholics Anonymous* or the "Big Book" which contains the stories of 44 recovering alcoholics and the *Twelve Steps and Twelve Traditions* which explains the twelve steps of A.A., which are the program's foundation for recovery. These books, as well as numerous pamphlets on A.A. and alcoholism, e.g., "This is A.A." and "44 Questions about A.A. and the A.A. Program of Recovery from Alcoholism," can be ordered from General Services Board of A.A., 468 Park Avenue, South, New York, N.Y. 10016, 212/686-1100, at local A.A. meetings, or at local A.A. offices.

"Facts About Alcohol and Alcoholism," "Alcohol: Some Questions and Answers" and other pamphlets on alcoholism, available from the National Clearinghouse for Alcohol Information, Box 2345, Rockville, Md. 20852, 301/468-2600.

Information is also available from the National Council on Alcoholism, 1511 K St. NW, Washington, DC, 20005, 202/737-8122.

Where To Call For Help

Consult your local information directory for the district office nearest you or call:

Alcoholics Anonymous World Services: 212/686-1100

Cocanon: 213/859-2206 or 212/713-5133

Families Anonymous World Services (for family members and friends of alcohol or drug addicted persons: 818/989-7841

Nar-Anon Family Group Headquarters: 213/547-5800

Narcotics Anonymous World Service, Inc. 818/780-3951

Further information on the effects of alcoholism on children can be obtained from Children of Alcoholics Foundation, 200 Park Ave., 31st Floor, New York, N.Y. 10166, 212/351-2680, and from The National Association of Children of Alcoholics (NACoA), 31706 Coast Hwy., No. 201, South Laguna, CA 92677, 714/499-3889.

Organizations Helping Veterans And Their Families

Veterans of the Vietnam War
National Headquarters
2090 Bald Mountain Rd.
Wilkes-Barre, PA 18702-9609
717/825-7215

Vietnam Veterans of America
2001 S Street, NW
Suite 700
Washington, D.C. 20009
202/332-2700
Most states have local chapters.

American Legion
1608 K Street, NW
Washington, D.C. 20006
202/861-2700

Provides help in obtaining a wide variety of services to veterans, including employment, Veteran's Administration benefits, medical care, discharge review, and Agent Orange.

Veteran's Affairs
941 N. Capitol
Washington, D.C. 20421
202/265-6280

Jewish War Veterans
1811 R St., NW
Washington, D.C. 20009
202/265-6280

Help for Agent Orange Cases
Law Firm of Ashcraft and Geriel
2000 L Street NW
Suite 700
Washington, D.C. 20006
202/223-6846

Veteran's Educational Project
P.O. Box 42130
Washington, D.C. 20015

VEP has a National Referral Directory which lists the network of organizations, attorneys, doctors, and others who offer assistance to veterans. Write VEP for listings in your state specifying the type of referral needed and the type of professional organization you are seeking. There may be a fee for the computer search.

American Veterans of World War II, Korea, and Vietnam (AMVETS)
4647 Forbes Blvd.
Lanham, MD 20706
301/459-9600

Offers free and personalized claims assistance, including appeals, community projects, insurance and travel plans, and other services.

Blinded Veteran's Association
1735 DeSales St. NW
Washington, D.C. 20036
202/347-4010

Offers information and referrals for health, education, tutoring, jobs, and legal assistance to blinded vets and their families.

Disabled American Veterans
807 Maine Ave. SW
Washington, D.C. 20024
202/554-3501

The DAV serves as a catalyst to obtain needed services for disabled veterans and their families.

Marine Corps League
National Headquarters
956 North Monroe St.
Arlington, VA 22201
703/524-1137

MCL offers employment counseling and job placement assistance along with referral data; helps Marines get VA and service connected benefits; and helps handicapped Marines with their rehabilitation.

Military Order of the Purple Heart
National Service Office
Veteran's Administration Regional Office
941 North Capitol St. NE
Room 1201A
Washington, D.C.20421
202/275-1338

Military Order of the Purple Heart
National Headquarters
54413B Backlick Rd.
Springfield, VA 22151
703/642-5360

Provides free assistance and counseling to all veterans and their families regarding veteran's benefits and how to apply for them; refers veterans to appropriate federal and state agencies for job counseling, job development, job referral, and employment. Provides information concerning employment programs for veterans.

National Veteran's Outreach Program
20 F St. NW
Washington, D.C. 20001
202/347-4885

Provides assistance in applying for veteran's benefits, upgrading discharges, obtaining or correcting military records for all veterans discharged or separated from the U.S. Armed Forces under other than dishonorable conditions. Also provides counseling and referral on social services which help veterans make the transition to civilian life and operates a self-help group for unemployed vets—VETNET. Special efforts are made to reach and serve Hispanic veterans.

Navy Federal Equal Opportunity Recruitment Program
Referral Bank
Department of the Navy
Naval Civilian Personnel Command
Capitol Region
801 North Randolph St.
Arlington, VA 22203
202/696-4567

Has a recruitment program and referral bank aimed at providing maximum employment opportunities for minority and female candidates, veterans (with 30% or more disability and those eligible for a veteran's readjustment appointment) and handicapped individuals.

Non-Commissioned Officers Association (NCOA)
Veteran's Employment Assistance Program
3543 West Braddock Rd.
Alexandria, VA 22302
703/671-3100

NCOA is an international organization which sponsors job fairs, health plans, and insurance and other services to its members. NCOA maintains a current listing of companies which are actively seeking veterans for employment.

Paralyzed Veterans of America
801 18th St., NW
Washington, D.C. 20006
202/872-1300

Provides a variety of services to paralyzed veterans, including advocacy, counseling, and help in obtaining VA benefits.

Prison Organization for Veteran's Affairs, Inc.
Box 52
Lorton, VA 22079
703/643-1111, ext. 2483
Ask for Program Coordinator

POVA provides assistance with employment, training and opportunities, work release, discharge upgrading, housing, and counseling for incarcerated veterans.

United States Office of Personnel Management
Federal Job Information Center
1900 E St., NW
Room 1416
Washington, D.C. 20415
202/653-8468

Offers federal job information to vets, including information on veterans' preference in appointments, credit for military service, jobs for preference eligibles only, special appointing authorities for disabled veterans and Vietnam-era veterans, as well as other services.

Veterans of Foreign Wars of the U.S.
National Veteran Service
200 Maryland Ave. NE
Washington, D.C. 20002
202/543-2239

The VFW has a national program of veteran's assistance regarding claims and employment referrals, as well as other services.

Veteran's Assistance Centers are located in each state. Check a local directory or call the nearest Vet Center for listings.

In some areas, the American Red Cross offers counseling and limited financial assistance to veterans whose claims are still pending. Check with the local office of the American Red Cross for further information.

Local universities and colleges, and local and state or county employment commissions, personnel departments, or labor departments sometimes have special offices for veterans. Check in a local directory or call the nearest Vet Center for more information.

This listing is reprinted from "Veterans Civil Council Services Directory," compiled by the University of the District of Columbia, Division of Student Affairs, Office of Veteran Affairs, Washington, D.C. with the permission of Mr. Richard M. Harrison, Director, Office of Veteran Affairs, University of the District of Columbia, Washington, D.C.

Veteran's Administration Medical Centers Nationwide

Alabama

700 S. 19th St.
Birmingham, AL 35233
205/933-8101

Loop Rd.
Tuscaloosa, AL 35404
205/553-3760

215 Perry Hill Rd.
Montgomery, AL 36193
205/272-4670

Tuskegee, AL 36083
205/727-0550

Alaska

235 E. 8th Ave.
Anchorage, AK 99501
907/271-4555

Arizona

7th & Indian School Rd.
Phoenix, AZ 85012
602/277-5551

3601 S. 6th Ave.
Tucson, AZ 85723
602/792-1450

500 Hwy 89, N.
Prescott, AZ 86313
602/445-4860

Arkansas

1100 N. College Ave.
Fayetteville, AR 72701
501/443-4301

4300 W. 7th St.
Little Rock, AR 72205
402/489-3802

California

2615 E. Clinton Ave.
Fresno, CA 93703
209/225-6100

11201 Benton St.
Loma Linda, CA 92357
714/825-7084

425 S. Hill St.
Los Angeles, CA 90013
213/688-3902

150 Muir Rd.
Martinez, CA 94553
415/228-6800

3350 La Jolla Village Dr.
San Diego, CA 92161
619/453-7500

16111 Plummer St.
Sepulveda, CA 91343
818/891-7711

4951 Arroyo Rd.
Livermore, CA 94550
501/661-2560

5901 E. 7th St.
Long Beach, CA 90822
213/494-2611

11301 Wilshire Blvd.
W. Los Angeles, CA 90073
213/478-3711

3801 Miranda Ave.
Palo Alto, CA 94304
415/493-5000

4150 Clement St.
San Francisco, CA 94121
415/221-4810

Colorado

1055 Clermont St.
Denver, CO 80220
303/399-8020

2121 North Ave.
Grand Junction, CO 81501
303/242-0731

Hwy 183 off Hwy 50
Ft. Lyon, CO 81038
303/456-1260

Connecticut

555 Willard Ave.
Newington, CT 06111
203/666-6951

W. Spring St.
West Haven, CT 06516
203/932-5711

Delaware

1601 Kirkwood Hwy
Wilmington, DE 19805
302/994-2511

District of Columbia

50 Irving St.
Washington, DC 20422
202/745-8000

Florida

1000 Bay Pines Blvd, N.
Bay Pines, FL 33504
813/398-6661

801 S. Marion St.
Lake City, FL 32055
904/755-3016

13000 Bruce B. Downs Blvd.
Tampa, FL 33612
813/972-2000

Archer Rd.
Gainesville, FL 32602
904/376-1611

1201 NW 16th St.
Miami, FL 33125
305/324-4455

Georgia

1670 Clairmont Rd.
Atlanta, GA 30033
404/321-0862

U.S. Hwy 80
Dublin, GA 31021
912/272-1210

2460 Wrightsboro Rd.
Augusta, GA 30910
404/724-5116

Hawaii

300 Ala Moana Blvd.
Honolulu, HI 96850

Idaho

500 W. Fort St.
Boise, ID 83702-4598
208/336-5100

Illinois

333 E. Huron St.
Chicago, IL 60611
312/943-6600

Buckley Rd. & Rt. 137
N. Chicago, IL 60064
312/688-1900

Roosevelt Rd. & 5th Ave.
Hines, IL 60141
312/343-7200

820 S. Damen Ave.
Chicago, IL 60612
312/666-6500

1900 E. Main St.
Danville, IL 61832
217/442-8000

Main St.
Marion, IL 62959
618/997-5311

Indiana

1600 Randalia Dr.
Fort Wayne, IN 46805
219/347-2511

E. 38th St.
Marion, IN 46952
317/674-3321

1481 W. 10th St.
Indianapolis, IN 46202
317/635-7401

Iowa

30th & Euclid Aves.
Des Moines, IA 50310
515/255-2173

1515 W. Pleasant St.
Knoxville, IA 50138
515/842-3101

Hwy 6 West
Iowa City, IA 52240
319/338-0581

Kansas

4201 S. 4th St. Trafficway
Leavenworth, KS 66048
913/682-2000

5500 E. Kellogg
Wichita, KS 67218
316/685-2221

2200 Gage Blvd.
Topeka, KS 66622
913/272-3111

Kentucky

Leestown Rd.
Lexington, KY 40511
606/233-4511

800 Zorn Ave.
Louisville, KY 40202
502/895-3401

Louisiana

Shreeveport Hwy
Alexandria, LA 71301
318/473-0010

510 E. Stoner Ave.
Shreveport, LA 71130
318/221-8411

1601 Perdido St.
New Orleans, LA 70146
504/568-0811

Maine

Rte 17 East
Togus, ME 04330
207/623-8411

Maryland

3900 Loch Raven Blvd.
Baltimore, MD 21218
301/467-9932

Perry Point, MD 21902

Old N. Point Rd.
Ft. Howard, MD 21052
301/477-1800

Massachusetts

200 Spring Rd.
Bedford, MA 01730
617/275-7500

17 Court St.
Boston, MA 02108
617/565-9400

N. Main St.
Northampton, MA 01060
413/584-4040

150 S. Huntington Ave.
Boston, MA 02130
617/232-9500

940 Belmont St.
Brockton, MA 02401
617/583-4500

Michigan

Southfield & Outer Dr.
Allen Park, MI 48101
313/562-6000

5500 Armstrong Rd.
Battle Creek, MI 49016
616/966-5600

1500 Weiss St.
Saginaw, MI 48602
517/793-2340

2215 Fuller Rd.
Ann Arbor, MI 48105
313/769-7100

H St.
Iron Mountain, MI 49801
906/774-3300

Minnesota

54th St. & 48th Ave. So.
Minneapolis, MN 55417
612/725-6767

8th St. & 44th Ave.
St. Cloud, MN 56301
612/252-1670

Mississippi

Pass Rd.
Biloxi/Gulfport, MS 39531
601/388-5541

1500 E. Woodrow Wilson Ave.
Jackson, MS 39216
601/362-4471

Missouri

800 Stadium Dr.
Columbia, MO 65201
314/443-2511

4801 Linwood Blvd.
Kansas City, MO 64128
816/861-4700

Hwy 67 North
Poplar Bluff, MO 63901
314/686-4151

915 N. Grand Blvd.
St. Louis, MO 63106
314/652-4100

Montana

Wm. St. Hwy. 12 W.
Ft. Harrison, MT 59636
406/442-6410

210 S. Winchester
Miles City, MT 59301
406/232-3060

Nebraska

2201 N. Broad Well
Grand Island, NE 68803
308/382-3660

600 W. 7th St.
Lincoln, NE 68510
402/489-3802

4101 Woolworth Ave.
Omaha, NE 68105
402/346-8800

Nevada

1703 W. Charleston
Las Vegas, NV 89102
702/385-3700

1000 Locust St.
Reno, NV 89520
702/786-7200

New Hampshire

718 Smyth Rd.
Manchester, NH 03104
603/624-4366

New Jersey

Tremont Ave. & S. Center
East Orange, NJ 07019
201/676-1000

Valley & Knollcroft Rd.
Lyons, NJ 07939
201/647-0180

New Mexico

2100 Ridgecrest Dr.,S.E.
Albuquerque, NM 87108
505/265-1711

New York

113 Holland Ave.
Albany, NY 12208
518/462-3311

Argonne Ave.
Bath, NY 14810
607/776-2111

800 Poly Pl.
Brooklyn, NY 11209
718/836-6600

Fort Hill Ave.
Canandaigua, NY 14424
716/394-2000

Old Albany Post Rd.
Montrose, NY 10548
914/737-4400

Long Island-Middleville Rd.
Northport, NY 11768
516/261-4400

Redfield Pkwy
Batavia, NY 14020
716/343-7500

130 W. Kingsbridge Rd.
Bronx, NY 10468
212/584-9000

3495 Bailey Ave.
Buffalo, NY 14215
716/834-9200

Beacon St.
Castle Point, NY 12511
914/831-2000

1st Ave. & E. 24th St.
New York, NY 10010
212/686-7500

Irving Ave. & University Pl.
Syracuse, NY 13210
315/476-7461

North Carolina

Riceville & Tunnel Rd.
Asheville, NC 28805
704/288-7911

2300 Ramsey St.
Fayetteville, NC 28301
919/488-2120

508 Fulton St.
Durham, NC 27705
919/286-0411

1601 Brenner Ave.
Salisbury, NC 28144
704/636-2351

North Dakota

Elmo & 21st Ave. N.
Fargo, ND 58102
701/232-3241

Ohio

17273 State Rt. 104
Chillicothe, OH 45601
614/773-1141

3200 Vine St.
Cincinnati, OH 45220
513/861-3100

10701 E. Boulevard
Cleveland, OH 44106
216/791-3800

4100 W. 3rd St.
Dayton, OH 45428
513/268-6511

2090 Kenny Rd.
Columbus, OH 43221
614/469-5663

Oklahoma

Honor Heights Dr.
Muskogee, OK 74401
918/683-3261

921 NE 13th St.
Oklahoma City, OK 73104
405/272-9876

Oregon

3710 SW U.S.
Veterans Hospital Rd.
Portland, OR 97207
503/222-9221

Hwy 62
White City, OR 97503
503/826-2111

New Garden Valley Blvd.
Roseburg, OR 97470
503/440-1000

Pennsylvania

Pleasant Valley Blvd.
Altoona, PA 16603
814/943-8164

Black Horse Rd.
Coatesville, PA 19320
215/384-7711

S. Lincoln Ave.
Lebanon, PA 17042
717/272-6621

Highland Dr.
Pittsburgh, PA 15206
412/363-4900

1111 E. End Blvd.
Wilkes-Barre, PA 18711
717/824-3521

New Castle Rd.
Butler, PA 16001
412/287-4781

135 E. 38th St.
Erie, PA 16504
814/868-8661

University & Woodland Ave.
Philadelphia, PA 19104
215/382-2400

University Dr. S.
Pittsburgh, PA 15240
412/683-3000

Puerto Rico

GPO Box 4867
San Juan, PR 00936
809/763-6316

Rhode Island

Davis Park
Providence, RI 02908
401/273-7100

South Carolina

109 Bee St.
Charleston, SC 29403
803/577-5011

Garners Ferry Rd.
Columbia, SC 29201
803/776-4000

South Dakota

I90 & Hwy 34
Fort Meade, SD 57741
605/347-2511

5th St.
Hot Springs, SD 57747
605/745-4101

2501 W. 22nd St.
Sioux Falls, SD 57117
605/336-3230

Tennessee

1030 Jefferson Ave.
Memphis, TN 38104
901/523-8990

Lamont St.
Mountain Home, TN 37684
615/926-1171

Lebanon Hwy
Murfreesboro, TN 37130
615/893-1360

1310 24th Ave. S.
Nashville, TN 37212-2637
615/327-4751

Texas

6010 Amarillo Blvd. W.
Amarillo, TX 79106
806/355-9703

2400 S. Gregg St.
Big Spring, TX 79720
915/263-7361

9th & Lipscomb
Bonham, TX 75418
214/760-0000

4500 S. Lancaster Rd.
Dallas, TX 75216
214/376-5451

5919 Brook Hollow Dr.
El Paso, TX 79925
915/541-7811

2002 Holcombe Blvd.
Houston, TX 77030
713/795-4411

Memorial Blvd.
Kerrville, TX 78028
512/896-2020

1016 Ward St.
Marlin, TX 76661
817/883-3511

7400 Merton Minter Blvd.
San Antonio, TX 78284
512/696-9660

1901 S. First
Temple, TX 76501
817/778-4811

Memorial Dr.
Waco, TX 76711
817/752-6581

Utah

500 Foothill Dr.
Salt Lake City, UT 84148
801/582-1565

Vermont

N. Hartland Rd.
White River Junction, VT 05001
802/295-9363

Virginia

Emancipation Dr.
Hampton, VA 23667
804/722-9961

1201 Broad Rock Blvd.
Richmond, VA 23249
804/230-0001

1970 Roanoke Dr.
Salem, VA 24153
703/982-2463

Washington

4435 Beacon Ave. S.
Seattle, WA 98108
206/762-1010

N. 4815 Assembly St.
Spokane, WA 99205
509/328-4521

American Lake
Tacoma, WA 98493
206/582-8440

77 Wainwright Dr.
Walla Walla, WA 99362
509/525-5200

West Virginia

200 Veterans Ave.
Beckley, WV 25801
304/255-2121

Milford & Chestnut St.
Clarksburg, WV 26301
304/623-3461

1540 Spring Valley Dr.
Huntington, WV 25704
304/429-6741

Route 9
Martinsburg, WV 25401
304/263-0811

Wisconsin

2500 Overlook Terrace
Madison, WI 53705
608/256-1901

County Trunk E.
Tomah, WI 54660
608/372-3971

5000 W. National Dr.
Milwaukee, WI 53295
414/384-2000

Wyoming

2360 E. Pershing Blvd.
Cheyenne, WY 82001
307/778-7550

Fort Rd.
Sheridan, WY 82801
307/672-3473

Veteran's Centers Nationwide

Alabama

1425 S. 21st St.
Birmingham, AL 35205
205/933-0500

110 Marine St.
Mobile, AL 36604
205/694-4194

Alaska

4201 Tudor Centre Dr.
Anchorage, AK 99508
907/271-3063

712 10th Ave.
Fairbanks, AK 99701
907/456-4208

905 Cook St.
P.O. Box 1883
Kenai, AK 99611
907/283-5205

Box 957
Mile 1/2 Knik Rd.
Wasilla, AK 99687
907/376-4318

Arizona

807 North 3rd St.
Phoenix, AZ 85004
602/261-4769

637 Hillside Ave.
Suite A
Prescott, AZ 86301
602/778-3469

727 North Swan
Tucson, AZ 85711
602/323-3271

Arkansas

1311 West 2nd St.
Little Rock, AR 72201
501/378-6395

California

859 South Harbor Blvd.
Anaheim, CA 92805
714/776-0161

157 East Valley Pkwy.
Escondido, CA 92025
619/747-7305

1340 Van Ness Ave.
Fresno, CA 93721
209/487-5660

2000 Westwood Blvd.
Los Angeles, CA 90025
213/475-9509

709 West Beverly Blvd.
Montabello, CA 90640
213/728-9966

616 16th St.
Oakland, CA 92504
415/763-3904

1111 Howe Ave.
Sacramento, CA 95828
916/978-5477

1540 Market St.
San Francisco, CA 94103
415/431-6021

1300 Santa Barbara St.
Santa Barbara, CA 93101
805/564-2345

1899 Clayton Rd. Suite 140
Concord, CA 94520
415/680-4526

P.O. Box 5189
Eureka, CA 95502
707/494-8271

251 West 85th Pl.
Los Angeles, CA 90003
213/753-1391

61 P. O. Box 843
Marina, CA 93933
408/384-1660

18924 Roscoe Blvd.
Northridge, CA 91324
818/993-8862

4954 Arlington Ave. Suite A
Riverside, CA 92504
714/359-8967

2900 6th Ave.
San Diego, CA 92103
619/294-2040

967 West Hedding
San Jose, CA 95126
408/249-1643

161 N. Mountain Ave.
Upland, CA 91786
714/982-0416

Colorado

207 Canyon Blvd.
Suite 201A
Boulder, CO 80302
303/440-7306

1820 Gilpin St.
Denver, CO 80218
303/861-9281

875 West Moreno
Colorado Springs, CO 80905
303/633-2901

400 Remington
Suite 100
Ft. Collins, CO 80524

Connecticut

370 Market St.
Hartford, CT 06120
203/240-3543

562 Whalley Ave.
New Haven, CT 06511
203/773-2232

16 Franklin St.
Room 109
Norwich, CT 06360
203/887-1755

Delaware

Van Buren Medical Center
1411 N. Van Buren St.
Wilmington, DE 19806
302/571-8277

District of Columbia

737 1/2 8th St. S.E.
Washington, DC 20003
202/745-8400

Florida

400 East Prospect Rd.
Ft. Lauderdale, FL 33334
305/563-2992

255 Liberty St.
Jacksonville, FL 32202
904/791-3621

Spectrum Centre
2311 10th Ave. N. #13
Lake Worth, FL 33461
305/585-0441

412 N.E. 39th St.
Miami, FL 33137
305/573-8830

5001 S. Orange Ave.
Suite A
Orlando, FL 32809
305/648-6151

15 West Strong St.
Suite 100C
Pensacola, FL 32501
904/479-6665

1800 Siesta Dr.
Sarasota, FL 34239
813/952-9406

235 31st St. North
St. Petersburg, FL 33713
813/327-3355

249 E. 6th Ave.
Tallahassee, FL 32303
904/681-7172

1507 W. Sligh Ave.
Tampa, FL 33604
813/228-2621

Georgia

65 11th St. N.E.
Atlanta, GA 30309
404/347-7264

8110 White Bluff Rd.
Savannah, GA 31406
912/927-7360

Hawaii

1370 Kapiolani Blvd.
Suite 201
Honolulu, HI 96814
808/546-3723

Idaho

103 West State St.
Boise, ID 83702
208/342-3612

1975 South 5th St.
Pocatello, ID 83201
208/232-0316

Illinois

547 West Roosevelt Rd.
Chicago, IL 60607
312/829-4400

1607 W. Howard St. #200
Chicago, IL 60626
312/764-6595

1600 Halsted St.
Chicago Heights, IL 60411
312/754-0340

1269 N. 89th St.
East St. Louis, IL 62203
618/397-6602

1529 46th Ave. #6
Moline IL 61265
309/762-6954

155 South Oak Park Ave.
Oak Park, IL 60302
312/383-3225

605 N. E. Monroe
Peoria, IL 61603
309/671-7300

624 South 4th St.
Springfield, IL 62703
217/492-4955

Indiana

101 N. Kentucky Ave.
Evansville, IN 47711
812/425-8511

528 West Berry St.
Fort Wayne, IN 46802
219/423-9456

2236 West Ridge Rd.
Gary, IN 46408
219/887-0048

811 Massachusetts Ave.
Indianapolis, IN 46204
317/269-2838

Iowa

3619 6th Ave.
Des Moines, IA 50313
515/284-4929

706 Jackson
Sioux City, IA 51101
712/233-3200

Kansas

412 S. Pattie
Wichita, KS 67211
316/265-3560

Kentucky

1117 Limestone Rd.
Lexington, KY 40503
606/276-5269

736 South First St.
Louisville, KY 40202
502/589-1981

Louisiana

2103 Old Minden Rd.
Bossier, LA 71112
318/742-2733

1529 N. Claiborne Ave.
New Orleans, LA 70116
504/943-8386

Maine

352 Harlow St.
Bangor, ME 04401
207/947-3391

175 Lancaster St.
Room 213
Portland, ME 04101
207/780-3584

Maryland

777 Washington Blvd.
Baltimore, MD 21230
301/539-5511

19 E. Mount Royal Ave.
Baltimore, MD 21202
301/837-3882

7 Elkton Commercial Plaza
South Bridge St.
Elkton, MD 21921
301/398-0171

1015 Spring St.
Suite 101
Silver Spring, MD 20910
202/745-8441

Massachusetts

200 North Main St.
Avon, MA 02322
617/580-2730

480 Tremont St.
Boston, MA 02116
617/451-0171

71 Washington St.
Brighton, MA 02135
617/782-1032

73 East Merrimack St.
Lowell, MA 01852
617/453-1151

181 Hillman St.
New Bedford, MA 02740
617/999-6920

1985 Main St.
Northgate Plaza
Springfield, MA 01103
413/737-5167

8 Worchester St.
West Bolyston, MA 01583
617/835-2709

Michigan

1940 Eastern Ave. S.W.
Grand Rapids, MI 49507
616/243-0385

1766 Fort St.
Lincoln Park, MI 48146
313/381-1370

20820 Greenfield Rd.
Oakpark, MI 48237
313/967-0040

405 E. Superior St.
Duluth, MN 55802
218/722-8654

2480 University Ave.
St. Paul, MN 55114
612/644-4022

Mississippi

121 W. Jackson St.
Biloxi, MS 39530
601/435-5414

158 E. Pascagoula St.
Jackson, MS 39201
601/353-4912

Missouri

3931 Main St.
Kansas City, MO 64111
816/753-1866

Montana

415 North 33rd St.
Billings, MT 59101
406/657-6071

929 S.W. Higgins Ave.
Missoula, MT 59803
406/721-4918

Nebraska

920 L St.
Lincoln, NE 68508
402/476-9736

5123 Leavenworth St.
Omaha, NE 68106
402/476-9736

Nevada

704 South 6th St.
Las Vegas, NV 89101
702/388-6368

341 South Arlington St.
Reno, NV 89501
702/323-1294

New Hampshire

103 Liberty St.
Manchester, NH 03104
603/668-7060

New Jersey

626 Newark Ave.
Jersey City, NJ 07306
201/656-6986

327 Central Ave.
Linwood, NJ 08221
609/927-8387

75 Halsey St.
Newark, NJ 07102
201/622-6940

318 East State St.
Trenton, NJ 08608
609/989-2260

New Mexico

4603 4th St. N.W.
Albuquerque, NM 87107
505/345-8366

1996 St. Michael's Dr.
Warner Plaza, Suite 5
Santa Fe, NM 87504
505/345-8366

211 West Mesa
Gallup, NM 87301
505/722-3821

New York

875 Central Ave.
West Mall Office Plaza
Albany, NY 12206
518/438-2508

226 East Fordham Rd.
Rooms 216-217
Bronx, NY 10458
212/367-3500

351 Linwood Ave.
Buffalo, NY 14209
716/882-0505

5-20 83rd St.
Elmhurst, NY 11373
718/446-8233

210 North Townsend St.
Syracuse, NY 13203
315/423-5690

116 West Main St.
Babylon, NY 11702
516/661-3930

165 Cadman Plaza, East
Brooklyn, NY 11201
718/330-2825

166 West 75th St.
New York, NY 10023
212/944-2917

294 South Plymouth Ave.
Rochester, NY 14608
716/232-3140

200 Hamilton Ave.
White Plains Mall
White Plains, NY 10601
914/684-0570

North Carolina

23 S. Brevard St.
Suite 103
Charlotte, NC 28202
704/333-6107

2009 Elm-Eugene St.
Greensboro, NC 27406
919/333-5366

4 Market Square
Fayetteville, NC 28301
919/323-4908

150 Arlington Blvd.
Suite B
Greenville, NC 27834
919/355-7920

North Dakota

1322 Gateway Dr.
Fargo, ND 58103
701/237-0942

108 East Burdick Expressway
Minot, ND 58701
701/852-0177

Ohio

2134 Lee Rd.
Cleveland Heights, OH
44118
216/932-8471

30 E. Hollister St.
Cincinnati, OH 45219
513/569-7140

11511 Lorain Ave.
Cleveland, OH 44111
216/671-8530

519 Hunter
Dayton, OH 45404
513/461-9150

Oklahoma

3033 N. Walnut
Oklahoma City, OK 73105
405/270-5184

1855 E. 15th St.
Tulsa, OK 74104
918/581-7105

Oregon

1966 Garden Ave.
Eugene, OR 97403
503/687-6918

2450 South/West Belmont
Portland, OR 97214
503/231-1586

Pennsylvania

G. Daniel Baldwin Bldg.
Suite 1 & 2
1000 State St.
Erie, PA 16501
814/453-7955

2705 North Front St.
Harrisburg, PA 17110
717/782-3954

500 Walnut St.
McKeesport, PA 15132
412/678-7704

1107 Arch St.
Philadelphia, PA 19107
215/627-0238

5601 North Broad St.
Room 202
Philadelphia, PA 19141
215/924-4670

959 Wyoming Ave.
Scranton, PA 18509
717/344-2676

954 Penn Ave.
Pittsburgh, PA 15222
412/765-1193

Puerto Rico

52 Gonzalo Marin St.
Arecibo, PR 00612
809/879-4510

Suite LC-8A & LC9
Medical Center Plaza
Rio Piedras, PR 00921
809/783-8794

35 Mayor St.
Ponce, PR 00731
809/879-3370

Rhode Island

172 Pine St.
Pawtucket, RI 02860
401/728-9501

South Carolina

1313 Elmwood Ave.
Columbia, SC 29201
803/765-9944

3366 Rivers Ave.
N. Charleston, SC 29405
803/747-8387

904 Pendleton St.
Greenville, SC 29601
803/765-2711

South Dakota

610 Kansas City St.
Rapid City, SD 57701
605/348-0077

115 North Dakota St.
Sioux Falls, SD 57102
605/332-0856

Tennessee

2 Northgate Park
Suite 108
Chatanooga, TN 37415
615/875-5114

1515 East Magnolia Ave.
Suite 201
Knoxville, TN 37917
615/971-5866

703 South Roan St.
Johnson City, TN 37601
615/928-8387

One North Third St.
Memphis, TN 38103
901/521-3506

Texas

2900 West 10th St.
Amarillo, TX 79102
806/376-3127

3134 Reid St.
Corpus Christi, TX 78202
512/888-3101

2121 Wyoming St.
El Paso, TX 79903
915/542-2851

4905A San Jacinto
Houston, TX 77004
713/522-5354

3208 34th St.
Lubbock, TX 79410
806/743-7551

3404 West Illinois
Midland, TX 79729
915/697-8222

1916 Fredericksburg Rd.
San Antonio, TX 78201
512/229-4120

3401 Manor Rd.
Suite 102
Austin, TX 78723
512/476-0607

5415 Maple Plaza
Suite 114
Dallas, TX 75235
214/634-7024

1305 West Magnolia
Suite B
Fort Worth, TX 76115
817/921-3733

717 Corpus Christi
Laredo, TX 78040
512/723-4680

1130 Pecan
Suite E
McAllen, TX 78501
512/631-2147

107 Lexington Ave.
San Antonio, TX 78205
512/229-4025

Utah

750 North 200 West
Suite 105
Provo, UT 84601
801/377-1117

1354 East 3300, South
Salt Lake City, UT 84106
801/584-1294

Vermont

359 Dorset St.
South Burlington, VT 05401
802/862-1806

Building #2,
Gilman Office Center
Holiday Inn Drive
White River Junction, VT 05001
802/295-2908

Virgin Islands

United Shopping Plaza
Suite 112-Christianstead
St. Croix, VI 00820
809/778-5553

Havensight Mall
St. Thomas, VI 00801
809/774-6674

Virginia

7450 1/2 Tidewater Dr.
Norfolk, VA 23505
804/587-1338

1030 W. Franklin St.
Box 83
Richmond, VA 23220
804/353-8958

320 Mountain Ave. S.W.
Roanoake, VA 24014
703/342-9726

7024 Spring Garden Dr.
Brookfield Plaza
Springfield, VA 22150
703/866-0924

Washington

1322 East Pike St.
Seattle, WA 98122
206/442-2706

North 1611 Division St.
Spokane, WA 99207
509/326-6970

4801 Pacific Ave.
Tacoma, WA 98408
206/473-0731

West Virginia

1591 Washington St. East
Charleston, WV 25301
304/343-3825

1014 6th Ave.
Huntington, WV 25701
304/523-8387

218 West King St.
Martinsburg, WV 25401
304/263-6776

1191 Pineview Dr.
Morgantown, WV 26505
304/291-4001

Wisconsin

147 South Butler St.
Madison, WI 53703
608/264-5343

3400 Wisconsin
Milwaukee, WI 53208
414/344-5504

Wyoming

641 East Second St.
Casper, WY 82601
307/235-8010

3031 Henderson Dr.
Cheyenne, WY 82001
307/778-2660

Reading List

Chapter 1

Recommended Reading

Brothers in Arms, William Broyles; Knopf, New York, 1986.

"The Grief of Soldiers: Vietnam combat veteran's self-help movement,"*American Journal of Orthopsychiatry*, 1973, 43(4): 640-653.

Long Time Passing: Viet Nam: The Haunted Generation, Myra MacPherson; Doubleday and Co., Inc., Garden City, NY, 1984.

The Ravens, Christopher Robbins; Crown Publishers, Inc., New York, 1987.

"Readjustment Problems Among Vietnam Veterans: The Etiology of Combat-Related Post-Traumatic Stress Disorders," Jim Goodwin, Psy.D.; Available from the Disabled American Veterans, National Headquarters, P.O. Box 14301, Cincinnati, OH 45214.

"The Road to Hell Ten," William Broyles; *Atlantic*, April, 1985.

Technical But Still Readable

Legacies of Viet Nam: Comparative Adjustment of Veteran's and Their Peers, The Center for Policy Research, Inc., New York City, March, 1981; A Study Completed for the Veterans Administration.

  Vol. I: Summary of Findings; Principal Investigators: A. Egendorf; C. Kadushin; R. Laufer; G. Rothbart; L. Sloan.

  Vol. II: Educational and Work Careers: Men in the Viet Nam Generation; Principal Investigators: G. Rothbart and L. Sloan.

  Vol. III: Post War Trauma: Social and Psychological Problems of Viet Nam veterans in the Aftermath of the Viet Nam War; Principal Investigator: R. Laufer.

  Vol. IV: Long Term Stress Reactions: Some causes, consequences and naturally occuring support systems., Principal Investigator: C. Kadushin.

  Vol. V: Dealing with the War: A view based on the individual lives of Viet Nam veterans: Principal Investigator: A. Egendorf.

Post Traumatic Stress Disorders: A Handbook for Clinicians, T. Williams, editor; Disabled American Veterans, Cincinnati, Ohio, 1987.

Strangers at Home: Vietnam veterans since the war, C.R. Figley and Seymour Leventman, eds.; Praeger, N.Y., 1980.

Stress Disorders Among Vietnam Veterans: Theory, Research and Treatment, C. R. Figley, editor, New York, Brunner/Mazel, 1978.

The Trauma of War: Stress and Recovery in Viet Nam Veterans, edited by S. Sonnenberg; A. Blank; J. Talbott; American Psychiatric Press, Inc., 1400 K. St., N.W. Washington, D.C., 20005.

Chapter 2

Technical But Still Readable

"Legacies Of A War: Treatment Considerations with Viet Nam Veterans And Their Families," P. Brown; *Social Work*, July-Aug., 1984, pp. 372-379.

"The Veteran System with a Focus on Women Partners," C. M. Williams; pp. 169-192, and "Family Therapy for Viet Nam veterans," by C. Williams and T. Williams, pp. 221-232 in *Post Traumatic Stress Disorders: A Handbook for Clinicians*, T. Williams, Ed., Disabled American Veterans, Cincinnati, Ohio, 1987.

Chapter 3

Recommended Reading

The Pleasure Bond: A New Look at Sexuality and Commitment, J. Masters and V. Johnson; Little Brown and Company, Boston, 1970.

Dr. Ruth's Guide to Good Sex, Dr. Ruth Westheimer, Warner Books, New York, 1984.

Technical But Still Readable

Handbook of Sex Therapy, J. Lo Piccolo; Plenum, New York, 1978.

Human Sexual Inadequacy, W. Masters and V. Johnson; Little and Brown and Company, Boston, 1970.

Principles and Practice of Sex Therapy, S. Leiblum and L. Pervin; The Guilford Press, New York, 1980.

The Psychology of Women, Judith Bardwick; Harper and Row, New York, 1971.

Psychology of Women: Behavior in a Biosocial Context, Juanita H. Williams; Second Edition, W. W. Norton, New York, 1983.

Chapter 4

Technical But Still Readable

"Fail: Bright women," M. Horner; *Psychology Today*, 1969, 3(6), pp. 36-38, 62.

"The measurement and behavioral implications of fear of success in women," M. Horner in J. Atkinson and J. Raynor, (eds.,) *Motivation and Achievement*, New York, Wiley, 1974.

"Multiple Role Women," B. Sigall and A. Matsakis; *The Counseling Psychologist*, Counseling Women III, Vol. 8, no. 1979, pp. 26-27.

Chapter 5

Recommended Reading on Drug Addiction

From Chocolates to Morphine: Understanding Mind Active Drugs, by Andrew Weil and Winifred Doren, Houghton Mifflin, New York, 1983.

The Tranquilizing of America, Richard Hughes and Robert Brewin, New York, Warner Books, 1979.

Recommended Reading On Alcoholism

Addictive Drinking: The Road to Recovery for Problem Drinkers and Those Who Love Them, Clark Vaughan, Penguin Books, 40 W. 23d St., New York, NY 10010.

The Big Book and *The Twelve Steps and Twelve Traditions*, Alcoholics Anonymous World Services, Box 459, Grand Central Station, New York, NY 10163.

Co-dependent No More, Melody Beatty, Hazelden Educational Materials, Box 176, Pleasant Valley Road, Center City, MN 55012-0176.

"Facts About Alcohol and Alcoholism," "Alcohol: Some Questions and Answers," and other pamphlets on alcoholism, available from the National Clearinghouse for Alcohol Information, Box 2345, Rockville, Md. 20852.

I'll Quit Tomorrow, Vernon E. Johnson; Harper and Row, New York, 1983.

Loving an Alcoholic: Help and Hope for Significant Others, Jack Mumey, Contemporary Books, 180 N. Michigan Avenue, Chicago, IL 60601.

Marty Mann Answers Your Questions About Drinking and Alcoholism, Marty Mann, Rev. Ed., Holt, Rinehart and Winston, New York, 1981.

Under the Influence: A Guide to the Myths and Realities of Alcoholism, Dr. James R. Milam and K. Ketchan, Bantam Books, New York, 1981.

Catalogues

Books, brochures and audio and video cassettes on all issues related to alcoholism, drug addiction and other forms of substance abuse are available through the following:

Al-Anon Family Group Headquarters
Box 862
Midtown Station
New York, N.Y. 10018-0862
212/302-7240.

Alcoholics Anonymous World Services
Box 459
Grand Central Station
New York, NY 10163
212/686-1100.

Hazelden Educational Materials
Box 176
Pleasant Valley Road
Center City, MN, 55012-0176
800/328-9000.

The Johnson Institute
510 First Avenue N.
Minneapolis, MN 55403
800/231-5165.

Comp-Care Publications
2415 Annapolis Lane

Minneapolis, MN 55441
800/328-3330.

Council on Alcoholism
1511 K St., NW
Washington, D.C. 20005
202/737-8122.

Chapter 6

Recommended Reading
The Angry Book, T. Rubin; Collier Books, McMillan, New York, 1970.

*Randy,*C. Matsakis; available from 319 Elm St., Takoma Park, MD. 20912.

Chapter 7

Recommended Reading
Battered Wives, Del Martin; Pocket Books, New York, 1976.

The Battered Woman, Lenore Walker; Harper and Row, New York, 1979.

Help for the Battered Woman, Lydia Savina, Bridge Publishing, Inc., S. Plainfield, New Jersey, 1987.

The Speaking Profits Us: Violence in the Lives of Women of Color, Center for the Prevention of Sexual and Domestic Violence, 1914 N. 34th St., #105, Seattle, WA 98103.

Wife-Beating: The Silent Crisis, Roger Langely and Richard Levy; E. P. Dutton, New York, 1977.

Technical But Still Readable
Battered Women: Issues of Public Policy: Consultation Sponsored by the U.S. Commission on Civil Rights, Jan., 1978, Washington, D.C.

Behind Closed Doors: Violence in the American Family, M. Strauss; R. Gelles; S. Steinmetz; Anchor Book, New York, 1970; M. Strauss; "Wife-Beating: How Common and Why?" *Victimology*, Vol. 2, No. 3-4, pp. 443-458, 1978.

Violence in the Family, Marie Borland (ed.); Atlantic Highlands, Manchester University Press, 1976.

The Violent Home, R. Gelles; London, Sage Publications, 1972.

Chapter 8

Recommended Reading
"The Battered (Military) Wife," Jane Sobie, *Ladycom* (present name, *Military Lifestyle*), August, 1980, pp. 43-46; 59-62.

Technical But Still Readable
Wife Abuse in the Armed Forces, A. West; W. Turner; E. Dunwoody; Center for Women Policy Studies, Washington, D.C., 1981.

Chapter 9

Suggested Readings: Books by Black or African women discussing race and sex oppression.

A *Question of Power*, B. Head; Heinemann Educational Books, Portsmouth, New Hampshire, 1974.

The Color Purple, A. Walker; Harbrace Paperback, San Diego, CA, 1982.

"Double Jeapordy: To Be Black and Female," by Frances Beal, in *Sisterhood is Powerful*, edited by Robin Morgan, Vintage Books, Random House, 1970, pp. 340-353.

The Joys of Motherhood, B. Emecheta; Braziler Press, New York, 1980.

Praise Song for the Widow, P. Marshall, 1983.

The Salt Eaters, T.C. Bambara; Random House, New York, 1980.

Sassafras, Cypress, and Indigo, N. Shange; St. Martin's Press, New York, 1982.

Their Eyes Were Watching God, Z.N. Hurston; University of Illinois Press, Urbana and Chicago, 1978.

PTSD among Black and Hispanic Viet Nam Veterans—General

Bloods: An Oral History of the Vietnam War by Black Veterans, Wallace Terry; Ballantine Books, New York, 1984.

Technical But Still Readable: PTSD among Black and Hispanic Vietnam Veterans

"Alcoholism in Black Vietnam Veterans: Symptoms of Post-traumatic Stress Disorder," James Carter; *Journal of the National Medical Association*, Vol. 74:7, 1982, pp. 655-660.

"Diagnosis and Treatment of Post-Traumatic Stress Disorder in Hispanic Viet Nam Veterans," Gegorio Pina, III, pp. 389-402, in *The Trauma of War:Stress and Recovery in Vietnam Veterans*, American Psychiatric Press, Inc., Washington, D.C.

"The Intercultural Setting: Encountering Black Vietnam Veterans," E.R. Parsons, in S. Sonnenberg; A. Blank; J. Talbott, *The Trauma of War: Stress and Recovery in Vietnam Veterans*, American Psychiatric Press, Inc., Washington, D.C., 1985, pp. 361-387.

"Post Traumatic Stress Disorder Among Viet Nam Veterans," Irving Allen, *Hospital and Community Psychiatry*, Jan., 1986, Vol. 37:1, pp. 55-60.

Chapter 10

Recommended Reading on Children and Family Violence

The Battered Woman, Lenore Walker, Harper and Row, New York, 1979.

Help for the Battered Woman, Lydia Savina, Bridge Publishers, South Plainfield, New Jersey, 1987.

Recommended Reading on Child Abuse And Neglect

"Everything You Always Wanted to Know About Child Abuse and Neglect," National Center on Child Abuse and Neglect, Department of Health and Human Services, P.O. Box 1182, Washington, D.C., 22013, 1984.

"Catalog of Materials," Clearinghouse on Child Abuse and Neglect Information, P.O. Box 1182, Washington, D.C., 22013, a listing of free and low cost pamphlets on child abuse and neglect.

Manchild in the Promised Land, Claude Brown; MacMillan, New York, 1965.

Technical But Still Readable

The Battered Child, R. Helfer and C. Kempe; Second Edition, University of Chicago Press, Chicago, 1974.

Child Abuse and Neglect, The Family and the Community, R. Helfer and C. Kempe; Ballinger Publishing Company, Cambridge, MA, 1976.

PTSD and Children, Spencer Eth and Robert Pynoos; American Psychiatric Press, Inc., Washington, D.C., 1985.

Recommended Reading on Children and Alcoholism

Adult Children of Alcoholics, Janet Woititz, 1983, Health Communications, 1721 Blount Road, Suite #1, Pompano Beach, FL, 33069; 800/851-9100.

Guide to Recovery: A Book for Adult Children of Alcoholics, Herbert Gravitz and Julie Bowden; Learning Publications Inc., Holmes Beach, FL, 1985.

A Primer on Adult Children of Alcoholics, Timmen L. Cermak, M.D.; Health Communications, Inc., 1721 Blount Road, Suite #1, Pompano Beach, FL, 33069; 800/851-9100.

Technical But Still Readable

Children of Alcoholism, Judith Seixas and Geraldine Youcha, Harper and Row, 10 East 53d St., New York, NY 10022.

"Effects of paternal exposure to prolonged stress on the mental health of the spouse and children," J.J. Sigal, *Canadian Psychiatric Association Journal*, Vol. 21, 1976, pp. 169-172.

"Impact of Post-traumatic Stress Disorder of World War II on the Next Generation," Robert Rosenheck, *The Journal of Nervous and Mental Disease*, Vol. 174:6, June, 1986, Serial No. 1243, pp. 319-327.

"Secondary traumatization in the children of Vietnam veterans with post-traumatic stress disorder," R. Rosenheck and P. Nathan; *Hospital and Community Psychiatry*, 36:5, May, 1985, pp. 538-539.

"The Viet Nam veteran and his preschool child: childrearing as a delayed stress in combat vets," Sarah Haley; *Journal of Contemporary Psychotherapy*, Vol. 14: 1, Spring/Summer, 1984, pp. 114-121.

Chapter 11

Recommended Reading

Feeling Good: The New Mood Therapy, David D. Burns; Signet Books, New American Collection, New York, 1980.

Technical But Still Readable

Suicide: Inside and Out, D.K. Reynolds and N.L. Farberow; University of California Press, Berkeley, CA, 1976.

The Suicidal Patient, Victor Victoroff; Medical Economics Books, Cradell, NJ, 1983.

Chapter 12

Technical But Still Readable

"Individual Psychotherapy with Viet Nam Veterans," pp. 125-164 and "Rap Groups and Group Therapy for Viet Nam Veterans," pp. 165-192 by John R. Smith in *The Trauma of War: Stress and Recovery in Viet Nam Veterans*, ed. by S. Sonnenberg; A. Blank; J. Talbott; American Psychiatric Press, Inc., Washington, D.C., 1985.

Post Traumatic Stress Disorders: A Handbook for Clinicians, edited by T. Williams, Disabled American Veterans, Cincinnati, Ohio, 1987.

"Stages of Treatment in PTSD," by Stephen T. Perconte, VA *Practitioner*, Feb. 1988, pp. 47-53.

Stress Disorders Among Vietnam Veterans: Theory, Research and Treatment, edited by Charles R. Figley; Brunner/Mazel, New York, 1978.

Chapter 13

Recommended Reading

Compassion and Self-Hate: An Alternative to Despair, T. Rubin, with Eleanor Rubin; Collier Books, MacMillan Publishing Company, New York, 1975.

Inner Joy: New Strategies for Adding Pleasure to Your Life, H. Bloomfield and R. Kory; a Jove Book, New York, 1985.

Living Alone and Liking It, L. Shahan; Warner Books, New York, 1981.

Necessary Losses, Judith Viorst; Fawcett Gold Medal Book, Ballantine Books, New York, 1986.

Why Do I Think I'm Nothing Without a Man? P. Russianoff; Bantam Books, New York, 1965.

Books of General Interest

Child Sexual Assault and Incest

Kiss Daddy Goodnight, L. Armstrong; Pocket Books, New York, 1978.

Voices in the Night, E. McNaron and Y. Morgan, eds.; Cleis Press, Pittsburgh, PA, 1982.

If I Should Die Before I Wake, M. Morris; J.P. Tarcher, Inc., Distributed by Houghton Mifflin Co., Boston, 1982.

Speaking Out, Fighting Back, Veri Gallager and Wm. Dodds; Madrona Publishers, Seattle, Washington, 1985.

Technical But Still Readable

Child Sexual Abuse: New Theory and Research, D. Finkelhor; Free Press, New York, 1984.

Sexually Victimized Children, D. Finkelhor; Free Press, New York, 1979.

Father-Daughter Incest, J. Herman; Harvard University Press, Cambridge, MA 1981.

Incest, K. Meiselman; Josey-Bass,San Francisco, 1978.

Sexual Violence: The Unmentionable Sin, Marie Fortune; The Pilgrim Press, New York, 1983.

"Victims of Incest and Rape," C. Courtois; *The Counseling Psychologist, Counseling Women III,* Vol. 8:1, 1979 pp. 38-40.

Help in Selecting a Therapist—General

Women and Madness, Phyllis Chesler, Avon Books, a division of the Hearst Corporation, New York, 1972.

Notes of a Feminist Therapist, E. Williams; Praeger Publishers, New York, 1976, p. 20.

Part One, Chapters 13 & 17, in *Help for the Battered Woman,* L. Savina; Bridge Publishing Inc., S. Plainfield, NJ, 1987.

Technical But Still Readable

Towards a New Psychology of Women, Jean Baker Miller; Beacon Press, Boston, 1976.

"Mother Blaming in Major Clinical Journals," P. Capland and I. Hall McCorquodale; *American Journal of Orthopsychiatry,* 55 (3), July, 1985, pp. 345-353.

"'Kinde, Kuche, Kirche' as Scientific Law: Psychology Constructs the Female," N. Weisstein; pp. 228-244 in *Sisterhood is Powerful* R. Morgan; Vintage Books, Random House, New York, 1970.

Eating Disorders—General

A catalogue of pamphlets and books on food addiction is available from Hazelden Educational Materials, Box 176, Pleasant Valley Road, Center City, MN 55012-0176, 800/328–9000.

The Nutritional Ages of Women: A Lifelong Guide to Eating Right for Health, Beauty and Well-Being, Patricia Long; MacMillan Publishing Co., New York, 1986.

Fat is a Family Affair, Judith Hollis; Harper and Row, San Francisco, 1985.

"Premenstral Syndrome," a report by the American Council on Science and Health, July, 1985 (Send $2 to ACSH, 47 Maple St., Summit, NJ, 07901).

Starving for Attention, Cherry Boone O'Neill; New York, Continuum Books, 1982.

Dying to Please: Anorexia Nervosa and Its Cure, Avis Rumney; McFarland, Jefferson, NC, 1983.

Technical But Still Readable

The Golden Cage: The Enigma of Anorexia Nervosa, Hilda Bruch; New York, Random House, 1979.

Anorexia Nervosa: A Multidimensional Perspective, P. Garfinkel and D. Garner; Brunner/Mazel, New York, 1982.

Treating and Overcoming Anorexia Nervosa, Steven Levenkron; Scriber, New York, 1982.

Eating Disorders: Obesity, Anorexia Nervosa, and the Person Within, Hilda Bruch; Basic Books, New York, 1979.

Endnotes

Introduction

1. Anonymous, "The Best Years of Our Lives," Vet Center, Fort Wayne, Indiana, 1985.

2. *Idem.*

3. Lyons, Richard, D., "Vietnam Veterans Turn to Therapy," The New York Times, Nov. 13, 1964.

4. Personal communication, Kerry Merback, National Readjustment Counseling Service, Feb. 1988.

5. *Idem.*

6. Jennings, Ben, as cited in "Veteran Centers Offer Refuge To All Who Served in Vietnam," by Marcie Ritz, *The Montgomery Journal*, Nov. 10, 1986, p. A-8.

7. Lyons, *op. cit.*; Houston Vietnam Veteran Leadership Program, "Vietnam Veteran Leadership Fact Sheet," compiled by Richard K. Kolb, Chairman, PO Box 77091, Houston, TX, March 20, 1985, pp.3-4, (data taken from "Veterans in the U.S.: A Statistical Portrait," 1980 Census; Blank, Arthur S., "Irrational Rections to Post-Traumatic Stress Disorder and Vietnam Veterans," pp. 69-98 in Sonnenberg, S.; Blank A.; Talbott, J., *The Trauma of War*, American Psychiatric Press, Inc., Washington, D.C., 1985; Harris, L. and Associates, "Myths and realities: A Study of Attitudes Toward Vietnam Era Veterans" Submitted by the Veteran's Administration to the Committee on Veteran's Affairs, US Senate, Senate Committee Print No. 29, US Government Printing Office, Washington, DC, 1980; Carter, J., "Message to Congress, Vietnam Era veterans" Oct. 10, 1978, Weekly Compilation, Presidential Documents 14, 1737-1742, 1978; Blank, A., "Discussion of Papers on the Psychological Problems of Vietnam Veterans" Annual Meeting of the American Psychiatric Association, San Francisco, 1980; Blank, A., "Vietnam Veterans—Operation Outreach," presented at the First Training Conference on Vietnam Veterans, St. Louis, Missouri, 1979.

Chapter 1

1. *Vietnam Veteran*, August 1980, as cited on p. 293 in Blank, Arthur S., Jr. "The Unconscious Flashback to the War in Vietnam Veterans: Clinical Mystery, Legal Defense and Community Problem," in *The Trauma of War: Stress and Recovery in Vietnam Veterans*, edited by Sonnenberg, S., Blank, A., Talbott, A., American Psychiatric Press, 1985, pp. 293-320.

2. Sorenson, Gary, "Hinterlands are home, not a hideaway, for Vietnam veterans," *Vet Center Voice*, Vol. VI, No. 9, October, 1985, p. 1.

3. *Diagnostic and Statistical Manual of Mental Disorders*, Third Edition, (DSM III-R), American Psychiatric Association, 1987, Washington, D.C., pp. 247-251.

4. Vercozzi, Carol, "The War that Refused to Die: Vietnam Again," Unpublished Paper, Department of Communications, Hartford, Massachusetts; p. 3, Silverman, Joel, "Post-Traumatic Stress Disorder," *Advanced Psychosomatic Medicine*, Vol. 16: 115-140, 1986.

5. DSM III, *op. cit.*, pp. 247-251, Vercozzi, Carol, "The War That Refused to Die: Vietnam Again," unpublished paper, Department of Communications, Hartford, MA; Silver-

man, Joel, "Post-Traumatic Stress Disorder," *Advanced Psychosomatic Medicine*, Vol. 16, pp. 115-140, 1986. Gaines-Carter, Patrice, "Salvadoran Pupils Here Still at War," *The Washington Post*, Tuesday, Oct. 15, 1985, pp. 1, 8. Terr, Leonore C. "Chowchilla Revisited: Effects of psychia trauma four years after a school bus kidnapping," *American Journal of Psychiatry*, 1983, 140:1543-1550. Wilkinson, Charles B., "Aftermath of a Disaster: The Collapse of the Hyatt Regency Hotel Skywalks," *American Journal of Psychiatry*, 1983, 140:1134-1139. Green, Bonnie L.; Grace, Mary C., et. al. "Levels of Functional Impairment Following a Civilian Disaster: The Beverly Hills Supper Club Fire," *Journal of Consulting and Clinical Psychology*, 1983, Vol. 51, No. 4, pp. 573-580. McFarlane, Alexander, C. "Post-traumic Morbidity of a Disaster: A study of cases presenting for psychiatric treatment," *Journal of Nervous and Mental Disease*, 1986, Vol. 174: 1, pp. 4-11.

6. Gaines Carter, Patrice, "Salvadoran Pupils Here Still at War," *The Washington Post*, Tuesday, Oct. 15, 1985, pp. 1, 8.

7. *Diagnostic and Statistical Manual of Mental Disorders*, Third Edition, (DSM III), American Psychiatric Association, 1980, Washington, D.C., pp. 236-238.

8. Haley, Sarah, "I Feel A Little Sad: The Application of Object Relations Theory to the Hypnotherapy of Post Traumatic Stress Disorders in Vietnam Veterans," Society for Clinical and Experimental Hypnosis, San Antonio, Texas, October 25, 1984.

9. Williams, Candice, "Peace Time Combat," in *PTSD: A Handbook for Clinicians*, edited by Williams, T., Disabled American Veterans, Cincinnati, Ohio, 1987, pp. 267-293.

10. Green, Bonnie; Grace, M.; Glesser, G., "Identifying Survivors at Risk: Long Term Impariment Following the Beverly Hills Supper Club Fire," *Journal of Consulting and Clinical Psychology*, 1985, Vol. 53: no. 5., pp. 672-678; Modlin, J., "PTSD: No Longer Just For War Veterans," *Post Graduate Medicine*, Vol. 79:3, Feb., 15, 1986, pp. 26-44; Mc Farlane, Alexander, "Post Traumatic Morbidity of a Disaster," *Journal of Nervous and Mental Disease*, 1986, Vol. 174, no. 1, pp. 4-14.

11. Williams, Candice, *op. cit.*, 1987, p. 267.

12. Bard, Morton, "Forward," in Williams, T., *PTSD: A Handbook for Clinicians, op. cit.*, p. iii.

13. Gerdemen, Eric, Assistant Regional Manager for Readjustment Counseling, Vet Center Program, Region II, Baltimore, Md., "PTSD and the Vietnam Veteran," Unpublished Paper, 1984.

14. The list of symptoms of PTSD is taken from a DAV (Disabled American Veteran's Project) called "The Forgotten Warrior Project," conducted by Dr. John Wilson at Cleveland State University and is cited in Rick Ritter's "Bringing the War Home: Vets Who Have Battered," Vet Center, Ft. Wayne, Indiana, 1984, p. 8.

15. Arnold, Arthur, "Diagnosis of Post-Traumatic Stress Disorder in Vietnam Veterans," in *The Trauma of War: Stress and Recovery in Vietnam Veterans*, edited by Sonnenberg, S.; Blank, A.; Talbott, A., American Psychiatric Press, 1985, p. 103.

16. Ziarowsky, Peter A. and Broida, Daniel C., "Therapeutic implications of nightmares of Vietnam combat veterans," *The V.A. Practioner*, July, 1984, Vol. 1, No. 7, pp. 63, 67, 68.

17. Ziarowsky, *et. al.*, pp. 67-68.

18. Arnold, *op. cit.*, p. 104.

19. Blank, *op. cit.*, p. 296.

20. Jaffe, R., Dissociative phenomenon in former concentration camp inmates, *International Journal of Psychoanalysis*, 49: 310-312, 1968.

21. Niederland, W.G., "Clinical observations on the survivor syndrome," *International Journal of Psychoanalysis*, 49: 313-315, 1968.

22. Grinker, R. R. and Spiegel, J. P. *Men Under Stress*, New York, McGraw, Hill, 1945.

23. Blank, *op. cit.*, p. 297.

24. Blank, *op. cit.*, p. 297.

25. Blank, *op. cit.*, p. 297.

26. Blank, *op. cit.*, pp. 295-296.

27. Blank, *op. cit.*, p. 305.

28. Blank, *op. cit.*, p. 104.

29. Arnold, *op. cit.*, p. 104.

30. Vercozzi, *op. cit.*, p. 3; Goodwin, Jim, Psy. D., *Continuing Readjustment Problems Among Vietnam Veterans: The Etiology of Combat Related Post-Traumatic Stress Disorders*, published by the Disabled American Veteran's National Headquarters, P.O. Box 14301, Cincinnati, Ohio, 45214, p. 6; Grinker, R. P. and Spiegel, J. P., *Men Under Stress*, McGraw Hill, New York, 1963, p. 28.

31. *Congressional Record*—Senate, S 10062-10072, July 15, 1987.

32. Goodwin, Jim, *op. cit.*, p. 5; Lipton, Merril, Shaeffer, W., "PTSD in the Older Veteran," *Military Medicine*, Vol. 151, Oct., 1986, 522-526.

33. Glass, A.J., "Introduction," in P.G. Bourne (Ed.), *The Psychology and Physiology of Stress*, N. Y. Academic Press, 1969, xiv-xxx.

34. Bourne, P.G., *Men, Stress, and Vietnam*, Boston, Little & Brown, 1970.

35. Futterman, S. and Pumpian-Midlin, E., "Traumatic war neuroses five years later," *American Journal of Psychiatry*, 1951, 108 (6): 401-408.

36. Thienes-Hontons, P., Watson, C., and Kucala T., "Stress disorder symptoms in Vietnam and Korean war veterans," *Journal of Consulting and Clinical Psychology*, 1982. 50, pp. 558-561; Caroll, Edward "Stress Disorder Symptoms in Vietnam and Korean War Veterans: A commentary on Thienes-Hontos, Watson, and Kucala," *Journal of Consulting and Clinical Psychology*, 1983, Vol. 51:4, No. 4, 616-618; Thienes-Hontos, P., "Stress-Disorder Symptoms in Vietnam and Korean War Veterans: Still No Difference," *Journal of Consulting and Clinical Psychology*, 1983, Vol. 51:4, 619-620.

37. Streimer, J. H., "The Psychosocial Adjustment of Australian Vietnam Veterans," *American Journal of Psychiatry*, 142:5: May, 1985, 616-618.

38. Bowman, Bruce, et. al., "Psychiatric Disturbances Among Australian Vietnam Veterans," *Military Medicine*, Vol. 150, 2: 77-79, Feb., 1985. Bowman, Bruce, "Post-traumatic Stress Disorder (Traumatic War Neurosis) and Concurrent Psychiatric Illness Among Australian Vietnam Veterans: A Controlled Study," *T.R. Army Medical Corps*, 1985, 131, pp. 128-131.

39. La Guardian, R., et. al., 1982, "Incidence of delayed stress among Vietnam era veterans: the effects of priming on response set," *American Journal of Orthopsychiatry*, 42 (3): 000-010; Frye, J. and Stockton, R., "Discriminant analysis of post-traumatic stress disorders among a group of Vietnam veterans," *American Journal of Psychiatry*, 1982, 139, pp. 52-56.

40. Harrington, David, "Who's Conning Whom?" *Veteran*, Washington, D.C., October, 1986, p. 22.

41. Houston Vietnam Veteran Leadership Program, "Vietnam Veteran Fact Sheet," compiled by Richard K. Kolb, Chairman, P.O. Box 77091, Houston, Texas, March 20, 1985, p. 4. (Data taken from "Veterans in the U.S.: A Statistical Portrait," 1980 Census.)

42. Lyons, Richard, D., "Vietnam Veterans Turn to Therapy," *The New York Times*, Nov. 13, 1964; Houston Vietnam Veteran Leadership Program, *op. cit.*, p. 3; Blank, Arthur S., "Irrational Reactions to Post-Traumatic Stress Disorder and Vietnam Veterans," pp. 69-98 in Sonnenberg, *et. al.*, *The Trauma of War, op. cit.*; Harris, L. and Associates, "Myths and realities: A Study of attitudes toward Vietnam era veterans," Submitted by the Veteran's Administration to the Committee on Veteran Affairs, U.S. Senate, Senate Committee Print No. 29, U.S. Government Printing Office, Washington, D.C., 1980; Carter, J. "Message to Congress, Vietnam era veterans" October 10, 1978, *Weekly Compilation, Presidential Documents* 14, 1737-1742, 1978; Blank, A., "Discussion of Papers on the Psychological Problems of Vietnam Veterans," Annual Meeting of the American Psychiatric Association, San Francisco, 1980; Blank, A., "Vietnam Veterans—Operation Outreach," presented at the First Training Conference on Vietnam Veterans, St. Louis, No., 1979. Walker, J. I., and Cavenar, J. O., "Vietnam Veterans: Their Problems Continue," *The Journal of Nervous and Mental Disease*, Vol. 170, No. 3, pp. 174-180, p. 176.

43. Jennings, Ben, as cited in "Veteran Centers Offer Refuge To All Who Served in Vietnam," by Marcie Ritz, *The Montgomery Journal*, Nov. 10, 1986, p. A-6.

44. Blank, Arthur, "Irrational Reactions to Post-Traumatic Stress Disorder and Vietnam Veterans," *op. cit.* in *The Trauma of War: Stress and Recovery in Vietnam Veterans*, edited by Sonnenberg, S. and Blank, A.

45. Walker, I, Cavenar, J.O., "Vietnam Veterans: Their Problems Continue," *The Journal of Nervous and Mental Disease*, Vol. 170, No. 3, p. 174-180; Figley, Charles, Ed., *Stress Disorders Among Vietnam Veterans*, Brunner Mazel, Publishers, N.Y., 1978; Yesavage, Jerome, "Dangerous Behavior by Vietnam Veterans with Schizophrenia," *American Journal of Psychiatry*, 140: 9, September, 1983, pp. 1180-1183.

46. Houston Vietnam Veteran Leadership Program, *op.cit.*, p. 4.

47. Gerdeman, *op. cit.*

48. Kolb, Richard K. Chairman, Houston Vietnam Veteran's Leadership Program of Houston, Inc., P. O. Box 77091, Houston, Texas, 77213, "Vietnam Veteran Statistics," March 20, 1985, p. 3.

49. Gerdeman, *op. cit.*, Vercozzi, *op. cit.*

50. Wilson, John, as cited in "Vietnam Veterans Turn to Therapy" by Richard D. Lyons, *The New York Times*, Nov. 13, 1984, p. 5.

51. Gerdeman, *op. cit.*

52. Kolb, *op.cit.*, p. 3.

53. Kolb, *op. cit.*, p. 4.

54. Kolb, *op.cit.*, p. 3.

55. *Idem.*

56. Wilson, *op.cit.*, p. 4, p. 2.

57. Downs, Frederick, *The Killing Zone: My Life in the Vietnam War*, New York, W.W. Norton and Co., 1978, as cited in Blank, A., "Irrational Reactions," *op. cit.*, pp. 72-73.

58. Vercozzi, *op. cit.*, Blank, "Irrational Reactions," *op. cit.*

59. Frye, S. and Stockton, R., "Discriminant analysis of PTSD among a group of Vietnam veterans," *American Journal of Psychiatry*, Vol. 139: 1, January, 1982, pp. 52-56.

60. Figley, Charles, "Delayed Stress Response," *Journal of Marriage and Family Counseling*, 4(3): 53-60, 1978.

61. Laufer, Robert S., "War Trauma and Human Development, The Vietnam Experience," in Sonnenberg, *et. al.*, The Trauma of War, *op. cit.*, pp. 31-67; Frye, *op. cit.*

62. Gault, W. B., "Some Remarks on Slaughter," *American Journal of Psychiatry*, 128:4, Oct., 1971, pp. 82-86.

63. Laufer, *op.cit.*, p. 48.

64. Houston Vietnam Veteran Leadersip Program, "Vietnam Veteran Fact Sheet," compiled by Richard K. Kolb, Chairman, P.O. Box 77091, Houston, Texas, March 20, 1985, p. 4. (Data taken from "Veterans in the U.S.: A Statistical Portrait," 1980 Census).

65. Futterman, *op. cit.*, p.402.

66. As cited in Pentland, Bruce and Dwyer, James, "Incarcerated Vietnam Veterans," pp. 405-416, in Sonnenberg, *et. al.*, *The Trauma of War*, *op. cit.*, p. 405.

67. Cruden, John, "Veteran's spiritual needs arise in counseling sessions," *Vet Center Voice*, Vol. VI, No. 11, December, 1985, p. 6-9; Sorenson, Gary, "Veterans struggle to integrate war and values," *Vet Center Voice*, Vol. VI, No 11, December, 1985, p. 5-6; Devine, Patrick, Fr., "PTSD shadows moral/spiritual dimension," *Vet Center Voice*, Vol. VI, No. 6, July, 1985, pp. 1, 9.

68. Melton, Roger, "Ideals, Death, Betrayal are central to PTSD Theme," Vet Center, Ft. Wayne, Indiana 46802, 1969; Marin, Peter, "Living in Moral Pain," *Psychology Today*, Nov. 1981, pp. 68-80.

69. Holloway, Harry C., Ursano, Robert J. "Vietnam Veterans On Active Duty: Adjustment in a Supportive Environment," pp. 323-338, in Sonnenberg, *et. al.*, *The Trauma of War*, *op. cit.*

70. Leventman, Seymour, "Epilogue: Social and Historical Perspectives on the Vietnam Veteran," pp. 291-295 in Figley, C., Ed., *Stress Disorders Among Vietnam Veterans: Theory, Research and Treatment*, Brunner/Mazel, Publishers, New York, 1978, p. 295.

Chapter 2

1. Gerdeman, Eric, "PTSD and the Vietnam Veteran," Unpublished paper, Vietnam Veteran Outreach Center, Silver Spring, Md. 20902, 1985, p. 1.

2. *Idem.*

3. *Idem.*p.2.

4. Anonymous, "The Best Years of Our Lives," Vet Center, Fort Wayne, Indiana, 1985.

5. Walker, J. and Cavenar, O., *op.cit.*, p. 174-180; Vercozzi, *op. cit.*, Gerdeman, *op. cit.*

6. Santoli, 1981, as cited in Vercozzi, *op. cit.*, p. 10.

7. Goodwin, Jim, "Readjustment Problems Among Vietnam Veterans," Disabled American Veterans, National Headquarters, PO Box 14301, Cinncinnati, Ohio 45214. Wilson, John, *Identity, ideology, and crises: The Vietnam veteran in transition*, Pt. 2, Cincinnati, Ohio Disabled American Veterans, 1978; Egendorf, A.; Kaduschin, C.; Laufer, R.; Rothbart, G.; Sloan, L.; *Legacies of Vietnam: Comparative adjustment of veterans and their peers* 5 volumes, New York: Center for Policy Research, 1981; Egendorf, A.; Laufer, R.; Sloan, L.; *Legacies of Vietnam: Comparative adjustment of veterans and their peers: overview of the report*, Washington, D.C., U.S. Government Printing Office, 1981; Penk, W., *et. al.*, "Interpersonal problems of Vietnam combat veterans with symptoms of PTSD," *Journal of Abnormal Psychology*, 1982, Vol. 91:6, 444-450; Penk, W., *et. al.*, "Adjustment

differences among male substances abusers varying in degrees of combat experience in Vietnam," *Journal of Consulting and Clinical Psychology*, 1981: 49:3, 426-437; Frye, T. S. and Stockton, R.A., "Discriminant analysis of PTSD among a group of Vietnam veterans," *American Journal of Psychiatry*, Vol. 139: 1, January 1982, pp. 52-56; Palmer, S. and Harris, D., "Supportive group therapy for women partners of Vietnam veterans," *Family Therapist*, 4(2), 3-11, 1983; Blank, Arthur S., "Psychological Aspects in the Vietnam War," in Charles A. Stenger (chair) *Vietnam Veterans: Traumatic effects and post war adjustment problems, treatment approaches,* Symposium presented at the meeting of the American Psychological Association, Montreal, Canada, Sept. 1980; Fairbank, John; Keane, T. M.; Malloy, P.Some Preliminary Data on the Psychological Characteristics of Vietnam Veterans with Posttraumatic Stress Disorders," *Journal of Consulting and Clinical Psychology*, 1983, Vol. 51, No. 6: 912-919; Keane, T. M. and Fairbank, J.A., "A Survey analysis of combat-related stress disorders in Vietnam veterans," *American Journal of Psychiatry*, 1983, 140, 348-350; Carroll, Edward, et. al. "Vietnam combat veterans with Post-traumatic Stress Disorder: Analysis of Marital and Cohabitating Adjustment," *Journal of Abnormal Psychology*, 1985: Vol. 94, No. 3, 329-337; VanKampen, Melodie; Watson, Charles; Tilleskjor, Curt; Kucala, Teresa; Vassar, Patricia; "The Definition of Posttraumatic Stress Disorder in Alcoholic Vietnam Veterans," *The Journal of Nervous and Mental Disease*, Vol. 173:3, 1986, pp. 137-144.

8. Cruden, John, "Vet Center staff members analyze homeless situation," *Vet Center Voice*, Vol. 8: No. 2, 1987, pp. 3-7.

9. Flynn, Charles and Teguis, Alexandra, "Grief and the Treatment of PTSD," unpublished paper, Manchester Community College, 1985. Address all correspondence to Charles Flynn, Department of Sociology and Anthropology, Miami University, Oxford, Ohio, 45056.

10. Rosenbeck, Robert, "The Role of Family Therapy in the Treatment of PTSD," Unpublished paper, presented at "Diagnosis and Management of Post-Traumatic Stress Disorders in the V.A.," V.A. Mid-Atlantic Regional Medical Education Center, Baltimore, Md., Aug. 21, 1985.

11. As cited in "The War That Has No Ending," by John Lagone, *Discover*, June, 1985, pp. 44-54.

Chapter 3

1. Masters, William and Johnson, Virginia, *The Pleasure Bond: A New Look at Sexuality and Commitment*, Little, Brown and Company, Boston, 1970; Moustakas, Clark, E., *Loneliness*, Spectrum Book, Prentice-Hall, Inc. Detriot, 1961; Bardwick, J., *The Psychology of Women*, Harper and Row, New York, 1971; Williams, J., *The Psychology of Women: Behavior in a Biosocial Context*, Second Edition, W. W. Norton, New York, 1983.

2. Masters and Johnson, *op. cit.*, p. 29.

3. Bardwick, *op. cit.*, Williams, *op. cit.*

4. Carroll, Edward M.; Rueger, Drue B.; Foy, David W., Donahoe, Clyde P, "Vietnam Combat Veterans with Posttraumatic Stress Disorder: An Analysis of Marital and Cohabitating Adjustment," *Journal of Abnormal Psychology*, 1985, Vol. 94:3, pp. 329-337.

5. Egendorf, A.; Kadushin, C.; Laufer, R.; Rothbard, G.; Sloan, L., *Legacies of Vietnam: Comparative adjustment of veterans and their peers*, Vol. 3, Center for Policy Research, Inc., New York, March, 1981; Yaeger, T.; Laufer, R.; Gallops, M., "Some problems associated with war experience in men of the Vietnam generation," *Archives of General Psychiatry*, Vol. 41, April, 1984, pp. 327-333.

6. Modelin, H., "Post Traumatic Stress Disorder: No Longer Just for War Veterans," *Postgraduate Medicine*, Vol. 79, no. 3, Feb. 15, 1986, pp. 26-29, 32, 37.

7. Matsakis, Aphrodite "The Effects of PTSD on Family Life," Research Project, Psychology Service, Veteran's Administration Medical Center, Washington, D.C. 1988.

8. Klonoff, H.; Mc Dougall, G.; Clark, C.; Kramer, P.; Horgan, J., "The Neuropsychological, psychiatric, and physical effects of prolonged and severe stress: 30 Years later," *The Journal of Nervous and Mental Disease*, Vol. 163: No. 4, pp. 246-252.

9. Masters and Johnson, *op. cit.*, Bardwick, *op. cit.*, Leiblum, Sandra R., and Pervin, Lawrence, A., Eds., *Principles and Practice of Sex Therapy*, The Guilford Press, New York, 1980.

10. Reich, Wilhelm, *The Function of the Orgasm: The Discovery of the Orgone*, The World Publishing Company, New York, 1971, pp. 138, 240.

11. Reich, *op. cit.*, p. 240.

12. Reich, *op. cit.*, describes the same masochistic thoughts in some of his patients, p. 81.

13. Kuhne, *et. al.*, as cited in "The Definition of Posttraumatic Stress Disorder in Alcoholic Vietnam Veterans," VanKampen, Melodie; Watson, Charles; Tilleskjor, Curt; Kucala, Theresa; Vassar, Patricia, *The Journal of Nervous and Mental Disease*, Vol. 174, no. 3; pp. 137-144, Kampen, *et. al., op. cit.*

14. Vercozzi, *op. cit.*, p. 8.

15. Reich, *op. cit.*, p. 82.

16. Reich, *op. cit.*, pp. 298-99.

17. Reich, *op. cit.*

18. Masters and Johnson, *op. cit.*, Masters W.H. and Johnson, V.E., *Human Sexual Inadequacy*, Boston,: Little, Brown & Company, 1970; O'Connor, J. F., *Sexual problems, therapy and progonostic factors*, in J.K. Meyer (Ed). *Clinical Management of Sexual Disorders*, Baltimore, Md., Williams and Wilkins, 1976; Leiblum and Pervin, *op. cit.*; Fischer, Joel and Gochros, Harvey, *Handbook of Behavior Therapy with Sexual Problems, Volumes 1&2*, Pergamon Press, New York, 1977.

19. Bardwick, *op. cit.*, Masters and Johnson, *The Pleasure Bond, op. cit.*

20. Walker, Lenore, *The Battered Woman*, Harper and Row, N.Y., 1979.

21. Bardwick, *op. cit.*, p.69.

Chapter 4

1. Wyman, Elizabeth and McLaughlin, Mary E., "Traditional Wives and Mothers," *Counseling Women III*, *The Counseling Psychologist*, Vol. 8. No. 1, 1979, pp. 24-26.

2. *Idem.*, Bardwick, Judith, *The Psychology of Women*, Harper and Row, New York, 1971.

3. "Twenty Facts on Women Workers," U.S. Department of Labor, Office of the Secretary, Women's Bureau, Washington, D. C., 1986.

4. Matsakis, A. and Sigall, B., "Multiple Role Women," *The Counseling Psychologist, Counseling Women III*, Vol. 8, no. 1979, pp. 26-27.

5. *Idem.*

6. Matsakis and Sigall, *op. cit.*, p. 26.

7. *Idem.*

8. *Idem.*

9. Bardwick, Judith, *The Psychology of Women,* Harper and Row, New York, 1971.

10. Matsakis and Sigall, *op. cit.,* p. 27; Horner, M. "Fail: Bright Women," *Psychology Today,* 1969 3(6), 36-38, 62, Horner, M., "The measurement and behavioral implications of fear of success in women," In J. Atkinson and J. Raynor (Eds.) *Motivation and Achievement,* New York, Wiley, 1974.

Chapter 5

1. Boscarino, Joseph, "Current Drug Involvement among Vietnam and non-Vietnam veterans," *American Journal of Drug and Alcohol Abuse,* 6(3), 1979, pp. 301-312. Nace, E. P.; O'Brien, C. P.; Mintz, J. et. al., "Adjustment among Vietnam veteran drug users two years post service," in *Stress Disorders Among Vietnam veterans: Theory, research and treatment,* C.R.Figley (ed.) Brunner/Mazel, 1978, pp. 71-128.

2. Boscarino, 1979, *op. cit.,* p. 302.

3. Nace, *et. al., op. cit.*

4. *Idem.*

5. Robins, L.N., *The Vietnam Drug User Returns, Special Action Office Monograph,* Series A, No. 2, 1974, U.S. Government Printing Office, Washington, D.C.; Robins, L.N. "Veteran's Drug Use Three Years After Vietnam," St. Louis, Department of Psychiatry, Washington University School of Medicine, 1974; Nace, *et. al., op. cit.*; O'Donnell, J. A.; Voss, H.J. H.; Clayton, R. R., "Young Men and Drugs—A Nationwide Survey," Washington, D.C. U.S. Government Printing Office, 1976. Ray, M.B., "The cycle of abstinence and relapse among heroin addicts," *Social Problems,* 1961, pp. 132-140; Waldorf., D., *Careers in Dope,* Prentice-Hall, Englewood Cliffs, New Jersey, 1973; O'Donnell, J. *et. al., op. cit.*; Duvall, H. J.; Locke, B. Z.; Brill, L. "Follow up study of narcotic addicts five years after hospitalization," *Public Health Rep.* 78: 1963, pp. 185-193.

6. Lacoursiere, Roy and Coyne, L., "Comment on Roy's 'Alcohol Misuse and PTSD (Delayed): An Alternative Interpretation of the Data,'" *Journal of Studies on Alcohol,* Vol. 45:3, 1984, pp. 283-237; Boscarino, op. cit., 1980; Branchey, L., Davis, W., and Lieber, C., "Alcoholism in Vietnam and Korea Veterans: A Long Term Follow Up," *Alcoholism: Clinical and Experimental Research,* Vol. 8: No. 6, Nov./Dec., 1984, pp. 572-575; Wish, E.; Robins, L.; Hesselbrock, M.; Heltzer, J.; "The course of alcohol problems in Vietnam veterans," in Seixas, F. (Ed); *Currents in Alcoholism,* Vol. 4, New York, Grune and Stratton, pp. 230-256; 1979; Robbins, L.; Hesselbrock, M.; Wish, E., "Polydrug and alcohol use by veterans and non-veterans," in Smith, D.E., Editor, A *Multicultural View of Drug Abuse,* Proceedings of the National Drug Abuse Conference, 1977, Cambridge, MA, GK Hall, 1978, pp. 74-90.

7. Sierles; Chen; Mc Farland; Taylor, *op. cit.*; Lindy, J.D.; Grace, M.C.; Green, B.J., "Building a conceptual bridge between civilian trauma and war trauma: Preliminary psychological findings from a clinical sample of Vietnam veterans." in B.A. Van Der Kolk (ed.) *Post-traumatic stress disorder: Psychological and Biological sequelae,* pp. 43-58, Washington, D.C., American Psychiatric Press, Inc. 1984; Lacoursiere, *et. al. op. cit.*; Schnitt, J., and Nocks, J., "Alcoholism Treatment of Vietnam Veterans with Post-Traumatic Stress Disorder," *Journal of Substance Abuse Treatment,* Vol. 1, pp. 179-189, 1984; Jelinek, J. M. and William, T., "Post-Traumatic Stress Disorder and Substance Abuse in Vietnam Combat Veterans: Treatment Problems, Strategies and Recommendations," *Journal of Substance Abuse Treatment,* Vol. 1, 87-97, 1984; Krystal, H.

"Psychoanalytic view on human emotional damages," in B. A. Van Der Kolk (Ed), *op. cit.*, pp. 1-28.

8. Robins, L. N., *The Vietnam Drug User Returns, U.S. Government Printing Office,* Washington, D.C., 1973; Nace, *et. al., op cit.*; Sanders, C. R., "Doper's wonderland: Functional drug use by military personnel in Vietnam," *J. Drug Issues* 3: 65-78, 1975; Boscarino, 1979, *op. cit.*

9. Holloway, H., and Ursano, R., in *Trauma of War, op. cit.*, p. 324.

10. Jones, F.D. and Johnson, A.W., "Medical psychiatric treatment policy and practice in Vietnam," in D. M. Mantell and M. Pilisuk, (Eds) *Journal of Social Issues: Soldiers In and After Vietnam,* 1975, 31(4), 49-65.

11. Goodwin, Jim, "The Etiology of Combat-Related Post-Traumatic Stress Disorders," In *Post-Traumatic Stress Disorders of the Vietnam Veteran,* Tom Williams, Ed., Disabled American Veterans, National Headquarters, P.O. Box 14301, Cincinnati, Ohio 45214, 1980, p. 9.

12. Holloway, *op. cit.*, p. 324.

13. *Idem.*

14. Vercozzi, *op. cit.*, Goodwin, *op. cit.*

15. Goodwin, *op. cit.*, p. 9.

16. Schnitt, J. and Nocks, J., *op. cit.*; Lindy, Grace, and Taylor, *op. cit.*; Lacoursiere, Godfrey and Ruby, *op. cit.*

17. Milam, J. and Ketcham, K., *Under the Influence: A Guide to the Myths and Realities of Alcoholism,* Bantam Books, N.Y., 1981, p. 33.

18. *Drug Abuse Facts,* Nelson Taxel, 1971, Woodmere, N.Y., 11598.

19. De Fazio, Victor and Pascucci, N., "Return to Ithaca: A Perspective on Marriage and Love in Post Traumatic Stress Disorder," *Journal of Contemporary Pyschotherapy,* Vol. 14: No.1, Spring/Summer, 1984.

20. Haley, Sarah, "The Vietnam Veteran and His Preschool Child, Childrearing as a Delays Stress in Combat Vets," *Journal of Contemporary Psychotherapy,* Vol. 14:1, Spring/Summer, 1984, pp. 114-121.

Chapter 6

1. Lagone, John, "The War That Has No Ending," *Discovery,* 6, pp. 44-47, 1985; Stein, Jeffrey, "Coming Home," *Progressive,* 45:10, April 1981; p. 10.

2. Wilson, J.P., *Identity, ideology and crises: The Vietnam veteran in transition,* (Pt. 2) Cincinnati, Ohio, Disabled American Veterans, 1978; Egendorf, A.; Kaduschin, C.; Laufer, R.; Rothbart, G.; Sloan, L., *Legacies of Vietnam: Comparative Adjustment of Veterans and their peers: Overview of the Report,* Washington, D.C., U.S. Government Printing Office, 1981; Penk, W., *et. al.* "Interpersonal problem of Vietnam combat vets with symptoms of PTSD," *Journal of Abnormal Psychology,* 1982, Vol. 91:6, 444-450; Penk, W., *et. al.* "Adjustment Differences among male substance abusers varying in degrees of combat experience in Vietnam," *Journal of Consulting and Clinical Psychology,* 1981; 49:3, 426-437; Carroll E., *et. al.,* "Vietnam veterans with Post-Traumatic Stress Disorder: Analysis of Marital and Cohabitating Adjustment," *Journal of Abnormal Psychology,* 1985, Vol. 94, No. 3, pp. 329-337.

3. Haley, Sarah, "When the patient reports atrocities," *Archives of General Psychiatry,* 30: 1974, pp. 191-194.

Chapter 7

1. Walker, Lenore, *The Battered Woman*, New York, Harper and Row, 1979.

2. Savina, Lydia, *Help for the Battered Woman*, S. Plainfield, New Jersey, Bridge Publishers Inc. (1987).

3. Walker, *op. cit.*

4. Savina, *op. cit.*

5. Borland, Marie (ed.), *Violence in the Family*, Atlantic Highlands, Manchester University Press, 1976.

6. Gelles, Richard, T., *The Violent Home*, London, Sage Publications, 1972.

7. Martin, Del, *Battered Wives*, New York, Pocket Books, 1976.

8. Walker, *op. cit.*, Savina, *op. cit.*, Borland, *op. cit.*

9. Strauss, Murray A., Gelles, Richard J., & Steinmetz, Suzanne K., *Behind Closed Doors: Violence in the American Family*, New York, Anchor Books, 1970; Langely, Roger and Levy, Richard, *Wife Beating: The Silent Crisis*, New York, E.P. Dutton, 1977; Strauss, Murray, "Wife Beating: How Common and Why?" *Victimology*, Vol. 2, No. 3-4, 1978, pp. 443-458.

10. Strauss, Gelles, and Steinmetz, *op. cit.*, Strauss, *op. cit.*, Walker, *op. cit.*, Langely and Levy, *op. cit.*, Gelles, *op. cit.*, Del Martin, *op. cit.*, Savina, *op. cit.*, Borland, *op. cit.*

11. "Analysis of Official Army Reports of Spouse Abuse: 1982" Army Family Advocacy Program, U.S. Army Community and Family Support Center, Alexandria, V.A. 22331-0521; MacLennan, Beryce, W., U.S. General Accounting Office, "Problems in Estimating the Nature and Extent of Family Violence in the Armed Forces," Research report: National Security Management; National Defense University, Washington, D.C.; April, 1985; *Battered Women, Issues of Public Policy*, Consultation Sponsored by the U.S. Commission on Civil Rights, Jan, 1978, Washington, D.C.

12. *Response*, Jan./Feb., 1984, vol. 7.

13. Stark, Evan and Flitcraft, Anne, "Medical Therapy as Repression: The Case of the Battered Woman," *Health and Medicine*, Summer/Fall, 1979; *Programs for Battered Women: Data Summary Report*, Minnesota Dept. of Corrections, St. Paul, Minn., 1982; Stark, Evan; Flitcraft, Anne; Frazier, William, "Medicine and Patriarchal Violence: The Social Construction of a 'Private' Event," *International Journal of Health Services*, 9:3, 1979.

14. Smith, William French, U.S. Attorney General, as cited in "Domestic Violence Fact Sheet," Southern California Coalition on Battered Women, 1986, Santa Monica, CA 90405.

15. Walker, *op. cit.*, Del Martin, *op. cit.*, Straus, *op. cit.*

16. Williams, C. M. "The 'Veteran system' with a focus on women partners: Theoretical considerations, problems, and treatment strategies," in T. Williams (Ed.), *Post-traumatic stress disorders of the Vietnam veteran*, Cincinnati, Ohio, Disabled American Veterans, 1980, pp. 73-124.

17. Ritter, Rick, "Bringing the War Home: Vets Who Have Battered," Vet Center, Fort Wayne, Indiana, 1980.

18. Matsakis, Aphrodite, "The Effects of PTSD on Family Life," Research Project, Veteran's Administration Medical Center, Washington, D.C., 1988.

19. Kaufki, Mark, as cited in "Anger dominates hostile, inappropriate social responses," by John Cruden, Vet Center *Voice*, Vol. 7: 10, 1986, p. 6.

20. Cruden, *op. cit.*

21. West, L.; Turner, Wm.; Dunwoody, E., *Wife Abuse in the Armed Forces*, Center for Women Policy Studies, Washington, D.C., 1981.

22. West, *et.al.*, *op. cit.*; Savina, *op. cit.*; Arkin, W. and Dobrosfsky, L. "Military Socialization and Masculinity," *Journal of Social Issues*, 34 (1978): 150-167; Horowitz, J. and Solomon, George F., "A Prediction of Delayed Stress Response Syndrome in Vietnam veterans," *Journal of Social Issues*, 31:4, 1975.

23. Ritter, *op. cit.*, p.1.

24. Ritter, *op. cit.*, p. 9.

25. Bliss, Shepherd, "The Military, Masculinity and the Men's Movement" (Response to the film, "Between Men," United Documentary Film, P.O. Box 315, Franklin Lake, N.J., 07417), Unpublished paper, available from Vet Center, Fort Wayne, Indiana, p. 6.

26. Savina, *op. cit.* p. 338.

27. Ritter, Rick and De Pew, Bobbie, "Masculinity and the Vietnam Vet," Fort Wayne Vet Center, Fort Wayne, Indiana, p. 5, as cited in Savina, *op. cit.*, p. 338.

28. Ritter and De Pew, *op. cit.*, p. 12, as cited in Savina, *op. cit.*, p. 338.

29. Goodwin, *op. cit.*; Figley and Sprenkle, *op. cit.*

Chapter 8

1. Sobie, Jane, "The Battered (Military) Wife," *Ladycom* (present name, *Military Lifestyle*), Aug., 1980, p. 43-46; 59-62. Beryce MacLennan, "Problems in estimating the nature and extent of family violence in the Armed Forces," U.S. General Accounting Office, 441 G. St., N.W., Washington, D.C. 20543, National Defense University, Washington, D.C., 1985; West, A.; Turner, William; Dunwoody, Ellen, *Wife Abuse in the Armed Forces*, Center for Women Policy Studies, Washington, D.C., 1981; "Analysis of Official Army Reports of Spouse Abuse," Department of the Army, Family Advocacy Program, U.S. Army Community and Family Support Center, Alexandria, Virginia 22331, 1984; Warren, Ava, "An Investigation of United States Army Programs for Men Who Batter," Doctoral Dissertation, Catholic University of America, Washington, D.C., 1982; Orlander, CRD, E. A.,"Amends: Abusive Men Exploring New Directions," *Military Chaplain Review*, Spring, 1986, Vol. 15: no. 2, pp. 43-53.

2. "Analysis of Official Army Reports of Spouse Abuse," *op. cit.*

3. West, *et. al.,* *op. cit.*

4. MacLennan, *op. cit.*, p. 8.

5. MacLennan, *op. cit.*, West, *et. al.*, *op. cit.*; Warren, *op. cit.*

6. Army Family Advocacy Report, *op. cit.*, p. 2

7. MacLennan, *op. cit.*, pp. 1-2.

8. Sobie, *et. al.*

9. West, *et. al.*, *op. cit.*

10. MacLennan, *op. cit.*, p. 7.

11. West, *et. al.*, *op. cit.*

12. Family advocacy program, Department of Defense Directive (No.: 6400.1), Washington, D.C., May 19, 1981; "Child sexual abuse action plan," Department of the Army, Advocacy Program, HGDA, 1986.

13. as cited in West, *et. al., op. cit.*, pp. 1-2.

14. West, *et. al., op. cit.*

15. Orlander, *op. cit.*, p. 44.

16. Orlander, *op. cit.*

17. Martin, Del, "Scope of the Problems," in *Battered Women: Issues of Public Policy: A Consultation,* sponsored by the U.S. Commission on Civil Rights, Washington, D.C., Jan, 30-31, 1978, p. 11.

Chapter 9

1. Carter, James, "Alcoholism in Black Vietnam Veterans: Symptoms of Posttraumatic Stress Disorder," *Journal of the National Medical Association,* Vol. 74, No. 7, 1982, p. 655-660; Terry, *op. cit.*

2. Terry, Wallace, *Bloods: An Oral History of the Vietnam War by Black Veterans,* Ballantine Books, New York, 1984; Carter, *op. cit.*

3. Terry, *op. cit.*; Irving M. Allen, "Posttraumatic Stress Disorder, Among Vietnam Veterans," *Hospital and Community Psychiatry,* January, 1986, Vol. 37:1, p. 55-60.

4. Allen, *op. cit.*

5. Goff, S.; Sanders, R.; Smith, C., *Black Soldiers in "The Nam,"* Harrisburg, PA., Stackpole, 1982 as cited in Allen, *op. cit.*, p. 56.

6. Terry, *op. cit.*, p. 39.

7. Allen, *op. cit.*, p. 56.

8. Allen, *op. cit.*, p. 55.

9. Terry, *op. cit.*

10. Allen, *op. cit.*, p. 57; Baskir, L., Strauss, W., *Chance and Circumstance: the Draft, the War, and the Vietnam Generation,* New York, Vantage, 1981.

11. Allen, *op. cit.*

12. Allen, *op. cit.*, p. 56.

13. Eisenhart, R., "You Can't Hack it, Little Girl," *Journal of Social Issues,* 30: 13-23, 1975; Allen, *op. cit.*

14. Allen, *op. cit.*, Carter, *op. cit.*, Parsons, Erwin, "The Intercultural Setting: Encountering Black Vietnam Veterans," in Sonnenberg, S.; Blank, A.; Talbott, J., *The Trauma of War: Stress and Recovery in Vietnam Veterans,* American Psychiatric Press, Inc., Washington, D.C., 1985, pp. 361-387.

15. Parsons, *op. cit.*, Allen, *op. cit.*

16. *Idem.*

17. Parsons, *op. cit.*, p. 366.

18. Allen, *op. cit.*, p. 56; Parsons, E.R., as cited in "The gook identification syndrome and post-traumatic stress disorder in Black Vietnam veterans," *The Black Psychiatrists of America Quarterly,* 13:14-18, 1984.

Endnotes | 411

 19. Parsons, 1985 *op. cit.*, Allen, *et. al.*, Carter, *et. al.*, Yaeger, Thomas; Laufer, R.; Gallops, M., "Some Problems Associated with War Experience in Men of the Vietnam Generation," *Archives of General Psychiatry*, Vol. 41, April, 1984, pp. 327-333.

20. Parsons, 1985, *op. cit.*, Terry, *op. cit.*

21. *Idem.*

22. Terry, *op. cit.*, p. xv.

23. Beale, Frances, "Double Jeopardy: To Be Black and Female," in *Sisterhood is Powerful*, edited by Robin Morgan, Vintage Books, Random House, 1970, pp. 340-353.

24. *Twenty Facts on Women Workers*, Fact Sheet No. 86-1, U.S. Department of Labor, Office of the Secretary, Women's Bureau, 1986, p.3.

25. "The American Woman," 1987-1988 Congressional Caucas for Women's Issues, as cited in *Time*, Aug. 3, 1987, p. 47.

26. The United Nations Decade for Women, 1976-1985, Employment in the U.S, *Report for The World Conference on the United Nations Decade for Women, 1976-1985*, U.S. Department of Labor, Office of the Secretary, Women's Bureau, July, 1985, p.13.

27. Helms, Janet, "Black Women," *Counseling Women III, The Counseling Psychologist*, Vol. 8, No. 1, 1979, pp. 40-41.

28. Beal, *op. cit.*

29. Helms, *op. cit.*, p. 40; Beale, *op. cit.*

30. Terry, *op. cit.*

31. Parsons, *op. cit.*

32. Halpern, Florence, *Survival: Black/White*, New York, Pergamon Press, 1973, p. 126, as cited in Parsons, 1985, *op. cit.*, p. 375.

33. Parsons, 1985, *op. cit.*, p. 380.

34. Parsons, 1985, *op. cit.*, p. 380.

35. Boyd, Julia, "Whose Reality?" *Aegis*, No. 42, 1987, pp. 40-42.

36. Escobar, Javier I., *et. al.*, "Post Traumatic Stress Disorder in Hispanic Vietnam Veterans," *The Journal of Nervous and Mental Disease*, Vol. 171, no. 10., Oct., 1983, pp. 585-596; Pina, G., "Diagnosis and Treatment of Post-Traumatic Stress Disorder in Hispanic Vietnam Veterans," pp. 389-402, in Sonnenberg, *et. al.*, *The Stress of War, op. cit.*

37. Harrington, David, "Healing in the Telling, Helping in the Listening," National Hispanic PTSD Conference, Chicago, Ill., Oct., 24, 1986, pp. 22-23.

38. Escobar, *et. al.*, *op. cit.*; Pina, *op. cit.*

39. *Twenty Facts, op. cit.*

40. Barajas, Lillian, as cited in Sorenson, G., "Educating spouses and partners plays important role," p. 7 *Vet Center Voice*, Vol. 8: No. 8, 1987, pp. 7-8.

41. Sorenson, *op. cit.*, p. 7.

42. Sorenson, *op. cit.*, p. 7.

43. Sorenson, *op. cit.*, p. 8.

Chapter 10

1. Anonymous, "Kid of a Vet," Handout # 17, Vet Center, 528 West Berry St., Fort Wayne, Indiana, pp. 1-2.

2. Shovar, G. Phil, "Medical Professionals," pp. 145-159, in *PTSD: A Handbook for Clinicians,* edited by T.M. Williams, Disabled American Veterans, Cincinnati, Ohio, 1987.

3. Shovar, *op. cit.,* p. 145.

4. Shovar, *op. cit.,* p. 146.

5. Allen, Irving, "PTSD Among Black Vietnam Veterans," *Hospital and Community Psychiatry,* Jan., 1986, Vol 31: 1, pp. 55-60.

6. Williams, Candice and Williams, T. "Family Therapy for Vietnam Veterans," pp. 195-209, in Sonnenberg, S.; Blank, S.; Talbott, J., *The Trauma of War: Stress and Recovery in Vietnam Veterans,* American Psychiatric Press, Washington, D. C., 1985, p. 198.

7. Williams, C. and Williams, T., "Family Therapy for Vietnam Veterans," p. 228, in *PTSD: A Handbook for Clinicians, op. cit.,* pp. 221-232.

8. Reppucci, Christine, James, Thomas, "Intervention with Children of Vietnam Veterans," Community Outreach to Vietnam Era Returnees (COVER), Charlottesville, Virginia, p. 1.

9. *Ibid.*

10. Rosenheck, R. and Nathan P., "Secondary traumatization in the children of Vietnam veterans with posttraumatic stress disorder," *Hospital Community Psychiatry,* 36:5, May, 1985, pp. 538-539.

11. Salom, Ellen, Vet Center North, 5601 N. Broad St., 2nd Floor, Philadelphia, PA., 19141, Personal Communication, May 15, 1987.

12. Van Der Kolk, Bessel, "Post-Traumatic Stress Disorder" in *Post-Traumatic Stress Disorder: Psychological and Biological Sequelae,* edited by Bessel A. Van Der Kolk, American Psychiatric Press, Inc., Washington, D.C., 1984; Silverman, Joel L., "Post-Traumatic Stress Disorder," *Advanced Psychosomatic Medicine,* Vol. 16, pp. 115-140, 1986; Rosenheck, Robert, "Impact of Posttrauamtic Stress Disorder of World War II on the Next Generation," *The Journal of Nervous and Mental Disease,* Vol. 174, No. 6, June, 1986, Serial No. 1243, pp. 319-327; Sigal, John J., "Effects of Paternal Exposure to Prolonged Stress on the Mental health of the Spouse and Children," *Canadian Psychiatric Association Journal,* Vol. 21, 1976, pp. 169-172; Barocas, Harvey and Barocas, Carol, "Manifestations of Concentration Camp Effects on the Second Generation," *American Journal of Psychiatry,* 130:7, July, 1973, pp. 820-821; Trossman, Bernard, "Adolescent Children of Concentration Camp Survivors," *Canadian Psychiatric Association Journal,* Vol. 13: 2, pp. 121-123; Sigal, John and Rakoff, Vivian, "Concentration Camp Survival, A Pilot Study of Effects on the Second Generation," *Canadian Psychiatric Association Journal,* Vol, 16, 1971, pp. 393-397.

13. Rosenheck, *op. cit.,* 1986, p. 322.

14. Suhr, Melanie, "Trauma in Pediatric Populations," *Advanced Psychosomatic Medicine,* Vol. 16: 1986, pp. 31-47; Paulauska, S.; Ottaviano, C.; Campbell, S., "Children of Divorce: Some Clinical Issues," Department of Psychology, Clinical Psychology Center, University of Pittsburgh, Pittsburgh, PA, 15260: Symposium presented at the Fifth Annual National Conference on Feminist Psychology, Pittsburgh, PA., March 2-5, 1978.

15. Suhr, *op. cit.,* p. 36.

16. Paulaskas, *et. al., op. cit.*

17. Rosenheck, 1986, *op. cit.*

18. Paulaskas, *et. al., op. cit.*, pp. 8-9.

19. Sigal, *op. cit.*, Trossman, *op. cit.*, Rosenheck, 1986, *op. cit.*, Freyberg, J.T., "Difficulties in Separation and Individuation as experienced by offspring of Nazi Holocaust Survivors," *American Journal of Orthopsychiatry* 50: 87-95, 1980.

20. Conn, Lois, "Self-Mutilation: The Symptoms and Its Management," *Treatment Trends: A Newsletter of Taylor Manor Hospital,* Ellicott City, Maryland, Vol. 1:1, Sept., 1986, pp. 1-3.

21. Haley, Sarah, "The Vietnam Veteran and His Preschool Child: Childrearing as a Delayed Stress in Combat Vets," *Journal of Contemporary Psychotherapy,* Vol. 14:1, Spring/Summer, 1984, pp. 114-121, p. 117.

22. Haley, *op. cit.*, p. 117.

23. Sigal and Rakoff, *op. cit.*, p. 395.

24. Haley, Sarah, "Treatment Implications of Post-Combat Stress Response Syndrome for Mental Health Professionals," pp. 254-264, in *Stress Disorders Among Vietnam Veterans: Theory, Research and Treatment,* Charles Figley, editor, Brunner-Mazel Publishers, New York, 1978, p. 263.

25. Van der Kolk, B.; Boyd, H.; Krystal, J., *et.al.,* "PTSD as a Biologically Based Disorder: Implications of the Animal Model of Inescapable Stress," p. 123-134 in Van Der Kolk, *op. cit.*

26. Shovar, *op. cit.*, p. 153.

27. Haley, *op. cit.*

28. Williams, T., "Therapeutic Alliance and Goal Setting in the Treatment of the Vietnam Veteran," pp. 25-34 in *Post Traumatic Stress Disorders of the Vietnam Veteran,* Disabled American Veterans, 1980, Cincinnati, Ohio.

29. Harrington, D. and Jay, J., "Beyond the Family: Value Issues in the Treatment of Vietnam Veterans," *Family Therapy Networker,* May/June, Vol. 6:3, 1982, pp. 13-15, pp. 44-45, p. 45.

30. Haley, *op. cit.*, p. 117.

31. Haley, *op. cit.*, p. 115.

32. Glover, H., "Guilt and Aggression in Vietnam Veterans," *The American Journal of Social Psychiatry,* Vol. 1, Winter, 1985, pp. 15-18.

33. Ellen Salom, Vet Center North, 5601 N. Broad St., 2nd Floor, Philadelphia, PA, 19141, Personal Communication, May 15, 1987.

34. Haley, *op. cit.*, p.116.

35. Sigal, *op. cit.*, p 171.

36. Rosenheck, 1985, *op. cit.*; Rosenheck, 1986, *op. cit.*; Silverman, *op. cit.*; Sigal, *op. cit.*; Epstein, H., *Children of the Holocaust,* New York, Putnam's, 1979.

37. *Idem.*

38. Rosenheck, 1985, *op. cit.*, p. 538.

39. Rosenheck, 1985, *op. cit.*; Rosenheck, 1986, *op. cit.*

40. Williams and Williams, 1985, *op. cit.*, p. 198.

41. Salom, *op. cit.*

42. Trossman, *op. cit.*, Silverman, *op. cit.*, Barocas and Barocas, *op. cit.*

43. Teguis, Alexandra, Presentation at The Vietnam Experience, Conference sponsored by the Springfield, Virginia, Vet Center, Disabled American Veterans, Washington, D.C., April 3-4, 1987.

44. Rosenheck, Robert, "The Role of Family Therapy in Treatment of PTSD," unpublished paper, presented at "Diagnosis and Management of Post-Traumatic Stress Disorders in the V.A.," V.A. Mid-Atlantic Regional Medical Education Center, Baltimore, Md., Aug. 21, 1985.

45. *Battered Women, Issues of Public Policy: A Consultation,* Sponsored by the U.S. Commission on Civil Rights, Jan., 1978, Washington, D.C.

46. Strauss, Murray, "Ordinary Violence, Child Abuse, and WifeBeating: What Do They Have in Common," in *The Dark Side of Families,* ed., David Finkelhor, *et. al.,* Beverly Hills, CA: Sage Publications, 1983; Walker, Lenore, *The Battered Woman,* Harper and Row, New York, 1979.

47. Savina, Lydia, *Help for the Battered Woman,* Bridge Publishers, South Plainfield, New Jersey, 1987.

47. Walker, *op. cit.,* p. 37.

49. Walker, *op. cit.*

50. Walker, Lenore, "Children as Victims: Prostitution and Pornography: Children as Victims of Violence," Battered Women's Research Center, Colorado Women's College, Symposium presented at the American Psychological Association, New York, NY, Sept., 1979.

51. *Idem.*

52. *Idem.*

53. *Highlights of the Official Child Abuse and Neglect Reporting,* 1985, American Association for the Protection of Children, American Humane Association, Denver, Colorado.

54. Strauss, Murray; Gelles, Richard; Steinmetz, Suzanne, *Behind Closed Doors: Violence in the American Family,* Garden City, NY, Anchor Press, 1980.

55. *Life Magazine,* Jan., 1988, p.121, "Outrage—The Death of an Innocent Exposes a Grim Reality: Child Abuse."

56. Corbett, Ann, "The Alcoholics' Legacy," The Washington Post, April 6, 1987, p.C 5.

57. *Idem.*

58. Rosenheck, 1985, 1986, *op. cit.*

59. Salom, *op. cit.*

60. Salom, *op. cit.*

Chapter 11

1. Reynolds, D.; Kalish, R.; Farberow, N., "A Cross Ethnic Study of Suicide Attitudes and Expectations in the U.S.," p. 36 in Farberow N., (Ed.), *Suicide in Different Cultures, op. cit.,* pp. 35-50.

2. Victoroff, V.M., *The Suicidal Patient: Recognition, Intervention, Management,* Medical Economics Books, Oradell, New Jersey, 1983; Berman, A. L., "Suicide," Staff Development Seminar, Counseling Center, University of Maryland, College Park, MD, April 17, 1987.

3. Reynolds, D.K. and Farberow, N.L., *Suicide Inside and Out*, University of California Press, Berkeley, California, 1976.

4. Victoroff, *op. cit.*

5. Smith, C. W. and Bope, E. T., "The Suicidal Patient: The Primary-Care Physician's Role in Evaluation and Treatment," *Postgraduate Medicine*, Vol. 79: 8, June, 1986, pp. 195-199, 202; Reynolds, *op. cit.*, Reynolds, D.K. and Farberow, N.L., *Endangered Hope—Experiences in Psychiatric Aftercare Facilities*, University of California Press, Berkeley, California, 1977.

6. Carney, C., also Salganik, A. "Teenage Suicide: The Despair, the Doubts, And the Haunting 'Why?'" *The Washington Post*, March 24, 1982; Victoroff, *op. cit.*

7. Berman, *op. cit.*

8. Smith and Bope, *op. cit.*

9. Bhatia, S., Khan, M., Sharma, A., "Suicide Risk: Evaluation and Management," *American Family Physician*, 34 (3), Sept.,1986, pp. 167-174.

10. Bhatia, *et. al.*, *op. cit.*

11. Stein, Jefferey, "Coming Home," *Progressive*, 45:10, April, 1981, p. 10.

12. Wolfgang, Martin E. "Husband-Wife Homicides," *Journal of Social Therapy*, 1956, pp. 263-271.

13. Savina, Lydia, *Help For the Battered Woman*, Bridge Publishing Inc., South Plainfield, NJ, 1987.

14. Wolfgang, Martin E., "Husband-Wife Homicides," *Journal of Social Therapy*, 1956, pp. 263-271.

15. Wolfgang, M. E., "Who Kills Whom?" *Psychology Today*, Vol. 3, 1969, p. 55,, 56, 72, 74.

16. Hearst, N.; Newman, T.; Hulley, S., "Delayed Effects of the Military Draft on Mortality," *The New England Journal of Medicine*, Vol. 314:10, March, 1986, pp. 620-624.

17. The Centers for Disease Control Vietnam Experience Study, "Postservice Mortality Among Vietnam Veterans," *Journal of the American Medical Association*, Feb. 13, 1987, Vol. 257, No. 6, pp. 790-795, p. 790.

18. Berman, *op. cit.*, Victoroff, *op. cit.*, Bhatia, *et. al.*, *op. cit.*, Smith and Bope, *op. cit.*

19. Burns, *op. cit.*, Iga, M. and Tatai, K., "Characteristics of Suicides and Attitudes toward Suicide in Japan," pp. 255-280, in *Suicide in Different Cultures*, Edited by Farberow, N.L., University Park Press, Baltimore, MD, 1975.

20. Berman, *op. cit.*, Victoroff, *op. cit.*, Smith and Bope, *op. cit.*, Burns, *op. cit.*, Bhatia, *et. al.*, *op. cit.*

21. Berman, *op. cit.*, Smith and Bope, *op. cit.*, O'Neill, *op. cit.*, Reynolds and Farberow, 1977, *op. cit.*

22. Berman, *op. cit.*, Burns, *op. cit.*, Schutz, Ben, "The Suicidal Patient," Staff Development Seminar, Veteran's Administration Medical Center, Washington, D.C., May 12, 1982.

23. Berman, *op. cit.*, Schutz, *op. cit.*, "Suicide," *op. cit.*

24. Schutz, *op. cit.*, "Suicide," *op. cit.*

25. Burns, *op. cit.*, p. 337.

26. Fisher, Kathy, "Sexual abuse victims suffer into adulthood," *APA Monitor*, Vol. 18:6, June 1987, p. 25.

27. Savina, *op. cit.*

Chapter 12

1. Silverman, Joel, "Post-Traumatic Stress Disorder," *Advanced Psychosomatic Medicine,* Vol. 16: 115-140, 1986; Yost, John, "The Psychopharmacologic Treatment of the Delayed Stress Syndrome in Vietnam Veterans," pp. 125-133, in *Post Traumatic Stress Disorders of the Vietnam Veteran,* edited by Tom Williams, Disabled American Veterans, Cincinnati, Ohio, 1980; Yost, J., "The Psychopharmacologic Management of Post-Traumatic Stress Disorder (PTSD) in Vietnam Veterans and in Civilian Situations," pp. 93-102 in *Post Traumatic Stress Disorders: A Handbook for Clinicians,* Williams, T., ed., Disabled American Veterans, Cincinnati, Ohio, 1987; Lipton, Merrill and Schaffer, W., "Post-Traumatic Stress Disorder in the Older Veteran," *Military Medicine,* Vol 151: 10., Oct., 1986, pp. 522-524; Falcon, Spencer, "Psychopharmacology and PTSD: Sharing a Perspective," Presentation at Diagnosis and Management of Post Traumatic Stress Disordes in the V.A., Aug. 21-23, 1985, Baltimore, MD.

2. Allen, Irvin, "PTSD Among Black Vietnam Veterans," *Hospital and Community Psychiatry,* Vol. 371, Jan., 1986, pp. 55-60.

3. Falcon, *op. cit.*; Yost, 1980, 1987, *op. cit.*

4. Falcon, *op. cit.*

5. Falcon, *op. cit.,* Yost, 1980, 1987,*op. cit.,* Allen, *op. cit.*

6. Harrington, David, "Healing in the Telling, Healing in the Listening," Paper presented at the National Hispanic PTSD Conference, Chicago, Illinois, Oct., 1986; Williams, T., "A Preferred Model for Development of Interventions for Pyschological Readjustment of Vietnam Veterans," pp. 37-48 in *Post-Traumatic Stress Disorders of the Vietnam Veteran,* edited by T. Williams, *op. cit.*; Lifton, R.J., "Advocacy and Corruption in the Healing Profession," pp. 209-230 in *Stress Disorders Among Vietnam Veterans,* C. Figley, ed., Brunner-Mazel Publishers, New York, 1978; Smith, J.R., "Rap Groups and Group Therapy for Vietnam Veterans," pp. 165-191, in Sonnenberg, S.; Blank, A.; Talbott, J., *The Trauma of War: Stress and Recovery in Vietnam Veterans,* American Psychiatric Press, Washington, D.C., 20005, 1985.

7. Smith, John R., "Rap groups and Group Therapy for Vietnam Veterans," *op. cit.,* p. 182.

8. Smith, John R., "Individual Psychotherapy with Vietnam Veterans," *op. cit.*; Smith, John R., "Rap Groups and Group Therapy for Vietnam Veterans," *op. cit.*; Lifton and Schaffer, *op. cit.*; Lifton, *op. cit.*

9. Gault., W.B., "Some Remarks on Slaughter," *American Journal of Psychiatry,* 128:4, Oct., 1971, pp. 450-454.

10. Lifton and Schaffer, *op. cit.,* p. 522.

11. *Idem.*

12. Williams, Tom, "Diagnosis and Treatment of Survivor Guilt," pp. 75-92, in *Post Traumatic Stress Disorders: A Handbook for Clinicians,* T. Williams, ed., Disabled American Veterans, Cincinnati, Ohio, 1987, p. 86.

13. Haley, *op. cit.,* Lifton, *op. cit.,* Smith, a, b, *op. cit.,* Williams, T., 1987, *op. cit.*

14. Williams, 1980, *op. cit.,* p. 40.

15. Newman, James, "Differential Diagnosis in Post Traumatic Stress Disorder: Implications for Treatment," pp. 19-34, in *Post Traumatic Stress Disorders: A Handbook for Clinicians, op. cit.*; Harrington, *op. cit.*; Jelinek, M.J. and Williams, T., "Post Traumatic Stress Disorders and Substance Abuse: Treatment Problems, Strategies and Recommen-

dations," pp. 103-118, in *Post Traumatic Stress Disorders: A Handbook for Clinicians, op. cit.*; Jelinek, J. and Williams, T., "PTSD and Substance Abuse in Vietnam Combat Veterans: Treatment Strategies and Recommendations," *Journal of Substance Abuse Treatment*, Vol 1, pp. 87-97, 1984; Schnitt J. and Nocks, J., "Alcoholism Treatment of Vietnam Veterans with PTSD," *Journal of Substance Abuse Treatment*, Vol. 1, 1984, pp. 179-189.

16. Newman, *op. cit.*; Schnitt, J. and Nocks, J., *op. cit.*; Jelinek and Williams, 1984, *op. cit.*, Harrington, *op. cit.*

17. Jelinek and Williams, 1987, *op. cit.*, p. 105.

18. Blank, Arnold, "Irrational Reactions to PTSD and the Vietnam Veteran," pp. 99-124 in *The Trauma of War, op. cit.*, Jelinek and Williams, 1987, *op. cit.*

19. Jelinek and Williams, 1984, 1987, *op. cit.*, Newman, *op. cit.*, Walker, J., Cavenar, J., "Vietnam Veterans: Their Problems Continue," *Journal of Nervous and Mental Disease*, Vol. 170:3, 1982, pp. 174-180.

20. Jelinek and Williams, 1987, *op. cit.*, pp. 105-106.

21. Jelinek and Williams, 1987, *op. cit.*, Newman, *op. cit.*, Walker and Cavenar, *op. cit.*

22. Langer, R., "PTSD in Former P.O.W.'s," p. 3550 in *Post Traumatic Stress Disorders: A Handbook for Clinicians, op. cit.*; Lifton, *op.cit.*; Smith, a, b., *op. cit.*; Lipton and Schaeffer, *op. cit.*; Ursano, R.J., "Vietnam Era Prisoners of War: Studies of U.S. Air Force Prisoners of War," pp. 339-358 in *The Trauma of War, op. cit.*; Van Der Kolk, Bessel, Ed., *Post-Traumatic Stress Disorders: Psychological and Biological Sequelae*, American Psychiatric Press, Inc., Washington, D.C., 1984.

23. Harrington, *op. cit.*; Harrington, D., "Group Therapy with Vietnam Veterans," Presentation, The Vietnam Experience, Conference sponsored by the Vet Center, Springfield, Virginia, Disabled American Veterans, April 3-4, 1987, Washington, D.C.; Gerdemen, Eric, Presentation, Vet Center, Silver Spring, MD, Oct., 1982.

24. Gerdemen, *op. cit.*

25. Menninger, Wm., as cited by Rick Ritter in *DMZ Vet Center*, Vol.3:2, p. 1, Vet Center, Fort Wayne, Indiana, March, 1985.

26. Lipton and Schaeffer, *op. cit.*, Smith, a,b, *op. cit.*, Bowman, Br., "Early Experiential Environment, Maternal Bonding and the Susceptibility to Post-traumatic Stress Disorder," *Military Medicine*, 151, 10:528, 1986.

27. Williams, Candice and Williams, Tom, "Family Therapy for Vietnam Veterans," pp. 195-209, in Sonnenberg, S.; Blank, A.; Talbott, J. *The Trauma of War: Stress and Recovery*, American Psychiatric Press, Inc. Washington, D.C., 1985, p. 200.

28. Lifton, *op. cit.*

29. Williams, Tom, "A Preferred Model for the Development of Interventions for Psychological Readjustment of Vietnam Veterans: Group Treatment," p. 41, in Williams, *op. cit.*

30. Harrington, *op. cit.*

31. Williams, *op. cit.*

Chapter 13

1. President's Commission on Mental Health, "Mental Health of Vietnam era veterans," Volume III, pp. 1321-1328, U.S. Government Printing Office, Washington, D.C., 1978 as cited on p. 100, in Williams, C., "The Veteran System with a Focus on Women

Partners: Theoretical Considerations, Problems, and Treatment Strategies," pp. 73-124, in *Post Traumatic Stress Disorders of the Vietnam Veteran*, edited by Williams, T., Disabled American Veterans, Cincinnati, Ohio, 1980.

2. Center for Policy Research, "The adjustment of Vietnam era veterans to civilian life," New York, 1979, as cited in Williams, C., *op. cit.*, p. 100.

3. Williams, C., *op. cit.*, p. 100.

4. Rawlings, Edna I. and Carter, Dianne K. "Divorced Women," pp. 27-28, in Counseling Women III, *The Counseling Psychologist*, vol. 8, no. 1, 1979; Williams, Elizabeth F., *Notes of a Feminist Therapist*, Praeger Publishers, NY, 1976; Miller, Juanita H., *Towards a New Psychology of Women*, Boston, Beacon, 1976.

5. Williams, E., *op. cit.*, p. ix-x.

6. Savina, Lydia, *Help for the Battered Woman*, Bridge Publishers, South Plainfield, NJ, 1987; Walker, Lenore, *The Battered Woman*, Harper and Row, New York, 1970.

7. *Idem.*

8. Schechter, Susan, "The Future of the Battered Woman's Movement," p. 22, *Aegis*, Summer/Autumn, 1980, pp. 20-25.

9. Newman, James, "Differential Diagnosis in Post Traumatic Stress Disorder: Implications for Treatment," pp. 19-34 in *Post Traumatic Stress Disorders: A Handbook for Clinicians*, edited by T. Williams, Ed., Disabled American Veterans, Cincinnati, Ohio, 45214, 1987, p. 23.

10. Newman, *op. cit.*

11. *Everything You Always Wanted to Know About Child Abuse and Neglect*, National Center on Child Abuse and Neglect (NCCAN), Department of Health and Human Services, PO Box 1182, Washington, D.C. 1984; Helfer, Ray and Kempe, C. Henry, *Child Abuse and Neglect: The Family and the Community*, Ballinger Publishing Company, Cambridge, MA, 1976; Martin, H. and Kempe, C. Henry, *The Abused Child: A Multidisciplinary Approach to Developmental Issues and Treatment*, Ballinger Publishing Company, Cambridge, MA, 1976; Armstrong, Louise, *Kiss Daddy Goodnight*, Pocket Books, New York, NY 1978; Rubinelli, Jackie, "Incest: It's Time We Face Reality," *Journal of Psychiatric Nursing and Mental Health Services*, April 1980, Vol. 18: No. 4, pp. 17-18;Cormier, Bruno, *et. al.* "Psychodynamics of father-daughter inces," *Canadian Psychiatric Association Journal*, Vol. 7, No. 5, pp. 203-217, October 1962; Weinberg, S., *Incest Behavior*, Citadel Press, New York, 1963; Savina, *op. cit.*

12. *Idem.*

13. *Idem.*

14. Williams, Candice, "The Veteran System with a Focus on Women Partners: Theoretical Considerations, Problems, and Strategies," p. 96, in *Post-traumatic Stress Disorders of the Vietnam Veteran*, Williams, T., Editor, Disabled American Veterans, Cincinnati, Ohio, 1980, pp. 73-124.

Epilogue

1. Richburg, Keith B., "Vietnam is pressing ahead with informal US exchanges," *The Washington Post*, Feb. 11, 1988, p. A 54.

2. Downs, F., "Vietnam: My Enemy, My Brother," *Washington Post*, Outlook, Jan. 31, 1988, D1-D22.

3. Richburg, *op. cit.*

4. Resnick, J.L., "Women and Aging," *The Counseling Psychologist,* Counseling Women III Vol. 8, No. 1, pp. 29-31.

Summary of the Vet Center Survey and Tables 1-9

1. Adapted from Candice Williams, Ph.D., "The Veteran System with a Focus on Women Partners," pp. 72-117, in *Post Traumatic Stress Disorders of the Vietnam Veteran,* edited by T. Williams, Cincinnati, OH, Disabled American Veterans, 1980.

2. Strauss, M., "Normative and Behavioral Aspects of Violence Between Spouses," *Victimology,* March 1977; Strauss, M., "Wife Beating: How Common and Why," *Victimology,M* Vol. 2, 1978.

3. Walker, Lenore, *The Battered Woman,* Harper and Row, New York, 1979.

4. NCCAN, *Everything You Wanted to Know About Child Abuse and Neglect,* NCCAN (National Center on Child Abuse and Neglect), Dept. of Human Services, Washington, D.C., 1983.

Index

ADCIO: 115

Adult children of alcohoics: 35, 106–107, 109–111, 192, 224, 257, 317

Agent Orange: 40, 230, 280, 311, 317

Al-Anon: 113, 114, 130, 321

Alcoholics Anonymous (AA): xxiii, 116, 220, 276, 287, 288, 290, 336

Alcoholism, definition and stages of: 107–108

Ambivalent feelings toward mother: 90, 102–103, 118, 185, 194, 215, 217

American Indian veterans: 182–183

Anniversaries, See Holidays and anniversaries

Antinauseants: 105

Anti-Oriental sentiment: xviii, 31, 106, 196, 206, 208, 215

Antipsychotic drugs: 105

Anti-war sentiments: xi, xix, 20, 29–30, 124, 133, 147, 174, 180, 182, 190

Arnold, Arthur L.: 12

Atrocities: 3, 21–23, 57, 123, 140, 152, 168, 202, 204, 226, 235

Australian Vietnam veterans: 14

Barajas, Lillian: 181, 182

Battered wives, or physical abuse of wives: xii, xvi, xxiii–xxiv, 1, 42, 43, 44, 64, 68, 71, 74, 115–116, 123, 126, 131, 178, 231, 232–233, 241, 252–253, 283–284, 291–293, 295, 307, 308, 325

Battered woman, definition of: 135, 137

Battering cycle: 134, 214–215, 284

Battering cycle, definition of: 214

Battering of physical abuse of wives, extent of: 137–138, 139, 145, 153–154

Blank, Arthur: 11

Bliss, Shepard: 140

Burns, David: 249

Child abuse: 126, 149, 153, 155

Child abuse committed by wife, extent of: 218

Child abuse committed by veteran, extent of: 217–218

Child abuse, extent of in U.S.: 218

Children: xvii, xxii–xxiii, 2, 10–11, 27, 32, 34, 37–38, 40–41, 86–87, 97, 100, 143, 144, 149–151, 168–169, 172, 227, 229, 231, 237, 245–249, 259, 260, 266, 269, 280, 297, 301, 305, 312, 314–315, 317–318, 319, 326, 327, 331, 332

Children and alcoholism: 87, 99, 106, 109–110, 117–119, 146, 290–291

Children and divorce: 275, 277, 295, 299–300, 301, 302, 306–307

Children and emotional problems: xxii, 88, 122, 126–128, 131

Children and school problems: xiii, xx, 85, 122, 126, 262–264

Children and therapy: 85, 127, 290–291

Children as step-children: xvii, 47

Children from violent homes: xxiii, 87, 133–134, 146, 150–151, 152, 153, 284, 317

Combat fatigue: 2

"Crazy" Vietnam veterans: xii, xvii, 9, 14, 84, 128, 226, 325

Death of buddy or war friends: 2, 38, 123, 124, 140, 152, 211, 238, 322

Death wish, See Suicide and suicidal thoughts

DEROS: 20, 105

DEROS, definition of: 4

Diagnosis of PTSD (or misdiagnosis): 11, 17–18, 105, 260, 285–286

Distancing during times of family loss or injury: 7, 39–44, 144

Drug abuse or drug withdrawal, symptoms of: 108

Dunwoody, Ellen: 154

Eating disorders: 18, 65, 81, 96–98, 129–130, 288, 290–291, 294, 300, 315, 317–320, 334–337

Employment problems of Vietnam veteran: xi, xxi, 2, 32, 74, 84–86, 89, 99, 108, 112, 124, 143, 156, 164, 170, 174, 179–181, 182, 187, 235–237, 245, 313

Extramarital affairs of the veteran: 51, 53, 63–64, 70–71, 109, 112, 124, 130, 156, 280

Extramarital affairs of the wife: 53, 60, 280

Family therapy: 85, 197–198, 199

Feelings of helplessness in the children: 11, 190

Feelings of helplessness in the veteran: 8, 28, 42

Feelings of helplessness in the wife: 122, 136, 157, 159–160, 177

Flashbacks: xi, 8–11, 37, 68, 78, 87, 135, 138, 189, 190, 217

Flashbacks, definition of: 8–9

Fragging of officers: 122

Gault, W. B.: 21–22

Geographical cure: 12, 299

Glover, H.: 202

God, religion, spirituality: xviii–xix, 2, 22, 23–25, 40, 122, 152, 165–167, 168, 172, 174, 176, 182, 226, 240, 246, 254, 270, 275, 278, 281, 282, 305, 314, 320

Good warrior ethos: 20, 23–24, 59

"Gook" identification syndrome, definition of: 169

"Gook" identification syndrome, Black veterans: 169, 182

"Gook" identification syndrome, Hispanic veterans: 181, 182

Grief repression, definition of: 36–37

Haley, Sarah: 5, 125, 200, 201, 202

Handicapped veterans, extent of: 17, 20

Harrington, David: 15, 187, 201, 271

Hearst, Norman: 233

Hermit: 2, 32, 45–46, 281

Holidays and anniversaries: xvii, xxiv, 2, 24–25, 30, 34, 36, 47, 126, 133, 144, 145, 232, 322

Homecoming: xiii, 20–21, 29–30, 163, 170

Homeless veterans: 32

Impacted anger in the veteran, definition of: 125

Impacted anger in the wife, definition of: 129

Incarcerated Vietnam wives: 112–115, 138–139, 188–189, 232–233

Irving, Allen: 167

Jay, Jeffery: 201

Jelinek, T. Michael: 260

Jennings, Bennett: xiii, 17

Kaufti, Mark: 139

Korean War veterans: 13–14, 18, 20

Loneliness: xxi, 1, 69, 151, 157, 275, 281, 303–304, 307, 308

MacLennan, Beryce: 154

Marriage counseling: 36–38, 47, 49, 255, 261–265, 269, 273–274, 281, 322–324, 328

Martin, Del: 158

Masturbation: 51, 54, 59, 236–237

McCullah, Robert D.: 155

Midlife crisis: 12, 144, 210, 268, 313,, 314, 320

Military training: 29, 134, 135, 140, 154, 167–168, 194

Nar-A-Non: 115

Narcotics Anonymous (NA): 288, 336

Newman, James: 447

Nguyen Van Linh: 311

No-talk rule: xix, xxiii, 58, 162, 190, 221, 222

Obesity and compulsive overeating, See Eating disorders

Orlander, Chaplain E. A.: 155

Overeaters Anonymous (OA): 335–337

Overprotectiveness of children: 37–38, 43

Overvaluation of children, definition of: 210

Parson, Erwin Randolph: 169, 177

"Pink cloud" phenomenon, definition of: 291

Pornography: 64, 71

Predisposition theory, definition of: 25

President's Commission on Mental Health: 279

Prisoners of War (POWs): xviii, 53, 57

Psychotropic drugs: 257

PTSD and WWI, WWII, and Korean veterans: 13–14, 192

PTSD among noncombatants: 4, 5, 9, 13, 14, 23, 105, 187, 219, 220, 258, 270

PTSD, definition of: 2–3

PTSD, symptoms of: 5–6

Re-experiencing the trauma, definition of: 6–8

Ritter, Rick: 138, 140

Romantic love: 62–63, 176, 214, 245, 256, 276

Rosenheck, Robert: 192, 194, 207, 208, 221

Safe zone: 4

Salom, Ellen: 191, 203, 223

Sauter, Sharon: 155

Savina, Lydia: 140

Schechter, Suzanne: 284
Secondary traumatization, definition of:
  191, 207
Sex: 33, 96, 140, 153, 165, 175, 176, 183,
  221, 227, 235, 236, 238, 266, 275, 288,
  301, 304, 306, 307
Sex role stereotyping, female: 73, 86,
  89–96, 115–116, 119, 122, 123, 128,
  131, 156, 157, 171–173, 176–177, 188,
  204, 213, 220, 273, 275, 282–283,
  314–315, 320, 325, 328–333
Sex role stereotyping, male: 18, 19, 20, 44,
  69–70, 89–96, 112, 135, 136, 139, 146,
  148, 156, 213, 233, 256, 273
Sexual abuse in the veteran: 57, 279
Sexual abuse in the wife: 55, 64, 114, 138,
  152, 155, 252–253, 291–293, 325, 334
Sexual functioning, veteran's problems:
  xxi, 33–34, 128
Sexuality, definition of: 74
Shell shock: 2, 13
Sigall, Brenda Alpert: 3320
"Slips": 296–297
Spiritual or moral healing: 257, 259
Strauss, Murray: 153
Suhr, Melanie: 193
Suicide and suicidal thoughts: xii, xxi,
  xxiii–xxiv, 9, 123, 152, 187, 211, 257,
  280, 308, 316
Suicide, characteristics of suicidal persons:
  237–238
Suicide, extent of in U.S.: 231
Suicide, extent of in Vietnam veterans:
  121, 231–232, 233
Suicide questions to ask: 240
Suicide signals: 238–239
Suicide, Vietnam wives: 145, 206, 214,
  294, 322

Teenage war: 19
Terry, Wallace: 167, 170
Trauma, definition of: 4, 258
Triggers: 2, 11, 12, 33, 45, 128, 201, 222
Turner, William M.: 154

"Uncover the trauma", definition of: 258

Vercozzi, Carol: 65
Victim-precipitated murder: 232
Vietnam as an excuse: 145–146, 276
Vietnam veterans, definition of: 103–104

Walker, Lenore: 74, 214, 217
The Wall: 128, 139, 312, 316–317
War neurosis: 2, 13, 23

West, Turner: 154
Westmoreland, General William: 170
Williams, Candice: 137–138, 188, 267, 294
Williams, Tom: 258–259, 260, 270, 271
Wolfgang, M. E.: 232, 233
Women as hostages: xvii, 10, 145
Women's Bureau of the U.S. Department
  of Labor: 171
World War I veterans: 13–14
World War II veterans: 2, 9, 13–14, 18–20,
  23, 45, 84, 147, 165, 167, 202, 207, 221